WEST

continued from front flap

coordinated as was the system of colonial administration, he shows it to have been more efficient than commonly supposed." This outstanding work is of unusual interest to historians and political scientists alike, "a real contribution to colonial history," as the same publication added, "with particular value in relation to modern problems."

About the Author:

Leonard W. Labaree, born in 1897, has been on the history faculty of Yale University since the start of his professional career. Now Farnam Professor of History at Yale, he was chairman of the department from 1942 to 1947. He is author also of *Royal Instructions to British Colonial Governors,* co-editor of *Mr. Franklin: A Selection from His Personal Letters,* and has been general editor of the Yale Historical Publications. Professor Labaree is editor of the projected Papers of Benjamin Franklin, sponsored by the American Philosophical Society and Yale University.

FREDERICK UNGAR
PUBLISHING CO.
105 EAST 24TH STREET, NEW YORK 10, N. Y.

ROYAL GOVERNMENT
IN AMERICA

AMERICAN CLASSICS

ROYAL GOVERNMENT IN AMERICA

*A Study
of the British Colonial System
before 1783*

LEONARD WOODS LABAREE

*Farnam Professor of History
Yale University*

FREDERICK UNGAR PUBLISHING CO.
New York

Printed in the United States of America

Library of Congress Catalog Card No. 58-9334

TO
MY MOTHER

CONTENTS

PREFACE

ALL but a very few of the English colonies in America during the seventeenth and eighteenth centuries were begun as private enterprises. Some were started by joint-stock trading companies, others by feudal proprietors, and still others by groups of private individuals unauthorized by the king. The constitutional systems of the early colonies were as numerous and as varied as the conditions of the times could possibly permit. But gradually private ownership gave way to royal control; charters were surrendered or annulled; unsanctioned settlements were absorbed by their duly constituted neighbors. Finally only a handful of colonies lay outside the direct administration of the crown. The royal province became the normal type of colony and a uniform constitutional system prevailed throughout most of British America. The institutions of some of these royal provinces have been analyzed by historians but the system of royal government as a whole has never been subjected to detailed examination. The purpose of this volume, therefore, is to study that system of government by the direct authority of the king which, sooner or later, was installed in nearly every colony. The analysis is not confined to any one province or group of provinces but includes every colony in which royal government was established before the close of the American Revolution—those in the West Indies as well as those on the continent, the colonies that remained loyal to the British crown in 1776 as well as those that declared their independence. In the chapters that follow I have tried to explain what the instruments were by which royal authority was exercised in America, what the machinery of royal government was and how it operated, what the governmental policies of the British officials were and what influences caused them to be adopted, and how the colonists reacted to these policies when the royal governors tried to apply them. Above all, I have concerned myself with that great contest between the assemblies and the crown over the royal prerogative, which is the central theme of the constitutional history of the colonies.

The period covered is roughly the hundred years or so from the establishment of the Lords of Trade in 1675 to the close of the American Revolution in 1783. Something appears here and there about the period before 1675 but the details of the political systems of the four provinces in the hands of the king before that date were so varied and the attitude of the English officials toward them so unsettled that the early years contribute little to the later story. The American Revolution, on the other hand, marks the close of one era and the beginning of another with its own problems and policies, the treatment of which I leave to other hands.

The topics dealt with have been definitely limited. The commissions and instructions to the governors, which necessarily form the basis of the study, contain many paragraphs on such matters as trade and commerce, Indian affairs, military and naval authority, religion and morals, and the land system, which receive only passing treatment in this study. To deal with all of them on the same scale that I have used for such subjects as the council, the assembly, legislation, and finance, would result in an enormous expansion of the volume and would lead to many digressions from the central theme. Detailed attention, therefore, is confined to those matters which relate directly to the governmental system and which comprised the essentials of the provincial constitution. I have had to pass over many important disputes either in complete silence or with such scant notice as to warrant criticism, especially from those interested in the history of individual provinces. In reply I can only plead the necessity of limiting the number of incidents that could be used to illustrate the major topics.

Of first importance to a study of the royal government in America is an analysis of the commissions and instructions to the governors appointed by the king. A detailed examination of every such document would have been desirable, but time and expense forbade. However, I have been able to reach approximate completeness in this respect. I have made a careful paragraph by paragraph examination and collation of two hundred and thirteen

—or ninety-two percent—of the two hundred and thirty-two sets of general instructions issued between 1624 and 1783, existing copies of which I have been able to locate. The examination of the instructions for fifteen of the twenty-four provinces that received royal governors at one time or another, has been complete, and these fifteen include all the more important provinces. More than half the instructions for the other nine colonies have been analyzed. I have not made quite such an extensive collation of the commissions and trade instructions, largely because it has seemed unnecessary on account of the great uniformity found in the approximately two-thirds of each group analyzed. In addition to these documents, the material used has been found chiefly in the correspondence of the governors with the home officials, in the records of the Board of Trade, the secretaries of state, and the privy council, and in the journals and acts of the provincial assemblies.

The form in which quoted passages appear may call for some explanation. Articles and phrases of the commissions and instructions were usually repeated to several governors, the same wording often appearing a hundred or more times during the period. The lack of standardized usages in spelling, capitalization, and punctuation in all English documents of the seventeenth and eighteenth centuries precluded the use of identically the same forms in any two commissions or instructions except by mere chance. No special significance can be attached to any one rendering. To avoid the meaningless selection of a single form in each case as well as to add to the clarity of the work, I have changed the spelling, capitalization, and punctuation in quotations from these documents to conform to modern American usage. Consistency and uniformity have then demanded a similar modernization in all quotations from other sources, with the exception of two or three cases in which the use of the original forms has seemed imperative. In no case, I believe, have I altered the sense in any way; often, I hope, I have been able to clarify it, especially in the letters of some of the more careless and illiterate governors.

I am grateful for this opportunity to acknowledge the assistance and cooperation I have received. This study, submitted in an earlier form as a doctoral dissertation at Yale University, has been completely rewritten and developed to its present form largely because of the generous action of the Yale Graduate School in appointing me Sterling Senior Fellow in 1926, which appointment enabled me to consult the manuscripts in London and to procure many necessary transcripts. Thanks are due to Miss Dorothy O. Shilton and Mr. Richard Holworthy of London for their interest and assistance in supervising the making and forwarding of these transcripts. The staffs of the Public Record Office, the British Museum, and the Yale University Library have been most courteous and helpful. The officials of the Division of Manuscripts in the Library of Congress showed great consideration and cooperation during the weeks spent with the invaluable collection of transcripts located there. I wish to acknowledge my gratitude to Mr. Albert Matthews of the Colonial Society of Massachusetts who sent to New Haven a large collection of transcripts made for that society. I have received many helpful criticisms and suggestions from Professors Wallace Notestein and Ralph H. Gabriel of Yale University and Professor Claude T. Lloyd of the University of New Hampshire, who have read various chapters in manuscript. Lastly, I owe the deepest debt of gratitude and affection to Professor Charles M. Andrews of Yale University, who first suggested the subject to me and who, at all times, has given me unsparingly of his time and invaluable counsel.

L. W. L.

New Haven, Connecticut,
July 28, 1929.

CHAPTER I

INSTRUMENTS OF ROYAL AUTHORITY

ALL students are familiar with the fact that the British constitution cannot be found in any single document or group of documents. Consisting as it does of a great body of law, both common and statutory, of a number of instruments of a non-legislative character, and of a steadily growing series of conventions, precedents, and clearly established forms of procedure, the constitution has at all times been found adaptable to changing conditions. Yet its characteristics have been definite enough so that one can describe with a certain degree of confidence the main features of the governmental structure at any given period.

There is one part of the constitutional system, however, which has always offered unusual difficulties and which, even in its relation to present-day affairs, seems to be subject to much doubt. The vast possessions of the crown, which found their beginnings early in the seventeenth century in the tiny settlement in Virginia, had made it necessary long before the American Revolution for the constitution of the mother country to provide in some special way, first, for the structure of local colonial government, and second, for a definition of the relationships between England and her dependencies. The Revolution itself clearly showed that this need had not been met to the satisfaction of all concerned, even after one hundred and fifty years of the existence of royal authority in America. The world today is watching with interest the efforts of British and colonial statesmen to meet the most recent developments of the same problem.

In spite of these uncertainties, the fact remains that every English colony has a constitution and has always had one, differing as it may from those of other colonies and from that of the mother country, but in a broad sense forming at the same time part of the constitution of the empire as a whole. At the present time this imperial constitution is a very complex affair, since peoples of every sort of territory, from great self-governing dominions, continental in expanse, to small and seldom-visited islands, mere specks upon the map, owe allegiance to the House of Windsor. But in the eighteenth century the constitution was simpler and the types of colonies were far more uniform. Royal, corporate, and proprietary colonies contained most of the transplanted population; the fishery of Newfoundland, the African slave posts, and the areas controlled by such corporations as the Hudson's Bay Company and the East India Company, none of which had many white inhabitants, marked the limits of British penetration. Among the royal provinces, which included the most important parts of this colonial world and which are the subjects of this study, the constitutional variations were few and generally insignificant. The political institutions of these provinces had grown from much the same origins and their governments stood upon a common footing in relation to the mother country. The home officials needed many more years of experience to teach them that differences in the economic, racial, and social conditions of the various parts of the colonial world made necessary many differences in the governmental systems.

However similar the constitutions of the royal provinces were to each other in the eighteenth century, they differed fundamentally from the constitution of England herself. The very origin and growth of the colonial constitutions are the keys to this divergence. In England interacting forces within the kingdom imposed changes from time to time upon a structure centuries old. Among the colonies the agencies involved were only partly local. External as well as internal conditions were responsible for the growth of the colonial constitution. In England the constitution grew out of the struggles between conflicting forces on the spot; in the colony the local forces of development, lacking sovereignty, were constantly checked by interests in England that attempted to establish and maintain institutions not in accord with colonial sentiment and growth. This pressure of external forces upon the development of political institutions was the primary obstacle to full self-expression of the colonial genius and explains most fully the difference in the fundamental characteristics of the English and colonial constitutions.

This external influence upon the colonies was expressed through various agencies in England—executive, legislative, and judicial—which were primarily concerned with the government of the realm itself, but which became more or less involved in the organization and administration of the trans-Atlantic dependencies. An analysis of the functions of these agencies and the machinery which they used in exercising that influence in colonial affairs is necessary to a proper understanding of the development of the colonial constitutional system.

Throughout the seventeenth century and the first six decades of the eighteenth, the colonies were recognized as dependencies of the English crown and not of the English people nor even of their representatives in parliament. Not until after the doctrine of parliamentary supremacy had become firmly established as a part of the British constitution itself, did parliament assume a direct and important part in ordering the internal affairs of the colonies. Until after the conclusion of the last intercolonial war parliament did not pass a single act dealing primarily with local colonial administration.[1] This is not to say that parliament did not try to regulate the external commerce of the colonies nor to pass laws on matters which involved the mercantile interests of England or the proper balance of the British mercantile empire. Parliamentary activity in this direction is well known. Nor is it intended to imply that English law did not prevail in the colonies. On the contrary, the Declaration of Independence shows how much the colonists esteemed their legal heritage when it asserts that the king had abolished "the free system of English law in a neighboring province [Quebec], establishing therein an arbitrary government and enlarging its boundaries so as to render it at once an example and fit instrument for introducing the same absolute rule into these colonies." Although there were some exceptions, English law generally was the basis of the colonial system.[2] But the points to be emphasized are that parliament

[1] It is, of course, well known that in 1650 parliament passed an act declaring that the colonies "ought to be subject to such laws, orders, and regulations as are or shall be made by the parliament of England." C. H. Firth and R. S. Rait, *Acts and Ordinances of the Interregnum,* II, 425–429; H. Scobell, *A Collection of Acts and Ordinances of General Use, Made in the Parliament, 1640–1656,* II, 132–134. But the very fact that it seemed necessary to make such a declaration at a time when the crown was in abeyance lends emphasis to the general doctrine that the colonies were dependent on the king and not on parliament.

[2] The opinion was widely held that the English common law and certain parts of the statute law did extend to the colonies. The best statement of this doctrine was rendered by Richard West, counsel to the Board of Trade, who declared in 1720: "The common law of England is the common law of the plantations, and all statutes in affirmation of the common law, passed in England antecedent to the settlement of a colony, are in force in that colony, unless there is some private act to the contrary, though no statutes made since those settlements are there in force, unless the colonies are particularly mentioned. Let an Englishman go where he will, he carries as much of law and liberty with him as the nature of things will bear." G. Chalmers, *Opinions of Eminent Lawyers on Various Points of English Jurisprudence, Chiefly Concerning the Colonies, Fisheries, and Commerce, of Great Britain,* I, 194–195. See also *ibid.,* I, 196–203, 220–221.

was not directly concerned in the administration of the plantations, and that, however often either house might call for reports on colonial conditions, they seldom embodied those reports in constructive legislation. Acts of parliament passed during the colonial period played a very minor rôle in the evolution of the internal polity of the colonies.

The English judiciary also had very little to do with the colonies. Appeals from the colonial courts to England —except in admiralty cases, and even in these after 1744[3] —lay to the privy council and not to the courts at Westminster. Appointments to the colonial bench, when made in England, followed on the recommendation of the secretary of state or of the Board of Trade. Hence practically all influence in judicial matters upon colonial institutions came from the executive branch of the home government rather than from its purely judicial organs.

The external influences brought to bear upon the shaping of a colonial polity, therefore, were primarily those of the English crown and its administrative organs. The royal prerogative was a major factor in the operation of the American governments. The administration of the colonies was the concern of the crown officials. It was the royal influence which most directly affected the development of the colonial constitution, and it was the prerogative with which the assemblies came most sharply into conflict. The study of the external factors in the colonial constitution is, therefore, primarily the study of the royal prerogative as it found expression in various types of diplomatic documents and as it affected, and in turn was affected by, the colonial or popular factors in the situation.

The actual exercise of the royal authority in the province was delegated to a group of officials, appointed for

---

[3] *Acts of the Privy Council of England, Colonial Series,* 1720–1745, § 608; 1745–1766, §§ 44, 95, 171, 197, 657.

the purpose, among whom one officer stands out preeminent in importance—the royal governor. Other appointees might be necessary to a satisfactory working of the system as it developed, and whenever need for them became apparent their positions were created and filled; but upon the governor alone rested the primary responsibility of representing the authority of the English crown and of securing obedience to royal orders. For this reason, the documents through which the governor derived his power and which told him how to carry out his duties held first rank among the components of the provincial constitution. But before these documents are analyzed they must first be classified in such a way as to show the function of each type and its relative authority and constitutional significance. This task involves some investigation into the subject of English diplomatics. Unfortunately specialists in this field have usually dealt exclusively with an earlier period of English history, leaving the centuries of American colonization largely unexplored.[4] Hence any classification and arrangement of the documents of immediate concern to this study can be only tentative, pending the time when they may be fitted into the larger groupings of general English diplomatic formulae of the seventeenth and eighteenth centuries.

Considering these instruments in the light of their origins, forms, functions, and constitutional importance to America, they may be grouped as follows:

I. Letters patent under the great seal of England (or Great Britain)
   (a) Charters
   (b) Commissions

[4] The authoritative works of Hubert Hall entitled *Studies in English Official Historical Documents;* and *A Formula Book of English Official Historical Documents:* Part I, *Diplomatic Documents;* Part II, *Ministerial and Judicial Records,* comprise almost the only works on this subject available

II. Instruments under the lesser seals or the sign manual
    (a) Writs or letters of privy seal
    (b) Instructions to governors
    (c) Royal proclamations
    (d) Commissions under the signet and sign manual
    (e) Royal warrants
    (f) Royal letters

III. Orders in council

IV. Commissions under the great seal of the Admiralty

V. Correspondence of officials and departments
    (a) Letters from the secretary of state
    (b) Letters from the commissioners of the Treasury
       and of the Admiralty
    (c) Letters from the Board of Trade

The royal charter is by far the most formal and authoritative instrument by which the king can express his will or grant powers and privileges. The importance of the charters given to individuals or corporations for colonies in America is too well known to need further comment here.[5] Furthermore, since most of these charters were revoked or surrendered before the territories in question became royal provinces, they lie outside the field of the present study. The only charter to play an important part in the history of a royal province was that granted to Massachusetts Bay in 1691.[6] This charter was the nearest ap-

to the general student. Valuable as these volumes are, they contain relatively little information on the instruments of the last three centuries and almost none at all on the documents relating to colonial administration. The nearest approach to a formula book on colonial diplomatics is Anthony Stokes, *A View of the Constitution of the British Colonies in North America and the West Indies* (London, 1783), which contains some typical documents and other useful information.

    [5] See especially, L. P. Kellogg, ''The American Colonial Charter,'' in *Annual Report* of the American Historical Association for 1903, I, 185–341.

    [6] F. N. Thorpe, *The Federal and State Constitutions, Colonial Charters and Other Organic Laws*, III, 1870–1886.

proach to the creation of a constitution for a royal province by means of a single document that we have before the passage of the Quebec Act in 1774.

The commissions issued in the form of letters patent under the great seal constituted the highest expression of the prerogative in all the royal provinces. For the most part, these commissions were issued for the purpose of establishing an individual in the office of provincial governor and of defining his powers. Other commissions under the great seal were given to certain inferior officers,[7] or to one or more appointees for various purposes such as the establishment of boundary lines between provinces,[8] or the trial of piracy.[9] But since these instruments usually referred to special, not general, powers, their influence upon colonial government was less important. The governor's commission, on the other hand, contained the grant to him of all powers necessary for establishing and maintaining a provincial government. Without this royal grant there could have been no legal political authority in the colony. Being a letters patent it was publicly read upon the governor's induction into office.[10] All officers and inhabitants were required to comply with its terms. In one important respect, at least, it differed from the charter. The charter was perpetual and only terminated upon

[7] For an account of the chief offices filled by letters patent under the great seal, see C. M. Andrews, *Guide to the Materials for American History, to 1783, in the Public Record Office of Great Britain*, I, 234–235.

[8] *E.g.*, for running the boundary between New York and New Jersey, 1767, *New Jersey Archives*, 1st series, IX, 630–636.

[9] *E.g.*, Public Record Office, Colonial Office, 5: 862, fos. 139–146 (Colonial Society of Massachusetts Transcripts); C.O. 324: 9, pp. 91–109 (Library of Congress Transcripts). The former series of transcripts is hereafter indicated by the symbol '' (Mass.) '' and the latter series by '' (L.C.).''

[10] The pomp and ceremony incident to the reading of the commission is described on pp. 86–88, below. See also A. Matthews, ''Notes on the Massachusetts Royal Commissions, 1681–1775,'' in *Publications* of the Colonial Society of Massachusetts, XVII, 2–111.

voluntary surrender or through established judicial process such as followed the issue of writs of *quo warranto* or *scire facias*, but the powers granted the governor were to be enjoyed only during the king's pleasure.[11] Consequently they lapsed either upon the death of the sovereign or upon a revocation under the great seal. This revocation, although occasionally an independent document,[12] was usually incorporated in the commission to the succeeding governor.

The governor's commission is a highly formal document, as befitted an instrument conveying such broad powers under the great seal. It begins with the royal superscription and style: "George the Second by the Grace of God of Great Britain, France, and Ireland, King, Defender of the Faith, etc.,"[13] followed by the address and salutation: "To our trusty and well-beloved Charles Pinfold, esq., greeting."[14] With the first royal appointment to a colony, a preamble or exposition next appears, setting forth the grounds on which the king had assumed the

[11] Some exceptions to this statement are to be found. Francis, Lord Willoughby of Parham, was appointed governor of Barbados and the Caribbee Islands for seven years in 1663 (C.O. 1: 17, no. 41) and on his death in 1667 his brother and heir, William, Lord Willoughby of Parham, was appointed to succeed him for the unexpired three years of his term (C.O. 29: 1, pp. 51–64). In 1675 Lord Culpeper received a grant of the governorship of Virginia in reversion after Sir William Berkeley (C.O. 5: 1355, pp. 299–303, L.C.). In 1679, after Berkeley's death Culpeper received a formal commission with a life tenure (*Calendar of Virginia State Papers*, I, 14–16) which was renewed in 1682 (*Virginia Magazine of History and Biography*, XXVI, 139–144, 260–266) but was revoked by inquisition, Aug. 16, 1683, for misbehavior and disobedience (C.O. 5: 1356, p. 188, L.C.). During the eighteenth century all governors were appointed during the king's pleasure.

[12] *E.g.*, revocation of the 1664 commission to Sir Thomas Modyford as governor of Jamaica in 1671, C.O. 138: 1, p. 85.

[13] The quotations here given follow the phraseology of the commission to Charles Pinfold, appointed governor of Barbados in 1756, C.O. 29: 17, pp. 137–174. Appropriate variations occurred in commissions of other dates and for other provinces.

[14] The form of address varies according to the rank of the appointee:

government.[15] Otherwise the grant to the preceding governor is mentioned and revoked at this point.[16] The actual appointment of the new governor is made in the movent clause which follows immediately.[17] The appointment is reenforced and safeguarded in a dispositive clause or injunction ordering the governor to execute his office "according to the several powers and directions granted or appointed you by this present commission and the instructions and authorities herewith given you," or according to such further powers and instructions as might later be given him under the signet and sign manual or by order in council, or according to such "reasonable laws and

A commoner, knight or baronet: "To our trusty and well-beloved"
A baron: "To our right trusty and well-beloved"
A viscount: "To our right trusty and well-beloved cousin"
An earl: "To our right trusty and right well-beloved cousin"
A duke: "To our right trusty and right entirely well-beloved cousin."
No marquis received appointment as a colonial governor before 1783. A member of the privy council is designated by the word "councillor" at the end of the address. Except in the cases of the very early governors, these commissions vary from the conventional letters patent of the period in that they are addressed to the appointee and not in the more general words of universal address, "To all to whom these presents shall come." See Thorpe, *Federal and State Constitutions, etc.*, III, 1870; Hall, *Studies*, p. 251, and *Formula Book of Diplomatic Documents*, p. 64.

[15] *E.g.*, "Whereas by reason of the great neglect of the proprietors of the Bahama Islands, the government of the said islands is fallen into great disorder and confusion . . ." Commission to Woodes Rogers, as governor of the Bahamas, 1718, C.O. 5: 189, p. 376 (L.C.).

[16] *E.g.*, "Whereas we did by our letters patents under our great seal of Great Britain bearing date at Westminster the [blank] day of [blank] 1746 . . . constitute and appoint Hen. Grenville esq. captain general and governor in chief in and over our islands of Barbados . . . now know you that we have revoked and determined and by these presents do revoke and determine the said recited letters patents, and every clause, article, and thing therein contained."

[17] *E.g.*, "And further know you that we, reposing especial trust and confidence in the prudence, courage, and loyalty of you the said Charles Pinfold, of our especial grace, certain knowledge, and mere motion, have thought fit to constitute and appoint you the said Charles Pinfold to be our captain general and governor in chief in and over our islands of Barbados . . ."

statutes'' as might be in force in the province at the time or should later be passed by the governor with the advice and consent of the council and assembly.[18] Next follows a series of clauses in which occur the specific grants of power, each normally introduced by some such words as ''we do by these presents give and grant unto you full power and authority to'' or ''our will and pleasure is that you may.'' The commission concludes with the clause announcing execution: ''In witness whereof we have caused these our letters to be made patent,'' and the attestation ''Witness ourself at Westminster the —— day of ——, in the —— year of our reign.'' In its engrossed form the commission occupies two or three sheets of parchment, of about the same size and shape as a modern newspaper page turned sidewards. The sheets are usually ornamented with deep borders adorned with the portrait of the king, coats of arms, lions, unicorns, and other symbols of the monarchy. The sheets are fastened at the top, and the great seal is appended at the bottom of the last sheet by a silken cord or ribbon.[19]

By the time of our colonial period the smaller seals and the sign manual were very commonly used on instruments of lesser importance. No consistent use of the different formulae can be recognized, however, and the diplomatic or constitutional relationships of the missives with which we have to deal are hard to determine exactly. A description of the documents and of their most common forms of authentication, together with a suggestion as to their probable constitutional standing is all that is at present possible.

Instruments under the privy seal rank next in authority

[18] This clause varies frequently in wording from colony to colony, but in general the substance is the same.

[19] For reduced facsimiles of the two pages of Queen Anne's commission to Lord Cornbury as governor of New York in 1702, see F. A. Ogg, *Builders of the Republic* (*The Pageant of America*, VIII), p. 25.

to those under the great seal. For colonial history, however, they have very little direct importance. As Mr. Hall points out, the administrative use of the privy seal was from the first chiefly associated with the fiscal business of the kingdom.[20] The Englishman, both mercantilist and governmental official, had a pronounced objection to any drain upon the Exchequer for the support of provincial government, therefore the privy seal could have little use in connection with colonial affairs. When payments from the Exchequer were authorized, however, the customary letter of privy seal was issued to the Treasury Board, thus initiating the procedure which led to the actual payment of the money. Sometimes, as in the case of the duty of four and a half percent levied in Barbados and the Leeward Islands, funds of colonial origin were lodged in the Exchequer and were likewise payable on letters of privy seal.[21] But so far as can be determined, only once was an attempt made to use a letter of privy seal to authorize the payment of money from a fund located in a colony and subject to appropriation by the assembly. In 1722, Charles Du Bourgay, appointed lieutenant governor of Jamaica, was given a letter of privy seal directing the payment to him of an annual salary of £1,000 out of the Jamaica revenues.[22] But even before he left England, Du Bourgay became convinced that such an instrument would be ineffec-

[20] Hall, *Studies*, p. 260.

[21] The salaries of many of the West India governors and of some other officials were paid from this or some other fund in the Exchequer, in which cases letters of privy seal were used. *Calendar of Treasury Books* and *Calendar of Treasury Books and Papers, passim.* For references to other letters of privy seal for expenditures relating to the colonies, see Andrews, *Guide to the Materials for American History, to 1783, in the Public Record Office of Great Britain*, II, 228–230.

[22] The king's bill for this letter of privy seal, addressed to the officers of the Treasury and to the receiver general of the revenues in Jamaica is in Signet Office 7: 181 (May, 1722); the letter itself is enrolled in the Treasury under date of May 4, 1722, in Treas. 52: 32, pp. 39–40.

tive for the purpose intended, a belief which was amply borne out by the event.[23] Apparently, the letter of privy seal was never successfully used as an instrument for expressing the royal will in the colonies.[24]

[23] On behalf of Du Bourgay, Lord Carteret, secretary of state, had asked the Lords of the Treasury to give "the proper directions for the payment of the said allowance in the usual manner." This request was minuted by the Treasury Board: "Prepare a p. seal for paying £1,000 p. ann. to Col. Du Bourgay as Lt. Gov. of Jamaica out of the revenues of that island in the form and manner as hath been before used." (Treas. 1: 238, no. 93). Examination of the record has failed to show that any similar document had ever before been issued, the probability being that in this case the Treasury officials assumed incorrectly that the procedure usual in England was applicable to the colonies. Less than a week after the issuing of the letter of privy seal, Du Bourgay memorialized Lord Carteret of his discovery that, according to the Jamaica Revenue Act of 1703, the receiver general was forbidden to issue money on any other authority than a warrant under the hand of the governor with the advice and consent of the council. He therefore prayed that an additional instruction be given to the governor directing him to issue such a warrant for Du Bourgay's salary, in accordance with the privy seal (C.O. 137: 14, p. 140). Such an instruction was accordingly issued (C.O. 138: 16, pp. 423–424). But when the governor and lieutenant governor arrived in the island, they found that there was no unappropriated surplus in the revenue fund available for this salary. Consequently the privy seal was displayed to the council and assembly with a request that funds be provided. Both bodies considered the instrument "extraordinary and unprecedented," not only because of its diplomatic form but also because of its demand of a salary for the lieutenant governor during the residence of the governor. Both bodies refused to honor it, although out of deference to Du Bourgay's person they granted him £1,350 "to defray his expenses in order to his returning back to Great Britain," whither he went in disgust. Assembly and council minutes, Jan. 17–Feb. 8, 1723, C.O. 140: 17 (unpaged), *passim*.

[24] The writ of privy seal was, of course, an important stage in the passage of a document under the great seal. But since this process was entirely completed in England and even in the cases of governors' commissions and other colonial documents, the writ of privy seal never reached the colony, the formulae employed do not require comment at this point. Mention should also be made of the fact that some governors erroneously referred to some other documents as "privy seals" when they were actually warrants under the signet and sign manual. See, for example, Thomas Handasyd to the Board of Trade, Jan. 7, 1703, C.O. 137: 5, no. 109; *Calendar of State Papers, Colonial Series*, 1702–1703, p. 536; same to same, Jan. 29, 1707, C.O. 137: 7, no. 37; *Cal. State Paps., Col.*, 1706–1708, § 735.

No form of royal authentication is more common on documents relating to colonial affairs than is the royal sign manual. Instructions to governors, proclamations, commissions to lieutenant governors, royal warrants, and letters, and various miscellaneous instruments, all bear the king's signature to attest their royal origin. Such documents are almost always countersigned by the secretary of state or some other ministerial officer, and usually they also bear the signet.[25] Although inferior in authority to instruments under the great seal and the privy seal, their influence upon provincial government was really greater, because of their constant use and the wide variety of matters with which they dealt.

Of this large class of documents the most important were the instructions to the governors. Briefly defined, the royal instructions were the formal expressions of the king's will as to the manner in which the powers granted in the commission were to be executed. The Board of Trade expressed the idea when they wrote Governor William Popple of Bermuda that the instructions were to be "the rule of your conduct in all matters relative to the powers given you by your commission."[26] For this reason they played a part in the constitutional history of the colonies which can hardly be over-emphasized. They fall into three categories: first, the general instructions, a long document in many articles or paragraphs, given to the governor with his commission and relating primarily to the civil government of the province; second, the trade instructions, a similar document but much shorter, relating to the enforcement of the acts of trade and navigation, given at the same time; and third, additional instructions,

[25] Although the countersignature of the secretary of state or another officer is usual, very occasionally a document bears only the name or initials of the monarch.

[26] Board of Trade to William Popple, Feb. 17, 1749, C.O. 38: 9, p. 4.

usually consisting of only a single paragraph, amending some article of the general or trade instructions or further clarifying the governor's duties, given at some date after the preparation of the other instructions. A fourth group, sometimes mentioned, is that of circular instructions. These were simply additional instructions which were sent simultaneously to a number of the governors in America with practically identical wording. The copy of a circular instruction received by any one governor normally bears no trace of its general character, but in all parts, including its heading, is similar to the usual additional instruction.[27]

There was less uniformity in the instructions than in the commissions, yet a definite formula was established and adhered to for certain parts of the document. In the upper left-hand corner of the first page of a set of instructions appears the king's signature or sign manual together with the signet. To the right of these are the title words: "Instructions [or additional instructions] to our trusty and well-beloved Joseph Dudley, Esq., our governor and commander in chief in and over our Province of New Hampshire in New England in America. Given at our Court at St. James's the 6th day of April, 1702, in the first year of our reign."[28] The text of the instructions follows

[27] The only indication that circular instructions were sent to more than one governor appeared in their preparation and entry in the records in the home offices. In the entry, the instruction to one governor, seemingly picked at random, was recorded in full, followed by the words "the like instruction to" and the names of the colonies, and sometimes of the governors, to whom duplicates were sent. Variations in wording to fit local conditions were indicated in the margin or in a note at the end of the entry. Occasionally the entire document as sent to each governor was recorded in full.

[28] *New Hampshire Province Laws,* II, 13. The trade instructions bear the lengthier title of "Orders and instructions to [name and title as in general instructions] in pursuance of several laws relating to the trade and navigation of the Kingdom of Great Britain and our colonies and plantations in America. Given, etc." There were, of course, numerous variations from these forms of headings, especially in the earlier period.

below. In documents of any length, as in general or trade instructions, a number of folio pages were used, the sheets being often bound together with thread and the text running along on both sides of each page in regular order. In nearly every case the final sentence of the instructions is followed by the words "By his Majesty's Command" and the countersignature of the secretary of state. The opening paragraphs of the general instructions contain a reference to the commission accompanying them and upon which they depend,[29] outline the governor's procedure for induction into office, and name the members of his council. The next group of paragraphs relates to the duties, powers, and regulation of the council. These are followed by articles treating of the assembly. The privileges of this body are outlined and the forms and limitations of its legislation defined. Matters of colonial finance, appropriations, and the rendering of accounts are usually considered in this connection. From this point the sequence of topics varies, but usually follows approximately this order: the administration of justice, inferior provincial officials, religion and morals, militia and local defence, maritime affairs, the land system, trade and commerce, and the devolution of the government on the death or absence of the governor. The instructions normally conclude with the grant of discretionary power to the governor and council in emergencies and with an injunction to keep in close communication with the secretary of state and the Board of Trade. Because of the variety of subjects touched upon, the general instructions are usually quite long. The average for the eighteenth century is about ten thousand words, divided into ninety or a hundred

[29] This was almost invariably in the following words: "With these instructions you will receive our commission under our great seal of Great Britain constituting you our captain general and governor in chief of our province of —— in America."

articles.[30] During the first third of the century the number of paragraphs tended to increase, but a gradual process of consolidation and elimination began about 1730 which ultimately brought about a considerable reduction. Except during the latter part of the seventeenth century the articles were regularly numbered, a practice so convenient for purposes of reference and record that one wonders why it was even temporarily abandoned.[31]

The phraseology of the instructions is formal and legalistic. Many articles are introduced by expository preambles explaining why the article is necessary or describing the complaints which brought about the change in policy indicated. "Whereas," "aforesaid," "notwithstanding," and similar bits of legal jargon are common. Once the phraseology of an article had become settled it was rarely changed except in minor particulars until some event took place which led to the reconsideration of the entire paragraph. Additions were made quite often, however, in the body of an article, but the older phrases and clauses were usually left intact. Before long the instructions had become thoroughly stereotyped and formal.

The additional and trade instructions regularly follow the same formulae as the general instructions. But they differed from each other in one respect. The trade instructions were repeated from governor to governor with even less change than was usual in the general instructions, but the additional instructions were almost

[30] The average number of paragraphs in the general instructions sent between 1700 and 1783 to the governors of all royal provinces was 93.5. The Massachusetts instructions were the shortest, averaging 63 articles, while the North Carolina instructions, with about double that average, were the longest.

[31] When references are given in this work to articles in instructions originally unnumbered, the writer has assigned numbers in accordance with the order in which the paragraphs occur in the original document.

never repeated as separate documents. Successive governors of a province often received identical trade instructions, but if an additional instruction reappeared in
a single province it nearly always took the form of a new
article in the general instructions to a succeeding governor. But the three types of instructions, taken together,
constitute the most important and the most numerous
body of instruments under the sign manual and signet
which went out from England to the colonies.

A second group of instruments under the sign manual
must be treated separately. Although relatively few in
number, the royal proclamations relating to the colonies
were sometimes of great importance to their political and
economic development.[32] The question may be raised as
to whether the royal proclamation should be classified as
an instrument under the great seal or under the sign
manual. The latter grouping seems to be more exact, since
the proclamation itself received only the king's signature.
In England, its promulgation was ordered by great seal
writs addressed to the sheriffs, to which copies of the
proclamation were attached. But those proclamations sent
to the colonial governors for publication never bore the
great seal.[33] The familiar phraseology and formulae of a
royal proclamation need no discussion here. In its relation

[32] The only collection of royal proclamations relating to the colonies which
has appeared in print was edited by Clarence S. Brigham and published as
volume XII of the *Transactions* of the American Antiquarian Society. This
volume includes 101 proclamations of which only 34 were issued between the
accession of William and Mary and the outbreak of the American Revolution.
The collection is not complete however.

[33] This and similar problems connected with the royal proclamation are
fully discussed by Robert Steele in his historical essay introducing the first
volume of *A Bibliography of Proclamations of Tudor and Stuart Sovereigns
. . . 1485–1714 (Bibliotheca Lindesiana,* vols. V and VI). On the above
question see p. xx. This work is unique, for of all diplomatic instruments of
the seventeenth and eighteenth centuries, the proclamation is the only one
that has undergone a thorough investigation.

to the colonial constitution the proclamation stands somewhat apart from other instruments. It represented neither
higher nor lower authority than the commission, since
each was an independent expression of the royal will. The
relationship must be found in the respective functions of
the two instruments. The commission was the authority
for the general government of a specified province; the
proclamation was a royal command in regard to some
particular matter, to be carried out in all the colonies, or
at least in a considerable number of them. Although the
proclamation may perhaps be said to occupy a position of
greater constitutional authority than the general instructions, the infinitely greater use of the latter and their
wider range of subject matter indicate their far greater
importance in colonial history.

A certain number of officials in the colonies received
their commissions not under the great seal but under the
sign manual and signet, countersigned by the secretary
of state. Of these royal appointees the most important
was the lieutenant governor.[34] By this term is here meant
an officer named to exercise all the powers granted to the
governor on the latter's death or absence from the province. There must also be included in the term the local
head of a division or part of what really constituted a sort
of federated province, as in the Leeward Islands and the
Ceded Islands. These distinctions must be made because
of the fact that instances are found where the actual chief
magistrate of a colony with a commission under the great
seal was entitled lieutenant governor.[35]

The lieutenant governor's commission is a very brief
document, for it merely served as authority for the ap-

[34] For lists of other officials with similar commissions, see Andrews, *Guide*,
I, 234.

[35] The most important cases of this nature are those of Cranfield, New
Hampshire, 1682; Beeston, Jamaica, 1692 (but named governor in 1699);

pointee to succeed to the powers of the governor in case
of need. Like all other sign manual documents it bears
at its head the king's signature or his initials. Either
above or below this is an impression of the signet. The
royal superscription and style, the address, and the
salutation are similar in form to the corresponding parts
of the governor's commission. In the earlier documents
an exposition follows, referring to the appointment of the
governor of the province, but this clause has disappeared
from most of the commissions of the eighteenth century.[36]
Next comes the actual appointment of the lieutenant governor, who is authorized "to execute and perform all and
singular the powers and directions" contained in the
governor's commission, upon the death or absence of that
official, "according to such instructions as are already
sent or shall hereafter from time to time be sent unto him
[the governor]" or according to such orders as the lieutenant governor himself might receive from the king or
the governor. After a warning to all officers and others
whom it might concern to give their obedience to the lieutenant governor, the document closes with a datal clause
and the countersignature of the secretary of state.[37] The

and the chief executives of Bermuda from Cony in 1684 through Pitt in 1727,
all of whom bore the inferior designation but whose commissions in other
respects were identical with other great seal commissions of their periods.
Two cases must be mentioned, however, in which lieutenant governors in the
usual sense of the term were appointed by commission under the great seal.
One was the commission to Lieutenant Governor Partridge of New Hampshire,
1696, which took this form because it included a revocation of the clause in
the commission to Governor Allen appointing John Usher as lieutenant governor (*N.H. Prov. Laws*, I, 515–516). The other was the commission to
Herbert Jeffreys as lieutenant governor of Virginia in 1676 when Governor
Berkeley's failing health made the presence of another man necessary to
cope with the situation following Bacon's Rebellion. *Virginia Magazine*, XVI,
356–359.

[36] This form was retained in Massachusetts and New Hampshire until
1727.

[37] The lieutenant governor's commission usually contains no elaborate

character and content of these commissions indicate their constitutional position. In the presence of a governor appointed under the great seal, the lieutenant governor had no real authority as such. His commission only gave him authority to exercise the powers specified in the governor's commission and to perform the duties of the latter according to his instructions when there was no governor in the province. The lieutenant governor's commission was of no constitutional importance when the governor was functioning. It only allowed its possessor to pick up the reins of authority when the governor laid them down.

The remaining documents under the signet and sign manual cannot be easily subdivided. They consist of instruments usually referred to as royal warrants or royal letters. The former term was more commonly used by contemporary officials, but the latter appeared often enough in connection with similar documents to make the two terms seem practically interchangeable. Only in the concluding words of warranty or valediction is there any variation in the formula, and even in this respect the distinction is not always clear. An epistolary form is the main characteristic of all documents of this class. The royal signature at the top is followed by a semi-personal address and salutation: "Trusty and well-beloved, we greet you well." The main body of the instrument uses the same expressions as the additional instruction or a single article of the general instructions. When an official warranty follows in the words, "And for so doing this shall be your warrant," the document may be safely

---

revocation of the commission to his predecessor. The expression "in the room of ——" does, however, frequently occur in the appointing clause. In some cases formal revocations under the sign manual are to be found as separate documents. For example, see that of 1709 revoking the commission of Richard Ingoldsby as lieutenant governor of New Jersey. *New Jersey Arch.*, 1st series, III, 474–475. A large percentage of the lieutenant governors died in office.

termed a royal warrant. The other form commonly used at the close is a valediction, "And so we bid you farewell," which would seem to indicate that the document ought to be called a royal letter. Neither usage nor content, however, is sufficiently uniform to allow of any such simple definition. In a few instances both forms appear in the same document, and occasionally both are omitted, so that no final conclusion can be drawn. In all cases, the datal clause stands next,[38] followed by the countersignature of the secretary of state. The missive was usually written on a folio of paper with the fourth page left blank. It was then folded in such a way as to conceal the contents and across the flaps was affixed the signet. The back was then endorsed with the name and office of the person to whom the document was to be sent.

Since instruments of this class bore the same authentication as did the instructions and the sign manual commissions, they held the same legal position and might be used for the same purposes. Indeed, it is impossible to say just why a given order should have taken the form of an additional instruction, a warrant, or a royal letter, and cases are to be found where each is used in a different occasion to signify the royal pleasure on the same subject.[39] However, some general principles may be suggested. First, the warrant or letter was used more often in the seventeenth century and the early part of the eighteenth, but the additional instruction became more common toward the latter part of the period and tended to supplant

[38] E.g., "Given at our Court at Kensington, the 20th day of November, 1707, in the sixth year of our reign."

[39] Thus an order of Feb. 2, 1702, directing the governors to send to England for trial any accessories of pirates they might apprehend, was in the form of a royal letter (C.O. 324: 7, pp. 165–171, L.C.), but a further order of June 5, 1716, to the governor of Jamaica not to seize the effects of certain persons accused and sent to England for complicity in piracy, was in the form of an additional instruction, C.O. 5: 190, pp. 348–349 (L.C.).

the epistolary forms. Second, any specific modification of
the general instructions was usually accomplished by an
additional instruction, while supplementary orders or
directions on matters not touched upon directly in the instructions were often first given in royal warrants or
letters. Third, there was a tendency, though never clearly
defined, to treat topics of major importance in the rather
more formal manner of additional instructions. The instruction was obviously the more important type of instrument.

Warrants and royal letters had a wide variety of uses.
Among the more common examples are the following: a
warrant directing the governor to swear a certain person
as a member of the council to fill a vacancy, or to issue a
commission under the provincial seal to fill some local
administrative or judicial office;[40] a warrant accompanying a new provincial seal, directing its use and calling for
the mutilation and return of the former seal; a license or
leave of absence to the governor to return to England for
a specified period of time; an order to the governor to
return to answer charges filed against him; directions for
the attitude or policy to be assumed by the governor in
some matter in dispute with the assembly; an order to
secure the passage of a certain act by the assembly; the
declaration of the confirmation or disallowance of a provincial law. Thus the warrants, letters, and other orders
may be said to constitute a body of directions and au-
thorizations closely allied to the instructions, supplementary to them, perhaps, but highly important for the exercise of the prerogative in America.

Nearly every matter of consequence relating to colonial
administration came, sooner or later, before the privy

---

[40] Such a warrant was commonly called a "mandamus," and in the West
Indies early in the eighteenth century it was frequently, but very incorrectly,
called a "privy seal."

council for decision. Whatever that body might agree to
do in any such case, their action invariably took the form
of an order in council. Orders approving drafts of commissions and instructions were necessary before those
instruments could pass the royal seals. Other orders were
issued referring reports, representations, appeals, and
colonial laws to the proper authorities for investigation.
In this way, the committee of the whole council, the Board
of Trade, the commissioners of the Treasury and of the
Admiralty, the attorney and solicitor general, and the
secretary of state received countless orders in council
dealing with colonial affairs. But we are not immediately
concerned with the orders which went to officials in England. Many orders in council, however, were sent to the
governors and other officers in the plantations. Such
orders form an important group of instruments of royal
authority in the colonial constitutional system. They were
used for much the same purposes as, and often inter-
changeably with, royal warrants, letters, or instructions.[41]
Constitutionally and legally, the order in council occupies
much the same position as these documents, although
ranking below those which bear the great seal.

The formula employed in the order in council is always
clearly recognizable. The heading runs: "At the Court
at ——, the —— day of ——, Present the King's Most
Excellent Majesty in Council," followed usually, though
not always, by the names of the members in attendance
on the day in question. In the body of the document the
king is always referred to in the third person. The au-
thenticity of the order is attested by the signature of one

[41] Thus the governor's commission directed him to execute the duties of
his office according to the commission itself, the general instructions and
"such further instructions and authorities as shall at any time hereafter be
granted or appointed you under our signet and sign manual or by our order
in our privy council." A large proportion of the orders in council sent to the
colonies related to the confirmation or disallowance of provincial laws.

of the clerks of the council and by the council seal, which, in the eighteenth century documents, usually occupies the upper left-hand corner of the first page.[42]

The commission to the governor as vice-admiral of his province was quite a different document from that official's commission for the civil government. The vice-admiralty commission was drawn up by the judge of the High Court of Admiralty on a warrant from the lord high admiral or the commissioners of the Admiralty. It was issued under the great seal of the Admiralty and not under the great seal of Great Britain. During the period when the Duke of York held the office of lord high admiral, the document was issued in his name, but thereafter it bore the superscription of the king. Until 1733 all vice-admiralty commissions were in Latin, but in that year the authorities took advantage of a permissive act of 1731 and began to issue the commissions in English.[43] Before that time there was in the document no movent clause in which the actual appointment was made, this function being performed by a title or heading at the beginning of the instrument, sometimes in English but more usually in Latin, in these or similar words: "Letters patent granted to William Phips, Knight, for the office of Vice Admiralty of the Province and Territory of Massachusetts Bay in New England."[44] This heading was omitted after 1733 and the appointment was thereafter made in a movent clause in the body of the document.[45] Likewise, the earlier

[42] See E. R. Turner, *The Privy Council of England in the Seventeenth and Eighteenth Centuries 1603–1784*, I, 124–127; II, 61–71; L. W. Labaree and R. E. Moody, "The Seal of the Privy Council," *English Historical Review*, XLIII, 190–202.

[43] 4 Geo. II, cap. 26. For the change to the use of English see A. Matthews, "Massachusetts Royal Commissions," in *Publications* of the Colonial Society of Massachusetts, II, xxvii.

[44] From commission to Phips, Mass., 1691, *Publ.* of Col. Soc. of Mass., II, 206, 373.

[45] *E.g.*, "We, confiding very much in your fidelity, care, and circum-

commissions have no expositions or notifications, but the powers conferred are introduced by participial phrases such as "ad cognoscendum et procedendum." The concluding words of the commissions issued after 1689 are significant of the different character of these documents. They are described as "given at London in the High Court of our Admiralty under the great seal of the same." The date follows and then the signature of the register of the court. Those commissions granted by James, either as Duke of York or later as king, were given at Whitehall, the seal is described as "representing an anchor,"[46] and the instrument was signed or initialed by James and countersigned by the secretary to the Admiralty.

This commission gave to the governor jurisdiction over all admiralty or maritime affairs within his province, with power of naming and appointing all necessary officers and ministers for carrying into effect the authority and exercising the jurisdiction granted.[47] The governor as vice-admiral was to take judicial cognizance of an extensive list of causes, including contracts between merchants and owners of ships, charterparties, agreements to be performed or entered upon beyond the seas, felonies within the admiralty jurisdiction of the province, admiralty droits and incidents, treasure trove, anchorages, and royal fish. The vice-admiral also had supervision of all rivers and ports and was charged with the enforcement of all

spection in this behalf, do by these presents, which are to continue during our pleasure only, ordain, constitute, and depute you, the said William Shirley, esq., . . . our vice admiral, commissary, and deputy in the office of vice-admiralty in our Province of Massachusetts Bay . . . and in the maritime parts of the same, and thereto adjoining, whatsoever, with power of taking and receiving all and every the fees . . ." (*Publ.* of Col. Soc. of Mass., II, 237).

[46] The Admiralty seal continued to display an anchor as its central device, but the commissions did not thus describe it after 1689.

[47] The appointment of judges, registers, and marshals of the vice-admiralty courts was excepted from this power until the reign of William and Mary.

statutes, ordinances, and customs of England affecting admiralty or maritime matters within the province. This broad grant of authority came, not directly from the king, but from the lord high admiral or the commissioners of the Admiralty, and within its peculiar sphere was as complete and final as if issued out of chancery under the great seal of Great Britain. No special instructions accompanied the document and the powers therein granted were not discussed at length in the general instructions to the governor.

The diplomatic instruments which have thus been described were sufficiently broad to provide for the general exercise of the royal authority in the colonies. But the specific duties of the governor made necessary a more regular and frequent contact with the administrative officials and departments at home. There was, therefore, an extensive correspondence across the Atlantic, the governor, on one side, describing colonial conditions and affairs, asking for advice or support in his movements, or recommending changes in the established policy of colonial government; the home officials, on the other, asking for information from America, commending or rebuking the governor for his actions, or ordering him to carry out specific points of policy not entirely covered in the more formal documents from the crown. This correspondence gives a more comprehensive view of the system of royal government than can possibly be gained from the commissions and instructions alone. These letters show how the system really worked out in practice, what its weak spots were, and why the royal prerogative finally lost most of its strength in the provinces through the growing power of the assemblies.

On the side of the British administration, the letters from the secretary of state were by far the most authoritative, because the secretariat was, of all departments, the

most closely associated with the king,[48] and a letter from
the secretary was almost equivalent to a letter from the
king himself. This fact is illustrated by the very language
used. Expressions such as "I am commanded by his Majesty to signify to you his Majesty's pleasure," or "His
Majesty has thought fit to direct," are common prelimi-
naries to orders from the secretary of state, but almost
never occur in letters of other officers. Diplomatically and
constitutionally, the secretary's letter to the governor
was, of course, inferior in rank to any document bearing
the sign manual or one of the royal seals.[49] On the other
hand, it was more authoritative than a letter from any
other official or department in England.

The correspondence of the commissioners of the Admiralty and of the Treasury with colonial officials was,
within the scope of the executive powers entrusted to
them, of an authoritative nature, and the governor was
expected to obey such commands as he might receive from
these bodies if they were not inconsistent with his commission and instructions. But neither the Treasury nor
the Admiralty was charged with the direction of colonial
policy, and since the governor owed neither his appointment nor his continuance in office to either of them, the
correspondence which took place was often more or less
perfunctory.

[48] Formal letters from the privy council to colonial officials are not considered here, because they were extremely rare, especially in the eighteenth
century. The few that were sent would, of course, rank above letters from
the secretary of state.

[49] Thomas Pownall declared in the House of Commons in 1770 and repeated in 1774 that a letter from a secretary of state could have no effect
as against a command or trust created by a commission, especially when that
trust was also given by a royal charter, and that, had he received such an
order while governor of Massachusetts Bay, he should not have obeyed it.
Parliamentary History, XVI, 991–992; XVII, 1285. No official seal appears
to have been used on the letters of the secretaries of state to the governors,
although occasionally a personal seal has been found.

The most important body of officials with whom the governor corresponded was the Board of Trade. The board was charged with the oversight of colonial affairs. Hence it wrote frequently to the governors, advising, commending, or rebuking them, recommending lines of action, requesting information, and urging a faithful discharge of duty in accordance with the instructions.[50] But the greatest weakness of the board lay in the fact that it was merely an advisory body with no right to act on its own initiative. As a result, its orders to the governor were seldom given in direct language unless previously authorized by the privy council. The board could never make a change in policy of its own accord. It had first to send a formal representation on the subject to the king. If the privy council favored the suggestion, they might order the Board of Trade to prepare the draft of an additional instruction or of a royal letter, they might propose a letter from the secretary of state, or they might send their own order in council to the governor to guide his actions. In a relatively small number of cases they referred the matter back to the Board of Trade with directions to write to the governor conveying the royal pleasure. On the other hand, the board often took occasion, when forwarding a more authoritative document to the governor, to add in a covering letter their own expectation that the order would be faithfully carried out by the governor. Their letters to the governors were signed by all the members present at the time of approval of the drafts. The seal of the Board of Trade does not appear to have been used to authenticate such documents, being reserved almost solely for reports

[50] At times the board's letters to the governors were frequent only in comparison with the letters of other officials. During the period of the "decline" of the board prior to 1752, its letters were not very numerous. Sometimes two years elapsed between letters to a single governor. During the twenty-three years from 1728 to 1750, the board wrote to the lieutenant governors of Virginia only twenty-five times. C.O. 5: 1366 (L.C.), *passim*.

and representations to higher authorities in England, such as the king, the privy council, or the houses of parliament.

Of all the instruments used to enforce the royal prerogative in America, the governor's commission and instructions were by far the most influential in the shaping of the provincial constitution. This fact was fully recognized on both sides of the Atlantic, at times grudgingly and with reservations in the colonies, always insistently and emphatically in England. Of the two instruments, the commission had naturally the more basic significance. It was declared by the Barbados assembly in 1665 to be "the principal of all records, acts, statutes, and proceeds in this island and of all matters tending to the security of their estates transacted since [the governor's] last arrival," and on this account they begged that it be recorded in the secretary's office in confirmation of all public transactions.[51] A similar view was expressed in 1747 by the attorney and solicitor general of Great Britain, Ryder and Murray, in an opinion called forth by the disputes over representation in the New Hampshire assembly. The law officers stated that "the right of sending representatives to the assembly [and consequently, we may add, the authority of the entire system of provincial legislation] was founded originally on the commissions and instructions given by the crown to the governors of New Hampshire."[52] It is true that the assemblies became more and more anxious to ignore this point and to assert their right, as local parliaments, to determine their own composition and legislative powers. But this subsequent attitude in no

[51] *Cal. State Paps., Col.,* 1661–1668, no. 1121. The practice of recording the governor's commission in the secretary's office was general in the royal provinces.

[52] Chalmers, *Opinions,* I, 272. See also similar opinions of various law officers, *ibid.,* I, 223, 268, 273, 301. The New Hampshire case is more fully dealt with below, pp. 180–184.

way detracts from the statement that historically and constitutionally the colonial legislative system was based on the commission to the governor. Consequently, even those organs of government which were created by act of assembly rested fundamentally on this instrument. With few exceptions, all forms of political activity may be traced to this source. The government of Massachusetts Bay, indeed, was founded on the royal charter of 1691 as well as on the governor's commission. In all colonies a few men, such as the customs officers, held their appointments by direct commission from England. The vice-admiralty courts were held by virtue of the vice-admiralty commission rather than by that of the civil commission.[53] But in all other respects the governmental system was based on the governor's civil commission. Nearly all political institutions were ultimately founded on this instrument which was thus the basic document of the provincial constitution.

The instructions ranked next in importance to the commission. Based upon the commission, explaining and defining its execution, the instructions inevitably had an influence upon colonial polity limited only by the extent to which they were observed and made effective. The home officials did not intend that the major portion of the instructions should be made public, so the responsibility for the observance of the instructions rested chiefly on the governor. But the obligation of obedience was not his alone. He was told to show some paragraphs to his council, and the members of that body were expected to advise him in the execution of his office and to support him in carrying out his orders. Even the assembly came within the scope of the instructions, which contained important

[53] Board of Trade to Lord Dartmouth, Oct. 26, 1711, C.O. 324: 9, pp. 484–488 (L.C.); *Cal. State Paps., Col.*, 1711–1712, § 141. See also, *ibid.*, 1701, § 1094; 1702, §§ 197, 504, 570, 743, 1005.

sections dealing with the organization, procedure, and law-making power of the elective branch of the legislature. If the assemblymen refused to obey the rules thus laid down, the governor was required to veto their bills and, if necessary, to dissolve them. The importance which the home officials attached to the instructions relating to the assembly is shown in a report of the privy council committee in 1760, which refers to the instructions on the method of passing private acts. Even though these rules related to a minor phase of legislative activity, the committee wrote of them not only as being "coeval with the constitution of the British colonies," but also as forming "an essential part of that constitution, which could not be set aside without subverting a fundamental principle of it."[54] The British authorities clearly looked upon the instructions as constitutional documents of the greatest importance which all members of the colonial government were expected to obey.

But the colonists did not always consider that the instructions had such vital constitutional significance. More than once an assembly refused to comply with an instruction or other royal order, not necessarily because the king had no right to issue it, but simply on the ground that he had been misinformed. Even the council took this stand at times, as when the Virginia council coolly disobeyed an instruction touching the disposal of quit-rents in that colony, declaring that experience had shown the method prescribed to be disadvantageous to the crown.[55] Of course, ulterior motives often explain the opposition that appeared, as when in 1711 the New Jersey council refused

[54] *Acts, Privy Coun., Col.*, 1745–1766, p. 449.

[55] Governor Nott to the Board of Trade, Dec. 24, 1705, C.O. 5: 1315, no. 11 (L.C.); *Cal. State Paps., Col.*, 1704–1705, § 1534; Lieut. Gov. Spotswood to the Board of Trade, Aug. 18, 1710, *Official Letters of Alexander Spotswood* (Virginia Historical Society *Collections*, I, II), I, 7–8.

to act favorably on a bill for relieving creditors of persons becoming bankrupt in England, the passage of which had been demanded by an instruction to Governor Hunter. In spite of the ready compliance of the lower house with this order, the council rejected the bill on the ground that the queen had been misinformed when she gave the instruction. But Hunter shrewdly hinted that the true reason for their attitude was that "some of them were personally too nearly concerned in the consequence of passing such a bill."[56] Such incidents show that even early in the eighteenth century the colonists were disinclined to consider the instructions as legally binding upon them.

This attitude on the part of the colonists became more and more apparent as the years went by, especially whenever the interests which the instructions were designed to protect came in conflict with the interests of the colonists themselves. By 1744 the situation had become so serious from the British point of view that parliament was asked to take action. In spite of repeated instructions against the issuing of paper bills of credit, many colonies —especially those in New England—authorized large quantities of such paper currency which they made legal tender. The depreciation that followed worked a great hardship to trade. A bill was therefore introduced into the House of Commons prepared by a committee two of whose three members were also members of the Board of Trade, prohibiting such issues in the future except for military emergencies.[57] To this bill was attached a rider requiring all governors, lieutenant governors, councils, and assemblies "to pay strict obedience to such orders and instructions as shall from time to time be transmitted to them or any of them by his Majesty or his successors,

[56] Governor Hunter to the Board of Trade, May 7, 1711, *New Jersey Arch.*, 1st series, IV, 54–55.
[57] *Commons Journal*, XXIV, 658, 681.

or by or under his or their authority.'"⁵⁸ Had this measure
passed it would have had the effect of giving the royal instructions all the force of law in the colonies and might
have resulted in an enormous extension of the prerogative
in America. But parliament was prorogued eight days
after the first reading of the bill so that the matter could
not be brought to an issue at the time. Not until five years
later was a similar bill introduced. In 1749, a committee,
again dominated by members of the Board of Trade, presented a new bill against paper currency in the colonies.⁵⁹
In this bill, however, the additional clauses relating to the
instructions were considerably modified, simply placing
the burden of enforcement on the shoulders of the governors, where, in the royal colonies at least, it already
rested according to their commissions.⁶⁰ Nevertheless, a
storm of protest came from the colonies and from their
agents in England, which apparently so aroused the anti-
prerogative group in the House of Commons that the bill
was allowed to die in committee after the second reading.⁶¹
When in 1751 parliament finally passed an act against
paper currency it related only to New England and contained no reference to the general enforcement of the
royal instructions in the colonies.⁶² Parliament had come

⁵⁸ *A Bill to Prevent the Issuing of Paper Bills of Credit in the British
Colonies and Plantations in America, to be Legal Tenders in Payments for
Money* [1744]. A printed copy of this bill is in the British Museum in a volume
labeled: *Parliamentary Papers Printed by Order of the House of Commons,
From the Year 1731 to 1800*, I, no. 19.

⁵⁹ *Commons Journal*, XXV, 746, 766.

⁶⁰ *A Bill to Regulate and Restrain Paper Bills of Credit in the British
Colonies and Plantations in America, and to Prevent the Same Being Legal
Tenders in Payment for Money; and for the Better Enforcing His Majesty's
Orders and Instructions Throughout the Said Colonies and Plantations* [1748-
49], in *Parliamentary Papers Printed by Order of the House of Commons,
From the Year 1731 to 1800*, I, no. 39.

⁶¹ *Commons Journal*, XXV, 792-794, 806-807, 813-815, 818, 819, 823,
830, 844, 853-854, 864, 871, 877, 882; *Parliamentary History*, XIV, 563-564.

⁶² 24 Geo. II, cap. 53.

to the rescue of the colonies and had prevented a broad extension of the prerogative.

This failure of the administrative officers in Great Britain to bolster up the declining authority of the instructions did not escape the notice of the colonists. In the years which followed, the assemblies showed more clearly than before their unwillingness to be bound by the governors' instructions. All through the eighteenth century the assemblies were becoming stronger and more able to contest the authority of the crown in matters of legislation and administration. Each success that they won strengthened their views of their own importance and weakened the effectiveness of the instructions. The thirty years or so before the American Revolution were years in which the balance of power in all the royal provinces, including the West Indies, was clearly shifting from the crown to the assemblies.

The constitutional history of the provinces in the eighteenth century is fundamentally the history of a series of controversies between the assemblies and the prerogative in which the former won victory after victory. The struggle reproduced in many ways the contest which had taken place in England between parliament and the crown. The gradual development of parliamentary sovereignty at the expense of the royal prerogative, which was a central feature of English constitutional history in the seventeenth and eighteenth centuries, was followed by a similar movement in the American colonies. Here the assemblies, slowly assuming a likeness to "the mother of parliaments" in organization, procedure, and function, and representing the local force in the constitution, were confronted by the royal governor, representing the king and armed with a commission and instructions as instruments of the prerogative. In the face of the British attitude toward the colonies, these local bodies could not hope to win the same degree of sovereignty that parliament had gained in England, except by open revolution. But before they took this final step they could and did win supremacy in many matters at the expense of the crown and by methods very much like those used by the parliament at Westminster.

Much of the story of the colonial struggle for supremacy has been told again and again. But the contest can never be fully understood without first studying the opposing forces. The British system of royal government was a vital factor in the history of the colonies. The royal prerogative, as expressed in the commissions and instructions, and as exercised by the governors, was foreign to the ideals which the Americans eventually adopted for their political system. In many of the royal provinces it finally went down to destruction. But during the century and a half in which it was maintained before the Revolution, the authority of the crown remained the basis of the provincial constitution.

CHAPTER II

LAUNCHING THE ADMINISTRATION

THE royal governor was the most important agent of the home government in the administration of the colonies. His office was twofold in character, since he was both the guiding head of a local government and the central link in the chain which bound the colony politically to the mother country. He had, therefore, to hold in a nice balance the frequently dissimilar interests and needs of the two peoples. His was a task for no mere placeman. The problems which confronted an incumbent of the office were often perplexing enough to demand statesmanship of a high order. Writers on colonial history have often maintained that honesty, disinterestedness, and real political ability were seldom if ever found in the persons of the various royal appointees. Such a statement, however, cannot be reconciled with the facts. Bearing in mind the nature of the governorship, the frequently inadequate financial return, and the eighteenth century idea that political office was a property right, one is rather led to wonder at the comparatively high quality of the men appointed. The British officials were more successful than might be expected in finding suitable men to fill these posts which required the exchange of the comforts of English life for the ruder, less cultured, more primitive society of a colonial capital, and in which the governor faced the almost certain prospect of a series of quarrels with a hostile assembly, should he fulfil his whole duty to the crown.

The men who were appointed to colonial governorships may be broadly divided into three groups. One included

provincials—men who by birth or long residence in
America had become familiar with colonial institutions
and colonial problems and whose sincere attachment to
the crown had been shown, often by years of devoted service. Many such appointments were in the nature of pro-
motions. After holding office for years as a member of the
governor's council, a man might advance to the senior
position on the board, in which post, or through later appointment as lieutenant governor, he might temporarily
administer the colony during the absence of the governor.
Loyalty and ability proven by such service were more than
once rewarded with appointment to the governorship of
the same or some other province. Such names as those of
Christopher Codrington, jr., governor of the Leeward
Islands, and Sir Henry Moore, governor of New York,
stand out among those of Americans who proved by the
general success of their administrations the wisdom of
their appointment from the colonial training school. But
with other native governors, such as Thomas Hutchinson
of Massachusetts Bay and Lewis Morris of New Jersey,
their American background and earlier political asso-
ciations were in themselves additional causes for antagonism and misunderstanding when duty forced the governors to oppose their fellow colonists.

A second group of colonial governors was composed of
men who were primarily military or naval officers, who
often held positions of civil authority chiefly to enable
them better to maintain their military leadership or to
repay them financially for the often unwelcome assign-
ment of an American command. Throughout the troubled
period of the Seven Years' War the governorship of
Virginia was held in succession by two of the commanders
in chief in America, the earl of Loudoun and Sir Jeffrey
Amherst. The only reason given by the Board of Trade
for recommending Amherst's appointment was that it was

"necessary and expedient" for the royal service that the commander in chief of his Majesty's forces in America be made governor of Virginia.[1] Neither Loudoun nor Amherst ever exercised direct control of the civil government of Virginia, both of them leaving the colony in the hands of the lieutenant governor and simply drawing their share of the salary and perquisites of the office. Sometimes naval officers were appointed as governors or lieutenant governors of provinces which were strategically important. Four such men held office in Jamaica and the same number administered the affairs of Nova Scotia.[2] In addition to such men, a number of governors or lieutenant governors could be named whose chief service was in connection with the long series of wars which marked the colonial period. The civil administrations of these men were largely incidental to their military commands, or, more frequently, followed afterward as rewards for services rendered. Included in such a list would appear the names of Lieutenant Colonel Lawrence Armstrong, lieutenant governor of Nova Scotia and acting governor for fifteen years; Major General the Honorable Robert Monckton, successively governor of Nova Scotia and New York; Rear Admiral Sir Charles Hardy, governor of New York; Major General Sir Guy Carleton (Lord Dorchester) and General Frederick Haldimand, governors of Quebec; and Lieutenant General Thomas Gage, governor of Massachusetts Bay. The list of appointees from military circles might be greatly extended.

[1] Board of Trade to the king, Sept. 12, 1759, C.O. 5: 1367, p. 390 (L.C.).

[2] In Jamaica: Captain Lord Archibald Hamilton (1711–1716); Rear Admiral, later Vice Admiral, Charles Knowles (1752–1756); Captain Sir William Trelawney (1768–1772); and Captain Sir Basil Keith (1774–1777). In Nova Scotia: Captain Lord William Campbell (1766–1771); Captain, later Rear Admiral, Mariot Arbuthnot, lieutenant and acting governor (1776–1778); Captain, later Rear Admiral, Sir Charles Hughes, lieutenant and acting governor (1778–1781); Captain Sir Andrew Snape Hamond, lieutenant and acting governor (1781–1782).

But by no means all of those with previous service in the army or navy were appointed to colonial office primarily for military reasons. In a period marked by frequent wars, many officers naturally had been in the armed forces of Great Britain at some time in their careers. In fact, as far as accurate information can be had, about one half of the governors and lieutenant governors of the royal provinces appointed before 1783 had at one time or another held commissions in the army or navy.[3] The service they had rendered might vary in extent and importance from that of the earl of Dunmore who had been a junior officer in the Third Footguards for three years during his young-manhood,[4] to that of Guy Carleton, who began his military career in 1742, served in America throughout the Seven Years' War and in the American Revolution, rose through the various ranks to lieutenant general in 1777 and general in 1783, and was elevated to the peerage as Lord Dorchester in 1786.[5] Nearly one half of these military officers held the rank of colonel or lieutenant colonel during their civil administrations. Military titles were very common among the royal governors.

The third and by far the largest group of governors was composed of Englishmen who owed their appointments to political connections at home. Many of the men with military histories actually belong in this category. The group was very largely made up of typical members

[3] Of the 243 men about whom definite information is available, 129 had served as officers in the army establishment and 15 had been officers in the royal navy.

[4] *Army Lists*, 1756, p. 32 (where he is listed as Lord Fincastle); 1757, p. 31; 1758, p. 45. Dunmore was governor of New York from 1769 to 1770 and of Virginia from 1770 to the Revolution.

[5] *Army Lists, passim;* G. E. Cokayne, *Complete Peerage*, III, 142–143; *Dictionary of National Biography*, IX, 93–95. Carleton held office as lieutenant governor and then governor of Quebec from 1768 until 1778 although out of the province some of this time. He was reappointed governor in 1786 and held office until 1796.

of the office-holding class in England, neither better nor
worse than the men who were carrying on the real administration of the mother country. Practically all such
men viewed political office as a property right rather than
as a public trust. Most of them looked upon the opportunity to head an American government as merely one step
in the forward progress of their political or financial
ambitions.[6] Many men desired the governorship because
it seemed to offer great money-making opportunities.
Often such men's hopes were doomed to disappointment,
especially in the smaller continental provinces where the
salary was anything but munificent and the perquisites
of office amounted to little. In other cases, especially when
the individual was not too scrupulous in his methods of
acquiring wealth, his hopes were better justified. A shrewd
governor might build up a comfortable fortune through

[6] It cannot be said that there ever existed a definite group of "professional" colonial governors, only two men in our period being really in that
class. These two, Sir Edmund Andros and Francis Nicholson, were unique in
the history of their times. The former, after serving in various court and
political offices in England during the early years of the Restoration, was
made governor of New York in 1674 by its then proprietor, the Duke of York.
In this position he served for seven years. After a short retirement he was
reappointed by his patron, now James II, as governor of the Dominion of
New England. Following the collapse of this experiment, Andros occupied the
governorship of Virginia until 1698 and was for a long time acting governor
of Maryland as well. He rounded out this long career as a royal administrator
by holding for two years the position of governor of the island of Jersey, retiring therefrom when he was approaching his seventieth birthday. Nicholson's career was still more striking. Beginning in 1688 as lieutenant governor of the Dominion of New England under Andros, he held in turn the
lieutenant governorship of New York, Virginia, and Maryland, and the governorship of Maryland, Virginia, Nova Scotia, and South Carolina. The only
extended interruption in this service was from 1705 to 1715, during part of
which time, however, he was engaged in important military enterprises in
America. He died in England in 1728 while still holding office as governor
of South Carolina. Other men occasionally held office for long terms of years
or in more than one colony, but there is no other case where it may be said
that the governorship of American provinces constituted a man's life work.

illegal trade, the operations of privateers, or the granting of improperly large tracts of land to himself and his friends.[7] In the larger West India islands the salaries and other rewards of office were higher than in most of the continental colonies. The governorship of either Jamaica, Barbados, or the Leeward Islands was therefore considered a more desirable position than that of any other province, with the possible exception of Virginia. But in most of the royal colonies the real profits were quite uncertain.

The general level of those who were appointed to colonial governorships was relatively high. There were those, of course, who through unworthy motives or actions incurred the hatred of the colonists and whose names served as a reproach for years to follow. Such a man was Lord Cornbury,[8] scion of the great house of Clarendon, whose peculations from the treasury of New York led the colonists to distrust the governors of the province for the next half century and thereby profoundly affected New York's political history. Such again was Daniel Parke of the Leeward Islands,[9] who, in spite of a laudable personal courage, was attacked and killed by inhabitants of Antigua who had become embittered by the severity of his rule and the immorality of his private life. Against such names, however, must be placed those of men like Robert Hunter,[10] who throughout his controversies with the New York assembly retained the friendship and esteem of its mem-

[7] The extent to which governors personally profited from their administrations is almost impossible to determine. In many cases their own statements conflict directly with contemporary accounts. For example, George Clinton of New York stated repeatedly in his letters home that his administration was impoverishing him, although it was generally believed in the province that he returned to England with a fortune "very little short" of £84,000, acquired in New York. Smith, *History of New York*, II, 159.

[8] Governor of New York, 1701–1708, and of New Jersey, 1702–1708.

[9] Governor of the Leeward Islands, 1705–1710.

[10] Governor of New York and New Jersey, 1709–1719, and of Jamaica, 1727–1734.

bers and who later secured from the Jamaica assembly legislation which none of his predecessors had been able to obtain; Henry Grenville of Barbados,[11] whose statue was erected at public expense in the town hall of Bridge-town upon his departure from the island;[12] and Thomas Pownall,[13] whose subsequent writings show him to have been one of the fairest and most discerning Englishmen to come in contact with the colonies. In general, the governors appointed by the crown compare not unfavorably in honesty and ability with the men now elected by the people of the several states of the Union.

Of the slightly more than three hundred governors general, governors, lieutenant governors, and deputy governors appointed by the crown for the English colonies during the period from 1624 to 1783, approximately one in every four was a peer or the son of a peer or belonged to one of the lesser titled classes. Forty-five of the total had gained political experience as members of the House of Commons at Westminster prior to their appointment, and nine others entered parliament after their return from America.[14] Forty-eight had matriculated at Oxford or Cambridge or at some other university or college in the British Isles, America, or the European continent. More than a score had been admitted to one or another of the Inns of Court. The Royal Society included

[11] Governor of Barbados, 1747–1753.

[12] Ralph Weeks, president of the council, to the Board of Trade, May 23, 1753, C.O. 28: 30. In writing of the ''excellent pattern of our most worthy governor,'' Weeks declared that within his experience of fifty years ''the island had not been blessed with such an administration, nor have six such years together passed over it in such an uninterrupted course of public tranquillity.''

[13] Lieutenant governor of New Jersey, 1755–1761 (only nominally after 1757), and governor of Massachusetts Bay, 1757–1760.

[14] By the Place Act (6 Anne, cap. 7, § 24) no man could sit in the House of Commons and hold office as governor or deputy governor of a colony at the same time.

fifteen governors in its membership. This group constituted a true cross-section of the British governing classes
and was composed of men in every way characteristic of
those who held office in Great Britain itself during this
period. Those who criticize the British government for the
sort of men sent over as provincial governors, should first
become familiar with the types of those who filled the
offices of equal standing in the mother country during the
same period.[15]

Except for the nine years between 1752 and 1761 when
the entire American patronage was in the hands of the
Board of Trade,[16] the nomination of governors was a
privilege of the secretary of state for the southern department. Applications for appointment, therefore, were
usually sent to this official. The ups and downs of British
politics accounted for a number of changes in governorships as the patron of first one candidate and then another
gained influence and power at Whitehall. As soon as news
of a vacancy became public, and often even before that,
letters and requests began to be received for the appointment of certain individuals to the position. These memorials were sent not only by the applicant for the position
himself but by anyone who might be interested in a particular candidate or who was in any way connected with
the province.[17]

In 1738, when the government of the Bahamas was ex-

[15] In his recent book, *The Structure of Politics at the Accession of George
III* (2 vols. London, 1929), L. B. Namier gives a vivid picture of the office-
seekers of Great Britain in the eighteenth century with particular reference
to membership in the House of Commons. The work well deserves perusal by
students of colonial history. The statements made in the text above concern
only the governors and lieutenant governors. Doubtless the lesser administrative offices in the colonies were often filled by very inferior men.

[16] *Acts, Privy Coun., Col.*, 1745–1766, pp. 154–157; C.O. 324: 38, pp. 311–
318.

[17] Many such applications and endorsements are found in the Newcastle
Papers in the British Museum. Only a few are mentioned here.

pected to be vacant soon, Martin Bladen, a member of the
Board of Trade, wrote to the duke of Newcastle, secretary
of state, recommending his son-in-law, John Tinker, for
the position. Among Tinker's qualifications were said to
be his experience of several years as agent for the Royal
African Company and the South Sea Company in South
America and his willingness, together with that of several
London merchants to whom he was related, to invest considerable sums in the development of the islands.[18] A few
months later a certain I. Frontin wrote to the earl of Essex requesting his recommendation to Newcastle for the
position. Frontin declared that he had the support of the
governor of the South Sea Company, who had "the chief
concern in those islands," and of Edward Walpole, son of
Sir Robert.[19] In forwarding this letter to Newcastle and
urging the appointment of Frontin, Essex wrote that the
applicant was "a very honest good sort of man and extremely unfortunate" and that he was also well known to
the duke of Devonshire.[20] In spite of this formidable support of Frontin's candidacy, the appointment went to
Tinker when the incumbent resigned in 1740.

In 1732, when it was noised about London that Governor Burrington was to be recalled from North Carolina,
the duke of Manchester wrote to Newcastle recommending
the appointment of Christian Cole, who had served as
British resident at Venice after Manchester's father's
embassy there.[21] That there was a financial motive behind
this application was indicated in a similar letter from the
duke of Kent, who wrote that Cole was "a very honest

[18] Martin Bladen to Newcastle, Sept. 25, 1738, British Museum, Newcastle Papers, VI, Additional Manuscript, 32,691, fos. 374–375.

[19] I. Frontin to the earl of Essex, Dec. 26, 1738, ibid., fos. 533–534.

[20] Essex to Newcastle, Dec. 28, 1738, ibid., fo. 535.

[21] Manchester to Newcastle, Oct. 7, 1732, ibid., II, Add. MS., 32,687, fo.
501.

intelligent and knowing person in all business" but that "his misfortune has been to have lost in the South Seas and again lately in the Charitable Organization, which makes him desirous to leave his own country and to go abroad and would be very happy to have your Grace's favor and protection for this employment, which I hear is but £500 a year salary."[22] Another and perhaps a less selfish reason for this appointment was urged by Lord Torrington, who stated his belief that Cole had "a disposition and a capacity to do good were he employed in a government that wants a reasonable man to settle a people that may want to be licked into some shape for his [their?] own happiness."[23] In view of this recommendation, the people of North Carolina may have deserved congratulations for a lucky escape when the appointment finally went to Gabriel Johnston, former professor of Oriental Languages at the University of St. Andrews, and the intimate friend of Lord Wilmington, president of the council.[24]

The appointment of William Shirley as governor of Massachusetts Bay was perhaps accelerated by a memorial of "sundry inhabitants of the Massachusetts Bay in New England now in London and merchants of London trading to New England,"[25] but it was primarily due to the personal solicitations of Mrs. Shirley, who had already secured sundry lesser favors for her husband from the

[22] Kent to Newcastle, Oct. 12, 1732, Newcastle Paps., II, Add. MS., 32,687, fo. 510. The duke of Kent was in error as to the salary of this position. Governor Burrington was entitled to draw £700 per annum from the quit-rents of the province, although he did not receive a penny until after the close of his administration. The salary of his successor, Johnston, was increased to £1,000, but was equally in arrears. See below, pp. 332–333.

[23] Torrington to Newcastle, Oct. 10, 1732, ibid., fo. 505.

[24] North Carolina Colonial Records, IV, iii; S. A. Ashe, Biographical History of North Carolina, IV, 187–193.

[25] C.O. 5: 10, no. 184 (L.C.), no date given.

duke of Newcastle.[26] A few years later, Jonathan Belcher, whom Shirley had supplanted, launched a campaign to get for himself the governorship of South Carolina. Although in his sixty-third year, he made the uncomfortable voyage to England and laid his case personally before Lord Chancellor Hardwicke and Henry Pelham, chancellor of the Exchequer and first lord of the Treasury, brother of the duke of Newcastle. He was supported in his appeal by some of the Quakers of England, for both Newcastle and Belcher had close relations with the Society of Friends. His letters stressed the financial losses in which his Massachusetts administration had involved him because of his loyalty to the crown, and he intimated that the then governor of South Carolina, James Glen, a "person of very little merit or pretensions," had held the office long enough.[27] After two years of such solicitation, Belcher won the governorship, not of South Carolina, but of New Jersey, in which province the Quaker element was strong. In this post he served during the remaining eleven years of his life.

A somewhat unusual motive for seeking colonial office was given by the earl of Kinnoul when he asked for the governorship of Barbados in 1738. He had served for some

[26] Chas. H. Lincoln, *Correspondence of William Shirley*, I, 6–43, *passim;* also Mrs. Shirley to Newcastle, July 19, 1738, Newcastle Paps., VI, Add. MS., 32,691, fo. 254; Newcastle to Mrs. Shirley, July 23, 1738, *ibid.*, fo. 262; Mrs. Shirley to Newcastle, Mar. 13, 1740, *ibid.*, VIII, Add. MS., 32,693, fos. 123–124. The application was also supported by Thomas Western in letters to Newcastle of Jan. 28, 1741, and May 15, 1741, *ibid.*, XI, Add. MS., 32,696, fos. 53–54, 530. It was ineffectually opposed by Governor Belcher's son, Jonathan, jr., then a barrister in London, in a letter to Thomas Townshend, teller of the Exchequer, dated April 30, 1741, which the latter apparently sent on to Newcastle, *ibid.*, fos. 430–431.

[27] Belcher to Newcastle, July 29, 1745, *ibid.*, XIX, Add. MS., 32,704, fo. 547; same to same, March 12, 1746, *ibid.*, XXI, Add. MS., 32,706, fos. 292–293; Belcher to Hardwicke, March 19, 1746, *ibid.*, fos. 314–315; Seventeen Friends in Sussex to Newcastle, Feb. —, 1746, *ibid.*, fo. 235.

time as British representative at Constantinople, but his embassy had ended in his recall the year before under conditions most unfavorable to his reputation. In applying to Newcastle, he defended strongly his conduct in Turkey and then added: "My lord, if the king is so good as to give me the government of Barbados at this time, it will justify me in the eyes of all the world; whereas, if I do not soon receive some such public mark of his Majesty's favor, the greater part of mankind will have reason to think that my accusers were in the right and that I did not discharge my duty in Turkey as I ought to have done; which will be very hard upon an innocent man. Therefore, as my reputation is concerned at this time as well as my support in the world, I must beg your Grace seriously to consider my case."[28] Possibly Newcastle did not care to clear Kinnoul "in the eyes of the world," for the latter was not appointed. More probably, reasons closely connected with the patronage system of Great Britain determined the choice of a governor for Barbados at this time, as not infrequently happened. For Sir Charles Wager, first lord of the Admiralty, wrote to Newcastle suggesting the appointment of Robert Byng, then a commissioner of the navy, and intimated that Byng's appointment was part of a plan to help another adherent, presumably by naming him to the post to be made vacant in the navy office.[29] This plan was eventually carried out.

Another instance in which considerations of British patronage and politics played a part related to Virginia. When the earl of Albemarle, governor general of Virginia, died in 1754, no less than five British noblemen were mentioned for the office, which for almost half a century had been a sinecure, bringing as it did, about fifteen hundred

---

[28] Kinnoul to Newcastle, Aug. 4, 1738, Newcastle Paps., VI, Add. MS., 32,691, fos. 284–287.

[29] Wager to Newcastle, Dec. 2, 1738, *ibid.*, fo. 502.

pounds a year to the titular governor who remained in
Europe and left the actual administration in the hands of
a lieutenant governor in the province. Among those who
wrote to Newcastle at this time was Lord Chancellor
Hardwicke, who urged that a resident governor be appointed, but suggested that, if the position was again to
be filled "in a court way," it be given to Lord Cholmondeley, as this would make vacant an Irish sinecure held
by the latter, which might be given to another influential
politician.[30] The Virginia governorship was finally be-
stowed upon the earl of Loudoun after his appointment as
commander in chief in America.[31]

An interesting hint of a bargain involving a governorship on one side and political support in England on the
other is to be found in a memorandum by Viscount Dup-
plin, a member of the Board of Trade and a supporter of
Newcastle, regarding the appointment of Thomas Pitt,
a brother of the later prime minister, as governor of South
Carolina. According to this paper, Henry Pelham, chancellor of the Exchequer, and Lord Halifax, president of
the Board of Trade, had apparently made a tentative
agreement that if the income of the South Carolina governorship could be increased from £1,900 to £2,400 to
equal that of the New York governorship, Pitt would be
appointed to the former office in exchange for his "giving
the government his interest in the several boroughs where
he is concerned."[32] The scheme fell through, however,

[30] Hardwicke to Newcastle, Dec. 29, 1754, *ibid.*, LII, Add. MS., 32,737,
fo. 514 (L.C.). Names suggested for the position made vacant by Albemarle's
death, include besides that of the late earl's eldest son and successor to the
title, and of Lord Cholmondeley, those of Earl Paulet, Lord Delawarr, and
Lord Mountfort, the last of whom was said to have "half asked for it."
Ibid., fos. 505–506 (L.C.).

[31] Board of Trade to the king, Feb. 10, 1756, C.O. 5: 1367, p. 163 (L.C.).

[32] "Memorandum relating to South Carolina," undated but probably of

probably because of the failure of the financial arrangements.[33]

When an individual had finally outdistanced his rivals and had won the appointment, he was prone to consider the position a property right in which he now had a vested interest. Buying and selling of offices was looked upon in England at this time as a legitimate form of business transaction, and there is no reason to suppose that colonial governorships were excepted from this attitude. There is a little evidence, although it is not conclusive, to show that traffic was actually carried on in these positions. For example, the agents for Massachusetts Bay were said to have paid £1,000 to Elezius Burges for the resignation of his appointment to that colony in favor of Samuel Shute, who was looked upon as being more friendly to the legislative and financial program of the majority party in the Bay Colony. It is not entirely certain, however, that this sum represented more than a liberal repayment to Burges of his expenses in getting his commission and instructions passed through the proper seals and offices.[34]

about 1753 or 1754, Newcastle Paps., CCCXLV, Add. MS., 33,030, fos. 346–347. Thomas Pitt had considerable political influence in Cornwall. See Lord Rosebury, *Chatham His Early Life and Connections*, pp. 16–18.

[33] An early instance of the keen competition which developed for colonial governorships is that of 1689, when new commissions were necessary for all provinces in consequence of the accession of William and Mary. At that time a total of sixteen names was submitted for the governorships of Jamaica, Barbados, the Leeward Islands, Virginia, New York, and Bermuda, in some cases one name being mentioned in connection with two provinces. That this list was only partial is clear from the fact that two of the six colonies named received governors not indicated on the list, and in a third case the successful candidate was superseded within three months after appointment by an altogether new nominee. C.O. 5: 1, pp. 901–923 (L.C.).

[34] See the article by Albert Matthews on "Colonel Elezius Burges" in *Publications* of the Colonial Society of Massachusetts, XIV, 360–372; also see Massachusetts Historical Society *Proceedings*, 1888, p. 192; Hutchinson, *History of Massachusetts Bay*, II, 215.

In another case, Lieutenant Governor George Clarke of New York offered one thousand guineas through his son to Lord Delawarr in 1740 for his commission.[35] How far the proposal went is not clear. At any rate, Delawarr never went to his colony, but his place was taken the following year by George Clinton and not by the lieutenant governor. There are several depositions to the effect that Lieutenant Governor John Pearne of Montserrat offered to sell his commission for £400, but absolute proof of an actual purchase in any case during the period is lacking.[36]

Even before the opening of the eighteenth century, the steps to be taken before a newly appointed governor could set out for his province had become fixed. Immediately upon his appointment he waited upon the king and kissed the royal hand in acknowledgment of the office conferred upon him. At the same time, the Board of Trade was directed to prepare the new governor's commission and instructions.[37] The former document was regularly the first to be prepared, and since changes from commissions to former governors were rare, the task seldom took very

[35] George Clarke, jr., to Lord Delawarr, June 20, 1740, *Documents Relating to the Colonial History of the State of New York*, VI, 163–164 (hereafter cited as *N. Y. Col. Docs.*).

[36] *Cal. State Paps., Col.*, 1712–1714, § 678 v, vi, vii. In a letter to the Board of Trade, March 3, 1705, Governor Nicholson said, ''I can safely swear that though I have had the good fortune and honor to have several employments in my lifetime, yet I neither directly or indirectly gave one farthing for obtaining them or afterwards to any person whatsoever for keeping them. . . . I hope that my paying the necessary fees and endeavoring to gratify those who have solicited the dispatch of my commission, instructions &c., after they were granted will not be accounted bribery,'' C.O. 5: 1314, no. 43, p. 9 (L.C.); *Cal. State Paps., Col.*, 1704–1705, § 924, p. 421.

[37] The order came either by a letter from the secretary of state or by an order in council. Before the organization of the Board of Trade, the commission and instructions were prepared by special committees of the privy council (*Cal. State Paps., Col.*, 1661–1668, § 847); by the secretary of state, (*ibid.*, § 637); or by the Lords of Trade (C.O. 5: 1355, pp. 266–273, L.C.).

long. In one case the commission was submitted to the
privy council on the very day on which the order for preparation was issued,[38] but the average time consumed was
from ten days to two weeks. The commission was submitted with a representation explaining what changes, if any,
had been made from that to the last governor of the same
province. Commonly this representation was merely perfunctory, stating that the commission was "in the usual
form." On reaching the privy council, either directly, or
indirectly through the secretary of state, the representation and commission were usually referred to the committee of the whole council, upon whose favorable report
an order in council was issued approving the draft and
directing the secretary of state to prepare a warrant for
the king's signature for passing the commission through
the seals. Occasionally some slight change was made in the
commission from the draft submitted, but this was seldom
of real importance.[39] The warrant, when properly signed,
was then sent to the attorney and solicitor general, who
prepared the "king's bill" and thus sent the commission
on its way through the seals.[40]

While the commission was being prepared, the Board
of Trade also had the general instructions under consideration. The drafting of this document generally took far

[38] Commission to Amherst, Virginia, submitted Sept. 12, 1759, C.O. 5:
1367, p. 391 (L.C.).

[39] For example, in the commission for Molesworth of Jamaica in 1689,
the king in council ordered the dropping of the word "conveniently" from the
clause directing the passage of laws "as near as conveniently may be agreeable to the laws of England." C.O. 138: 6, p. 185. In 1701 the words empowering the governor to put to death "according to the law of arms" such
enemies as he might capture, were ordered changed to "according to law."
C.O. 138: 10, p. 170.

[40] The procedure involved in passing a document through the seals is
described in Hall, *Studies*, pp. 267–269; *Formula Book of Diplomatic Documents*, pp. 114–118; Andrews, *Guide*, I, 268–273; Sir H. C. Maxwell-Lyte,
Historical Notes on the Use of the Great Seal of England, pp. 93–96.

more time and serious attention than did that of the commission. As the instructions were to be a detailed working guide to the administrative conduct of the governor in the province, it was important that each draft include all the changes in policy of the home government since the last general instructions had been prepared, and that it be made to fit any altered conditions in the colony itself. Therefore, the Board of Trade regularly introduced—in modified form if necessary—such additional instructions, royal letters, or even orders in council as had been issued during the interval dealing with matters of more than temporary importance. Correspondence of the governors or other officials of recent years was considered and any suggestions that might have been made were borne in mind.[41] Often, of course, such proposals had already been embodied in additional instructions, but action was sometimes delayed until a new governor was appointed. When the former governor happened to be in England at the time the board was at work upon the documents for his successor, the occasion was often taken to get his firsthand opinion upon the instructions which he had used.[42]

The newly appointed governor was also frequently given a chance to make suggestions and comments upon his own instructions while they were being prepared. Of the fifteen governors appointed for Jamaica between 1677

[41] Lord Culpeper's marginal comments on his 1679 instructions as governor of Virginia were useful in this connection. Against one of these which required him to suggest a better form of tax than that on polls and tillables then in force, he wrote proposing an impost on brandy and liquors imported, C.O. 5: 1355, p. 335 (L.C.). In his instructions of 1682 (art. 32) he was accordingly directed to recommend such a tax to the Virginia assembly, C.O. 5: 1356, pp. 30–61 (L.C.).

[42] Former Governor Hunter of New York and New Jersey, for example, made some important comments in 1720 upon the instructions under preparation for his successor, William Burnet. *N. Y. Col. Docs.*, V, 540–541; *Journal of the Commissioners for Trade and Plantations*, 1718–1722, pp. 167, 175, 185–186, 194–196, 198–199 (hereafter cited as *Board of Trade Journal*).

and 1727, memorials concerning changes in their instructions have been found from seven, and an eighth appeared personally before the board.[43] Most prominent of these was Sir Nicholas Lawes, a former resident and chief justice of Jamaica and member of its council. More recently, as a London merchant, he had been engaged in trade with the island and had repeatedly been consulted by the Board of Trade on Jamaica affairs. Soon after his appointment as governor, the board called him before them and offered him a copy of the draft instructions with a request that he submit his observations thereon in writing. This resulted in a series of memorials to which the board gave careful consideration. In the end they adopted many of his suggestions.[44] The board seems always to have listened with especial attention to the suggestions of prospective governors who had themselves had experience in America, whether connected or not with the provinces to which they were going. Thus, when Robert Dinwiddie, formerly surveyor general of the customs for the southern department in America, was preparing to return as chief executive of Virginia in 1751, he was allowed to examine the instructions and suggest additions. He did so and several of his proposals became permanent features

[43] C.O. 138: 3, pp. 159–160 (Carlisle, 1677); C.O. 138: 5, pp. 242–260, 300–301; C.O. 138: 6, p. 115 (Albemarle, 1686); C.O. 138: 6, pp. 178–182 (Molesworth, 1689); C.O. 137: 5, no. 41 (Selwyn, 1700); C.O. 138: 15, pp. 1–6, 59–60, 216–219 (Pitt, 1716); *Board of Trade Journal*, 1718–1722, p. 322 (Portland, 1721); C.O. 137: 16, fo. 339 (Hunter, 1727); see also the next note for Lawes, 1717. Henry Cunningham, appointed governor in 1734, also appeared before the board asking for a change in one article, but he did not make his request until after the draft was completed, *Board of Trade Journal*, 1728/9–1734, pp. 418–421, 425.

[44] "Observations on the Instructions of his Majesty to his Governor of Jamaica," received Aug. 29, 1717, C.O. 137: 12, no. 59. See also *ibid.*, nos. 68, 75, 93; C.O. 138: 15, pp. 288, 326–329, 338–340, 341–344; minutes of the Board of Trade, July 11, Aug. 30, 1717, *Board of Trade Journal*, 1714/5–1718, pp. 246, 262.

of the general instructions to the governors of that colony.[45] Not every prospective governor was consulted in this way, but the board was generally willing to hear what the appointees had to say and to accept their suggestions whenever possible.

But the governors, past and prospective, were not the only persons whose views were considered in the preparation of general instructions. Every individual or organization having any interest or authority in the colonies might make suggestions, many of which were regularly incorporated in the form of new articles or of alterations in those already existing. One of the most influential of these persons was the bishop of London, within whose jurisdiction all the American colonies fell. Practically all the instructions on matters of religion and morals can be traced back to original proposals of one or another of the occupants of the see of London. As they were members of the privy council committee on plantation affairs in the seventeenth century, many of their early suggestions were made verbally, but formal memorials and letters attest the bishops' interest in the instructions when they themselves were absent from the meetings of the committee. When instructions were being prepared for the earl of Carlisle as governor of Jamaica in 1677, the bishop requested the addition of clauses requiring that no ministers be received in the island without his license, that such ministers as he might send properly licensed be not rejected without sufficient cause, and that all ministers

---

[45] Dinwiddie to the Board of Trade, Aug. —, 1751, C.O. 5: 1327, p. 417 (L.C.). Among other instances of suggestions asked for and received are the following: Andros (Va.) to the Board of Trade, April 7, 1692, on the disposal of the quit-rents of Virginia for military service, *Calendar of Treasury Papers*, 1557–1696, p. 231; questions submitted to Jonathan Belcher (Mass.) on the paper currency problem, to assist the board in preparing his instructions of 1730, C.O. 5: 916, p. 263 (Mass.); *Board of Trade Journal*, 1728/9–1734, pp. 89, 90, 97.

be admitted as members of their respective vestries.[46] The first and third requests were granted and the resulting instructions were regularly given to all subsequent governors. Further proposals were made in 1679 and 1685.[47] In 1698 the bishop sent to the Board of Trade through the earl of Bridgewater a number of suggestions for changes in the instructions to Governor Nicholson of Virginia.[48] When shown the articles as finally drafted by the board, he protested to the secretary of state that the instruction about collating to benefices was not strong enough to protect the king's prerogative against the encroachments of the vestries.[49] No change was made, however, and the problem remained to trouble the successive governors and bishops for years to come.[50]

Among the official bodies in England which were often consulted in the preparation of general or additional instructions were the Commissioners of the Admiralty, of the Treasury, and of the Customs, each of which bodies was vitally concerned in some aspect of American affairs. The first named had, naturally, a special interest in the governor's maritime authority and jurisdiction. The Admiralty Board considered all matters in any way related to the naval power of Great Britain as being within their special province. Following a memorial by the Admiralty

[46] Minutes of the Lords of Trade, Nov. 10, 1677, C.O. 138: 3, pp. 157–158; *Cal. State Paps., Col.*, 1677–80, § 475.

[47] C.O. 324: 4, pp. 47–48, 75 (L.C.); *Acts, Privy Coun., Col.*, 1613–1680, § 1331; bishop of London to William Blathwayt, Apr. 15, 1685, and minutes of Lords of Trade, Apr. 27, 1685, C.O. 324: 4, pp. 143–144 (L.C.); *Cal. State Paps., Col.*, 1685–1688, §§ 130, 153.

[48] C.O. 5: 1309, pp. 285–287 (L.C.); *Cal. State Paps., Col.*, 1697–1698, § 585.

[49] Bishop of London to Sir Philip Meadows, Aug. 9, 1698, C.O. 5: 1309, pp. 339–340 (L.C.); *Cal. State Paps., Col.*, 1697–1698, § 737.

[50] See, for example, letters from Robert Dinwiddie to the Board of Trade, June 5, 1751, C.O. 5: 1327, pp. 461–462 (L.C.), and to the earl of Holderness, same date, C.O. 5: 1338, no. 79 (L.C.).

to the privy council in 1728 touching the preservation of
the woods in North America as a source for masts, an
additional instruction was sent to the governors of all the
northern colonies ordering them to aid the surveyor
general of the woods in the fulfillment of his duties. This
instruction was incorporated in the subsequent general
instructions to the governors of Massachusetts Bay, New
Hampshire, and Nova Scotia.[51] When the Admiralty felt
that a colonial statute was harmful to the naval service,
they were quick to complain to the king and try to get relief by instruction to the governor. In 1766, for example,
they learned of a recent Virginia act abolishing a drawback formerly allowed there upon the rum used in vict-
ualling ships of the royal navy. They memorialized the
king at once and secured an instruction to Governor Amherst forbidding the imposition of any tax on victuals or
liquor imported unless all supplies for the royal ships of
war were specifically exempted.[52] An article to the same
intent was included in the general instructions to the succeeding governors.[53]

In the same way, the views of the lord high treasurer
or the Commissioners of the Treasury were considered
in the framing of instructions. In 1670 the Commissioners
of the Treasury asked for changes in a number of paragraphs in the instructions to Sir Thomas Lynch as lieutenant governor of Jamaica to provide that reports on

[51] *Acts, Privy Coun., Col.*, 1720–1745, § 143. For the additional instructions,
April 5, 1728, see *New Hampshire Province Laws*, II, 240. Instructions to
Belcher, Mass., 1730, art. 44, C.O. 5, 192, pp. 361–400 (L.O.); instructions
to Belcher, New Hampshire, 1730, art. 57, *N. H. Prov. Laws*, II, 467–490;
and instructions to Philips, Nova Scotia, 1729, art. 20, C.O. 5: 189, pp. 417–
434 (L.C.).

[52] Additional instructions, submitted June 18, 1766, C.O. 5: 1368, pp. 306–
308 (L.C.).

[53] Instructions to Botetourt, Va., 1768, art. 23, C.O. 5: 1368, pp. 491–541
(L.C.); instructions to Dunmore, Va., 1771, art. 25, Mass. Hist. Soc. *Collections*, 4th series, X, 630–667.

various financial matters be sent to the Treasury officials
in England, thereby assuring the supervision of the island's fiscal system by the home authorities.[54] Robert
Hunter asked in 1707 that he be given an instruction allowing him to draw half salary as governor of Virginia from
the death of his predecessor, and the Board of Trade referred this application to the lord high treasurer for consideration.[55] In the end it was felt that this would be an
unwise precedent and the Board of Trade so reported
to the secretary of state.[56] In 1721 the Commissioners of
the Treasury undertook a general survey of all the articles in the various governors' commissions and instructions relating to the royal revenue and to the effects of
pirates seized in America.[57] Although no changes seem
to have been made at once as a result of this investigation,
probably several of the alterations made in the instructions during the next few years were due to this manifesta-
tion of interest on the part of the Treasury.

Possibly the Commissioners of the Customs were more
vitally concerned in American affairs than any other of
the British bodies with the exception of the Board of
Trade itself. Charged with important duties connected
with the enforcement of the navigation acts, and inti-
mately concerned with all matters relating to the trade of
the British mercantile world, as the Commissioners of
the Customs were, they felt it their duty to keep in close
contact with the Board of Trade as well as with the
customs officers in America. Any complaints from the

[54] "Additions to Sir Thomas Lynch's Instructions made by the Commissioners of the Treasury, Dec. 28, 1670," C.O. 1: 25, no. 105.

[55] William Popple, secretary of the Board of Trade, to William Lowndes,
secretary to the lord high treasurer, April 7, 1707, C.O. 5: 1362, p. 120 (L.C.);
Cal. State Paps., Col., 1706–1708, §§ 856, 1145.

[56] Board of Trade to the earl of Sunderland, July 16, 1707, C.O. 5: 1362,
pp. 253–255 (L.C.); Cal. State Paps., Col., 1706–1708, § 1147.

[57] C.O. 324: 10, pp. 293–294 (L.C.).

latter officials about their relations with the governors or others in the colonies were immediately forwarded to the Board of Trade for remedy. When in 1717 the surveyor general in America reported that the surveyors, collectors, and other customs officers were being forced to neglect their regular duties in order to serve on juries, in the militia, or in various "parochial" offices, the commissioners asked the Board of Trade for an instruction against this practice.[58] The board responded to this request with the addition of an instruction to all subsequently appointed governors of royal provinces.[59] A similar complaint in 1770 about the taxation of the salaries of customs officers in Massachusetts Bay, led to the introduction of an article prohibiting such taxation in the instructions to Governor Hutchinson and to his successor, General Gage.[60] In the same spirit of cooperation the Board of Trade was anxious to consider the opinion of the Customs Commissioners on any points in the general instructions which might affect their branch of the royal service in America.[61]

Similarly, the Board of Trade welcomed the assistance of other officers of the home government in the preparation of instructions, either general or additional. In par-

[58] Charles Carkesse to William Popple, July 20, 1717, C.O. 137: 12, no. 71.

[59] In this case the Board of Trade did not consider the matter sufficiently important to warrant an additional instruction, but contented themselves with introducing the article into each set of general instructions subsequently prepared, with the result that it was not found in the instructions for all royal colonies until ten years later. Alured Popple to Charles Carkesse, March 7, 1727, C.O. 324: 11, pp. 34–36 (L.C.).

[60] Instructions to Hutchinson, Mass., 1771, art. 27, C.O. 5: 203, pp. 481–511 (Mass.); instructions to Gage, Mass., 1774, art. 27, C.O. 5: 205, pp. 427–461 (Mass.).

[61] Alured Popple wrote to Charles Carkesse on Oct. 3, 1727, enclosing four articles of the 1715 instructions to Orkney of Virginia, requesting the opinion of the Customs Commissioners as to whether these articles were proper to be repeated, since they apparently infringed on the right of the surveyor general to appoint and supervise his subordinates in the colonies, C.O. 5: 1365, pp. 367–371 (L.C.). The articles were continued unchanged until 1756.

ticular, the auditor general of the plantation revenues,[62] the receiver general of the rights and perquisites of the Admiralty,[63] and, above all, the attorney and solicitor general of Great Britain[64] left their impress upon the development of the instructions. The responsibility rested with the Board of Trade, but the real work was essentially cooperative.

By far the most important single influence upon the development and expansion of the instructions was that of the British merchants. The Board of Trade proved itself to be a thoroughly mercantilist body, ever responsive to conditions of trade and the opinions of the merchants. Those Englishmen who were engaged in trade with America considered the colonies to be their particular preserves and sincerely believed that the interests of British commerce were paramount to any considerations of local needs or desires. The fact that the Board of Trade reflected this view is one of the fundamental reasons why the governors' instructions produced so much antagonism in the colonial assemblies. As early as 1733 the board stated its attitude in a representation to the House of Lords on the relation of the laws, manufactures, and trade of the colonies to the trade of England: "We beg leave to acquaint your Lordships that besides these general [i.e., trade] instructions, this board has never failed to repre-

[62] Horatio Walpole to Newcastle, June 18, 1754, Newcastle Paps., L, Add. MS., 32,735, fos. 487–489 (L.C.).

[63] *Acts, Privy Coun., Col.*, 1720–1745, § 130.

[64] The clause in the commissions of 1702 relative to the oaths to be taken by all governors was prepared by the attorney general, C.O. 324: 8, pp. 159, 162–164 (L.C.). The opinion of the law officers was also taken on instructions relating to pardons, appeals, and other judicial questions, *Cal. State Paps., Col.*, 1710–1711, §§ 764, 767, 774–776; *Board of Trade Journal*, 1708/9–1714/5, pp. 257, 258, 259. Advice on the preparation of commissions and instructions was also sought from the specially appointed counsel to the Board of Trade. John Pownall to Richard Jackson, Dec. 10, 1771, C.O. 324: 18, pp. 392, 426–430 (L.C.); *N. J. Arch.*, X, 370–371.

sent their sense of particular grievances and point out the best methods of redress of them, as often as we have received complaints upon such occasions either from incorporated bodies or private traders, which from the variety of accidents attending trade in the several governments in America, have been very frequent, and have given rise to several other instructions, some of which are general to all the governors of the plantations and others peculiar to respective provinces, as the reason of things or the exigency of the case may have required.''[65]

Although the merchants concerned themselves in all matters which might conceivably affect their interests, the chief target of their attacks was the legislation of the assemblies laying duties on British imports into the colonies or relating in any way to British trade or navigation. Practically every instruction which directed the governor to veto bills of this nature can be traced back to the passage of such a law in some one province. Almost invariably the merchants protested against the law and asked that it be disallowed and that an instruction be sent the governor forbidding such legislation in the future. Sometimes the instruction was first sent to the offending colony alone and was extended to others only as need was later felt; at other times the board took the precaution to issue at once a circular instruction to the governors of all the provinces. In 1731 the merchants of London placed before the king their difficulties in collecting their just debts in the colonies, complaining at the same time of laws which laid lower import duties on the ships and goods of the inhabitants of the respective provinces than on those of other British subjects. When this petition was referred to the Board of Trade, the acting secretary asked the merchants to lay before the board all the facts and specific laws upon which

[65] C.O. 5: 5, fo. 72 (L.C.); C.O. 324: 12, pp. 61–62 (L.C.).

they based their complaints.[66] From the information thus obtained the board prepared a report which fully supported the merchants' charges. The board admitted that many of the laws establishing preferential rates were "of very ancient standing" and could not now be disallowed, but they declared that, in the more recent cases, they had always listened to complaints and, whenever the laws seemed "prejudicial to the trading interest of Great Britain," they had recommended disallowance. They promised to continue this practice. In the meantime they proposed an additional instruction to all governors strictly forbidding the passage of any laws for preferential duties and reenforcing the instructions already given against bills which affected the trade or shipping of Great Britain.[67] Such an additional instruction was issued at once and with slight changes was incorporated in the general instructions to nearly all royal governors until well after the close of the American Revolution.[68]

Naturally the colonists were antagonized by instructions which so clearly represented British rather than colonial interests. Naturally they tried to get such instructions repealed. But their appeals were almost invariably turned down. In 1772, for example, the Virginia House of Burgesses asked for permission to lay an additional duty upon the importation of slaves although such a duty had been prohibited by instructions ever since 1731.[69] In asking that this instruction be withdrawn the Burgesses declared:

[66] B. Wheelock to Humphrey Morice, Micajah Perry, and Richard Harris. Sept. 1, 1731, C.O. 324: 11, pp. 246–247 (L.C.).

[67] *Board of Trade Journal*, 1728/9–1734, pp. 229, 233, 245–248, 265, 268–270; Board of Trade to the king, Jan. 21, 1732, C.O. 324: 11, pp. 248–253 (L.C.).

[68] The circular instruction, May 5, 1732, is printed in *N. H. Prov. Laws*, II, 491–492.

[69] Circular instructions, Dec. 10, 1731, C.O. 5: 195, pp. 249–250 (L.C.). Virginia laws laying such duties had been disallowed as early as 1724 and as recently as 1770, C.O. 5: 1319, pp. 222–253, 255–256, 259–263, 279, 283, 315,

"We are sensible that some of your Majesty's subjects in Great Britain may reap emoluments from this sort of traffic [the slave trade], but when we consider that it greatly retards the settlement of the colonies with more useful inhabitants and may in time have the most destructive influence, we presume to hope that the interest of a few will be disregarded when placed in competition with the security and happiness of such numbers of your Majesty's dutiful and loyal subjects.'"[70] Even such a loyal official as the earl of Dunmore, governor of Virginia, supported the House of Burgesses in this petition. Two years later he felt that he must again remonstrate against the situation, which "cannot fail of renewing the uneasiness which they [the assembly] often express at finding the representation of a set of self-interested merchants and the accounts of the exigencies of the colony which these people take upon them to give, listened to preferably to those which proceed from the people of the colony themselves.'"[71] But the "interest of a few" was of supreme importance in England when those few happened to be a well-organized "set of self-interested merchants." The Board of Trade and the privy council turned deaf ears to the American petitioners, thus helping to alienate those planter aristocrats who were so active a few years later in expelling the British government from Virginia.

The constant repetition of instructions from one governor to the next without material change naturally led to the retention of many clauses the original purposes of which had been fulfilled and of articles which had become obsolete for other reasons. On a few occasions the home officials became aware of this fact and took steps toward

---

325, 329, 434 (L.C.); additional instructions to Botetourt, Va., Dec. 10, 1770, C.O. 5: 1375, pp. 125–127 (L.C.). See below, pp. 238, 241–242.

[70] C.O. 5: 1350, pp. 91–93 (L.C.).

[71] Dunmore to Secretary of State Dartmouth, March 20, 1774, C.O. 5: 1352, p. 67 (L.C.).

a complete revision of the general instructions. They then sent letters to the governors asking what instructions needed revision or elimination because they were either inadequate or obsolete. The British authorities sent such letters three times before 1783: once in 1752, on the reorganization of the Board of Trade;[72] again in 1768, on the appointment of the earl of Hillsborough as secretary of state for the colonies;[73] and finally in 1782, when the dissolution of the Board of Trade and the concluding struggles of the American Revolution had brought the period almost to its close. At that time Thomas Townshend (Lord Sydney) ordered certain governors in the West Indies and elsewhere to consider their general instructions and to report all articles which were contrary to law or established custom or which ordered the passage of laws already in force, in order that all future instructions might be "consistent with the actual state and circumstances of the colony or island."[74]

The governors do not seem to have responded to these requests very satisfactorily. The best results were obtained by the letter of 1752, to which the governors of five of the thirteen royal colonies returned answers.[75] Three of these were extremely detailed and showed much thoughtful attention. The letters of the other governors generally failed even to mention the request for advice. Altogether, the lack of cooperation was deplorable.

The home officials made no attempt to revise the instructions for all the provinces at the same time. They postponed action in each case until, in the natural course of

[72] Board of Trade to the governors, June 3, 1752, *N. Y. Col. Docs.*, VI, 760–761.

[73] Hillsborough to the governors, June 21, 1768, *ibid.*, VIII, 77.

[74] Townshend to the governors of Jamaica, Leeward Islands, Bermuda, and Nova Scotia, Sept. 16, 1782, C.O. 5: 242, pp. 437–438 (L.C.).

[75] Detailed reports came from Henry Grenville of Barbados (C.O. 28: 30); William Popple of Bermuda (C.O. 37: 18); and James Glen of South Carolina

events, a new set of instructions became necessary.[76] At first glance the changes made after 1752 appear to have been numerous and important, but more careful examination shows that the Board of Trade made no radical alterations in its policy. A word-by-word comparison of the instructions given to Governor Henry Grenville of Barbados in 1746 with the revised set issued to his successor Charles Pinfold in 1756 gives results typical of the other revisions. In this case the board had the benefit of an elaborate report prepared by Grenville, who was one of the island's most successful governors. Of the ninety-nine articles in the earlier set of instructions, seventy were repeated to Pinfold without change. Grenville had recommended the dropping of two of these and the modification of a third. Seven articles were rephrased without change in content and thirteen were altered to a greater extent, in three cases on the recommendation of Grenville. The remaining nine articles were dropped entirely, six of them as a result of the governor's report. The instructions to Pinfold contained two new paragraphs, one of which, however, was essentially the regrouping of clauses eliminated from other articles.[77] These changes represented a more exten-

(C.O. 5: 374). A brief reply came from Charles Knowles of Jamaica (C.O. 137: 25). George Clinton of New York promised to submit a report but apparently failed to do so (*N. Y. Col. Docs.*, VI, 764–766). The most thorough report was that of Popple, who had served in the Board of Trade office for several years prior to his governorship.

[76] In the case of Bermuda, however, so many additional instructions had been sent Gov. Popple by 1755 that the Board of Trade decided to issue a new set of general instructions in the middle of his term. *Acts, Privy Coun., Col.*, 1745–1766, § 280; general instructions to William Popple, Bermuda, 1755, art. 1, C.O. 38: 9, pp. 52–144.

[77] Instructions to Grenville, Barbados, 1746, C.O. 5: 200, pp. 219–235 (L.C.); instructions to Pinfold, Barbados, 1756, C.O. 29: 17, pp. 178–298. This analysis compares closely in result with that for New York where political conditions were much more critical than in Barbados and from the governor of which the board received no elaborate report. Of George Clinton's instructions of 1741, 67 articles out of 97 were repeated verbatim to Osborn in 1753, 4

sive revision of the general instructions than was customary from one governor to the next, even when a ten-year
period intervened. But the significant fact remains that
none of these changes involved any important alteration
in policy. None of them dealt with the vital problems of
the relation between governor and assembly, the scope of
provincial legislation, or the subordination of the colony
to the mother country. The Board of Trade clearly made
no effort to bring the instructions into harmony with existing conditions and the developing self-assertiveness of
colonial life. In spite of its renewed energy and fresh
blood, the reorganized Board of Trade remained a body
of typical British officials, imbued with the spirit of mer-
cantilism and anxious to maintain the royal prerogative
in the colonies at its highest point.

The revision of 1768 was even less extensive than that
of 1752 and came at a time when new issues were compli-
cating the problem of colonial administration. The suggestion of 1782 was defeated before it could be carried
through by the resignation of the ministry which had
sponsored it. Thus the effort of the earl of Halifax and
his colleagues in 1752 remains the most important attempt
made to revise the general instructions during the period.
Occurring as it did just before the outbreak of the last
intercolonial war, during which Great Britain needed
every particle of support she could get from her colonies,
it offered a golden opportunity to gain the perpetual good
will of the assemblies through a modification of the colonial policy in a spirit of sympathetic understanding of the
real conditions of colonial life. Since the home authorities
failed to make any changes in this direction, the instructions continued to be objects of ever growing resentment

showed alterations in phraseology, 16 were modified in content, and 10 were
omitted. Osborn received 12 new paragraphs. Instructions to Clinton, N. Y.,
1741, C.O. 5: 198, pp. 531–582 (L.C.); instructions to Osborn, N. Y., 1753,
C.O. 5: 200, pp. 875–974 (L.C.).

to the local legislative bodies. Their members took advantage of every request for men or money for the war to secure in return a closer grip on the reins of government. They repeatedly forced the governors to disobey the instructions in order to get the assemblies' help for the war. As a result, the representatives lost nearly all the respect they had left for the king's orders to his governors. In the new conditions which followed the peace no one was strong enough or wise enough to restore the old relations, and few perceived the true meaning of the colonists' new attitude. Thus the year 1752 is not without significance in the movement which culminated in the Revolution.

But the responsibility for this situation can by no means be placed wholly upon the Board of Trade. Not only did this board have to remain responsive to the desires and requests of the merchants, but its work was always subject to review by a higher and even less liberal authority, the privy council. Every representation, every report, every draft of a commission or an instruction, was sent to the council where the action of the board received formal approval or disapproval by order in council. The final responsibility rested with this body, in relation to which the Board of Trade stood merely in an advisory capacity.

When the board had completed the draft of a set of general instructions, they forwarded it to the privy council together with a representation outlining the changes which they had made from the instructions to the preceding governor and explaining why they had made these changes. The board usually sent these documents up two or three months after they had been notified of the appointment. On receiving the representation and the instructions, the privy council referred both to its committee where the real consideration took place. Generally the committee reported back full approval of the work of the Board of

Trade. But if the committee disagreed with the board on some proposed article, its members felt no hesitation in making a change. Although exceptions may be found, these modifications were usually less liberal to the colonists than the original proposals of the Board of Trade. After all, the board was in closer touch with American affairs than was the council committee and was more likely to be influenced by the difficulties which the governors met in carrying out the instructions. Often enough interested and influential persons were able to get support in the committee for proposals which the board had turned down.[78] When the committee had studied the draft instructions it presented its report at a plenary session of the privy council, where its recommendations were invariably approved by order in council. The instructions were then turned over to the secretary of state whose clerks prepared the final copy. When the king had personally signed the instrument and when the signet had been affixed, the instructions were complete.

With the preparation of the commission and the general instructions and their passage under the proper seals,

[78] The volumes of the *Acts of the Privy Council, Colonial Series,* contain, in whole or in part, most of the representations of the Board of Trade and the reports of the committee in cases of important changes made by either body in the instructions. Typical cases of alterations made by the council committee in drafts of instructions prepared by the Board of Trade include the following: the elimination of parts of two articles in the instructions to Governor Hart of the Leeward Islands, 1721, one, article 62, which would give the right of licensing ministers for American service to others than the bishop of London; the other, article 66, which would give the governor the right to license schoolmasters in the islands if properly qualified persons with the same bishop's license were lacking (*ibid.,* 1720–1745, § 19); the dropping of an article in the instructions to Governor Bernard of New Jersey, 1758, which would permit the colony to issue paper bills of credit in times of military emergency under proper safeguards as to sinking funds, etc., and the restoration of the former article which absolutely prohibited such an issue without a suspending clause (*ibid.,* 1745–1766, § 348; *N. J. Arch.,* IX, 49).

the chief documents needed by the new governor were ready for his departure. But two other important instruments, the trade instructions and the vice-admiralty commission, were prepared and regularly delivered to him at the same time. The trade instructions, like the civil commission and the general instructions, were entrusted to the Board of Trade to prepare. The board reported to the House of Lords in 1734 that the first set of instructions to the governor relating to the enforcement of the acts of trade and navigation, issued in 1685 and 1686, "were prepared by a committee of the lords of the privy council [the Lords of Trade] with the assistance of the Commissioners of the Customs."[79] The Board of Trade added that from its own inception it had always prepared the trade instructions, but this statement was not literally true. The responsibility certainly rested on the board, but much of the real work continued to be done by the Commissioners of the Customs. The draft of the trade instruc-

[79] Representation on the laws, manufactures, and trade of the colonies which might affect that of England, sent to the House of Lords, Jan. 23, 1734, C.O. 5: 5, fo. 71 (L.C.); C.O. 324: 12, p. 58 (L.C.). In this representation the board stated that these trade instructions mentioned "former instructions upon those subjects to the governors of the plantations which do not appear in our records." Such earlier instructions are still missing and the only reference to them in 1685 is to be found, not in the trade instructions prepared in that year, but in a circular letter from the Lords of Trade to the governors, April 10, 1685, referring to the seizure of foreign ships trading to the colonies, which trade was reported as continuing "notwithstanding the several injunctions that have been signified from time to time for the due observance of the acts of trade and navigation," C.O. 324: 4, pp. 142–143 (L.C.). This is almost certainly a reference, not to a formal set of trade instructions in the sense later understood, but to various circular letters to the governors relative to illegal trade. Among these are the following: from the privy council, June 4, 1663, *Acts, Privy Coun., Col.*, 1613–1680, § 601; C.O. 5: 903, pp. 11–15 (Mass.); from the king, Aug. 25, 1663, C.O. 1: 17, no. 72 (Mass.); from the Lords of Trade, April 6, 1676, C.O. 138: 3, pp. 49–50; C.O. 324: 4, pp. 37–39 (L.C.). But instructions of a formal character were issued to the customs officers appointed in the colonies to collect the plantation duty in 1673, *Cal. Treas. Books*, 1672–1675, pp. 451–452.

tions issued to all governors in 1697 was prepared by the
Commissioners of the Customs and submitted by them to
the Lords of the Treasury and by the latter referred to
the Board of Trade for comment.[80] The board noted dupli-
cations of some parts of the general instructions and of
royal letters already sent and suggested a few changes,
but in general they approved highly of the proposed instructions, which were finally sent without important
modification.[81] An additional instruction, explanatory of
one article of these instructions, was proposed by the
Commissioners of the Customs the next year, prepared by
the Board of Trade, and dispatched to all the governors.[82]

From this time on, the preparation of trade instructions to new governors was a simple matter. Usually the
old instructions were reissued without significant change.
But if acts of parliament bearing on colonial trade had
recently been passed, the secretary of the board was directed to write to the Commissioners of the Customs asking for their suggestions as to what changes in the instructions the new legislation made necessary. The Board
of Trade then considered the proposals offered by the
commissioners and used such of them as seemed desirable
as the basis of new articles or of changes in those already
drawn.[83] The board also included such further amend-

[80] C.O. 324: 6, pp. 142–162 (L.C.); Cal. State Paps., Col., 1696–1697, §§
838, 1007.

[81] Marginal comments by the Board of Trade on this draft are found in
C.O. 324: 6, pp. 145–162 (L.C.). The board expressed the opinion that these
instructions ''were very useful to the end intended and proper to be dispatched
according as the Lords of the Treasury shall think fit.'' William Popple to
William Lowndes, May 20, 1697, ibid., pp. 166–167 (L.C.); Cal. State Paps.,
Col., 1696–1697, § 1036.

[82] C.O. 324: 6, pp. 348, 360–361, 369–370, 379–380 (L.C.); C.O. 324: 26,
pp. 231–233 (L.C.).

[83] Such periodic references of the trade instructions to the Commissioners
of the Customs took place in 1700 (C.O. 324: 7, pp. 305–306, L.C.); 1701
(C.O. 324: 8, pp. 8–15, L.C.); 1710 (C.O. 137: 12, no. 71); 1721 (C.O. 29: 14,

ments as seemed desirable to themselves. The final draft thus prepared was sent to all governors until a new revision seemed necessary. The document was so standardized that there was very little difference, if any, in the forms sent to the governors of different provinces.[84] The final steps of approval of the trade instructions and the authentication of the document were the same as in the case of the general instructions.

The responsibility for preparing the vice-admiralty commission rested, not with the Board of Trade, but with the Admiralty officers. On the appointment of a new governor, either the Board of Trade or the secretary of state notified the Commissioners of the Admiralty and asked that the usual powers of vice-admiralty be granted to the appointee.[85] This body then issued a warrant directing the judge of the High Court of Admiralty to grant the usual commission. The document itself, however, was prepared by the solicitor of the Admiralty.[86] Although

pp. 106–107, 109–110, 118–119; C.O. 28: 17, fos. 134–135); 1727 (C.O. 324: 11, pp. 34–36, L.C.); 1736 (C.O. 324: 12, pp. 225–226, L.C.); and 1752 (C.O. 324: 15, pp. 324–325, L.C.). Subsequent cases have not been located. Of course the board did not always accept outright all the proposals of the customs officers. In 1701 they adopted only one out of five suggested new paragraphs, and in 1710 they stated that they were willing to accept one of the four proposed changes if the Customs Commissioners considered it "absolutely necessary."

[84] When the first instructions for the new governments established in 1763 (Quebec, East and West Florida, and Grenada) were prepared by the Board of Trade, they made many important changes in the general instructions from the forms usually given, but they reported that the trade instructions they had prepared were "exactly conformable" to those given the governors of other royal provinces. Board of Trade to the king, Nov. 3, 1763, C.O 5: 563, pp. 33–34 (L.C.).

[85] For example, William Popple to Josiah Burchett, secretary to the lord high admiral, April 18, 1707, C.O. 5: 1362, p. 138 (L.C.); *Cal. State Paps., Col.,* 1706–1708, § 866; Hillsborough to the Lords of the Admiralty, Dec. 15, 1770, C.O. 5: 1376, p. 127 (L.C.).

[86] See Andrews, *Guide to the Materials for American History, to 1783, in the Public Record Office of Great Britain,* II, 35.

no formal instructions were issued with these commissions,[87] a number of other documents were sent to the governors from time to time in explanation of their various maritime powers and duties. Among these were lists of fees to be taken by officers of the Admiralty in the colonies upon condemnation of prizes there;[88] commissions for the trial of pirates;[89] copies of commissions and instructions issued in England to private ships of war, for the guidance of the governor in granting letters of marque in his colony;[90] and instructions to the governors from the Commissioners of the Admiralty regarding the issuing of Mediterranean passes.[91] The provincial governor did not entirely lack advice from the Admiralty.

Although the total number of documents given to the new governor on his departure varied from time to time, it was generally large.[92] To get these papers together promptly required a degree of organized effort and co-

[87] J. Burchett to W. Popple, March 10, 1719, C.O. 324: 10, pp. 241–242 (L.C.); *Board of Trade Journal*, 1718–1722, pp. 43–44, 48.

[88] W. Popple to Lieut. Gov. Spotswood, Va., May 24, 1710, C.O. 5: 1363, p. 183 (L.C.); *Cal. State Paps., Col.*, 1710–1711, § 247.

[89] These commissions were probably more often issued under the great seal than under the seal of the Admiralty, but the latter form was common toward the end of the period. See commission to William Leyborne, governor of Grenada, and others, Sept. 3, 1772, C.O. 5: 204, pp. 6–19 (L.C.).

[90] Circular letter from the Board of Trade to the governors, Aug. 30, 1710, C.O. 5: 1363, p. 203 (L.C.); *Cal. State Paps., Col.*, 1710–1711, § 372. Copies of such commissions and instructions as were issued in 1739 are printed in *N. H. Prov. Laws*, II, 498–506. According to the general instructions to all governors from 1727 to the end of the period, copies of these instructions and commissions should have been sent to each governor upon his appointment, but this was not always done. Complaint of this neglect was eventually made by the Board of Trade to the Admiralty. A. Popple to J. Burchett, Aug. 12, 1735, C.O. 324: 12, pp. 134–135 (L.C.). See also Connecticut Historical Society *Collections*, I, 307–308, 312–313.

[91] J. Burchett to W. Popple, June 11, 1700, C.O. 324: 7, pp. 240–244 (L.C.). Copies of these instructions are given in *ibid.*, pp. 245–256 and in C.O. 323: 3, no. 69 (Mass.); see *Cal. State Paps., Col.*, 1700, §§ 528, 528 i.

[92] For example, a "list of papers delivered to Lord Botetourt, lieutenant and governor general of Virginia, August the 21st 1768" gives twenty-five

operation not always found among British officials of the period. Sometimes important documents were neglected and the governor left without them.[93] There are even cases on record when the governor sailed without his general instructions and was told to use those given to his predecessor.[94] One governor, Lord Culpeper, left for Virginia before his commission had been delivered to him. But the cause of delay in this case seems to have been Culpeper's neglect to pay the fees of the various offices through which the commission had to pass to receive the great seal.[95]

items, among which the civil and vice-admiralty commissions are not included. The documents included instructions, circular letters, reports of the Board of Trade, lists of councillors, and other officers in Virginia, copies of acts of parliament, and a map of North America. C.O. 5: 1375, pp. 65–68 (L.C.).

[93] In spite of the numerous documents given to Botetourt in 1768, as indicated in the preceding note, he did not receive a commission for the trial of piracy. Acting Governor Nelson reported in 1770 that there had been none in the colony since the administration of Sir William Gooch, which had ended in 1749. Nelson to Hillsborough, Nov. 15, 1770, C.O. 5: 1348, pp. 369–370 (L.C.).

[94] This happened in the cases of Sir Henry Moore, New York, 1765 (*N. Y. Col. Docs.*, VII, 794), and of Peter Heywood, commander in chief of Jamaica, 1716. The latter did, however, receive a brief set of instructions of four articles only, which directed him to use the general instructions to Lord Archibald Hamilton, whose administration Heywood was sent over to investigate, C.O. 5: 190, pp. 344–346 (L.C.). In some other cases the Board of Trade decided definitely not to prepare a complete set of instructions for the governor of a new colony, conditions in which were as yet unknown. They preferred instead to refer the governor to a copy of the instructions used in some other colony, with directions to observe them as far as possible. In this way, Governor Philips of Nova Scotia was told to guide himself by the Virginia instructions, both after his original appointment in 1719 and after his reappointment in 1729, C.O. 324: 11, pp. 201–203 (L.C.); instructions to Philips, 1719, art. 10, C.O. 5: 189, p. 421; *Acts, Privy Coun., Col.*, 1720–1745, § 116; instructions to Philips, 1729, art. 10, C.O. 5: 194, p. 438 (L.C.). In similar fashion, the first two royal governors of the Bahamas were ordered to follow the instructions to the governor of Jamaica. Instructions to Rogers, Bahamas, 1718, art. 6, C.O. 5: 189, pp. 382–383 (L.C.); instructions to Phenney, 1721, art. 6, C.O. 5: 191, pp. 123–125 (L.C.).

[95] William Blathwayt to the attorney general, Oct. 31, 1682, C.O. 5: 1356, p. 90 (L.C.); *Cal. State Paps., Col.*, 1681–1685, § 764. Ordinarily no gov-

This system of requiring fees proved to be a great burden to the newly appointed governors of the provinces. In spite of a protest against it by the Lords of Trade in connection with the Culpeper case in 1682, the system remained in force throughout the period. Because of the commonly accepted notion that public office was a property right and because of the low salaries paid to most of the clerical officials in England, every appointee of the crown was expected to pay large fees for preparing and sealing his commission and other instruments. Just what these fees totaled is impossible to say exactly. They seem to have varied from time to time. The fees charged Culpeper in 1682 for passing the commission alone were stated to have come to £61 0s 10d.[96] In 1698 Governor Nicholson of Virginia received an unitemized bill from his agent for over £160 for procuring his commission, but Nicholson suspected that the entire sum was not a legitimate charge.[97] Lord Delawarr stated that his New York commission of 1737 had cost him above £600, although this figure may have been meant to include the cost of his New Jersey commission and both sets of instructions as well.[98] When the expense of the other instruments was added to that of the commission, the total outlay became a serious matter. Delawarr's successor in the New York

ernor would have departed without his commission, for lacking that instrument he could not enter into his office. Culpeper, however, already had been inducted into office by virtue of an earlier commission.

[96] *Cal. Treas. Books*, 1681–1685, pt. I, p. 666. The offices among which this sum was to be distributed were those of the secretary of state, signet, privy seal, attorney general, and hanaper, and the Crown Office.

[97] Nicholson to the Board of Trade, March 3, 1705, C.O. 5: 1314, no. 43, p. 9 (L.C.) ; *Cal. State Paps., Col.*, 1704–1705, p. 422.

[98] Delawarr to Newcastle, May 21, 1741, Newcastle Paps., XII, Add. MS., 32,697, fo. 31; Delawarr to Lord Chancellor Hardwicke, May 21, 1741, *ibid.*, fo. 56. In these letters Delawarr was asking that he might retain the office of governor of New York (whither he had never gone) until he had collected the costs of his commission and instructions out of the perquisites of the office.

office, George Clinton, estimated the cost of his commission and instructions in 1741 at more than £400 and the other expenses of equipment and preparation at over £1,100, a total which he contemplated with sorrow especially in view of the fact that he had recently been hiding from his creditors.[99] In the same year the friends of Benning Wentworth, named governor of New Hampshire, undertook to raise £300 for his commission and instructions to make possible his paying various private creditors before leaving England.[100] Even the Board of Trade refused to transact business without charge to the governor or other individual benefited. In 1731 a table of fees was established to replace the system of gratuities formerly in vogue in that office. The new table was said to effect a reduction in the actual expenses of the appointee. By this list the draft of a governor's commission or of his trade instructions cost six guineas and a draft of his general instructions double that sum.[101] Although some of the governors undoubtedly exaggerated their estimates in the hope of getting sympathy, probably few governors of the eighteenth century were able to depart before paying out at least two or three hundred pounds, even if no outright bribery or purchase of the appointment was involved.

When the various documents had been prepared but

[99] Clinton to Newcastle, May 7, 1740, Newcastle Paps., VIII, Add. MS., 32,693, fo. 268; June 30, 1741, ibid., XII, Add. MS., 32,697, fo. 261.

[100] John Tomlinson to Theodore Atkinson, May 9, 1741, Documents and Records Relating to the Province of New Hampshire, V, 929–930 (hereafter cited as N. H. Prov. Paps.).

[101] Some of the other items were: representation for recommending councillors in the plantations, 4 guineas; representations on private business or for securing the approval of private acts of the assemblies at the request of the persons concerned, 2 guineas; entering patents for employments in the plantations, 2 guineas; copies of papers, 10 shillings. Acts, Privy Coun., Col., 1720–1745, p. 320. See also Board of Trade Journal, 1728/9–1734, pp. 201, 232.

before the newly appointed governor left for America or in any way assumed the duties of his office, he was required to take certain oaths before the privy council. This procedure began in 1674 when the Council of Trade and Foreign Plantations recommended to the king that Sir Jonathan Atkins, soon to sail for Barbados, and all other governors and lieutenant governors, be required before their departure to take the oaths of allegiance and supremacy and the test, as well as oaths for the due execution of their commands and for the fulfillment of their duties under the navigation acts.[102] Every governor had to take these oaths. Those who were in England when they were appointed took them twice, once before the privy council, and again before the provincial council upon inauguration. Governors actually in America when appointed were sworn before the local council only. Although the wording of the oaths was changed from time to time in conformity with acts of parliament, the procedure remained the same throughout the period.[103]

When the new governor had taken the oaths and his departure for America was assured, he was entitled to certain donations. The most notable of these was a gift or loan of communion silver and of Bibles, prayer-books, altar cloths, and other "furniture" for the royal chapel in his province. The first reference which has been found to this practice is in the report of the Lords of Trade to the king on a commission and instructions for Lord Culpeper of Virginia in 1679, in which they recommended "that upon the departure of the Lord Culpeper, [the king] would send a mace and a sword into Virginia with furniture for his Lordship's chapel." The entire report

---

[102] *Cal. State Paps., Col.*, 1669–1674, § 1221.

[103] See the appendices to the *Acts of the Privy Council, Colonial Series*, where, in the lists of governors appointed, the words "oaths taken" indicate the dates on which the ceremony was performed. The oaths were generally taken on the same day that the general instructions were formally approved.

was approved and orders were given for making the grant.[104] During the next few years the privy council ordered many Bibles, prayer-books, and other ecclesiastical volumes to be delivered to various new governors for the use of the provincial churches.[105] But as far as the available records show, the practice did not become standardized for all the royal colonies until the first quarter of the eighteenth century.[106] Upon being notified of the appointment of a new governor, the lord chamberlain or the vice-chamberlain of the royal household usually issued two warrants, each later confirmed by Treasury order, one to the master of the jewels for communion plate and the other to the master of the great wardrobe for "chapel furniture." The items issued from the Jewel House regularly included two flagons, a chalice, a paten, and a receiver for the offerings, valued at about £80. The rather miscellaneous list of "chapel furniture" was usually described as including "one large Bible, two large and twelve small common prayer-books, two cushions for the reading desk, a cushion and cloth for the pulpit, a carpet for the altar, all of crimson damask with silk fringe, two linen cloths for the altar, and two surplices," which together cost about £110.[107] While these grants were specifically for the use of the royal chapel in the province, they

104 Order in council, March 14, 1679, C.O. 5: 1355, pp. 266–273 (L.C.); *Acts, Privy Coun., Col.*, 1613–1680, § 1250.

105 *Acts, Privy Coun., Col.*, 1680–1720, § 31; C.O. 5: 1356, pp. 263–264. In addition to Bibles and Books of Common Prayer, the most usual items were Books of the Canons of the Church, Books of the Thirty-Nine Articles, and Tables of Marriage.

106 Although there are occasional entries in the Lord Chamberlain's Books in the Public Record Office (L.C. 9: 44 and 45) of plate issued about 1700, they are not frequent before 1713 nor regular before 1730.

107 In addition to the entries in the Lord Chamberlain's Books there are frequent references to the warrants for plate and furniture in the volumes of the *Calendar of Treasury Books and Papers* for the years which they cover (1729–1745).

were issued personally to the governor and he was made responsible for their safe-keeping. In spite of the fact that one man might administer two provinces at the same time, as occurred in the cases of Massachusetts and New Hampshire until 1741 and of New York and New Jersey until 1738, he received only a single grant.[108] On the other hand, no matter how soon one administration might succeed another within a province, the new appointee was entitled to receive a new grant upon his departure for America.[109] Apparently a retiring governor was expected to return his equipment to the officials from whom he received it, although this regulation was certainly often broken.[110] One

[108] The grant was made as to the governor of the larger province in each case, which fact led to a protest by Lieut. Gov. Dunbar of New Hampshire in 1735. He asserted that King's Chapel in Boston had received two donations since his own arrival in New Hampshire, but that the Anglican church in Portsmouth had been unable to get a minister appointed by the Society for the Propagation of the Gospel or "his Majesty's wonted bounty in books and ornaments for the communion table and pulpit and governor's seat." Dunbar to Newcastle, Dec. 5, 1735, C.O. 5: 10, no. 51 (L.C.). But no grant was made for New Hampshire until the appointment of Benning Wentworth as the first separate governor in 1741.

[109] Sometimes in the early period one governor transferred his plate and furniture to his successor upon the latter's arrival. For example, see *Maryland Archives*, XXV, 45. But of the 96 governors newly appointed between 1730 and 1783, all but 7 received communion plate from the Jewel House. L.C. 9: 44, 45, *passim*.

[110] The entries in the Lord Chamberlain's Books indicate that the plate was "to be returned on demand," but only occasional notation was made of such return. In one case, at least, a governor was detected in the act of converting the plate to his own private use. The culprit was Governor Douglas of the Leeward Islands, who was proven to have shipped back secretly to England the communion silver allowed him, declaring that it was "old-fashioned plate his wife had no occasion for." It was recovered, restored to the island, and eventually returned to the Jewel House. *Acts, Privy Coun., Col.*, 1680–1720, p. 689; L.C. 9: 44, fo. 164. In 1689 complaint was made to the privy council that the Bibles, prayer-books, etc. sent to Barbados some years before had been embezzled. After investigation, orders were given the attorney general to proceed in law against Sir Richard Dutton, the governor in whose administration the books had been taken to the island. *Acts, Privy Coun., Col.*, 1680–1720, § 293.

could hardly have expected Governor Benning Wentworth of New Hampshire to return to the master of the great wardrobe in 1767 the two surplices presented to him twenty-six years before.[111]

Some governors also carried with them to America gifts from the king to the Indians in or near the provinces. This was done by a few governors of Virginia and Nova Scotia and was a regular practice on the part of those of New York. The eight or nine hundred pounds which the governors of this province received were laid out for guns, powder, ammunition, and other supplies primarily designed to assist the Iroquois in their capacity as allies of the British against the French.[112]

The production of these tokens of the royal bounty upon the governor's arrival in the province doubtless gave him some pleasure. But occasionally he received a still more gratifying return for the expenses of his appointment, even before he left England. The governors of the West Indies, more fortunate than their colleagues on the continent, were often allowed to draw part of their salaries while still in the mother country. The Board of Trade reported adversely on the request of Robert Hunter in 1707 to receive half salary from the death of his predecessor in Virginia, eight months before his own appointment. The reason given for this refusal was that such

111 In 1713 Thomas Harley, secretary to the Treasury, wrote to the Board of Trade on behalf of the lord treasurer asking what care was taken for the preservation of the chapel furniture allowed the governors. The Board of Trade replied that they had never been consulted in the matter, but that they supposed "the proper officers who issue the said furniture have taken care that the same be preserved." *Cal. State Paps., Col.*, 1712–1714, §§ 367, 371.

112 Warrants for such gifts are numerous in the various Treasury *Calendars*. See also, representation of the Lords of Trade, Feb. 18, 1679, C.O. 5: 1355, p. 270 (L.C.); instructions to Culpeper, Va., 1679, art. 12, *ibid.*, pp. 326–356; instructions to Philips, Nova Scotia, 1719, art. 22, C.O. 5: 189, pp. 417–434 (L.C.); instructions to Philips, Nova Scotia, 1729, art. 23, C.O. 5: 194, pp. 434–452 (L.C.).

a precedent might cause delay on the part of newly appointed governors in sailing for America.[113] Nevertheless, the custom became well established for those men named governors of the West India colonies to draw half salary either from the date of the death or other actual withdrawal of their predecessors from the government, or from the date on which their own commissions had passed the privy seal.[114] Not content with the concession of a salary grant before assuming office, the governors of a few provinces were able to get additional subsidies to prepare them for the journey to America. The Treasury Board made a special allowance to John Tinker, governor of the Bahamas, in 1740 "for equippage for his going over," or, as he himself put it, "for the extraordinary

[113] Board of Trade to Sunderland, July 16, 1707, C.O. 5: 1362, pp. 253–255 (L.C.); *Cal. State Paps., Col.*, 1706–1708, § 1047.

[114] The date of the privy seal was customarily, though not invariably, used because a copy of the commission in the form of a writ of privy seal was sent to the treasury as well as to the chancery and payments were reckoned from the date of this writ. For examples of such advance payment see, *Cal. Treas. Books and Paps.*, 1731–1734, pp. 338, 340, 352, 489, 496, 505, 512. A good illustration of the variation in practice between the island and continental colonies is found in the case of William Cosby, appointed governor of the Leeward Islands in 1731 (privy seal dated June 22) and transferred to New York in 1732 (privy seal dated March 27) before he had departed for the West Indies. He drew half salary as governor of the Leeward Islands for the nine months ending on Lady Day (March 25), 1732, after which his successor, William Mathew, received half salary until arrival in the islands. Meanwhile Cosby petitioned the Lords of the Treasury to be allowed to receive half salary as governor of New York since the death of his predecessor there, which event had occurred eight days after Cosby's Leeward Island appointment. To this request the Treasury agreed but only "if it has usually been done." When Cosby arrived in New York, he found that the acting governor, Rip Van Dam, had been drawing the full salary since the death of the last governor and now refused to turn half of it over to Cosby. A lawsuit was commenced by Cosby against Van Dam, which, although never brought to a conclusion, resulted in much bitterness within the province. *Cal. Treas. Books and Paps.*, 1731–1734, pp. 185, 226, 317, 321, 336, 493, 501, 644; *N. Y. Col. Docs.*, V, 944; VII, 499; VIII, 250, 257–258; William Smith, *History of New York*, II, 4–24.

expense of his commission and instructions.''[115] What appears to have been an outright gift of £1,500 ''as a mark of royal favor'' was made to each of the seven governors of Barbados appointed between 1721 and 1742.[116] The governors in the West Indies were indeed well taken care of.

The fear expressed by the Board of Trade that a grant of half salary to Governor Hunter before reaching his government would result in long delay does not seem to have been well founded, if we may judge by the examples of those to whom such concessions were made. The average amount of time consumed between the signing of the general instructions—usually one of the last steps in preparing the official documents—and the actual beginning of the administration in America, does not vary greatly from province to province, nor from the beginning of the period until 1783, although individual cases of long delay are found in almost every province. The general average of all cases for which dates may be found is something less than six months. The governors of Barbados and the Leeward Islands, to whom advances in salary seem to have been most commonly made, had a record, if anything, slightly better than the average.[117]

[115] *Cal. Treas. Books and Paps.*, 1739–1741, pp. 263, 330.

[116] *Ibid.*, 1742–1745, p. 14. Of these seven men, two, Walter Chetwynd and Sir Orlando Bridgman, never left England and another, Lord Belhaven, was lost at sea on his way out. Among the Newcastle Papers is a letter from the duke of Rutland to the secretary of state, July 26, 1732, which, although partly illegible, seems to refer to a proposal for depriving Lord Howe of the allowance made to his three predecessors in the Barbados government. Rutland urged that Howe be not made the sufferer from the king's ''denial of an usual allowance'' and pointed out that if the grant was made, Howe could ''cross the sea with a prospect of the bettering his fortune without running the hazard of ruining his family if he miscarry by the way, or pay nature's tribute soon after his arrival.'' Newcastle Paps., II, Add. MS., 32,687, fo. 460.

[117] The dates used in this computation are from C. M. Andrews, ''List

Unquestionably, however, the governors were often loath to begin the long voyage across the Atlantic. They naturally had many matters of a personal nature to attend to before they could leave their homes for the five or six years' absence which appointment to colonial office usually involved. Some men clearly disliked to embark on the ocean voyage, which, at best, was uncomfortable and, at worst, was really dangerous. The experience of John Montgomerie served as a warning to others not to sail after the winter storms had begun. For, although his destination was New York, his vessel was driven to the West Indies and he was forced to spend the winter with his retinue at Barbados in expensive and unrewarded idleness.[118] Two governors, Robert Hunter in 1707 and William Henry Lyttelton in 1755, were captured by the French while on the way to America.[119] Most disastrous of all, the ship carrying Lord Belhaven to Barbados in 1721 was wrecked off the Lizard before the voyage had well begun, with the loss of two hundred and forty lives, including that of the governor himself.[120] It is impossible to say how much time usually elapsed after a governor learned of his appointment and before he actually set sail, since neither date is often found exactly stated, but the average must have been between six and seven months,

of the Commissions, Instructions, and Additional Instructions to the Royal Governors and Others in America,'' *Annual Report* of the American Historical Association for 1911, pp. 393–528, subject to correction in a very few cases by other information.

[118] Governor Worsley of Barbados to the Board of Trade, April 9, 1728, C.O. 28: 19, fos. 190–191. With this experience in mind, a subsequent governor of New York, George Clinton, refused to sail later in the year than the end of August. Clinton to Newcastle, July 31, 1741, Newcastle Paps., XII, Add. MS., 32,697, fo. 376. But for unexplained reasons he did not actually depart until nearly two years later.

[119] *Acts, Privy Coun., Col.*, 1680–1720, p. 585; 1745–1766, p. 278.

[120] *Ibid.*, 1720–1745, p. 815; G. E. Cokayne, *Complete Peerage*, II, 308.

of which two or three were consumed in the preparation of the necessary documents.[121]

As soon as it became practically certain when the governor would be ready to sail, the Admiralty received orders to prepare a frigate or other warship for the transportation of the appointee, his retinue, and his baggage.[122] The Admiralty then undertook to find out how much space would be required. In this the needs of the governors varied. As might be expected, commoners going to the less wealthy provinces on the continent were more modest in their demands than members of the nobility destined for the more luxurious life in the West Indies. Joseph Dudley, when going to Massachusetts in 1702, needed accommodations only for himself, five servants, and one hundred thirty tons of goods.[123] But the earl of Inchiquin was allowed to take to Jamaica in 1690 seventy-five servants and three hundred fifty tons of goods.[124] Perhaps the record was set by a predecessor in the same island, the duke of Albemarle, who received free transportation for no less than one hundred servants and five hundred tons of

[121] In arriving at this conclusion, the figures for New York alone have been fully analyzed, but, by general comparison, they seem typical of all other provinces. Assuming that the date upon which the Board of Trade was notified of the appointment corresponded closely with that of the man's own receipt of definite word, and allowing for a transatlantic voyage of eight weeks—a liberal estimate—it appears that the governors of this province from Bellomont (1697) through Moore (1765) spent an average of thirty-two weeks in England before sailing. If we omit the exceptional case of Clinton, the average is reduced to about twenty-five weeks.

[122] Occasionally, a privately owned ship might be chartered for the trip, or the governor advanced a sum of money and permitted to arrange his own sailing.

[123] J. Burchett to Dudley, Feb. 19, 23, Mar. 30, 1702, Admiralty 2: 402 (Mass.). In this case and in those of Inchiquin and Albemarle, here mentioned, the "ton" referred to was the nautical measure of capacity, equivalent to 40 cubic feet.

[124] C.O. 138: 6, pp. 306–308; *Cal. State Paps., Col.*, 1689–1692, §§ 461, 464, 488, 495, 599.

goods.[125] Among the articles listed in the invoices of these and other governors are pictures, books, guns, musical instruments, horses, and coaches. Francis Russell, like other Barbados governors, assured himself of warmth and fuel in that semi-tropical island by carrying with him twenty chaldrons, or about twenty-five tons, of coal.[126] Fortunately for them, the governors were exempted from all customs charges in transporting their effects out of the kingdom.[127]

When the governor had finally taken himself and his family aboard ship his connections with the home officials were severed until he reported his arrival in America. Whether all governors were accorded special honors as soon as they had passed the Narrow Seas, in virtue of their commissions as vice-admirals of their provinces, is not certain, but some of them, at least, raised their flags as such as soon as they had passed the Lizard.[128] Any de-

[125] C.O. 138: 5, pp. 245–246, 250, 254–255; *Cal. Treas. Books,* 1685–1689, pp. 1258, 1355, 1463. The Treasury reimbursed the Navy Board to the extent of £1,000 for the costs of this voyage. For a vivid description of the preparations attendant upon the departure of this governor, so highly stationed in English society, see Estelle Frances Ward, *Christopher Monck Duke of Albemarle,* pp. 273–278.

[126] *Cal. State Paps., Col.,* 1697–1698, § 113. A chaldron of coal was 36 bushels or about 25½ hundredweight. Russell also took 2 coaches, 21 horses, and 32 persons.

[127] Sometimes this was effected by an outright payment of the normal duties "at the king's charge," as in the case of Governor Grey of Barbados in 1698, when the charges amounted to £22 6s. 11d. *Cal. Treas. Paps.,* 1697–1701, pp. 142–143. At other times the Commissioners of the Customs were ordered simply to seal the governor's baggage on its presentation or to pass it customs free, as was done in the cases of Albemarle in 1687 and of Viscount Howe of Barbados in 1732. *Cal. Treas. Books,* 1685–1689, p. 1355; *Cal. Treas. Books and Paps.,* 1731–1734, p. 301.

[128] Culpeper asked "that he might have the same honor and privilege that all his Majesty's lieutenants, governors general, and commanders of the plantations in America have of wearing a flag in the maintop as soon as he is sailed out of the limits of the Narrow Seas." Thereupon the privy council ordered the Commissioners of the Admiralty to inform themselves whether

ficiency in pomp and ceremony on the high seas was amply made up upon arrival in the province. Usually the vessel sailed directly to the capital town, although sometimes the last part of the journey was necessarily made by land. But whatever the nature of the approach, the occasion marked a red-letter day in the life of the community. The reception began with a salute of seventeen guns from the artillery in the fort to which the vessels in the harbor replied either by discharging their guns or by dressing ship until, as one contemporary described the scene, they were "blazoned with a rich variety of colors."[129] Unless the day was too far advanced, the new governor landed at once at some convenient wharf where he was met by the acting governor, the members of the council, such assemblymen as happened to be in town, and other dignitaries. Many other "gentlemen," although not of official position, often joined in the gathering at the water's edge. When suitable greetings and compliments had been exchanged, the governor and his new associates began a parade or procession to the statehouse or other public building where the inauguration was to take place.

In case the governor arrived by land he was usually met at the boundary line of the province by a delegation

any governors had actually exercised this privilege, and if so, to grant it to Culpeper. The final decision in this case is not known. C.O. 5: 1355, pp. 376–377 (L.C.); *Acts, Privy Coun., Col.*, 1613–1680, § 1318. Culpeper had no commission as vice-admiral. According to Miss Ward's account, the duke of Albemarle raised an admiral's flag as soon as he had passed the Lizard. Ward, *Christopher Monck*, p. 278. On Feb. 15, 1712, Josiah Burchett, secretary of the Admiralty, wrote the governors that their vice-admiralty commissions did "in no way entitle them to the right of hoisting a flag on board any of her Majesty's ships more than the vice-admirals of the maritime counties of this kingdom" (Adm. 2: 411, p. 351), but this seems to refer to warships stationed in or calling at the plantations, and not to those transporting the governors thither.

[129] Boston *Weekly News Letter*, Aug. 6–13, 1730 (no. 189). Contemporary accounts in the newspapers of several provinces have been drawn upon for this description of the inaugural ceremonies.

from the council and by other officers. The militia companies of the various towns along the way turned out to do him honor and sometimes troops of cavalry escorted him throughout the entire journey to the capital. Arrived at the end of his trip, the governor received the same greeting as if he had come by water.

The procession through the streets to the statehouse was a colorful affair. The local militia, hastily summoned, had been placed under arms and now formed double lines along the route of march. In many provinces there was a special body of troops who served as escorts to the governors on these and other state occasions. The half-military, half-social character of these organizations, like that of their modern counterparts, is perhaps best illustrated by the description of one of them furnished by a royal governor. The company of Horse Guards in Barbados, wrote Charles Pinfold in 1762, was composed of "the principal merchants and people of Bridgetown, whose duty it is to wait on the governor's person on alarms, reviews, and other public occasions. It is commanded by a colonel, 2 lieutenant colonels, 2 majors, 4 exempts, 2 adjutants, and private gentlemen, 80."[130] Similar organizations in colonial times included, among others, the Horse Guards and Cadet Corps of Boston, the Grenadiers and Halberdiers of New York, and the Light Infantry Company of Charleston, South Carolina.

Headed by these forces and accompanied by those officials who had come to meet him, the governor made his dignified way, receiving as he passed the salutes of the militia officers and the acclamations of the assembled spectators. The streets and windows were, of course, crowded with people and the houses were hung with carpets and other impromptu decorations. It cannot be said that inauguration weather was any better then than now. The re-

[130] Pinfold's answers to queries, 1762, C.O. 28: 32 (unpaged).

ception committee was forced to meet Governor Franklin of New Jersey in sleighs; nevertheless, it was said that the inauguration "was conducted with as much decency and decorum as the severity of the season could possibly admit of."[131] The optimistic writer of the Boston *Weekly News Letter* thus cheerfully describes the thunderstorm which accompanied the inauguration of Governor Belcher of Massachusetts: "While the pomp was making its orderly procession, the guns which were bursting in every part of the town were answered in mild and rumbling peals by the artillery of heaven, which introduced the plentiful and refreshing showers that succeeded a very dry season."[132]

When the column reached the building which housed the council chamber, the chief persons entered and as many others as possible crowded into the room.[133] Silence was commanded and his Majesty's commission was publicly read. The new governor then took the oaths of office required by this document—the same obligations which he had already taken before the privy council. In turn the governor then customarily administered the oaths to the members of the council named in his instructions. After this had been done, the new chief executive performed the first official act of his administration. In imitation of the kings of England upon their accession to the throne and for the same reasons, he issued a proclamation announcing his appointment and ordering the continuance in office of all officers and ministers until further order. The seal of the province was affixed and the proclamation was read from the balcony or steps of the building. The reappear-

---

131 Wayman's *New York Gazette*, March 7, 1763.

132 Boston *Weekly News Letter*, Aug. 6–13, 1730 (no. 189).

133 On the comparatively few occasions when the former governor was in the province at the inauguration of his successor, he seems to have played, with few exceptions, the gentlemanly and sportsmanlike part in welcoming the newcomer. He customarily met the new governor at the steps of the statehouse and accompanied him throughout the remaining ceremonies.

ance of the governor out of doors was greeted by a salute of three volleys from the muskets of the assembled militia and by the loud huzzas of the enthusiastic populace. In some provinces the procession then reformed, headed by the mace, as in Jamaica, or the sword of state, as in South Carolina, and marched to the harbor fortifications where the commission was again read and saluted by the cannon.

The ceremonies were apparently always brought to a close at some prominent coffee house or tavern, whither the leading citizens proceeded to the accompaniment of ringing church bells and booming artillery.[134] Here a lavish dinner and entertainment were provided at public expense. Sometimes, when the accommodations of the leading hostelry were insufficient to provide for all those entitled to share in this part of the program, the lesser lights were assigned to other public houses and there furnished with "an elegant dinner." The viands and the vintages provided at such an inaugural repast may not have seemed exactly ambrosial to a governor accustomed to the more sumptuous banquets of London's court circles, yet the cordiality of the reception and the conviviality of the occasion must have proved ample recompense to one tired by weeks of monotonous sailing across the ocean. Speeches of welcome were made, his Majesty's health and other loyal toasts were offered, and now and then, a poem written in honor of the new governor was read to the assembled guests.[135] The general celebration continued through-

[134] In the Massachusetts Archives appears the following item relative to the inauguration of Governor Shirley in 1741: "The Province of the Massachusetts, Dr. To 9 sextons ringing their bells at his Excellency's access to the government half a day each by order - - £4 10." Mass. Arch. XLIX, 44–45.

[135] In its account of the official dinner tendered to Governor Burnet, son of the famous bishop of Salisbury (Sarum), and successor in the Massachusetts government to Lieutenant Governor Dummer, the *Weekly News Letter* stated that "after dinner M. Byles presented his Excellency with a poem introduced by the Rev. Mr. Colman." On the same page of the paper is

out the evening. The public buildings were "beautifully
illuminated," fireworks were displayed, and bonfires were
built. The populace might share in the rejoicing even
though the state dinner was restricted to the privileged.

For as much as a week afterward, the governor was
the recipient of a stream of congratulatory addresses from
all those bodies and organizations which might lay claim
to his attention. The clergy or associated ministers of the
community, the justices of the provincial courts, the members of the bar, the merchants of the town, and, in a few
provinces, the president and fellows of the college, all

printed the following gem which was probably the previously mentioned
work of Byles:

> "Immortal WILLIAM sav'd the British Isle,
> Groaning in Romish Chains, and Bid it smile,
> And when th'infatuate Tribe grew mad again,
> And fain would Re-assume the broken Chain:
> Great *Sarum's* Eye Pierc'd quick the deep Designs,
> Warded the Ruin, Sapp'd the fatal Mines!
> Blest *Phospher!* Usher'd in the GEORGIAN Sun; ⎫
> The happiest Light that e'er on *Britain* Shone! ⎬
> And then Retir'd and Resign'd his own. ⎭
> But that blest Saint's bright Light can ne'er Expire
> Whilst his Fam'd Son, Rap't with Prophetick Fire,
> Unvails the Secret Mysteries of Fate,
> Long wrapp'd in Pitchy Clouds Impenetrate.
> He the Almighties deep Decrees Unseals,
> Th'Evolv'd and Unevolv'd Events, Reveals.
>   When Sylvian Salvages, by Rome Enrag'd,
> Our Frontiers harras'd, in Fierce Wars engag'd:
> Great DUMMER 'rose and stop'd the raging Flouds,
> And Bound and Tam'd the Tygers of the Woods!
> Rent with dire Chasms, that urged impending Fate; ⎫
> He clos'd the Wounds, and heal'd the Bleeding State; ⎬
> Where no Attempts before were Fortunate: ⎭
> The Traffick Medium Plung'd in numerous Ills:
> We mourn'd Decennial more than Weekly Bills:
> The Trade and Commerce sunk in deep Distress;
> But still, 'twas He reviv'd and brought redress;
> Nor can our Body justly now Complain,
> When Scarce a single Joint is left in Pain:

paid their respects to the new chief executive. Their addresses and the gracious replies of the governor were usually printed in full in the local newspapers of the succeeding weeks. In New York the mayor and corporation of the city went to the extreme of hospitable reception, not only by inviting the governor to dine formally with them at some convenient date, but by presenting him with the freedom of the city, suitably engrossed, with the seal of the corporation enclosed in a costly gold box.[136] The people as a whole continued to show the greatest interest in the new official, actuated not only by curiosity but by the hope

> We're very Happy! ————————————
> ————————————Yet Great BURNET's name,
> Swells big the Sails of Hope as well as Fame!
> Perhaps the Trading Medium will Demand
> Some Master stroke from your Superior Hand.
> Perhaps a fixed Frontier Barrier too,
> If possible, may be atchiev'd by You.
> Our Golden Churches, sure, will shine more bright
> Rejoycing Long in your auspicious Light.
> The KING's high Favours bless the prosperous State;
> Whilst the KING's Friend's our powerful Advocate.
> Unnumber'd Blessings flow the Peaceful Land,
> Triumphing in your just and wise Command!
> And thus Great Sir! our Hope, and Crown and Joy!
> Whilst you, your mighty Powers for us employ.
> A tyde of Love, in every Breast shall spring;
> And each glad Tongue your grateful Praises sing:
> The joyous Land with every Blessing crown'd,
> The Fields & Floods shall your blest Name resound.''
> —Boston *Weekly News Letter,* July 18–25, 1728 (no. 82).

It is a painful duty to record that Burnet's name was not blessed for long in Massachusetts. He was forced to quarrel with his first assembly over his salary and the privy council of Great Britain took cognizance in 1730 of the fact that, in spite of his death the year before, neither he nor his children had ever received a penny from the provincial assembly by way of salary. C.O. 5: 871 (unpaged) (Mass.); *Acts, Privy Coun., Col.,* 1720–1745, p. 260.

136 See *Minutes of the Common Council of the City of New York,* under the years and months of the respective governors' inaugurations. The gold box presented to Governor Tryon, the last royal governor, was valued at 20 pistoles, *ibid.,* VII, 292.

that his administration might bring an improvement in such conditions as they disliked. For example, two weeks before the arrival of Sir Henry Moore in New York in 1765, a mob had hung and then burned together the effigies of Lieutenant Governor Colden and the devil, in part at least, as a protest against the Stamp Act. But when Moore's disapproval of the new law became known shortly after his arrival, a crowd of "many thousands" again assembled in the commons, built a huge bonfire, and rent the air with cries of "Long live Henry Moore and a speedy repeal of the Stamp Act!"[137]

Of course, the real test of a governor's success lay not in the cordiality of his reception but in the conduct of his administration. Often the first meeting of the assembly dissipated all hopes that the new broom would sweep clean the causes of former difficulty or that the new instructions would indicate a change of British policy on some disputed point. But optimism would not down. With each new arrival the colonists looked forward to an improvement in the relations between governor and assembly. The rigidity of the British system of colonial government and the inflexibility of the instructions seemed for the moment to be forgotten. Whatever the future might hold in store, the omens were favorable and the new governor began his work on a tidal wave of popularity.

[137] *New York Mercury*, Nov. 18, 1765.

CHAPTER III

CAPTAIN GENERAL AND GOVERNOR IN CHIEF[1]

WHILE the newly inaugurated governor was still receiving the congratulations and addresses of the inhabitants, he would naturally be studying the situation and the novel position in which he found himself. For, unless he was himself a provincial or had previously served in some official capacity in America, he was likely to find much that was strange in his social and political surroundings and much that was perplexing in the functions of his office.

The social and cultural conditions of the province would almost certainly appear to him crude and backward, relieved though they might be by the presence of a few persons with English education and point of view. Some compensation for this situation was to be found in the fact that the governor and his lady took precedence over all persons in the society of his province. Regardless of how far down he might belong in the social hierarchy of Great Britain, he took first place in all colonial functions as official representative of the king within the province.[2]

---

[1] The official title of the governor varied somewhat from province to province. "Captain general and governor in chief" was most common, although "lieutenant and governor general" was used for Virginia from 1683 until 1756 and "lieutenant governor and commander in chief" for Bermuda from 1684 until 1738. For lists of the forms used in addressing governors at different dates see: C.O. 5: 5, fos. 143–144, 239, 241, 243–244; C.O. 324: 57, pp. 13–15 (L.C.).

[2] An interesting series of rules "compared and adjusted from the several acts and Statutes made and provided in England, for the settlement of the precedency of Men and Women in America By Joseph Edmunson Mowbray, Herald" is printed in Anthony Stokes, *A View of the Constitution of the British Colonies in North-America and the West Indies* (London, 1783),

He rejoiced in the title of "His Excellency" and he might
receive on all official occasions a salute of seventeen guns.
A certain pride in these facts was pardonable in the man,
especially if he added to it a dignified expression of cordiality and good will to the people and society of the province. Many governors, be it said, did so comport themselves as to win the respect, esteem, and even the affection
of the inhabitants. Although the governors might grumble
privately at the expense incurred, they frequently gained
reputations for ease of access and hospitable entertainment. Some may have carried this policy to extremes from
unworthy motives, as Governor Henry Grenville hinted
in 1747 when he wrote his brother: "The truth is I keep
'em at a distance, suffer no freedoms with my person, or
authority, and will not allow my house to be a banqueting
place for them; all which is directly contrary to the general system of all my predecessors, who having improper
selfish ends in view, combed them for favors instead of
being courted by them."[3] In spite of his policy, Grenville
proved a most popular and well-loved governor. But some
men lost the opportunity of helpful social contact by a

p. 190. Each title in the printed list is followed by the words "his wife" or
"their wives" as the case may be. The order of precedence was:

Governor of the province	Baronets
Lieutenant governor	His Majesty's attorney general
President of the council	Judge of the admiralty
Members of his Majesty's council	Secretary of the province
Speaker of the Commons House of Assembly	Members of the Commons House of Assembly
Chief justice	Mayor
Treasurer	Aldermen
Associate judges	Members of the corporation

Members of the assembly and crown officers had no peculiar rank outside
of their own province. A widow of a former governor had no precedence as
such. A governor of one province or his wife had no precedence in another
which he or she might visit.

[3] Henry Grenville to George Grenville, Dec. 31, 1747, Huntington Library,
Stowe MSS. (unclassified).

policy of seclusion or of disdain for the people of the community. So it was with George Clinton, according to the historian of New York, William Smith, who wrote: "In a province given to hospitality, he erred by immuring himself in the fort, or retiring to a grotto in the country, where his time was spent with his bottle and a little trifling circle, who played billiards with his lady and lived upon his bounty."[4] For their policy in these matters the governors and their wives had little to go by except their own judgments, yet in general they were successful in avoiding extremes in either direction and in taking their natural place as leaders of the provincial society in which, for the time being, they were placed.

The political situation which the new governor met upon his arrival was apt to be more perplexing and complicated than the social. Although the governmental system of the royal province bore natural similarities to that of Great Britain, there were nearly always new problems to face, of which British experience had given him little understanding. There were details of administrative machinery, local traditions and prejudices, factional rivalries, long-standing controversies, and individual personalities with which the governor had to acquaint himself as soon as possible. With regard to some of these matters he had doubtless been prepared before leaving home. The Board of Trade, the London merchants, and colonials temporarily residing in England had frequently given him some insight into the affairs of his new domain. But in other respects information could only be gained at first hand after his arrival. The wise governor applied himself to a study of local politics as soon as possible.

In regard to the actual frame of government and the policies which the home officials expected him to pursue, the new executive had definite guides in his commission

4 William Smith, *History of New York*, II, 158.

and instructions. In fact, so far as written documents went, these instruments were the basis of the provincial constitution. In them was to be found all the authority necessary for the establishment and maintenance of a system of royal government. Except in the case of Massachusetts with its charter of 1691, there were no documents above these to which appeal could be taken, and on their terms rested the legislative power—and hence the laws—of the provincial assembly. Both the governor and the inhabitants of the province, therefore, had decidedly more than a passing interest in their contents.

Of the two, the commission was distinctly of higher authority than the instructions, but paradoxically, its public reading at the governor's inauguration was seldom awaited with much curiosity. This apparent apathy is partly explained by the fact that the commissions varied little from governor to governor. The form of the document was fixed even before the close of the seventeenth century, after which changes were rare and seldom of real importance. Furthermore, as everyone versed in governmental matters knew, the commission was general in its grant of powers while all vital details were contained in the instructions. The commission was so broad in character that it might almost serve as the basis for the constitution of a twentieth century self-governing dominion, but the instructions expressed the real policy of the British government and defined the actual manner in which the eighteenth century governor was to execute his powers. Hence the commission held far less significance than the other document for the practical politicians of the colony.

But, unlike the commission, the instructions were not designed for public examination. They were for the eyes of the governor only, or, in part, for those of the members of the council. At first the rule was not clearly laid down as to just which instructions the council was to see. In 1680 Sir Richard Dutton, prospective governor of Barbados, asked the Lords of Trade that he be required to show the council only those articles relating to measures in which their advice and consent were necessary. The Lords of Trade agreed and framed the instruction accordingly but they added a clause permitting him to show such other articles to the council as he should think convenient for the royal service.[5] The rule as stated in Dutton's instructions was later given to other governors, and in time became an accepted principle in all provinces. Although the chief executive was thus definitely told to communicate certain articles to the council, his discretion remained large. Councillors sometimes complained that the governor was withholding instructions which he ought to show the council, but the chief executive rarely allowed the members of that body to remain ignorant of the articles relating to its powers and duties. As to the rest of the document, the wise governor usually exercised caution. To let the councillors know just what directions he had received from home might provide his opponents ammunition with which to attack his administration. For this reason one chief executive declared that a governor "ought to keep very fair with all the council, or at least the major part of them, and seem to let them know everything, but withal that they may think he hath more instructions and orders."[6] Because of this feeling that they should be kept secret, Thomas Pownall, private secretary to Sir Danvers Osborn of New York, refused to surrender

[5] *Cal. State Paps., Col.*, 1677–1680, § 1535; instructions to Dutton, Barbados, 1680, art. 5, C.O. 29: 3, pp. 37–53.

[6] Francis Nicholson, lieutenant governor of Virginia, to the Lords of Trade, July 1, 1699, C.O. 5: 1310, no. 2 (L.C.). Nicholson was charged four years later by six Virginia councillors with keeping his instructions too secret. Memorial concerning Nicholson's maladministration, May 20, 1703, C.O. 5: 1314, no. 5 (L.C.); *Cal. State Paps., Col.*, 1704–1705, p. 92.

the governor's instructions after the latter's suicide to anyone but the lieutenant governor personally, although he readily delivered the commission to the entire council.[7] The Bermuda instructions from 1755 on contained an article requiring especial precautions against allowing the document to become public "to the great prejudice of his Majesty's service."[8] In general, the contents of the instructions were intended to be kept secret unless a conflict with the assembly or some similar event forced the governor's hand. He might then lay before the legislature the articles concerned in support of the position he had taken. And even then his judgment in so doing might not be approved in England. The Board of Trade once severely criticized Governor Knowles of Jamaica for showing an instruction to his assembly, as the board thought, needlessly. "We think it necessary to observe," they wrote, "that there ought to be no communication of his Majesty's instructions without it is either specially directed or is evidently and absolutely necessary to their execution."[9] The principle was thus well established that the governor ought to use great care in letting his instructions become public.

But when, in the secrecy of his closet, the governor perused his instructions, he found food for much thought. Novice though he might be in political matters, he could by careful study find in them most of the rules which he was to follow in the conduct of his office. They indicated

[7] Pownall to the Board of Trade, Oct. 14, 1753, *N. Y. Col. Docs.*, VI, 802–803.

[8] *Acts, Privy Coun., Col.*, 1745–1766, p. 304; instructions to Wm. Popple, Bermuda, 1755, art. 3, C.O. 38: 9, pp. 52–144. This instruction had been suggested by Popple himself in his "Observations on the Instructions" in 1754, but he had proposed even more drastically than was finally agreed to that any acting governor who should permit instructions to become public improperly should forfeit his place. C.O. 37: 18 (unpaged).

[9] Board of Trade to Knowles, Jan. 31, 1754, C.O. 138: 20, pp. 4–5.

the course he was to pursue in the maintenance of the prerogative and the attitude he was to take toward the council and assembly. Together with his commission, his instructions showed the extent and the limitations of the power and authority conferred upon him.

Wrought into the very fabric of these instruments was the principle that the governor was the direct representative of the British crown in the province. In all that concerned the royal interest, be it executive, legislative, or judicial in its bearings, the governor was responsible for the exercise of the prerogative. To pass this prerogative on to his successor unimpaired was his most important obligation. He was expected to set aside all thoughts of personal interest whenever necessary. Governor Burnet expressed the idea in his first speech to the Massachusetts assembly when he said: "The governor is but [the king's] officer, to act by his instructions and to have no inclinations, no temptations, no bias, that may divert him from obeying his royal master's commands."[10] To act thus might, and sometimes did, require sacrifices that were difficult to make. Jonathan Belcher, Burnet's successor and obviously a self-seeker, complained bitterly at not being permitted to draw his salary in the form offered by the assembly. "I think it cannot be judged just, reasonable, or honorable," he wrote the Board of Trade, "that I must live upon air or consume my own fortune while I am so faithfully serving the crown."[11] In contrast to this attitude, however, stands that of Daniel Parke of the Leeward Islands, who, reprobate though he was, valiantly upheld his interpretation of the prerogative in spite of threats against his life, and finally met death rather than leave Antigua where he had been ordered to make his

10 *Journals of the House of Representatives of Massachusetts*, VIII, 246.
11 Belcher to the Board of Trade, Oct. 29, 1731, *Belcher Papers*, I, 15 (*Collections* of the Massachusetts Historical Society, 6th series, VI).

principal residence.[12] To stand within the province as the king's own representative and the guardian of his power was, then, the first and greatest duty of the royal governor.

Only brief mention need be made here of those parts of the commissions and instructions which dealt with the governor's powers in connection with the council and assembly and with legislation, finance, and the administration of justice, as these subjects will be treated at length in later chapters.[13] The governor was the head of the local legislature, standing in much the same relation to the council and assembly as did the king to the lords and commons in Great Britain. He might summon, prorogue, and dissolve the assembly. The commission required that he get the consent of the council only for summoning the legislature, although the governor usually took their advice before putting an end to the session. He was armed with the powerful weapon of an absolute veto which he was expected to employ vigorously in the defense of good government and British interests. In financial matters the governor's authority was theoretically great. Entire control of appropriations and expenditures was supposed to be conferred upon him and his council by the requirement, given in all the commissions and repeated in all the general instructions, that money should be paid out only by warrant of the governor and council. But the ingenuity and persistence of the assemblymen reduced this power in many provinces to a minimum of executive control. In judicial matters the governor not only exercised general oversight through the right to create and regulate the lower courts with the council's assistance, but with the latter body he constituted the highest court within the province, from which appeals could only go to the privy council in Great Britain, and not then except in cases of

[12] *Cal. State Paps., Col.,* 1710–1711, §§ 204, 228, 623 ii, 683.
[13] See chapters IV–VII, IX, below.

moment. The governor's powers thus touched every phase of political life in the province.

In order to carry on the government and uphold the prerogative the governor needed assistants, and to the officials appointed for this purpose the commission and instructions made frequent reference. The most important group of advisers to the governor were the members of his council. Many of his specific powers were ordered to be executed only with the advice and consent of this body. Its members acted also as the upper house of the legislature, and, as has already been mentioned, they formed with the governor the highest court of appeals within the province. The names of the councillors, usually twelve in number, were given in his general instructions,[14] and in normal cases were substantially the same as those of the councillors at the close of the preceding administration. The new governor, therefore, found his advisory body ready formed upon his arrival. But his influence over its composition was often considerable because of the power given him by his commission and instructions to make nominations to fill vacancies, to make temporary appointments when the active membership dropped below a certain figure, and to suspend individual members when need should arise. The relations between the governor and the councillors were designed to be close and intimate.[15]

In addition to the council other officers were necessary to assist the governor and to maintain the royal authority. That these men should be under the close control of the chief executive was important for the sake of efficiency and centralized administration. To this end the governor was empowered by his commission to appoint "judges,

[14] This was not true, of course, in the case of Massachusetts Bay, where until the act of 1774, the councillors were annually elected by the assembly. In some of the earlier seventeenth century cases the councillors were named in the commissions instead of in the instructions.

[15] This subject is more fully discussed in the next chapter.

and in cases requisite, commissioners of oyer and terminer, justices of the peace, and other necessary officers and ministers.''[16] By the instructions from 1702 until the revision of 1752, the advice and consent of the council were required for all judicial appointments, after which the approval of a minimum of three members of that body was specified in most provinces.[17] The governor was forbidden to express any limitation of time in the commissions which he granted. This rule also was clarified after 1752 by a positive instruction to grant all judicial commissions during pleasure only. The assemblies then began to insist that the tenure of office by judges be during good behavior, as was the practice in England, but the governors were usually able to enforce an additional instruction forbidding this tenure.[18] The governor was instructed not to exercise himself, either personally or by deputy, any subordinate office or to permit any other person to execute more than one office by deputy. In contrast to the restraints imposed upon his appointive power, the restriction placed upon his right to suspend or remove his appointees was slight. The instructions only required that removal be for

[16] In Virginia, the Dominion of New England, the Leeward Islands, and the Floridas, sheriffs were also specifically mentioned in the lists; in Barbados and the Bahamas, provosts marshal.

[17] In the Leeward Islands from 1753 on, and in all of the royal governments established after 1763 (East and West Florida, Quebec, Grenada, Dominica, and St. Vincent) the consent of the ''majority of the members of our council signified in council'' was required by the instructions. It should be pointed out, as former Governor Pownall told the House of Commons in 1774, that technically the power of appointment was vested in the governor alone by his commission. ''His commission gives him full power to act—if he acts without the advice of his council, he does indeed break through his instructions, and may incur his Majesty's displeasure, but yet the appointment is good to all intents and purposes.'' *Parliamentary History*, XVII, 1284.

[18] Circular instructions to all governors of royal provinces, Dec. 15, 1761, *N. J. Arch.*, 1st series, IX, 322–326, 329–330; *N. Y. Col. Docs.*, VII, 479; *Colonial Records of North Carolina*, VI, 591–592. See also pp. 388–401, below.

cause, which the governor was to report immediately to the Board of Trade "in the fullest and most distinct manner." With so much of power over the inferior officers of the province, the chief executive was presumably in a strong position to enforce a proper administration of the government.

But the governor's authority over many inferior officers proved in time to be seriously limited. The home officials found themselves irresistibly tempted to take charge of the extensive patronage which the existence of royal government in America provided. As a result, a large number of the more important posts in all the colonies, but especially in South Carolina and the West Indies, were filled by nomination of the secretary of state or the Board of Trade during its period of ascendancy.[19] Sometimes appointments were made directly by commissions under the great seal or the sign manual and signet; in other cases, warrants were issued to the governors directing them to grant commissions to the nominees under the provincial seal. The governor was forbidden by his instructions to interfere with these patent officers in the enjoyment of their positions, although he might suspend them for misbehavior and, during such suspension or in case of death, appoint temporary substitutes. The system was a direct infringement upon the discretionary power of appointment lodged in the governor by his own commission.

Various evils grew out of the situation which were des-

[19] A list of the places which might be filled by the secretary of state, undated, but apparently of about 1747, is illuminating. Ninety-two offices are mentioned, the incumbents named with the date of their appointment, and the character of the tenure specified whether for life or during pleasure only. The largest group was that of South Carolina with 15 offices named. The others were: Jamaica, 12; the Leeward Islands, 10; Barbados, 8; North Carolina, Virginia, and Placentia (Newfoundland), 6 each; New York and Cape Breton, 5 each; Nova Scotia, 4; New Jersey, Massachusetts, and New Hampshire, 3 each; the rest scattered. C.O. 5: 5, fos. 227–230 (L.C.). See also Andrews, *Guide*, I, 234–236.

tined to have a serious and lasting effect upon royal government in America. Many of these patent officers ignored the clauses in their commissions requiring them to reside in the colonies. Instead of going to America they appointed deputies who performed their duties with a maximum of financial return to the principals in England and a minimum of efficient service in the colony. The compensation to these deputies was usually so low that they were frequently forced to serve in two or more offices, thus further decreasing their efficiency. This situation came to the attention of the Lords of Trade as early as 1679 when a proposal was made to grant to one man, residing in England, the two Jamaica offices of clerk of the crown and of the peace and clerk of the markets and fairs. The Lords of Trade represented to the king that the offices ought not to be served by deputy while the patentee resided in England. Furthermore, they pointed out that the governor's instructions forbade him to permit any person to execute more than one office by deputy.[20] A general inquiry into the patent offices in the colonies was ordered, in the course of which most of the governors roundly denounced the prevailing system.[21] But no permanent good was accomplished, as was shown by the fact that twenty years later the agents of Jamaica petitioned that no patents be granted for offices in the island except to men who would actually reside there.[22] The Board of Trade supported this request and an order in council was issued in 1699 requiring all patent officers to reside in their provinces and execute their offices personally except "in case of sickness or other incapacity." Letters to this effect were ordered written to the governors and the requirement inserted in

20 Lords of Trade to the king, Nov. 13, 1679, C.O. 324: 4, pp. 67–69 (L.C.); *Cal. State Paps., Col.,* 1677–1680, §§ 1182, 1183; *Acts, Privy Coun., Col.,* 1613–1680, § 1325.

21 *Cal. State Paps., Col.,* 1677–1680, §§ 1269, 1270, 1279, 1362, 1418.

22 *Ibid.,* 1699, § 69.

all future patents.[23] But again the rule was cheerfully ignored with impunity by all who could command even a little influence at Whitehall. Even men who held offices in England were sometimes appointed to colonial positions and no one expected them to go to America. As late as 1763 the Board of Trade—some of whose members were themselves among the offenders—was still petitioning that patent officers be obliged to a constant residence in their provinces.[24] Absenteeism was constant, flagrant, and unchecked.

Perhaps even more serious than this absenteeism itself was the fact that officials thus independently appointed from Great Britain were totally irresponsible to the governors, who were charged with the general oversight of administration. ''Where there is no dependence, obedience seldom follows,'' wrote Governor Atkins of Barbados in 1680,[25] and in the course of the next century the truth of his words was again and again illustrated.

Especially unsatisfactory was the independent appointment of the naval officer in many provinces. The governor was charged, both by law and by his trade instructions, with the enforcement of many details of the navigation acts. For this purpose there had grown up the post of naval officer, or clerk of the navy office, under the governor's control and supervision. This official attended to many of the matters for which the governor was responsible under the law. The trade instructions warned the governor that any neglect or failure properly to enforce the law would involve the loss of his office, the forfeiture of £1000, and also ''the most rigorous marks'' of his Majesty's displeasure. Hence the governor considered it particularly important that he himself should appoint the

[23] C.O. 324: 7, pp. 30–32 (L.C.); *Cal. State Paps., Col.*, 1699, §§ 91, 104, 552–558.

[24] Board of Trade to the king, June 8, 1763, C.O. 5: 65, pp. 165–166 (L.C.).

[25] Atkins to the Board of Trade, *Cal. State Paps., Col.*, 1677–1680, § 1362.

naval officers and be able to remove them at will. What was the governor's dismay, therefore, when warrants began to appear for the appointment of nominees of the secretary of state to the office. Governor after governor protested bitterly but to no avail. Particularly distressing was the case of Jonathan Belcher, who had appointed his own son-in-law to the position of naval officer in Boston, only to be forced to remove him and install in his place "an insolent jackanapes," Benjamin Pemberton by name. Nepotism did not bother Belcher, but having to turn his children "out of so much bread" did. The further thought that Pemberton's conduct of the office might cause the loss of his own position and a fine of £1000 added to the grief of the close-fisted New Englander. But in spite of his appeals to everyone with whom he thought he had any influence, Belcher was unable to get the office restored. In the end, Pemberton held the office until Belcher's name had become but a memory in Massachusetts.[26] In all the provinces the naval office eventually passed out of the governor's control.

Most important of all in its bearing upon the governor's position in the province was the direct loss of local patronage when lucrative positions were filled from Great Britain. The axiom that the man who can appoint to a large number of profitable offices will command a strong political following was as true then as it is now. In the eighteenth century the cause of royal government required that the governor build up such a following within his province, even though its members were moved by personal ambition rather than by disinterested loyalty.

26 For Belcher's letters on this subject see *Belcher Paps.*, I, 376–378, 385–386, 405, 413; II, 155–156, 167–170, 173–174, 177–178, 180–181, 191. See also Pemberton to Newcastle, Oct. 8, 1733, Add. MS., 32,688 (Newcastle Paps., III), fos. 474–475. Warrants for Pemberton's appointment are in C.O. 324: 36, pp. 417–418, C.O. 324: 37, pp. 515–516; C.O. 324: 40, pp. 74–75; C.O. 324: 41, pp. 234–236; and C.O. 5: 920, pp. 40–43 (Mass.).

Support of the governor was most surely to be found among those whom he appointed or could appoint to local office. He found it especially discouraging, therefore, when the patronage was slowly taken from him and post after post was filled by appointees over whom he had no influence and whom he could not remove. The bad effects of the system became more and more apparent as the Revolution approached. The earl of Dunmore wrote late in 1774—and many leading Virginians were said to agree with their governor—that "if it had been thought fit to vest all the power of this nature which this government affords in the hands of the governor, I should have had the means of keeping down the attempts of party and faction which have put the public affairs of this colony in the alarming situation in which they actually stand."[27] This view was perhaps exaggerated, but it can be matched by a declaration made in the House of Commons a few months earlier by George Johnstone, the outspoken former governor of West Florida: "In that country, sir, the governor is nothing more than a mere cipher; he has no support in any proposition he makes, no places to give away, and yet you blame him for not keeping up his authority."[28] Perhaps the fairest summary of the effects of the whole situation was likewise made in the House of Commons at about the same time by George Byng, son of the former governor of Barbados: "It was now become a fashion, he said, to give away those places of emolument to men of this country, with reversions to one, two, or three sons; to men who had never been of the least service to this country in his apprehensions. . . . Whilst places

[27] Dunmore to Dartmouth, Dec. 24, 1774, C.O. 5: 1353, pp. 73–75 (L.C.).
[28] *Parliamentary History*, XVII, 1188. Any of Johnstone's remarks on colonial affairs must be judged in the light of the fact that he had been removed from office in 1766 for declaring war on the Indians without first receiving the sanction of the British ministry. Lord Shelburne to James Grant, governor of East Florida, Feb. 19, 1767, C.O. 5: 548, pp. 265–266.

continue to be given away to men of this country the emoluments of which arise from the labor and sweat of an American brow, it will undoubtedly, and very properly, annihilate the power of any supreme officer in that country. Men look up to their superiors, and obey their directions according to the emoluments received from them; and when once there is no dependence in it, there will be no obedience.'"[29]

The depression which this lack of control over civilian officials might occasion in the mind of the new governor would be partly relieved upon examining those clauses in his commission and instructions which related to his authority in military affairs. His commission named him captain general and commander in chief of his province and endowed him with all the powers belonging to this rank. All officers of the provincial military forces were under his command and subject to his authority. He might employ all persons residing within the province for its defense, and, in case of necessity, transport them to any of the American possessions of the crown for service against the common enemy. With the advice of the council he might establish forts or other defenses and provide them with ordnance and other equipment.[30] The governor was empowered to execute martial law in time of invasion or other military emergency, but his instructions forbade him to do so without the advice and consent of the council. He had no power to enforce martial law upon the provincial troops in time of peace, but the instructions recommended that the assembly pass laws for the regulation of the militia much as parliament did for the forces in Great Britain. The governor was made responsible for

---

[29] *Parl. Hist.*, XVII, 1194.

[30] The commission did not state who was to supply the necessary funds for this purpose. In point of fact, the assemblies, through their control of the purse, came to exercise much power in this connection.

the efficient organization of the militia and for their adequate training, a duty which the individualism and lack of subordination of the Americans made particularly difficult, if not almost impossible. His instructions also appointed him custodian of the military supplies which might be furnished by the Board of Ordnance, to whom he was directed to make regular reports as to the conditions of the fortifications and the stores of war. In theory, at least, the governor's control over the purely local and provincial military organization was practically complete.

The governor's authority over troops of the British establishment was not so clear. Until well along in the eighteenth century almost the only units of the army regularly stationed in the continental colonies were the independent companies, such as those in New York and South Carolina, over whom the royal governors usually exercised fairly complete control.[31] In the West Indies there were often larger units which sometimes were commanded by the governors and at other times were independent of their authority. But from the time of the third intercolonial war until the Revolution there was always a large number of British regulars in America whose officers seldom were responsible to the governors in any way. From 1755 until the Revolution there was almost constantly a British commander in chief in America who was inclined to look upon the governors simply as liaison officers between himself and the assemblies and who successfully established his right to command all men in arms in the provinces in spite of the terms of the governors' commissions.[32] Under such conditions the governors

[31] Independent companies were also stationed in Bermuda and the Bahamas among the island provinces during most of the period. The governors regularly held commissions as captains of these companies.

[32] The subject of the relations between the governors and the commander in chief in America is to receive extensive illustration in a forthcoming treatise by Dr. Stanley M. Pargellis on ''The Earl of Loudoun and the Seven

yielded first place in military authority and precedence to
the commander in chief, although they still retained their
independence in civil matters.[33]

The governor's naval powers were considerably less
extensive than his military. He had, it is true, a commission as vice-admiral of his province, but the authority
therein granted was judicial rather than naval, giving
him oversight of the vice-admiralty court and not of the
vessels of the royal navy within provincial waters.[34] From

Years' War.'' See also C. E. Carter, ''The Significance of the Military Office
in America, 1763–1775,'' in *American Historical Review*, XXVIII, 475–488.

[33] A table of precedence for the military service in America, given under
the royal sign manual, Dec. 17, 1760, is printed in Stokes, *A View of the
Constitution*, pp. 188–189, and is here reproduced in abbreviated form:

1. Commander in chief of the British forces
2. Royal governors when in their respective provinces
3. General officers on the staff
4. Royal governors when out of their respective provinces
5. Lieutenant governors and presidents of councils when acting governors
   in their respective provinces
6. Colonels
7. Lieutenant governors and presidents of councils when acting governors but out of their respective provinces
8. Lieutenant governors when not acting governors but in their respective
   provinces
9. Lieutenant governors when not acting governors and out of their
   respective provinces
10. Governors of charter colonies when in their respective colonies
11. All field officers under the rank of colonel
12. Lieutenant governors of proprietary governments when out of their
    respective provinces
13. Governors of charter colonies when out of their respective colonies.

All royal governors and lieutenant governors and all proprietary lieutenant
governors were to take rank within their respective grades according to the
dates of their commissions, but governors of charter colonies according to the
dates of their charters.

A controversy over the interpretation of this table of precedency took
place in New York between Governor Moore and General Gage in 1767. See
N. Y. Col. Docs., VIII, 15–19, 73, 97–99, 101, cited by Carter, *Amer. Hist.
Rev.*, XXVIII, 486.

[34] Josiah Burchett, secretary of the Admiralty, wrote the governors on
this point, Feb. 15, 1712: ''The commission the aforesaid governors have or

the time of Charles II, the governor's civil commission entitled him to appoint captains and masters of ships and to confer upon them power to execute martial law upon members of their crews. Throughout the eighteenth century the governor's instructions allowed him to grant commissions to privateers, but the flags borne by such vessels had to be of a special design to distinguish privateers from ships of the royal navy.[35] In early times there was some confusion as to the authority of the governor over officers of the navy stationed in the province. But beginning in 1689 the commissions specified that the governor's jurisdiction did not extend to the personnel of the navy, except that, should the commander of a vessel refuse or neglect to obey the written orders given him by the governor, the latter might suspend him and send him to England in custody for trial. Much friction and many disputes followed upon this arrangement, which was unsatisfactory to both parties. Conditions were probably at their worst in Jamaica. Merchants of this island petitioned in 1696 for closer control of officers of the navy by the governor. The situation was mischievous, they said, "every captain over a sixth rate or a fire ship huffing and hectoring the governor and the whole island, as if each of those little commanders were a petty king or at least governor of the place, acting as they please without all control."[36] Similar complaints came from the governor

may receive from the lord high admiral or the commissioners of the Admiralty constituting them vice-admirals of her Majesty's islands and plantations does in no degree entitle them to the right of hoisting a flag on board any of her Majesty's ships more than the vice-admirals of the maritime counties of this kingdom." Adm. 2: 411, p. 351 (Mass.).

[35] There was some doubt during the late seventeenth century as to the source of the governor's authority to grant commissions to privateers although the power was frequently exercised. See *Cal. State Paps., Col.*, 1689–1692, §§ 2528, 2529, 2553.

[36] Proposals of the Jamaica merchants [Sept. 18, 1696], C.O. 137: 4, no. 18; *Cal. State Paps., Col.*, 1696–1697, § 233.

and the agents of the island.[37] But instead of granting
closer control to the governors, the Admiralty Board
followed a reverse course in 1702. Beginning with that
date the commissions omitted entirely the provision that
the naval commanders must obey the written orders of
the governor, although the instructions intimated that
such authority would be specially conferred upon the governor by the lord high admiral or the commissioners of the
Admiralty.[38] Even these instructions were dropped after
1718. Three years before this date the Board of Trade
reported to the secretary of state complaints of friction
between the governor of Jamaica, Lord Archibald Hamilton, and the naval commander there, Sir Hovenden
Walker. They asked that officers of the navy on American
service be instructed "to live in good understanding with
the said governors during their stay there" and suggested
further that the governor's power be restored as it was
before 1702.[39] But the commissioners of the Admiralty
replied to the secretary's letter of inquiry that "many
inconveniences" had followed the earlier arrangement.
They did instruct their captains "to employ the said ships
in such manner as may be most for the service of the islands or governments, and therein to advise with the gov-

[37] "Considerations Relating to Jamaica" by the agents and merchants
trading thereto, Oct. 16, 1696, C.O. 137: 4, no. 22; *Cal. State Paps., Col.*,
1696–1697, § 324. See also *ibid.*, 1689–1692, § 2643; 1693–1696, § 2022, p.
576; 1696–1697, § 768. It should be pointed out that the governor's commission authorized him to arrest and punish according to law officers and
sailors who committed offenses on land. This clause continued unchanged
throughout the eighteenth century. There were complaints against some
governors on behalf of officers of the navy. Sir William Phips of Massachusetts was recalled in 1694 in part because of his high-handed treatment of one
such officer. Royal letter to Phips, Feb. 15, 1694, C.O. 5: 858, no. 17 (Mass.);
Cal. State Paps., Col., 1693–1696, §§ 689, 708, 862, 1666.

[38] I have been unable to find any such grant of power by the Admiralty
to the governors as is indicated in these instructions.

[39] Board of Trade to Secretary Stanhope, March 15, 1715, C.O. 138: 14,
pp. 201–202.

ernors and follow their directions.'' This, they said, was the proper way to handle the situation.[40] With this statement the subject was perforce dropped, although further complaints occasionally appeared throughout the century.[41] The governor's naval authority was thus limited to such local vessels as he might himself commission.

A responsibility of a very different sort which was placed upon the governor by his commission was the custody of the great seal of the province. He was authorized to use the seal upon all papers which required this form of authentication. All public documents of the province, such as commissions, legislative acts, and proclamations, were passed under the seal. In addition, many instruments of more private concern, such as patents for land, licenses of various sorts, and decrees issued out of the provincial chancery had to be validated in the same way. Substantial fees were charged for the use of the seal and the income from this source was one of the most important perquisites of the governor. Lieutenant Governor Fauquier of Virginia reported in 1763 that the fees attached to the office of governor of Virginia produced more than £1000 sterling a year, a large portion of which sum undoubtedly came from the use of the seal.[42] The custody of this symbol of authority was therefore a desirable privilege as well as an important duty.

In all colonies where the title to the soil rested immedi-

[40] Commissioners of the Admiralty to Stanhope, March 26, 1715, C.O. 137: 10, no. 70 i; C.O. 138: 14, pp. 215–216.

[41] The greatest subject of controversy between the governors and the officers of the navy was that of impressment within the colonies. This matter is so extensive and complicated as to preclude treatment here. It is enough to say that the navy officers were eventually deprived of the power of impressment without the governor's consent.

[42] Fauquier's answers to queries, Jan. 30, 1763, C.O. 5: 1330, pp. 558–559 (L.C.). During the administration of Fauquier's predecessor, Robert Dinwiddie, a bitter controversy had raged over his demand of a fee of one pistole (about 20s sterling) for every land patent granted. In New York as

ately in the king, the governor's commission placed on him the authority for granting land. He was required, however, to take the advice of his council, with whom he was to consult on all questions of quit-rents, terms of disposal, and conditions of settlement. But discretion in such matters was more apparent than real, for the instructions usually contained long sections, sometimes running into a dozen or more articles, specifying the exact manner in which such grants were to be made. The details of these regulations varied from province to province and from period to period. For the entire subject they are so important, and yet so detailed, that a memorandum of about 1766 among the secretary of state's papers could assert with approximate truth that "the governors derive their power of granting land solely from their instructions," and that "a fresh instruction may either erase, diminish, or entirely annul the governor's power of granting lands."[43]

But even the very limited discretion allowed by these instructions was further curtailed toward the end of the period. After the close of the Seven Years' War, reduced officers, British noblemen, and others who claimed special consideration flooded the privy council with petitions for grants of lands in America. These were referred to the council committee and to the Board of Trade, upon whose recommendations the actual grants were made by the council itself. The Board of Trade repeatedly declared that this practice was dangerous because of the impossibility

elsewhere, the fees varied from time to time. Lord Bellomont received 12s for each grant of land in 1700 but Sir Henry Moore took 25s (about 18s sterling) for every 100 acres in 1767. Bellomont to the Board of Trade, July 26, 1700, *N. Y. Col. Docs.*, IV, 686-687; Moore to the earl of Shelburne, April 25, 1767, *ibid.*, VII, 921.

[43] C.O. 5: 216, pp. 1-6 (L.C.). The document can only be dated from the various extracts which it gives from the instructions to individual governors relating to the granting of land.

of judging in England "of the abilities of each particular proponent with that precision which follows the rules of proceeding in those colonies where the power of granting lands is constitutionally vested in his Majesty's governors and councils, under the limitations and directions prescribed in his Majesty's instructions.'"[44] Nevertheless, between 1764 and 1777 the privy council approved grants of land to the astonishing total of over five million acres, nearly a third of which were to be laid out within provinces which had been occupied by the British for at least half a century.[45] Although much criticism had arisen in England over the exorbitantly large grants made by the governors of many colonies during the last part of the seventeenth century and the early part of the eighteenth, the activities of these governors and their councils, fraudulent and pernicious as they often were, stand favorable comparison with the later grants authorized by the privy council itself. In both cases the colonies were ruthlessly exploited for the benefit of a few individuals. Yet the grants made by the early governors were nearly always to persons in America who might be expected to make some show, at least, of developing the tracts assigned them, while the grants made by the privy council were for the most part to residents of Great Britain whose only interest was that of the outright speculator. However, in spite of this violation of the governor's right to grant lands himself, the great bulk of the grants in the royal colonies throughout the colonial period came from the

[44] Board of Trade to the privy council committee, June 6, 1765, C.O. 324: 17, pp. 458–461 (L.C.). See also *Acts, Privy Coun., Col., Unbound Paps.,* §§ 646, 715, 778.

[45] These figures have been derived by totalling the grants actually made as indicated in *Acts, Privy Coun., Col.,* 1745–1766, app. V, and *ibid.,* 1766–1783, app. V. No account has been taken of the applications referred to the Board of Trade without final action being noted, nor of the considerable number of grants made before 1764 or after 1777.

governors and councils. And because the proper distribution of land to bona fide settlers is always such a vital factor in the growth of any frontier community, the activities of the governors and councils in this connection were among their most important functions in the province.

The new governor also found that his commission and instructions made him responsible for overseeing the religious and moral life of the province. He was made the local representative of the king as head of the Established Church. His commission gave him the right of collating to ecclesiastical benefices and his instructions empowered him to issue licenses for marriage and for the probating of wills. The latter document also laid upon him various duties connected with the Anglican churches in the community. In spite of the fact that general diocesan jurisdiction over all the American colonies was vested in the bishop of London, the governor's instructions directed him to see that the Book of Common Prayer was read every Sunday and holy day; that the sacraments were administered according to the rites of the Church of England in all orthodox churches; that parishes were settled and churches established; and that maintenance, parsonages, and glebes were provided for the clergy. The governor was also to see that the ministers were members of their respective vestries; that those who preached or administered the sacraments were in due orders; and in case any minister gave cause for scandal, either because of his doctrine or manners, that the best means be used for his removal.[46] The governor's relation to the clergy and to the Established Church was thus made very close.

Although many of these instructions were first intro-

[46] These directions were omitted from the instructions to all the governors of dissenting Massachusetts and from those to the governors of New Hampshire before 1761. The clause in the commission conferring the right of collating to benefices was omitted from all Massachusetts commissions and from those for New Hampshire before 1715.

duced at the suggestion of the bishop of London, his jurisdiction and that of the governor inevitably came into conflict from time to time. The exact extent of the bishop's
authority in America was never defined except during the
episcopate of Bishop Gibson who received a special commission from the king in 1727 empowering him or his
commissaries to visit, try, and punish the provincial
clergy.[47] But at other times the bishops appointed commissaries in some of the predominantly Anglican colonies
to exercise general oversight of the ministers. The powers
of these ecclesiastical officers seemed to encroach upon
those of the governors and bitter antagonism between the
two officials was not infrequent. However, the commissary
only rarely held an ecclesiastical court, for but one such
ecclesiastical official, Garden of South Carolina, exercised
the privilege in the continental colonies,[48] and, except for
one possible case in Barbados about 1737, no commissary
ever seems to have done so in the West Indies. An earlier
attempt by Commissary Gordon of Barbados in 1717 met
with the united opposition of both governor and assembly.
The latter became so aroused that it passed an act in 1719
"to quiet the minds of the inhabitants against their terrors
of an ecclesiastical court," whereby the holding of such
a court was forbidden.[49] Candor requires the statement

[47] A. L. Cross, *The Anglican Episcopate and the American Colonies*, p.
289. The commission was renewed in 1728 by George II, *N. Y. Col. Docs.*, V,
849–854.

[48] Garden started four processes against four irregular clergymen and
held two actual trials. Two of the clergymen proceeded against refused to
stand trial after the preliminary steps had been taken and resigned their
livings. Two others were actually tried and convicted. One of these, George
Whitefield the evangelist, was suspended from his office (1740); the other
was suspended from both office and living. Cross, p. 313.

[49] The trouble in Barbados began about 1717 with the appointment of
William Gordon as commissary and with his attempts to set up an ecclesiastical
court, which, it was feared, would try laity as well as clergy. The Barbados
agents issued dire warnings of the effect of such a court, which they said,
would clash with the civil government and the laws of the island. (Barbados

that few governors tried very hard themselves to raise the
tone of the worldly minded provincial clergy. Yet the conflict between the governor and the commissary over jurisdiction was an important factor in the agitation for an
American diocese with a resident bishop.[50]

The governor's instructions also pointed out his duty
toward the laity of the province. Beginning as early as
1626 the governors were urged to labor for "the extirpat-
ing of vice and the encouragement of virtue and good-
ness" among the inhabitants.[51] During the decade of

agents to the king, [Aug.] 1717, C.O. 28: 15, no 11.) The Board of Trade
wrote to Secretary of State Addison that Gordon was a thorough reprobate,
that one of the other members of the proposed court was a lunatic, and that the
third was a man of little account. The board urged that the bishop employ
his activities toward improving the clergy rather than the laity of the island
"since the lives and conversation of the laity will, in all human probability,
much sooner be reformed by the pious examples of their spiritual pastors
than by any ecclesiastical censure or coercion from the secular arm." (Board
of Trade to Addison, Oct. 17, 1717, C.O. 29: 13, pp. 413–422.) The bishop of
London rose to the defense of his commissary and declared that Gordon
had never once exercised his authority for an ecclesiastical court. (C.O. 28:
15, no. 46; C.O. 29: 13, pp. 500–503. See also C.O. 28: 15, nos. 14, 15, 17; and
Acts, Privy Coun., Col., 1680–1720, § 1310.) In 1737 the assembly was induced
to suspend part of the act of 1719 for a period of three years during which
time one clergyman was prosecuted and censured, but, according to Governor
Pinfold in 1765, the case was handled with so much personal malice that
twenty-eight years later it was still spoken of with detestation. Pinfold
himself removed a rector from his living after conviction in a civil court for
assault and was immediately challenged for want of power to make such a removal. (Pinfold to the Board of Trade, Sept. 3, 1765, C.O. 28: 32).

[50] In a long letter to Hillsborough, Jan. 11, 1771, Richard Terrick, bishop
of London, reviewed the history of ecclesiastical jurisdiction in the colonies
and urged the appointment of an American bishop. Pending such action,
Bishop Terrick proposed an instruction to the governors for a new method
of handling cases of delinquent clergymen which would prevent disputes. The
governor was to call in two councillors and two clergymen, one of whom was
preferably to be the bishop's commissary. They were to cite the accused
clergyman before them, hear the evidence, suspend the minister if necessary,
and report the whole case to the privy council for final disposition. (C.O. 5:
1349, pp. 25–31, L.C.) The proposal was never adopted.

[51] Instructions to Yeardley, Va., 1626, art. 17, *Va. Mag.,* II, 393.

1670–1680 the various instructions on this subject were consolidated. For the next half century the instructions ordered the governors "to take care that drunkenness, debauchery, swearing, and blasphemy" were severely punished and that no one was admitted to public office whose "ill fame and conversation" might bring scandal thereupon. Either the governors were only half-hearted in their attempts to enforce this instruction, or else their efforts were largely in vain, for in 1727 the bishop of London became much disturbed over the state of morals in the colonies. At his request a new instruction was prepared and sent to all governors ordering them to execute vigorously all laws against blasphemy, sexual irregularity, sabbath-breaking, and drunkenness, and to urge the assemblies to pass such further laws as might be necessary to suppress vice in its various forms. The instruction also directed the governors to encourage their assemblies to erect schools "in order to the training up of youth to reading and to a necessary knowledge of the principles of religion."[52] But as far as the evidence goes, this instruction was no more effective than those which had preceded it. Few of the governors openly condoned vice, but they were not selected for their interest in moral uplift and their position gave them, after all, little opportunity to lead in movements for reform.

Throughout the century before the Revolution the instructions paid some attention to the welfare of the dark-skinned inhabitants and neighbors of the provinces. With

[52] This was first prepared as an additional instruction for all royal governors and was so submitted by the Board of Trade to the privy council committee, June 6, 1727, but the death of George I soon afterward necessitated new general instructions for all governors and this article was included therein. (C.O. 324: 11, pp. 40–41; *Acts, Privy Coun., Col.*, 1720–1745, § 117.) It was included in all general instructions until after the Revolution, except that a somewhat shorter article to the same effect was given to the governors of provinces acquired in 1763.

the assistance of the council and assembly every governor was to "facilitate and encourage" the conversion of Indians and negroes to Christianity.[53] Until after the revision of the instructions in 1752 nearly all the governors were told to get laws passed to restrain the "inhuman severities" of masters and overseers toward their slaves. These laws were to make the wilful killing of Indians and negroes punishable with death and to provide a "fit penalty" for maiming them. Indifference might meet the attempts of the governor to improve the morals of the whites, but open antagonism was very likely to appear if he took up too seriously the cause of the less favored races. Public sentiment did not favor the conversion of slaves, although some helpful legislation was passed here and there. Merchants interested in the fur trade, whether British or colonial, disliked all attempts of missionaries or others to dam up the devastating flow of liquor to the Indians.[54] There were laws to punish undue severity toward slaves in many provinces but, as Governor Grenville of Barbados pointed out in 1752, the death penalty for killing a negro or Indian was generally opposed. The assembly of his island had never passed a law to that effect

[53] The instructions to the governors of New York from 1703 until the Revolution specifically urged that the governor, council, and assembly provide "for the maintenance of some ministers to inhabit among the Five Nations of Indians in order to instruct them and also to prevent their being seduced from their allegiance to us by French priests and Jesuits." In like manner other instructions to various governors of continental provinces dealing with Indian relations represented a mixture of humanitarian, economic, and political motives.

[54] One of the few governors to make serious attempts to educate and convert the Indians was Alexander Spotswood, lieutenant governor of Virginia. But his efforts, which were part of a broad scheme for handling Indian relations in his province, were frustrated by the jealousies of British merchants. See his letters to Dartmouth, Nov. 11, 1711, *Spotswood Letters*, I, 123–126, and to the bishop of London, Nov. 11, 1711, Jan. 27, and June 4, 1715, *ibid.*, I, 127–129; II, 88–93, 113–114; *Executive Journals of the Council of Colonial Virginia*, III, 363, 365, 388–389, 397.

"from the apprehension of the dangerous effects it might have on the spirits of the negroes, by lessening that awe in which they ought to stand of their masters and perhaps inciting them to insurrections." Grenville added a suggestion that "as the security of the island does in a great degree depend upon keeping the slaves, now grown very numerous, in a due state of subjection," the instruction ought to be given up.[55] Largely because of this advice the instruction was soon discontinued. For once the British authorities realized that nothing was to be gained by keeping up a recommendation in which no one—unless possibly the negroes themselves—was likely to be seriously interested. The influences which were responsible for such humanitarian instructions as these were not strong enough to bring about their strict enforcement.

Passing reference has already been made to the governor's duties in connection with the enforcement of the navigation acts.[56] These measures imposed many tasks upon the governor. He was to take bonds of the shipmasters for transporting enumerated commodities to legal destinations; to see that vessels engaged in colonial trade were of English or plantation build and were manned with the required proportion of Englishmen; to satisfy himself that cargoes imported into the province had been loaded in England and cleared by the customs authorities there; to register all vessels built within his colony; and to send to England periodically lists of all ships entered or cleared, of cargoes imported or exported, and of bonds issued or canceled within his jurisdiction. Most of these duties devolved in time upon the naval officer, but the responsibility remained with the governor. To aid him in this work he was given a set of trade instructions which epitomized the laws and to a certain extent explained his

[55] Grenville's observations on his instructions, Dec. 14, 1752, C.O. 28: 30.
[56] See above, pp. 104–105.

duties. He also received copies of all acts of parliament which touched upon colonial trade. Few in number in the seventeenth century, these statutes multiplied until, in 1761, the trade instructions listed no less than ninety-three enactments, including extensions and renewals, which the governor was expected to master. Merely to read them was a formidable task in itself. During the generation or so in which the colonial world was getting adjusted to the system, the more diligent governors earned for themselves much hatred in America by enforcing these laws. But during the eighteenth century the governors' letters made fewer and fewer references to such problems. This fact was in part due to the increasing share which the naval officers and customs officials took in trade administration, but even more to the gradual adjustment of colonial commerce to the system. The governor's task in this respect was materially lightened as the years went by.

But aside from the enforcement of acts of parliament, the governor's commission and instructions gave him many powers and duties connected with trade. His commission empowered him to appoint fairs and markets,[57] and to establish ports and harbors for shipping and the movement of commerce. The same document authorized him to set up customs houses and warehouses and to create all necessary offices related thereto. His instructions directed him to examine rates and duties payable upon imports and exports, to prevent the engrossing of commodities ''as tending to the prejudice of that freedom which trade and commerce ought to have,'' and with the consent

[57] Acts establishing such fairs and granting freedom from arrest to persons attending them were sometimes passed by the assemblies with clauses recognizing the royal prerogative. The Board of Trade was inclined to view such acts with little disfavor. See Board of Trade to the king, July 29, 1768, C.O. 5: 1368, pp. 364–365 (L.C.).

of the council to establish regulations for the improvement of trade. The governor was told to encourage all lawful traders in general and the Royal African Company and other slave traders in particular. He was expected to give British merchants every protection, to guard against hostile legislation by the provincial assembly, and to make easy the collection of just debts. In the minds of those Englishmen who gave any thought at all to the colonies, these communities existed primarily, if not entirely, for the benefit of the trade of the mother country. The governor's responsibility was to Great Britain and not to the colony. In case of a clash of British and colonial interests, British merchants and governmental officials considered it axiomatic that the governor should support the former and oppose the latter. And most governors did. But some of them, especially after they had resided in America for several years, saw that there were two sides to the question and acted accordingly. Such men seldom met with favor in Great Britain since they had violated the spirit if not the letter of their instructions in which British commercial interests were so greatly emphasized.

Lastly, the instructions made clear that the governor was the connecting link between the colonial government and the home officials. In addition to a general requirement to correspond regularly with the secretary of state and the Board of Trade, the instructions ordered him to send frequent accounts of the wants and defects of the province with suggestions as to how the home government might contribute to its prosperity. He was to transmit annually a statement regarding population, listing the numbers of inhabitants under various classifications as to age, sex, military availability, freemanship, bondage, and slavery. He was also to send an account of the numbers born, christened, and buried. In addition to several kinds of inventories, accounts, and other reports connected with his regular duties, the Board of Trade expected the governor to submit at frequent intervals full answers to a series of queries dealing with every phase of the governmental and economic life of the province. The repeated complaints of the Board of Trade and secretary of state show clearly that many governors took these duties lightly. Many of them were more lax in their reports and correspondence than in any other part of their official business. Yet the governors were, and had to be, the most important sources of information for the British officials on all aspects of provincial affairs.

The duties of the governor were extensive and his powers almost dangerously great. As direct representative of his royal master he was naturally endowed with prerogatives which in Great Britain belonged solely to the king. After the Revolution of 1689 the ministers of the crown, controlling but in turn controlled by parliament, came to exercise many of these powers in the king's name. But in the province the governor encountered no agency which had legal competence to control his actions. He was accountable only to the king and ministers in Great Britain. He might prove tyrannical, but few of the statutes designed to protect the English subject from oppression extended to the colonies. At first no machinery existed for punishing him for his misdeeds. A series of unfortunate incidents in the late seventeenth century, growing out of the appointment of several greedy and unfit governors, led to the passage of an act of parliament in 1700 designed to meet the situation in the future. This measure, "An Act to Punish Governors of Plantations in this Kingdom for Crimes by them Committed in the Plantations,"[58] provided that any governor guilty of oppressing English subjects beyond the seas within his province or of any other crime or offense contrary to the laws of the realm or

[58] 11 & 12 William III, cap. 12.

of the province should be tried before the court of king's bench or before royal commissioners and a jury in whatever county the king should direct in his commission. The punishment to be inflicted was to be the same as was usual for similar offenses committed in England. Until the passage of this act the governor had been in effect above the laws of his province and outside the jurisdiction of the courts of England. But this act definitely placed him under the laws of the province and of England and provided a jurisdiction in which he might be tried.

The machinery thus created was used to the full only once in our period. The case was that of Walter Douglas who had been sent as governor to the Leeward Islands in 1711 after the murder of Governor Parke. Douglas, who had been an army officer, not only proved unfitted for the delicate task of restoring harmony but was greedy, vindictive, and unscrupulous as well. The charges lodged against him included false arrest, use of the queen's pardon as a means to enrich himself, false entry in the council register, acceptance of improper presents from the assemblies, and —most scandalous of all—embezzlement of the communion silver issued to him upon his departure for the Leeward Islands. He was ordered home, tried before the king's bench, fined, and sentenced to five years' imprisonment.[59] After his release he went to France and spent his remaining years in retirement.[60] While Douglas was in prison awaiting trial, the Jamaica governor, Lord Archibald Hamilton, came under fire. He was charged with various crimes, especially with implication in piracy. His inveterate enemy, Peter Heywood, was appointed temporary commander in chief with power to investigate the charges and to send Hamilton home in custody if a trial

[59] *Acts, Privy Coun., Col.*, 1680–1720, pp. 650–652, 687–690; *Cal. State Paps., Col.*, 1711–1712, §§ 350, 355, 392; 1712–1714, §§ 1, 36, 127, 129.
[60] V. L. Oliver, *The History of the Island of Antigua*, I, 212.

seemed warranted.[61] Nothing loath, Heywood arrested his
former superior after a one-sided investigation and sent
him back to England. But at a hearing before the Board
of Trade, while under bail, Hamilton was able to clear
himself of the charges and was never brought to trial.[62]
That his career was not seriously impaired is indicated by
the fact that a few months later he entered parliament
where he sat for thirty years and by the further facts that
he served as a commissioner of the Admiralty for nine
years and as governor of Greenwich Hospital for the last
eight years of his life.[63] Hamilton was apparently the only
governor besides Douglas whose punishment under the act
of 1700 was even seriously considered, at least before 1783.
This fact does not mean that some other governors did
not betray their trusts or act oppressively. But it does
seem to indicate that conditions never again became so
bad, at least to British eyes, that criminal prosecution became necessary. Whatever hostile colonials might think
of their governors, the British officials never considered
another governor deserving of such severe punishment.

With the exception of a few men in the seventeenth century, every governor held his commission during the
king's pleasure, which meant that he might remain in
office until the secretary of state and other officials at
Whitehall were ready to supplant him. A few governors
were recalled for disobedience or inefficiency; some asked
permission to resign because of ill health or a desire to
enter other employment. Several administrations came

[61] Instructions to Heywood, Jamaica, 1716, art. 4, C.O. 5: 190, pp. 344–
346 (L.C.).
[62] Board of Trade Journal, 1714/5–1718, (Oct. 2, 1717) pp. 269–275;
Board of Trade to Secretary Addison, Oct. 24, 1717, C.O. 138: 15, pp. 504–
508. For other documents on this case see C.O. 137: 11, nos. 16, 17, 25, 26;
C.O. 138: 14, pp. 418–429, 454–458.
[63] Charnock, Biographia Navalis, III, 15–17; Parliamentary Papers:
Lists of Members of Parliament.

to an end when the governors were transferred to other provinces. Of the one hundred and thirty governors whose American service had ended before the beginning of the Revolution, forty—that is, almost a third—died while actually in office. The rest of the governors, probably including more than half of them all, were superseded because of politics or patronage in England, or simply because they had outlived their usefulness in America. The longest consecutive term was that of Benning Wentworth, who governed New Hampshire for twenty-five and a half years; the shortest was that of Sir Danvers Osborn who committed suicide two days after being inaugurated in New York.[64] The average length of an administration was almost exactly five years, a figure which compares very closely with that of the average length of service of the presidents of the United States.[65]

The governor was not permitted to leave America without the previous consent of the crown. An order of 1680, amended in 1688, required that this permission be given by order in council or by warrant under the royal signet and sign manual. The verbal authority of the king was not to be deemed sufficient.[66] The governors of the southern colonies and of the West Indies were usually allowed by

[64] Other administrations of noteworthy duration include those of Sir William Berkeley, Virginia, 36 years, but interrupted for 8 years by the Puritan interregnum; William Mathew, jr., Leeward Islands, 3 years as lieutenant governor, followed immediately by 19 years as governor; John Tinker, Bahamas, 17 years; Gabriel Johnston, North Carolina, 18 years; William Shirley, Massachusetts, 14 years, followed later by 9 years in the Bahamas; Edward Trelawney, Jamaica, 14 years.

[65] In determining the average for governors, all men have been eliminated who were in office at the outbreak of the Revolution, since the conditions which brought about the end of their administrations were generally abnormal, in the West Indies as well as on the continent. The twenty-nine men who have served as president of the United States up to March 4, 1929, have held office on the average for four years and ten months each.

[66] *Cal. State Paps., Col.*, 1677–1680, § 1573; 1685–1688, § 1720.

their instructions to go to New York or some other cooler province in case of sickness, and some of the Nova Scotia governors were likewise permitted to go to Carolina. Some governors, such as Henry Grenville of Barbados, received permission to go to England just before a successor was appointed, since this seemed a more graceful way of laying down the administration than to wait in the province for the arrival of the new governor.[67] In periods of crisis the British officials were loath to let a governor return to England even temporarily. At the time of the Stamp Act disturbances the Board of Trade told Lieutenant Governor Fauquier of Virginia that the king could not possibly grant his request to spend twelve months in England for the recovery of his health and the settlement of his personal affairs.[68] And in 1773 Lord Dartmouth told the earl of Dunmore that in the future permission would not be granted a governor to go to England unless he was willing to resign immediately upon his arrival.[69] Although there were some important exceptions to the rule, the governors were expected to remain on the spot as long as they held office.[70]

Upon the death of a governor or his withdrawal from the province the administration devolved upon the lieutenant governor, if such an official existed in the colony. In some provinces, such as Nova Scotia, Massachusetts,

[67] Henry Grenville to George Grenville, May 6, 1752, Huntington Library, Stowe MSS.

[68] Board of Trade to Fauquier, Nov. 29, 1765, C.O. 5: 1368, pp. 291–292 (L.C.).

[69] Dartmouth to Dunmore, Feb. 3, 1773, C.O. 5: 1351, pp. 28–29 (L.C.). But on Nov. 8, 1775, Dartmouth wrote a circular letter to the governors of the revolting colonies permitting all royal officers to withdraw if their personal safety required it. C.O. 5: 242, pp. 95–96 (L.C.).

[70] The most important exceptions were in the case of Virginia whose governors from 1709 to 1768 held the office as a sinecure and never came to the province.

New Hampshire, and New York, lieutenant governors were quite regularly appointed, but in others the office was only rarely filled. In the Leeward Islands and later in the Ceded Islands there was regularly a lieutenant governor for each separate island and a lieutenant general who commanded the entire group in succession to the governor. During a large part of the eighteenth century the lieutenant governor of St. Christopher held the office of lieutenant general of the Leeward Islands, although by a separate commission. Until 1733 the lieutenant general was to be followed in the succession by the lieutenant governor of Nevis, but after that date each lieutenant governor was entitled to succeed in the order of priority of his commission.[71] In all cases of devolution the lieutenant governor exercised all the powers of a full governor, according to his predecessor's commission and instructions, except that he was entitled to only one-half the salary and perquisites of the office.

If, upon the death or absence of the governor, there was no lieutenant governor in the province, or if he too should die or go away, the administration then came into the hands of the council. Prior to 1707 the instructions directed that the entire council should act in such cases, although the senior resident councillor was to preside. The council was to perform only such acts as were immediately necessary. Uncertainty as to exactly what powers the president was to enjoy under this arrangement led to great confusion in Barbados and eventually to a change in the rule itself. When Sir Bevil Granville left the island in 1706 the council agreed to a series of fourteen articles, defining the powers of the senior councillor, William Sharpe. For the most part, the councillors allowed him far more latitude than was usual and certainly more than the words

[71] Commission to Mathew, Leeward Islands, 1733, C.O. 5: 195, pp. 265–284 (L.C.).

of the governor's commission and instructions implied.[72]
His opponents later declared that they had accepted this
agreement partly out of respect and a desire to keep the
peace and partly out of fear of losing their places.[73] They
soon began to regret their concession and to complain that
Sharpe had gone even further than they had at first
agreed. He was acting in every way as a full-fledged governor. Consequently, they refrained from coming to council meetings so that Sharpe was forced to act on the advice
of only two councillors. The controversy was brought to
the Board of Trade and privy council. After investigation
in England the home authorities supported Sharpe in all
his actions and discharged the complaints against him.[74]
In the meantime they prepared and sent a circular instruction to all governors, which provided that in the
future the administration was to devolve upon the senior
councillor resident in the province at the time of the vacancy, who was to have and exercise the usual powers of
the governor.[75] The council as a whole was no longer to
share in the administrative authority.

But time showed that this arrangement gave the acting
governor too much power instead of too little. In 1720 the
government of Barbados devolved on the eldest councillor,
Samuel Cox, after something of a contest. As soon as Cox
came into power he promptly suspended seven members

[72] Barbados council minutes, Sept. 4, 14, Oct. 1, 1706, C.O. 28 : 9, no. 93 ii.

[73] Representation of William Cleland, James Colleton, and John Holder,
Barbados councillors, to President Sharpe, Dec. 3, 1706, C.O. 28 : 9, no. 94 iv;
same to the queen, Jan. 2, 1707, C.O. 28 : 9, no. 101 i; C.O. 29 : 10, pp. 446–
453; *Cal. State Paps., Col.*, 1706–1708, §§ 697 iv, 831 i.

[74] Board of Trade to the queen, May 28, 1707, C.O. 28 : 11, pp. 2–24;
Cal. State Paps., Col., 1706–1708, § 948 i; *Acts, Privy Coun., Col.*, 1680–1720,
§ 1022.

[75] Circular instructions, May 3, 1707, *N. J. Arch.*, III, 169–170. In Massachusetts, the succession in the whole council remained unchanged in accordance with the charter of 1691.

of the council, putting his adherents in their places. He
also removed several justices of the peace and militia
officers. In spite of being ordered to readmit the suspended
officials, Cox continued to make his administration "one
long series of tyranny and oppression," according to his
enemies.[76] Lord Belhaven was appointed governor in 1721,
but was shipwrecked on the way out. The next governor,
Henry Worsley, did not arrive to restore peace until 1723.
After a trial lasting a month, Worsley removed Cox from
the council and declared him incapable of holding similar
office for the future.[77] To prevent such a situation from
ever arising again, the Board of Trade changed the instructions to Belhaven and Worsley and to all subsequent
royal governors in America. Thereafter the senior councillor, upon whom the administration should fall, was
forbidden to dissolve the assembly or to perform any
other act not immediately necessary. He was not to remove any councillor, judicial officer, or other official without the consent of at least seven members of the council,
and even with such consent he was at once to report his
reasons for the removal to the Board of Trade.[78] These
precautions were wise. The president of the council was
almost always a member of a faction. Jealousies and disputes were almost bound to arise, and unless the power of
an acting governor was distinctly limited, such a man,
who expected to be superseded before long in any case,
could not be trusted to deny himself the pleasure of re-
venge upon his enemies. As one Barbados councillor wrote,

[76] C.O. 28: 15, nos. 90, 99; C.O. 28: 17, fos. 29, 31–32, 52, 53, 59, 63–67,
71–73, 86, 88, 91, 124, 128, 130, 170, 187, 206, 207; C.O. 29: 14, pp. 101–105.

[77] Worsley to the Board of Trade, July 16, 1723, C.O. 28: 17, fos. 314–316.
The minutes of the hearing are in *ibid.*, fos. 339–533.

[78] Board of Trade to Secretary Carteret, reporting on Belhaven's instructions, Aug. 9, 1721, C.O. 29: 14, p. 145; instructions to Belhaven, Barbados,
1721, art. 30, C.O. 5: 191, pp. 14–74 (L.C.).

"president government" was as susceptible to misuse from the love of power as any other, "and to gain these sweet morsels, factions are always increased."[79] Temporary administrations are weak at best and those which took place in the provinces show clearly the need of the steady and impartial hand of a royal governor.

The governor's position itself was hard enough. He was equipped with broad powers derived from the royal prerogative in England. But the home government limited in many ways his free exercise of these powers, especially through the independent appointment of inferior officers in his province. He was not in fact the sole responsible head of administration which the words of his commission seemed to imply. The presence of such officers might serve as a check upon arbitrary rule by the governor, but from his point of view it was far more likely to be a source of friction and inefficiency. Another difficulty in the governor's position was the fact that he really had to serve two masters and, to be successful, had to reconcile their often conflicting interests. He was responsible to the crown and to the officials at home for the proper exercise of the royal prerogatives, but his daily contacts were with the people of the province. Their cooperation and good will were necessary to his success in office. Loss of confidence with either group brought endless trouble and often final disaster to his administration. Sir Thomas Robinson gave expression to what must have been the experience of many governors, when he was recalled after five years in Barbados. While his successor's vessel lay in the roadstead he wrote: "If a governor lies under the fatal necessity of disobliging a majority of representatives by doing his duty on one hand, or on the other of gaining their favor

[79] William Cleland to the Board of Trade, Feb. 10, 1707, C.O. 28: 10, no. 5; C.O. 29: 10, p. 481.

by a breach of duty, his doom is fixed, since he must either fall a victim to the unjust rage of those men for what is right or to his Majesty's just displeasure for doing what is wrong."[80] Only a man of exceptional tact and winning personality could avoid entirely the pitfalls which beset his path.

Not every governor realized at first the difficulties before him. As he read his commission and instructions his powers might seem ample to his task. As he listened to the addresses of welcome which followed his inauguration the hearty support of the people might seem assured. But if he desired a long and peaceful administration he would do well to heed the advice of Francis Nicholson, writing after eleven years' experience as governor of several provinces:

Whoever shall be governor in these parts must not pretend it in all respects, by having read or studied learned, judicious, or cunning books for policy in government, to understand the government in all points; but he must have some sense of the practical, too, to qualify him to be a good governor. But with humble submission, I think it absolutely necessary for his Majesty's interest and service that the governor or commander in chief may be esteemed by the people, or at least the major part of them, to be a lover of them and their country; and not that he be sent or comes to make or retrieve a fortune; which character, no doubt, he may get amongst them, if he behaves himself generously and not be covetous; but above all distributes equal justice, endeavoring what in him lies to obey his Majesty's royal commission, his instructions, and your Lordships' to him. . . . Such a governor or lieutenant governor in chief, I think, is every way bound in duty, interest, and gratitude to make it his whole business so that all his actions may tend to God's glory, to his Majesty's interest

[80] Robinson to the Board of Trade, April 13, 1747, C.O. 28: 27 (unpaged). Writing in somewhat the same vein, Governor Christopher Codrington, jr., declared in 1701 that he acted during his administration as if he "were walking between red hot irons." *Cal. State Paps., Col.*, 1701, § 112.

and service; and after those two most great and important affairs, to do the country which he governs all the good he can. And if he either willfully or wittingly fails in any of them, let him have St. Paul's curse of *Anathema maranatha.*[81]

[81] Nicholson to the Board of Trade, July 1, 1699, C.O. 5: 1310, no. 2 (L.C.); *Cal. State Paps., Col.,* 1699, p. 311 (much abridged).

CHAPTER IV

HIS MAJESTY'S COUNCIL

CLOSER to the governor than any other agency in the management of local affairs stood the provincial council. It shared in almost every branch of governmental activity into which the governor's duties carried him. For some purposes the council served as a check upon the chief executive, for others it was intended to be a support and bulwark to his authority. From the British point of view it was, next to the governor, the most important unit in the political framework of the province.

The council was a unique institution in its powers and in its composition. It served in a threefold capacity with executive, legislative, and judicial duties. It was the governor's advisory board, the upper house of the assembly, and the highest court of appeals in the province. Many of the powers granted to the governor by his commission and instructions could be executed only with the advice and consent of the council. In normal cases these included among other things the summoning of assemblies, the appointment of inferior officers, the issuing of money from the provincial treasury, the creation of courts of justice, and the establishment of martial law in time of war. In many other matters the governor was expected to take the advice of the council, although he was not bound thereby. In its executive capacity the provincial council resembled the privy council of the mother country, although its powers were perhaps more clearly defined and limited. As a branch of the legislature, the council had functions similar to those of the House of Lords. Although membership was not hereditary, neither was it elective or representative as was the case with both the House of Commons and the lower house of the provincial assembly. The council was entitled to an equal voice in all legislation. It never seriously pressed the right to initiate money bills, although it tried, with little success, to amend them. In this connection the analogy of the council to the House of Lords was closer than its members or the British government would have liked. As the highest court within the province the council also resembled to a certain extent the House of Lords sitting as the high court of parliament. But being a smaller, newer body, its judicial organization was more compact and artificial. This threefold capacity in which the council served naturally led the British officials to look upon it as a body only less important to the welfare of the province than the governor himself.

Because of this importance of the council, the selection of its members was a matter for extreme care, especially since a councillor, once appointed, normally served for life. But it was never a representative body, in the sense that its members were even indirectly chosen by a local electorate; nor was it British, in the sense that its members were sent over from England for the purpose of serving upon it. The council consisted regularly of a group of colonials, usually twelve in number, appointed by the king. The duty and privilege of naming councillors devolved upon the Board of Trade. This body could not be expected to have personal knowledge of the men available in America. The board had to rely upon the recommendations of those more closely in touch with the personalities in the province. The most important source of information was the list supplied by the governor. During the first half of the eighteenth century the instructions required every governor to keep the Board of Trade constantly supplied with a list of twelve men suitable for appointment to the council.[1] A further article directed him in his choice of councillors, judges, and all other important officers, to name only men "of good life, well-affected to our government, of good estates and abilities, and not necessitous people or much in debt." Some variations in these words occurred from time to time. The most important of these was the substitution of the expression "and of abilities suitable to their employments" for the phrase "or much in debt," which change was made about the middle of the century. When economic conditions kept almost every important planter chronically in debt to his English correspondents, it was certainly far more desirable that the local offices be filled by capable men rather than by the very few who happened to have balances on the credit side of their ledgers.

The plan of having the governors keep the names of twelve potential councillors before the Board of Trade caused much difficulty and was eventually modified. Many governors found it impossible to name so many men of the proper caliber at the same time in addition to the actual members of the council. Governor Edward Trelawney of Jamaica wrote of a further difficulty in 1751. He pointed out that a governor's nomination was looked upon as a recommendation, the later withdrawal of which would be considered an affront, even though the governor might change his mind about the candidate's qualifications. Furthermore, he said, the keeping of a long list so far in advance of vacancies would prevent the appointment to the council of recent arrivals in the island, although their

[1] In New York and New Hampshire prior to 1727 only six names were required. In the Leeward Islands the governor was to keep the board supplied with the names of six men from each of the four islands within the group, since each island had its own council.

admission to the council would secure them to the governor's interest before they sought to join the opposition in the assembly.[2] These arguments led the Board of Trade to alter the instruction to all governors. Thereafter the chief executive was told to nominate three men at the time of reporting each vacancy.

But the governor was by no means the only one whose recommendations were received or acted upon. British merchants, army officers, the bishop of London, and other interested persons proposed the names of those they desired to see appointed to the council.[3] They also used their influence to prevent the naming of objectionable individuals. When the patrons of the Jamaica Coffee House in London heard of the proposed appointment of a certain man of unsavory reputation, a "clamor" arose and they took effective steps to prevent the appointment.[4] The suggestions and comments on candidates that came from other colonists were particularly valuable and important. They were received by letter or by direct questioning at the Board of Trade, when such colonists happened to be in England.[5] Some men were not above proposing them-

[2] Edward Trelawney to the Board of Trade, Sept. 1, 1751, C.O. 137: 25.

[3] Examples of such recommendations follow: Micajah Perry, tobacco merchant of London, to Newcastle, recommending John Taloe for the Virginia council, May 12, 1731, C.O. 5: 1344 (L.C.); Duke of Bolton to the Board of Trade, April 27, 1708, recommending Mr. Betts for the Jamaica council, C.O. 138: 12, p. 259; *Board of Trade Journal*, 1704–1708/9, p. 485; Bishop of London to Wm. Popple, June 21, 1711, recommending Col. William Hill for the Virginia council, C.O. 5: 1316, p. 86; *Cal. State Paps., Col.*, 1710–1711, § 894.

[4] Benjamin Harris to Wm. Popple, Sept. 27, 1717, C.O. 137: 12, no. 73; *Board of Trade Journal*, 1714/5–1718, pp. 277–278.

[5] Under date of Jan. 5, 1715, the *Board of Trade Journal*, 1708/9–1714/5, pp. 585–586, gives a splendid illustration of such oral examination of persons well acquainted with the affairs of a province. Six individuals connected with Barbados—the agent, the former attorney general of the island, a member of the council, and three merchants, at least one of whom had lived in Barbados —were called before the board and asked their opinions of three candidates for the council. The witness who was also a councillor recommended four

selves as fit members of the provincial council.[6] Through the names supplied in these various ways the Board of Trade kept lists which usually give fairly complete histories of the nominations and their ultimate disposal. Different columns indicate the names of those proposed and their sponsors, whether the governor or another individual. Another column lists the members of the council in office at the time. When the governor reported the death of a councillor or a vacancy for any other reason, the name of the individual concerned was struck through on the council list with a notation of "dead," "left the island," "suspended," or some other explanatory words. When the board had decided on the substitute to be appointed they caused his name to be crossed off the list of persons recommended and entered at the foot of the column of councillors, often with the date upon which his name was proposed to the king. Notification of the death of those on the "recommended" list also resulted in the cancellation of their names. Information of various sorts concerning the members of the council was often noted opposite their names, such phrases as "in England," "absent," "very old," "infirm," "seldom able to attend," appearing frequently. By means of such lists the Board of Trade was able to keep up-to-date information constantly at hand and to supply immediately either a single name to fill a vacancy or an entire list for the instructions to a new governor.[7]

other persons as fit for the office. Those most familiar with island affairs were also asked their opinions of another member of the council.

[6] Francis Oldfield's petition [Sept. ?] 1708, C.O. 138: 12, p. 331; *Cal. State Paps., Col.*, 1708–1709, § 138 i; Thomas Bernard to the Board of Trade, Sept. 25, 1713, C.O. 138: 14, p. 40; *Cal. State Paps., Col.*, 1712–1714, § 477. Both these men were admitted to the Jamaica council.

[7] This description is taken from a number of such lists covering the different colonies and various periods in the eighteenth century, collected together in C.O. 324: 48. To aid in keeping these lists up to date the board directed the governors in 1738 to report semi-annually on the death or absence

The fact that their instructions directed them to recommend suitable men for the council led many governors to believe, or at least to expect, that only their nominations would be considered. But the Board of Trade quickly disabused them of this notion. Not only did the board consider themselves free to adopt the proposals of others than the governors, but they felt it their duty to get all possible information to guide them in making their selections.[8] Lieutenant Governor Fauquier expressed the attitude of the governors quite freely and fairly in a long letter to the board protesting against the appointment of Robert Burwell to the Virginia council without his recommendation. Fauquier admitted that Burwell was a man of good family, resided near enough to attend council meetings, and was "of a very fair character," but in the judgment of the governor and other members of the council, he lacked essential qualifications of mind and was afflicted with an "unwarrantable impetuosity of temper." Fauquier declared that he had no personal axe to grind in his recommendations, having come to Virginia "an utter stranger to the whole country." His nominations were based solely on his conception of the service of king and country. But he felt that the royal interest would suffer greatly if the colonists learned that the governor's recommendations were ignored. Such knowledge would weaken the influence of the governor, who was, besides, presumably much more to be depended upon in his recommendations than a private person, serving his own interests. The governors "are in his Majesty's power, but if a private man can obtain his wishes to serve his friend, will he not afterwards laugh in his sleeve and despise con-

of councillors. Board of Trade to Lt. Gov. Gooch, Va., Aug. 9, 1738, C.O. 5: 1366, p. 292 (L.C.); Board of Trade to Gov. Belcher, N. H., Aug. 10, 1738, C.O. 5: 917, p. 255 (Mass.).

8 Board of Trade to Gov. Belcher, N. H., Oct. 10, 1732, C.O. 5: 917, pp. 72–74 (Mass.).

sequences?'"[9] To this argument the board replied denying
that the governor had any "implicit right" of filling
vacancies, although "in general great respect is due and
indeed paid to the recommendations of his Majesty's
governors, but it would be carrying that respect too far
if the recommendations were construed to preclude a
nomination to his Majesty of any other person even in
preference to the governor's recommendation.'"[10]

There was, of course, much truth in Fauquier's contention that the regular adoption of his recommendations
would increase his influence and strengthen his support
among those who sought appointment. His authority
would conversely be weakened by knowledge that influential friends in England were more helpful than cooperation with the governor in the province. On the other hand,
the Board of Trade realized that some governors played
favorites and that their letters did not always give un-
biassed accounts of colonial disputes and personalities.
Consequently the board attempted to steer a middle
course, acting in each case upon the situation as it arose.[11]
The question in general was but part of the larger problem of the colonial patronage which proved so troublesome, and in which the governor usually felt that he was
not receiving the consideration due to his position.

The governor was usually more concerned over a prospective councillor's place of residence than was the
Board of Trade. The matter was more important in a
large colony such as Virginia, or one as far north as New

[9] Fauquier to the Board of Trade, July 31, 1762, C.O. 5: 1330, pp. 331–
334 (L.C.).

[10] Board of Trade to Fauquier, Mar. 11, 1763, C.O. 5: 1368, pp. 222–223
(L.C.).

[11] When the earl of Hillsborough became secretary of state for the colonies, he tried to solve the problem by reporting to the governor the names of
candidates proposed and requiring the governor's approval before making an
appointment. Hillsborough to Gov. Botetourt, Va., April 14, 1770, C.O. 5:
1348, pp. 174–175 (L.C.).

Hampshire, where travelling conditions, especially in winter and spring, were not of the best. When the councillors were scattered, the governor was often put to it to get a quorum together, even though a meeting was expected and announced weeks in advance. The topography of Virginia was such that its many broad rivers served to hinder rather than to help rapid transportation from one part of the colony to another. But the men of influence and ability who would be the natural candidates for the council lived in various parts of the province. In 1744 Lieutenant Governor Gooch prepared a list of the ten men then composing the Virginia council showing how far each one lived from Williamsburg. Only one man lived in the capital. One was from the Northern Neck, one hundred fifty miles away. The average distance was over forty miles, which meant at least two days' travel during much of the year.[12] In spite of repeated protests from the governors and a promise from the Board of Trade to consider the question of residence in their future appointments,[13] the situation, if anything, became worse in Virginia. Lieutenant Governor Fauquier reported in 1767 that five of the eleven councillors were from the Northern Neck.[14] In other provinces the condition was similar though usually less acute. The Board of Trade found great difficulty in preserving a balance in the council between up-country planters and seaboard merchants, without seriously weakening the efficiency of the body as a whole.

Whenever a commission and instructions for a new governor became necessary, the Board of Trade went carefully over the list of councillors. They noted vacancies

[12] Enclosure in letter of Gooch to the Board of Trade, Dec. 21, 1744, C.O. 5: 1326, p. 201 (L.C.).

[13] Board of Trade to Fauquier, Feb. 17, 1761, C.O. 5: 1368, p. 16 (L.C.). The difficulty was very serious in Virginia at this time.

[14] Fauquier to Lord Shelburne, July 30, 1767, C.O. 5: 1345, pp. 381–382 (L.C.).

through death or other reasons and considered the names of any men suspended by the former governor. The places of suspended councillors might be restored to them, left open for investigation and report by the new governor, or filled by other nominations, as circumstances seemed to warrant. The board filled all vacancies, bringing the total membership up to twelve men whose names they incorporated in their draft of general instructions.[15] Only very rarely did the privy council make changes in the Board of Trade's list, and then usually in connection with suspended councillors, when the board's decision seemed unwise.[16] When a vacancy occurred during the middle of a governor's administration the Board of Trade prepared a special representation informing the king of the circumstances and proposing a candidate for the place. This representation was then laid before the privy council and was approved by order in council. This order directed the secretary of state to prepare a warrant to the governor to admit the individual to the council. The warrant was in form a royal letter signed at the top with the sign manual and at the bottom with either the king's initials or the countersignature of the secretary of state. The paper was then folded so as to conceal the contents and the royal signet affixed in such a way as to seal the folds together.[17]

[15] Prior to 1677 the councillors were sometimes named in the commission, but at the request of the earl of Carlisle, appointed governor of Jamaica in 1677, the names were transferred to the instructions, making suspension and removal easier since a fresh document under the great seal would not be necessary. *Cal. State Paps., Col.,* 1677–1680, §§ 474, 480; *Acts, Privy Coun., Col.,* 1613–1680, p. 746.

[16] For this reason the privy council altered the lists of councillors in the instructions to Lord Belhaven as governor of Barbados in 1721 and to Edward Trelawney as governor of Jamaica in 1737, C.O. 28: 17, fos. 258–259; C.O. 29: 14, pp. 140–147; C.O. 138: 18, pp. 136–137; *Acts, Privy Coun., Col.,* 1720–1745, p. 823, § 411.

[17] For a description of this document and the formula used see Stokes, *View of the Constitution,* pp. 237–238.

This document, usually spoken of as a "mandamus," constituted the only legal authority for the admission of a new councillor except the instructions themselves.[18] Although the nomination of the Board of Trade was approved by an order in council, a copy of this order was not in itself sufficient authority for the governor to act. In order to secure the speedy preparation and dispatch of his warrant a prospective councillor had to employ an agent in England to solicit the issuing of the document, pay the required fees, and see that it was sent to the governor.

This rule once caused a tempestuous scene in the New Hampshire council. Joseph Dudley was governor of that province as well as of Massachusetts at the time. He seldom went to the northern colony, although he tried to prevent the lieutenant governor, John Usher, from taking too active a share in its control. At various times beginning in December, 1705, the privy council had approved the nominations of five men to the New Hampshire council, but in May, 1710, the Board of Trade wrote Dudley that the proper warrants had not been issued because no agents had appeared to pay the necessary fees, and solicit their dispatch.[19] In the same month Dudley received copies of the orders in council approving the nomination of two of these men, Mark Hunking and Richard Waldron. Since three of the seven men then forming the council were incapacitated by age or gout and since a meeting of the council and assembly was necessary in view of the proposed expedition against Port Royal, Dudley decided to make

[18] Lieut. Gov. Colden of New York expressed the general view in a letter to Halifax, May 8, 1764: "It has been an established rule to admit no person to a seat in his Majesty's council, otherwise than by the king's pleasure signified under his sign manual and signet and no instance I believe can be given to the contrary." N. Y. Col. Docs., VII, 623.

[19] Board of Trade to Dudley, May 2, 1710, C.O. 5: 913, pp. 236–242 (Mass.); Cal. State Paps., Col., 1710–1711, § 215.

use of these orders. Accordingly he swore the two men
into the council on one of his visits to New Hampshire.[20]
Some time after Dudley had returned to Massachusetts,
Lieutenant Governor Usher appeared at the council
board and found Waldron, his bitter enemy, seated there.
A violent quarrel soon broke out between them. Usher
demanded to be shown the authority for Waldron's presence and the order in council was produced. But Usher
was quick to perceive that the document merely ordered
the secretary of state to prepare the proper warrant and
did not in itself authorize the admission of Waldron. He
scornfully asked whether a warrant under her Majesty's
signet had been received. He was answered in the negative.
Waldron's temper had been steadily rising and he now
announced that he had known of the order for many years
but that "he would not take it out for he was not covetous
of it." Usher, matching wrath with wrath, promptly
suspended Waldron, since the latter apparently judged
"her Majesty's honor not worth the charge." The suspended councillor arose, clapped on his hat, and with
mocking courtesy took his leave of the lieutenant governor. But Usher fired the parting shot by retorting as
Waldron left the room, "It is very saucily with your hat
on!"[21] When Dudley heard of the lieutenant governor's
action he was incensed, but Waldron, who had learned his
lesson, refused to return to the council until a proper
warrant arrived about a year later. Dudley and the councillors continued to reproach Usher, and the latter filled
letter after letter with illiterate but spicy comment on his
fellows until the administrations of both men had come

[20] Gov. Dudley to Henry Newman, May 28, 1711, *Cal. State Paps., Col.*,
1710–1711, § 860.

[21] New Hampshire council minutes, Nov. 21, 1710, *N. H. Prov. Paps.*, II,
621–622. See also *Cal. State Paps., Col.*, 1710–1711, §§ 283, 348, 509, 510,
510 i, iii.

to an end. But Usher was technically in the right for an
order in council was not adequate authority for the induction of a councillor.

The councillors were very jealous of rank and precedence among themselves. Under ordinary circumstances
there was no question as to seniority at the council board,
since each member took his place according to the date of
his first membership. But sometimes doubts arose as to
just what date should be reckoned as the beginning of a
councillor's tenure. As far as evidence is available the
council itself seems invariably to have held that the date
of taking the oaths of office at the council board should
determine the matter.[22] The Board of Trade and the privy
council insisted upon the date of the royal mandamus.[23]
The question might be raised in either one of two ways:
a royal appointee might delay presenting himself to be
sworn until some man with a warrant of later date had
been admitted; or he might find that, since the date of his
warrant, the governor had admitted a man of his own
appointment to bring the council up to the required number of seven. In either case the question was perplexing

[22] Lieutenant Governor Dinwiddie of Virginia informed the Board of
Trade in 1756 that ''it has always been a constant custom that the councillors in this dominion always took their seats at the board from the time
they were sworn in and admitted a member of the council without any regard
to the date of their mandamus.'' This practice, he said, could be proved by
many precedents. Dinwiddie to the Board of Trade, Feb. 24, 1756, *Dinwiddie
Papers*, II, 353–354 (in *Collections* of the Virginia Historical Society, new
series, IV).

[23] A year before Dinwiddie's letter, quoted in the previous note, the Board
of Trade had written the king that it appeared to them ''to have been the
general custom for the members of your Majesty's councils in the several
colonies and plantations in America to take place according to the date of the
royal mandamus whereby they are appointed.'' Board of Trade to the king,
Feb. 5, 1755, C.O. 5: 1367, p. 139 (L.C.). An order in council was issued
supporting the board's position and applying this rule to a specific Virginia
case. It was this order which called forth Dinwiddie's statement. *Acts, Privy
Coun., Col.*, 1745–1766, § 262.

and was never settled by an authoritative and final ruling. As late as 1766 it aroused bitter controversy in Barbados. One royally appointed councillor absolutely refused to sit when he discovered that he was to rank below the acting governor's son-in-law, who had been admitted after the date of his mandamus in order to bring the number of resident councillors up to seven.[24] A somewhat different question of seniority arose when a councillor who had once surrendered his membership was readmitted by a new mandamus. He would naturally desire to rank from the date of his first appointment, but the Board of Trade generally felt that his second warrant should determine his seniority. They did, however, make occasional exceptions.[25] Aside from the mere matter of personal pride among the disputing councillors, the question of seniority had a real importance. On the death or absence of the governor and lieutenant governor, the administration devolved upon the senior councillor as president. To a newly appointed councillor his own succession to the government might seem a remote contingency, but occasionally experience showed that the coveted position might not be so far off as one might suppose. Within a year and a half after Governor Hunter's death in Jamaica in 1734, John Gregory, the fifth councillor named in Hunter's instructions of 1727, had succeeded to the presidency of the

[24] The case was peculiarly complicated from the fact that, if the president's son-in-law were not to be deemed a councillor in full standing, as the royal appointee insisted, there would not have been a quorum of the council to do business and the latter could not have been sworn. Pres. Samuel Rous to the Board of Trade, Sept. 6, 1766, enclosing minute of Barbados council, Sept. 2, 1766, C.O. 28: 32; Gedney Clarke to the Board of Trade, Sept. 5, 1766, C.O. 28: 32. No reply from the board has been found.

[25] In 1731 John Ayscough, who had once been acting governor of Jamaica but had since left the island, was restored to first place in the council after a long discussion between the Board of Trade and the privy council committee. C.O. 137: 19, *passim* (unpaged); C.O. 138: 17, pp. 271–272, 308–310, 312–313; *Acts, Privy Coun., Col.*, 1720–1745, § 230.

island. Death or infirmity had ended the careers of the four senior councillors.[26] With such possibilities, the contests over precedence are not surprising.

Perhaps the greatest difficulty which the governor faced in connection with the council was that of keeping together a quorum. The commissions for the island provinces specified that five councillors were to constitute a quorum. On the continent the figure was usually fixed at three, but the governor's instructions directed him not to act with less than five except in emergencies. As already indicated, distant residence was one obstacle to regular attendance in some provinces. Generally, illness was a far greater factor in reducing the number present at council meetings. "As to the councillors here," a distracted Jamaica governor once wrote, "I think that they are no sooner put into the council, but they are troubled with one distemper or another, which they pretend makes them incapable of doing their duty, so that I am the hardest put to it to get a council when there is a necessity for it."[27] Gout, that all too prevalent malady of the eighteenth century, was responsible for the adjournment of many council meetings without quorums. The two factors of distant residence and illness, together with indifference to duty on the part of the councillors, were the burden of many a governor's complaints. In 1707 a crisis in Barbados led the Board of Trade to take action. During the presidency of William Sharpe three members of the council quarreled with him to the extent of withdrawing and refusing to attend subsequent meetings. Their action, together with the absence of other councillors from the island, made it impossible for the acting governor to get a quorum together. All governmental business thus came to a standstill. Among their

26 John Gregory to the Board of Trade, Oct. 25, 1735, C.O. 137: 22.
27 Thomas Handasyd to the Board of Trade, June 4, 1710, *Cal. State Paps., Col.*, 1710–1711, § 253.

other proposals to the privy council in connection with
this controversy the Board of Trade suggested that the
governors be given power to compel the councillors to
attend.[28] The privy council approved and a circular royal
letter was sent to all governors empowering them to suspend councillors who should absent themselves from meetings without due cause and should persist in such absence
after proper warning.[29] This letter was repeated as an
article in all subsequent general instructions, but its beneficial effects seem to have been slight. Governors sometimes threatened, but seldom cared to use the power thus
entrusted to them, probably because of the bad feeling
such action would engender.[30]

The greatest reason for the councillors' failure to attend meetings lay, however, in their absence from the
province. This fact was especially true in connection with
the West Indies. The great sugar planters—the very type
most commonly appointed councillors—developed the

[28] Board of Trade representation, May 28, 1707, C.O. 29: 11, p. 24; *Cal.
State Paps., Col.,* 1706–1708, § 948 i.

[29] Order in council, Aug. 4, 1707, C.O. 28: 10, no. 36; circular letter to the
royal governors, Oct. 23, 1707, C.O. 324: 9, p. 148 (L.C.), *Cal. State Paps.,
Col.,* 1706–1708, §§ 1085, 1153.

[30] On Dec. 30, 1724, the Duke of Portland, governor of Jamaica, wrote
to the Board of Trade a long account of his troubles with the council. During
the preceding year members had failed to attend eight out of ten regular
monthly meetings and by their absence from legislative sessions had forced
adjournments of the assembly in times of crisis. Yet he would be sorry, he
said, to turn them out according to his instruction. Of the twelve members,
four were off the island, one had recently resigned, one lived one hundred
twenty miles away across the mountains by roads which were entirely cut
off in the rainy season, and one lived seventy miles away with similar road
conditions. Only five lived near by and two of these were "very sickly and
often afflicted with the gout." C.O. 137: 16, fos. 39–42. A year later Portland
complained of the appointment of another man whose distant residence would
make his attendance infrequent, "which is a difficulty I already too much
labor under. I wish they had as great a desire to attend as they are solicitous
to have a place at the board as a pretence only to be idle." Portland to the
Board of Trade, Dec. 18, 1725, C.O. 137: 16, fo. 148.

custom of residing for years at a time in England, where
they lived in luxury from the profits of their plantations.
Such absentees cared nothing for their obligations to the
island government as members of the council, though they
fought vigorously when it was necessary in order to retain the prestige of membership. As early as 1680, when
preparing instructions for Sir Richard Dutton as governor
of Barbados, the Lords of Trade attempted to meet the
situation by a clause directing Dutton to inform his councillors that absence from the island for two years without
the written permission of the king would cause the forfeiture of their seats.[31] In time this instruction was extended to include all royal provinces and underwent some
modification. From about 1720 on, the rule was that a
councillor would lose his seat if he absented himself from
the province for twelve months without the governor's
written permission secured in advance, or for two years
without a leave of absence under the royal sign manual.[32]
But this instruction was seldom rigidly enforced. In spite
of repeated complaints from the Board of Trade, the
secretaries of state often failed to inform that body of the
granting or renewing of leaves of absence, so that the
board did not always know what places to treat as open
to reappointment.[33] But even when they did know, they
were often lenient, and the secretaries of state on their

[31] Instructions to Dutton, Barbados, 1680, art. 11, C.O. 29: 3, pp. 37–53.
The instruction was probably introduced because of a complaint of absenteeism sent by Governor Atkins of Barbados in 1678, *Cal. State Paps., Col.*,
1677–1680, § 825.

[32] The instruction was first given in this form to Governor Lawes of
Jamaica in 1718, art. 11, C.O. 5: 189, pp. 334–375. After 1752 it was always
joined into one paragraph with the clause empowering the governors to suspend councillors who wilfully absented themselves from council meetings.

[33] In 1707, in 1715, and again in 1747, they begged the secretary of state
for information on leaves of absence granted to councillors. C.O. 138: 12, pp.
184–186; *Cal. State Paps., Col.*, 1706-1708, § 1220; C.O. 324: 10, p. 65; C.O.
5: 402, pp. 120–121.

part apparently had no hesitation about renewing leaves of absence almost indefinitely. Perhaps the most extraordinary case was that of George Clarke, jr., secretary of New York and member of the council there. Although he remained in England from about 1740 on without returning to the province, and although two governors asked that he be superseded in the council, he was allowed to hold his seat until 1770, a period of thirty years.[34] But sometimes the Board of Trade did insist that absent councillors return or lose their places. In 1747 they ordered circular letters sent to twelve absentees warning them that their places would be filled if they could not produce proper leaves of absence.[35] Five of these men were removed within a year and two others died soon afterward.[36] But a year after this general round-up, the governor of the Leeward Islands reported that out of a total of fifty-one men who had been appointed to the four councils under his supervision only twenty-seven were present.[37] In 1754 the secretary of the Board of Trade warned Abel Dottin, a Barbados councillor who had been in England for twelve years, to return to the island at once on pain of forfeiting his place.[38] Dottin replied that his affairs would not permit of his immediate return and coolly added that he hoped his continued absence would be "attended with no inconvenience to the island."[39] But absenteeism

[34] N. Y. Col. Docs., VI, 163; VII, 675, 843, 916; Acts, Privy Coun., Col., 1766–1783, p. 570.

[35] Circular letter from Thomas Hill, secretary to the Board of Trade to twelve councillors, Aug. 17, 1747, C.O. 324: 12, 302–303 (L.C.). A similar letter was sent by John Pownall in 1767 to seven councillors, C.O. 324: 18, pp. 67–68 (L.C.).

[36] Acts, Privy Coun., Col., 1745–1766, pp. 781–799.

[37] William Mathew to the Board of Trade, Sept. 30, 1748 (inclosure), C.O. 152: 26.

[38] John Pownall to Abel Dottin, May 23, 1754, C.O. 29: 17, p. 116.

[39] Dottin to Pownall, June 4, 1754, C.O. 28: 30.

was at this time particularly serious in Barbados, as Dottin must have known, so the board recommended and secured his removal.[40] Yet in spite of such sporadic efforts on the part of the Board of Trade to keep the councils filled with residents, the governors of almost every province continued to report slender attendance, adjournment without quorums, and inability of the supreme courts to function through lack of judges. As late as 1768 conditions in Barbados were so bad that the assembly petitioned the king on the subject. A quorum of the council was almost out of the question, they said, "even when the most urgent affairs have cried aloud for dispatch," since all but five councillors, in addition to the senior councillor who was acting governor, were in England, and one of these five was "valetudinary."[41] When the popular assembly considered the councillors' absence a grievance requiring the king's attention, the condition had become serious indeed.

The governor had one other means of keeping up the numbers of resident councillors. In case there should at any time be less than seven members of the council actually within the province, his commission allowed him to admit other men to bring the total number on hand up to seven.[42] He was to report such appointments back to England for royal confirmation or disapproval, pending which the individuals were to be deemed councillors to all intents and purposes. This provision was sometimes very effective

[40] Board of Trade to the king, Oct. 31, 1754, C.O. 29: 17, pp. 121–122; Acts, Privy Coun., Col., 1745–1766, p. 784.

[41] Barbados assembly to the king, n.d., enclosed in Hillsborough to the Board of Trade, Jan. 27, 1768, C.O. 28: 33. Of the six absentees, the Board of Trade reported that one had already gone back, another had declared his intention of returning at once, one had a royal leave of absence good for seven months more, and one was "in the service of his country" in parliament. The remaining two were removed. Board of Trade to the king, Jan. 29, 1768, C.O. 29: 18, pp. 401–403; Acts, Privy Coun., Col., 1766–1783, p. 562.

[42] In Nova Scotia and Virginia the figures were fixed at nine instead of seven.

in maintaining the necessary quorum. But it was by no means a panacea. Appointment by the governor was not always welcome to the ambitious colonial. The home government might, and frequently did, confirm him in his office as a regular member, but often enough it did not. To be appointed by the governor and later removed by the king would hardly enhance a man's prestige or self-esteem. Then, too, such appointments were in a sense only temporary. If the allotted number of royally named councillors should return to the province, the governor's man would have to drop out, in spite of whatever useful service he might have performed. Such a prospect was almost equally distressing. But far more important than the man's possible unwillingness to serve, was a practical difficulty which often prevented the governor from using this power when it was most needed. He was not allowed to appoint councillors unless the number of members actually within the province dropped below seven. When illness, remote residence, and indifference, rather than the absence of councillors from the province, prevented a quorum, the governor could not act. If, when there were seven residents, any three failed to appear at a meeting, his hands were tied. In such cases—and they were common enough to cause frequent complaint—the governor's appointive power was utterly valueless.

There can be no doubt but that poor attendance at council meetings seriously lessened the efficiency of the administration. More than that, it helped to lower the prestige of the royal element in government and to magnify the popular share, especially in connection with legislation. An upper house of the assembly which frequently consisted of only five or six appointed men, of whom any three or four could determine the fate of all bills, was not such a body as to inspire great respect or confidence among the colonists. Almost inevitably the voters tended to put their faith in the elective branch of the legislature and to support it in its controversies with the aristocratic council and the royal governor.

The council served as a check upon the governor but it was by no means independent of his control. As early as 1673 Sir Jonathan Atkins, governor of Barbados, received power by his commission to suspend councillors from the board.[43] During the rest of the seventeenth century the suspending power of the governors was almost unlimited. The instructions simply required that removal be for "good and sufficient cause" and that the governor transmit to the king a statement of his reasons with the charges and proofs and the answer of the accused. But investigation of the evidence in England three thousand miles or so away was hardly likely to prove an effective check upon the governor's arbitrary actions. With such freedom from restraint as this arrangement actually gave him, the governor was often able to dominate his council. He might easily convert it into an instrument for the promotion of selfish designs upon the province. Such, at least, was the opinion of the Board of Trade soon after their organization toward the close of the century. In preparing instructions for Francis Nicholson as governor of Virginia in 1698 they decided to modify the system so as to make the council a more effective check upon the governor in case "an ill man" should come to occupy that post. In order to make the councillors "less liable to arbitrary and ill-grounded recalls," they required that the governor spread upon the council books his reasons for suspending a coun-

---

[43] Commission to Atkins, Barbados, submitted Dec. 19, 1673, C.O. 29: 1, 153–162. The earlier governors in the West Indies also had full power to suspend or expel members of their councils, but the situation was somewhat different in view of the fact that these governors selected their own councils in the first place without the necessity of confirmation by the crown. In Virginia, where the council was always named by the crown, the suspending power was not granted until 1679.

cillor together with the charges, proofs, and defense. But they recognized that occasions might arise when such publication would be impolitic. The governor was then to transmit all information, and especially his reasons for secrecy, to the home government.[44] This instruction was repeated to all governors until 1715 when a further restriction upon the suspending power seemed desirable. In most of the new sets of instructions issued after the accession of George I, the governor was forbidden to suspend a member of the council without the consent of a majority of that body. Within a year Lieutenant Governor Spotswood of Virginia had occasion to become much annoyed with this new limitation. He had what he considered excellent reasons for suspending a certain councillor but was unable to get rid of him since more than half the other councillors were relatives of the culprit.[45] Such family control of provincial councils was not uncommon. This incident and the expressed attitude of other governors led the Board of Trade to clarify the instruction by again permitting the governor to act alone if his reasons for suspension were "not fit to be communicated to the council."[46] As the instruction now read, the governor was to suspend only for good cause, which, in normal cases, was to receive the approval of a majority of the

[44] Board of Trade to the lords justices, Aug. 23, 1698, C.O. 5: 1359, pp. 254–259 (L.C.); *Cal. State Paps., Col.*, 1697–1698, § 767; instructions to Nicholson, Va., 1698, art. 9, C.O. 5: 1359, pp. 266–303 (L.C.). The suggestion of publicity before suspension had originally come from Henry Hartwell, a Virginia councillor, though not in the form actually adopted. *Cal. State Paps., Col.*, 1696–1697, § 1320 ii.

[45] Spotswood to the Board of Trade, May 23, 1716, *Spotswood Letters*, II, 154–155 (in *Collections* of the Virginia Historical Society, new series, II).

[46] Memorandum by Secretary of State Methuen to the Board of Trade, read Oct. 16, 1716, C.O. 137: 12, no. 4; observations of Sir Nicholas Lawes on the Jamaica instructions, read Aug. 30, 1717, C.O. 137: 12, no. 59; instructions to Lawes, Jamaica, 1718, art. 10, C.O. 5: 189, pp. 334–375 (L.C.).

council and to be entered on the record with all pertinent data. But if necessity arose the governor might suspend a councillor without bringing the council as a whole or any of its other members into the case, though he was to send a full report back to the authorities in England under any circumstances. The instruction was repeated to all governors throughout the period without any other important change.[47]

The governor's power was one of suspension only. The home government always reserved the right to review his actions. Usually the Board of Trade agreed with his decision and recommended the final removal of the suspended councillor. Engagement in illegal trade, obstructive tactics in council, and violent opposition to the governor were among the important causes for such removals.[48] But sometimes the home authorities felt that the governors had acted with prejudice or malice, or that in the subject under dispute the governor was wrong and the councillor right. Then the governor usually had the disagreeable duty of restoring to his place the councillor whom he had so unwisely removed. A large percentage of reversals occurred in connection with suspensions by senior councillors who, while acting governors, seized the opportunity to dislodge their enemies from office. In reaching their decision the Board of Trade always tried to act with full justice to both parties. They succeeded fairly well in making both governor and council feel that there was a tribunal in Great Britain anxious to check arbitrary

[47] From 1752 on the instructions specified that the consent of the council to a suspension was to be given in open council after a full hearing. This method had been implied in the earlier instructions but had not always been followed.

[48] See, for example, the wholesale removal of five councillors of New York for various illegal practices, ordered by additional instructions to the earl of Bellomont, Nov. 10, 1698. Three of the five men had been first suspended by the governor. *N. Y. Col. Docs.*, IV, 424.

government on the one hand and unwarranted obstruction on the other.

A further protection to the councillors lay in the instruction which required the governor to allow entire freedom of debate and vote in council. To determine just how far this instruction was obeyed is difficult. As far as complaints to the home government show, there was very little violation of the rule during most of the eighteenth century. There were, however, several instances during the period around 1700 in which the governors interpreted the instructions with little liberality. One such case from Barbados illustrates both the Board of Trade's interpretation of this instruction and their willingness to reinstate councillors improperly suspended by a governor. The presidency of William Sharpe in 1706 and 1707 between the administrations of Sir Bevil Granville and Mitford Crowe aroused much bitter feeling within the island. One result of this situation was the change in the rule for the devolution of government, which has been alluded to in a preceding chapter.[49] During this period the assembly passed, with the support of the Sharpe faction, a paper money bill which provoked serious opposition and was finally disallowed in England. The new governor, Mitford Crowe, arrived in 1707 with instructions to investigate complaints of misbehavior on the part of the councillors and to suspend such of them as he should find guilty of the charges against them.[50] Crowe sided at once with Sharpe's opponents and proceeded to suspend Sharpe and three of his fellow councillors because they voted for the paper money bill.[51] But the former president's administration had recently been fully investigated and

[49] See above, pp. 128–129.

[50] Instructions to Crowe, Barbados, 1707, art. 12, C.O. 29: 10, pp. 216–311.

[51] Governor Crowe to the Board of Trade, Aug. 8, Oct. 8, 1707, C.O. 28: 10, nos. 39, 56; *Cal. State Paps., Col.*, 1706–1708, §§ 1090, 1131.

vindicated in England. The Board of Trade held that Crowe's action was a direct violation of the councillors' privileges and of the instruction requiring freedom of debate and vote: "So that if councillors in the plantations must be accounted criminals barely for voting in their legislative capacity . . . it will be difficult to find persons of any tolerable ability to serve her Majesty in these stations." Sharpe and his friends had indeed voted for an improper law, but their action had been "only an error in judgment" and they had since tried their best to remedy the harm done. The board therefore recommended their reinstatement.[52] A royal letter to this effect was dispatched and Crowe unwillingly restored the four men to the council.[53] But intense hostility continued to mark the relations between the governor and these councillors, two of whom, together with another of their group, he again suspended unwarrantably. Only repeated peremptory orders from the queen and finally his recall convinced the governor that he could not dictate to his council.[54]

During these years there were a few other complaints against governors for limiting freedom of debate or for punishing councillors for their votes. But in general such breach of privilege was rare. The governor was usually able to get along with his council reasonably well. The members of that body would naturally be conservatives and supporters of the royal authority, since these quali-

[52] Board of Trade to Sunderland, Oct. 28, 1707, C.O. 29: 11, pp. 147–149; *Cal. State Paps., Col.*, 1706–1708, § 1163.

[53] Royal letter to Crowe, Jan. 24, 1708, C.O. 28: 10, no. 57; *Cal. State Paps., Col.*, 1706–1708, § 1303; Crowe to the Board of Trade, May 18, June 27, 1708, C.O. 28: 11, nos. 11, 18; *Cal. State Paps., Col.*, 1706–1708, §§ 1482, 1591.

[54] The story of Crowe's further contests with these councillors is summarized with appropriate references in the prefaces to *Cal. State Paps., Col.*, 1706–1708, 1708–1709, 1709–1710. The editor makes the case against Crowe appear very strong, but it should be noted that the privy council eventually dismissed the charges against him as not proven. *Acts, Privy Coun., Col.*, 1680–1720, p. 581.

fications were looked for in prospective councillors. Many
of them owed their appointment to the solicitations of the
governor or to one of his predecessors. The British government intended that the governor and council should
work together in harmony. There were numerous exceptions, but a spirit of cooperation and mutual support
marked their normal relationships.

The governor presided in the executive and judicial
sessions of the council. This right was not specifically
given to him by his commissions and instructions but was
inherent in his office and in the nature of the council itself. Except in legislative matters the council had no independent functions to perform. All executive authority
was given to the governor, even when it was to be exercised "by and with the advice and consent of the council."
The court of appeals consisted of the governor and council and not of the council alone. Hence there was no constitutional reason for the council to meet by itself except
when it sat as the upper house of the assembly. On the
few occasions when a provincial council attempted to hold
executive sessions without the presence of the governor,
that official entered an immediate protest. Complaints
came especially from New Hampshire, New York, and
Massachusetts.[55] The most important case was that of the
Massachusetts council. At the time when the excitement

[55] Lieut. Gov. Usher complained that the New Hampshire council was in
the habit of meeting without the presence of governor, lieutenant governor,
or president of the council, even when one or another of these officials was
in the province. The members seemed to think that "if any three or four meets
they are a council and [have] as full power as governor in council." He asked
that all their acts in this capacity be declared void. Usher to the Board of
Trade, Aug. 5, 1710, *Cal. State Paps., Col.*, 1710–1711, § 335. Governor Clinton
of New York reported that while he was at Albany with a quorum of the
council negotiating with the Indians, the rest of the councillors, who constituted a majority, remained in New York City and acted in an executive
capacity entirely without his authorization. Clinton to the Board of Trade,
June 22, 1747, *N. Y. Col. Docs.*, VI, 355.

over the Townshend Acts was at its height, the council met without summons of the governor and signed a petition protesting against the levying of duties by parliament. In reporting this incident, Governor Bernard expressed the opinion that the council could have been acting only in its legislative capacity since he had not been present.[56] But the practice of meeting without the governor became so common in Massachusetts during the next few years and the council's pretensions to executive authority at these sessions grew so bold that an article was added to the instructions to Governor Hutchinson in 1771, forbidding such "unjustifiable and unconstitutional proceedings."[57] The instruction was couched in such strong terms that it should have warned the councillors that the home officials might soon feel impelled to abolish the elective council of the province entirely, as they actually did by act of parliament only three years later.

But the royal council occupied a very different position as a legislative body from what it did as an executive or judicial organ. The colonial legislature consisted of three branches—the lower house, commonly called the assembly; the upper house, or legislative council; and the governor, who exercised an absolute veto over the bills which passed the other two branches. The mutual independence of the three was, in theory, complete. But the council was not actually independent of the governor if that official presided in the upper house as he did in the executive and judicial council. Kings of England did, indeed, occasionally attend the deliberations of the House of Lords, but not in the capacity of presiding officers, and the practice

[56] Francis Bernard to the Board of Trade, Dec. 5, 1768, C.O. 5: 758, pp. 49-52.

[57] Instructions to Hutchinson, Massachusetts, 1771, art. 5, C.O. 5: 203, pp. 481-511 (Mass.). The instruction was repeated verbatim to Gage in 1774, C.O. 5: 205, pp. 427-461 (Mass.).

died out with the end of the Stuart line. But in the seventeenth and early eighteenth centuries the governors of many royal provinces not only often attended the legislative council but presided there. Sometimes, though not always, their presence was resented. Charges were made that they were able by indirect methods to limit freedom of speech and to influence votes. Six members of the Virginia council signed a complaint against Governor Nicholson in 1703 which included a section headed: "His behavior in the upper house of assembly." Then followed this statement: "Whereas that house humbly conceives that they ought to be left to the freedom of their own debates, without being swayed and overawed by the governor's interposition; he is not only constantly present, but takes upon him to preside and debate, and state the question, and overrule as if he were still in council, which the said house takes to be a great encroachment on their liberties and privileges."[58] Similar complaints came now and then from other provinces.

Less commonly, though more seriously, the question was raised of the governor's right to vote in the legislative council, either as a regular member, or as the presiding officer in case of a tie. Such a right, in addition to his usual veto power, would give him a share in legislation wholly unwarranted by the theory of the constitution. In a sense, of course, this problem was comprised within the other, for if a governor could not even sit in the legislative council he certainly could have no vote there. The legal problems involved did not receive an authoritative answer until the eighteenth century was well advanced. A controversy in New York gave occasion for an opinion by the law officers of the crown. In 1733 the senior councillor and former acting governor, Rip Van Dam, complained that

[58] Memorial of complaint by six Virginia councillors, May 20, 1703, C.O. 5: 1314, no. 5 (L.C.); *Cal. State Paps., Col.*, 1704–1705, § 247.

Governor Cosby had not allowed the council to sit and act as a separate branch of the legislature, that the governor had taken it upon himself to act as their president in order to influence their debates, and that Cosby had insisted on all bills and messages from the lower house being brought to him personally as presiding officer of the council. By these and other methods Cosby had rendered the council useless as a legislative body and had virtually given himself a second negative voice in the law-making process in addition to that regularly his as a third branch of the legislature.[59] Van Dam's charges, though doubtless true, had been actuated by personal enmity toward the governor, because of Cosby's attempt, immediately on arriving in the province, to collect from Van Dam half the profits of the acting governorship since the last governor's death. On Van Dam's side in the controversy were ranged three of the most prominent councillors, Lewis Morris, later governor of New Jersey, whom Cosby removed from the chief justiceship; James Alexander, a wealthy merchant, prominent in the affairs of New York and New Jersey; and Cadwallader Colden, the later lieutenant governor. The other councillors supported Cosby in the ensuing struggle. In answer to Van Dam's charges they drafted a statement declaring that the governor had only acted according to custom in presiding over the legislative council. Van Dam himself had so presided when acting governor before Cosby's arrival. In fact, the council had never considered themselves as more than a committee in the absence of the governor. Debate had always been free and Cosby had made no innovations.[60]

Out of the charges and countercharges which followed

[59] Rip Van Dam's "Articles of Complaint against Governor Cosby," Dec. 17, 1733, *N. Y. Col. Docs.*, V, 975–976.

[60] Seven members of the New York council to Newcastle, Dec. 17, 1733, *ibid.*, pp. 979–980.

grew the famous Zenger trial which went far to establish
the principle of freedom of the press. The original issue
was referred back to England. The Board of Trade supported Cosby to the extent of removing his three opponents from the council but did not uphold his pretensions
to the presidency of that body. At the direction of the
board, the secretary wrote to the attorney and solicitor
general asking their opinion upon the points at issue.[61] The
law officers replied that "it is inconsistent with the nature
of this government, with the governor's commission, and
his Majesty's instructions that governors should in any
case whatsoever sit and vote as a member of the council."
When the senior councillor was acting governor, he also
must refrain from acting as a councillor.[62] After receiving
this opinion the secretary of the Board of Trade wrote to
Cosby telling him that when the council was acting in an
executive capacity he was to sit and advise with them, but
that when the council sat as a branch of the legislature he
was neither to sit nor vote with them. "It would in fact be
taking away the privilege of the council in vesting two of
the three parts of the legislature in one person and consequently destroying that constitution so prudently established by his Majesty's commission and instructions for
the government of his American colonies." The secretary
also told Cosby not to expect bills to be presented to him
from the assembly before passage by the council.[63] The
Board of Trade proposed to the king that all the governors
be directed to conform themselves to the opinion of the law
officers, but the privy council was unwilling to take action
without further investigation.[64] Therefore no uniform

[61] Alured Popple to Attorney General Willes and Solicitor General Ryder,
Dec. 18, 1735, C.O. 324: 12, pp. 126–128 (L.C.).

[62] Willes and Ryder to Popple, Jan. 15, 1736, *N. Y. Col. Docs.*, VI, 41–42.

[63] Popple to Cosby, Jan. 23, 1736, *ibid.*, pp. 39–40.

[64] Board of Trade to the king, Feb. 6, 1736, *ibid.*, pp. 40–41; *Acts, Privy
Coun., Col.*, 1720–1745, § 371.

practice was established throughout the colonial world although the governors of New York and of some other provinces did not afterward attend the legislative sessions of their councils.

The controversy in New York has a special significance which should not be passed by without mention. Although the dispute eventually involved everything from the perquisites of the governor to the freedom of the press, Cosby looked upon it as an attack upon the prerogative by the three opposing councillors. Nothing could have been farther from the truth. The activities of these men throughout their lives proved that they were ardent advocates of the crown and supporters of the prerogative. They opposed the governor from motives largely personal but he treated their attacks as if these were directed against the authority of the crown. Such an attitude was all too common among the governors. An avaricious or an obtuse governor (and Cosby was both of these) might easily construe the personal enmity of his opponents, however loyal to the interests of the king they might otherwise be, as an attempt to weaken the prerogative and destroy the royal authority. This belief could not help but lessen the cooperation between governor and council and in itself lower the prestige of the administration. The great majority of controversies which took place between governors and members of their councils related originally, as did this one, to personal interests and not to the fundamental authority of the governors as representatives of the prerogative. In this fact lies the greatest distinction between such quarrels and those in which the assemblies were directly involved.

The members of the council received no financial rewards for their services in an executive capacity. The policy of the home government was opposed to allowing the assemblies to vote salaries to the councillors.[65] In some

[65] Lieutenant Governor Spotswood expressed the common British view

provinces they did receive an allowance for the days in
which they sat as part of the legislature or for their services in the court of appeals. But their chief rewards came
in other ways. Not the least of these was the honor and
prestige of membership in his Majesty's council. On formal occasions the councillors took precedence immediately
after the governor and lieutenant governor.[66] In some
provinces they seem to have been entitled to a salute of
eleven guns.[67] Such distinction was eagerly sought after
in regions where social castes had not become permanently
defined but where democracy was as yet an unknown
ideal.[68] More mercenary, though not more selfish, was the
desire of some men for protection from lawsuits which
council membership might give. The Board of Trade appreciated the dangers in this situation, and did its best to
prevent such a misuse of the royal appointment. In 1704

in 1711 in discussing a recent revenue act of Virginia: "And though there
was formerly a law in this country ascertaining the salary of the council,
yet I have not suffered any such establishment to be inserted in this act,
because it is certainly more agreeable to that dependence which they ought
to have on the crown that they should owe their support as well as their promotion entirely to her Majesty's bounty, and not to claim it by a law here."
Spotswood to the Board of Trade, March 6, 1711, *Spotswood Letters*, I, 49;
Cal. State Paps., Col., 1710–1711, § 710.

[66] See above, p. 92, note 2.

[67] The Board of Trade wrote Gov. Knowles of Jamaica, Oct. 15, 1754, that
a certain councillor, whom Knowles had reported as having left the island
without permission, told them that the governor had dined with him before
sailing, recommended him as a passenger to the ship's captain, "and when
he passed the fort, ordered him a salute of eleven guns." C.O. 138: 20, pp.
93–94.

[68] Governor Edward Trelawney of Jamaica complained to the Board of
Trade, March 23, 1740, that the principal gentlemen in Jamaica had for
some unstated reason become "extremely averse" to accepting seats in the
council. C.O. 137: 23. At this the board expressed surprise and concern and a
hope that "upon reflection they [the proposed councillors] will be induced
to think more favorably of a post which has hitherto been esteemed an honor
to those that have been possessed of it." Board of Trade to Trelawney, Aug.
8, 1740, C.O. 138: 18, p. 323.

they asked Queen Anne to declare under her signet and sign manual "that no councillors in the plantations have or ought to have by virtue of their places any privilege which may tend to the interrupting of justice or to the giving them any protection to the detriment of other your Majesty's subjects in the recovery of their rights in the several plantations."[69] Although nothing came of this proposal, the board continued to keep a watchful eye upon the councils in order to prevent any abuse of privilege. In 1708, for example, when complaints reached the board from Jamaica, they wrote Governor Handasyd asking by what law or usage the councillors claimed a privilege of not being sued for debt without the previous permission of the council.[70] In reply the governor denied that there had been any such privilege claimed or granted in the seven years since he had come to the island, except the same privilege granted to members of the assembly of freedom from arrest or suit during sessions of the legislature.[71] The board expressed satisfaction with this answer but promised to consider the question further if new complaints should reach them.[72] In Virginia and eventually in New Hampshire, the pretensions of the councillors to freedom from judicial process were serious enough to necessitate an instruction on the point. This provided that a letter signed by the governor, secretary, or the clerk of any court of record to a councillor was to be as binding in law as a writ or subpoena. Failure to obey such a special summons would subject the councillor, except during sessions of the

[69] Board of Trade to the queen, Oct. 26, 1704, C.O. 29: 9, pp. 74-75; *Cal. State Paps., Col.*, 1704–1705, p. 296.

[70] Board of Trade to Handasyd, March 25, 1708, C.O. 138: 12, pp. 235–236; *Cal. State Paps., Col.*, 1706–1708, § 1410.

[71] Handasyd to the Board of Trade, July 20, 1708, C.O. 137: 8, no. 23; *Cal. State Paps., Col.*, 1708–1709, § 56.

[72] Board of Trade to Handasyd, Nov. 25, 1708, C.O. 138: 12, p. 338; *Cal. State Paps., Col.*, 1708–1709, § 208.

legislature, to the ordinary forms of process with their attendant penalties.[73]

The most desirable reward for a loyal councillor came through his appointment to an administrative or judicial office within the disposal of the governor. Such an appointment was mutually advantageous. The salary or fees attached to the position might serve as a fitting return for faithful attendance upon the council, while the income would depend not upon the caprice of the assembly but upon a proper discharge of the duties of the office and loyal support of the governor or the ministry in England. Prompt removal might follow disobedience. Among the positions most frequently granted to councillors were those of receiver general, naval officers, clerks of various sorts, and judges in the inferior courts.[74] Although councillors very often held such offices, thereby increasing their importance in local affairs, the converse by no means always followed that occupants of administrative or judi-

[73] A minute of the general court of Virginia (the council in its judicial capacity) March 27, 1678, provided for summoning a councillor before itself by letter of the governor or secretary, but made no provision for summons before a lower court. C.O. 5: 1309, no. 23 (L.C.). Complaints against this arrangement in 1697 led to the introduction in the following year of an instruction to Governor Nicholson (art. 38) providing for the new system. C.O. 5: 1359, pp. 266–303 (L.C.). The same instruction was sent to Governor Benning Wentworth of New Hampshire in 1761, art. 14, *N. H. Prov. Laws*, III, 251–281.

[74] A curious instruction was given to all royal governors of Virginia and Maryland between 1698 and 1737 forbidding them to appoint councillors to the positions of naval officer or collector of the duty of two shillings per hogshead on tobacco exported. (See instructions to Nicholson, Va., 1698, art. 88, C.O. 5: 1359, pp. 266–303, L.C.) The Board of Trade framed the article in an effort to check frauds in the tobacco trade, particularly by prohibiting the holding of these two administrative offices by one man. The clause against councillors holding either of these offices seems to have arisen from a misunderstanding of the duties of the offices. Governor Nott protested against the rule in 1705 but it was not dropped until the instructions of 1756. Nott to the secretary of state, Dec. 24, 1705, C.O. 5: 1340, no. 19 (L.C.); *Cal. State Paps., Col.*, 1704–1705, § 1535.

cial posts were made councillors either *ex officio* or in ordinary. In fact, *ex officio* councillorships were rare. The most important exception was that of a resident lieutenant governor who was almost always named senior councillor. The surveyor general of the customs, the superintendent of Indian affairs, the chief justice, and, in the West Indies, the commanders of naval vessels in provincial waters, were sometimes made councillors extraordinary in one or more provinces, but they were usually prohibited from succeeding to the presidency in the ordinary course of seniority. Very clearly, the council was not to be looked upon as a body of administrative officials brought together because of the positions which they held. Its members were primarily councillors, although they might hold other offices either as rewards for services rendered or because the custom of the time or the scarcity of able men made pluralism inevitable. Herein the provincial council differed radically from the institution which was developing contemporaneously in Great Britain—the cabinet council.

The provincial body was modeled rather after the House of Lords and the privy council. It inherited many of the weaknesses which were at that very time diminishing the importance of those two institutions, but it never acquired the elements of strength which contributed most to their vitality. It stood halfway between the assembly, which was an elective body in large measure representative of the freeholders of the province, and the governor, who was the agent of the king and the bearer of the prerogative. Since its composition was determined from above and reflected only accidentally, if at all, the wishes of a majority of the voters, it could inspire the confidence of the lower house no more surely than could its prototypes inspire that of the House of Commons. And because of a more equitable system of representation in America its members could not in turn control the membership of the elective body as effectively as did the leading peers in the eighteenth century. On the other hand, the provincial council was composed of colonials—prominent, usually wealthy, and often men of real political ability, but nevertheless colonials. The home government, anxious for the welfare of British mercantile interests, could not therefore always count on the support of the council when colonial interests might be affected by pending measures. The tradition of the prerogative was less strong in America than in Great Britain, and provincial councillors were far less to be trusted with its exercise than were the aristocrats who dominated the government at home. Therefore, the British officials resisted every tendency to make the executive council more than an advisory body. They opposed every suggestion which would take from the governor the actual responsibility for the maintenance of the prerogative and vest it in the council. They made it clear that the provincial council was not to follow lines of development similar to those of the British cabinet.

This attitude naturally contributed to the ineffectiveness of the council as an institution of government, however necessary such a policy was to safeguard British interests. Regardless of whether the council advised the governor to carry out a certain policy, to consent to a legislative bill, or to perform any other function of government which might possibly infringe upon his instructions, the final decision must rest with him alone. The councillors occasionally denied this principle, insisting that their advice was binding both negatively and affirmatively upon the governor. He was forbidden by his instructions to perform certain acts without their consent, and they felt that logically he should do all things which a majority of the council recommended him to do. Even the governor sometimes sought to justify himself by similar arguments, especially when local sentiment strongly opposed the expressed royal policy. But such views brought sharp replies from Great Britain, as Lieutenant Governor Fauquier of Virginia once learned to his chagrin. A bill was passed in 1759 by the burgesses and council laying a duty on slaves imported from Maryland, Carolina, and the West Indies for the personal use of the importer. Fauquier knew well enough that one of the instructions forbade him to assent to any bill imposing a duty on slaves payable by the importer, and he knew further that neither commission nor instructions required the council's approval of a veto. But the bill was very popular in the colony. So he summoned the council, produced the instruction in question, and stated his objections to the measure. He then asked the councillors to give him their opinions in writing if they thought he should approve the bill in spite of the instruction. Ostensibly to his great surprise, seven of the eight councillors present advised approval, whereupon Fauquier affixed his signature and forwarded the act to the Board of Trade together with copies of the councillors' opinions.[75] But the board refused to let him shift responsibility in this way. They wrote him at once, charitably admitting that his action had evidently arisen from a misapprehension or misconstruction of his instructions, but pointing out the "very dangerous and pernicious tendency and consequence" of such a policy on his part: "The cases in which the advice and consent of the council are required in any acts of government are precisely marked out in the instructions; in all other cases of duties enjoined by these instructions the governor alone is accountable for his own conduct; and if it should ever be admitted that the advice and opinion of the council can dissolve the governor from the obligation he is under of

[75] Fauquier to the Board of Trade, Dec. 17, 1759, C.O. 5: 1329, pp. 396–397 (L.C.).

obeying those instructions by which the negative voice in the passing of laws is limited and restrained, the interest of the crown and the mother country must depend solely for security upon the uncertain wills, interests, and inclinations of the members of the council, and what the consequences of such a system would be are too obvious to mention.''[76]

The refusal of the home authorities to allow the provincial council to develop into a responsible body whose advice would finally determine the policy of the provincial executive, was further emphasized by Secretary Hillsborough. In a letter to Governor Bernard of Massachusetts in 1768, he wrote that the latter's evident doubts as to his power to act in any case without the advice and opinion of the council could not be substantiated by a careful perusal of the commissions and instructions. Hillsborough thought that the admission of a right in the council to be consulted on all occasions would establish in it ''a power and authority inconsistent with the spirit of the constitution.''[77]

The council, which in theory was such an important part of the constitutional system of the royal provinces, became in fact less and less significant as time went on. In the Virginia commissions of the early seventeenth century the royal governor was little more than the first among the councillors. But as his office grew, theirs declined. The development of the elective assembly further lessened their importance as legislators. When contests over the prerogative became more and more frequent, the antagonists were almost always the assembly on one side and the governor on the other. The councillors usually stood by, aiding one or the other, or remaining neutral according to their

[76] Board of Trade to Fauquier, June 13, 1760, C.O. 5: 1367, pp. 405–407 (L.C.).

[77] Hillsborough to Bernard, Jan. 11, 1768, C.O. 5: 757, pp. 169–175 (Mass.).

inclinations, but seldom leading in the fight. While the determination of policy and the actual exercise of the prerogative in Great Britain was passing into the hands of a group of officials—the cabinet—the corresponding powers in the province remained primarily in the person of a single man—the royal governor. As Hillsborough wrote to Bernard: "It is you to whom the crown has delegated its authority, and you alone are responsible for the due exercise of it."

CHAPTER V

THE PROVINCIAL ASSEMBLY

The dissolution of the Virginia Company in 1624 led to the temporary suspension of representative government in the colony. But four years later, Charles I permitted the House of Burgesses to be summoned again for certain limited purposes. At that moment the first step was taken toward the permanent inclusion of an elective legislature in the constitutional system of the royal provinces. From this beginning grew an institution which was destined to have a tremendous influence upon the government and the political ideals of the provinces throughout the next century and a half. The elective assembly represented the local and popular interests in colonial government, while the governor, and to a lesser extent the appointive council, represented the prerogative. Sooner or later these forces were bound to come in conflict. Unless some satisfactory compromise was then worked out, the contest would surely continue until one group or the other had established its supremacy by political means, or, these failing, by force of arms. In nine royal provinces on the continent a military victory finally gave the local and popular forces complete and absolute independence. That armed conflict did not take place elsewhere at the same time was due to various factors, especially the overwhelming strength of British naval control in the West Indies. In no way did it result from any lack of antagonism between royal and local interests in the government of these provinces. The disputes continued there until in the following century changing conditions in the colonies and wiser administration in

Great Britain made more peaceful solutions possible.[1] But the great struggle between the prerogative and the assembly took place in every royal province.

During the second and third quarters of the seventeenth century the clash of interests appeared only occasionally. The home authorities were so preoccupied with affairs in England that they could give little thought to the colonies. Then, too, England had acquired colonial dependencies only comparatively recently. Her administrators could not adopt a consistent policy until time and experience in the control of several royal provinces had shown what was the most desirable course to follow. Conditions both in England and America were not suitable for a fixed colonial policy until well along in the reign of Charles II. Beginning about 1670, and more especially after 1675, the English authorities seem for the first time to have made a serious study of political conditions in the colonies. They began to adopt certain principles for the control of the royal provinces and to embody these principles in the commissions and instructions issued to the governors. Royal government of the colonies, in the form it was to take for a century and more, really began with this period.

The Lords of Trade, who were responsible for most of what was done at this time, interested themselves especially in the regulation of the assembly. Before this period the commissions and instructions to the governors dealing with the assembly had been vague, indefinite, and very few in number. But beginning with the instructions to the

---

[1] In some respects the final solution does not yet seem to have been reached, especially for those colonies which possess representative institutions but not responsible government. For example, a dispatch to the *New York Times*, July 22, 1928, dated "Nassau, Bahamas, July 17," describes a bitter contest between the royal governor and the elective assembly of that colony, growing out of the control of appropriations and involving questions of parliamentary privilege. Nothing but names and dates indicates that the dispute was not one of many which took place over similar matters in all the royal provinces two hundred years ago.

earl of Carlisle for Jamaica in 1678, the Lords of Trade drew up more and more precise directions to the governors for the control and limitation of the popular bodies in their provinces. With very few exceptions the instructions given during these years were retained throughout the colonial period, altered and expanded from time to time, indeed, to meet the needs of later years as the royal authorities saw them, but still keeping the essential characteristics of the earlier age. The ten or twelve years before the Revolution of 1689 marked the establishment of a fixed British policy toward the assembly.

Even at this period there was a difference between the British and American views of the assembly, a difference which became more and more pronounced with the passing years. Those on the two sides of the Atlantic were never able to reach a common understanding of the nature and origin of the representative body. The colonists felt that, as Englishmen, they had a right to share in making laws and laying taxes through agents of their own election. They believed that the summoning of an assembly by a royal governor in accordance with his commission and instructions was nothing but the recognition of this right and that this right could not legally be denied them. Therefore, the assembly, though called into being by a royal act, was just as fundamental and essential a part of the provincial constitution as the king's own representative. Its position, they thought, should be equally independent and assured. But the ministers and agents of the crown saw the matter in a different light. They generally admitted the right of all Englishmen to a share, actual or theoretical, in legislation and taxation. But they would not concede that the only means to accomplish that end was a local assembly exercising powers equivalent to those of parliament. In their opinion parliament itself might pass laws for or impose taxes upon the colonies, as it

actually did after 1763. Or a local elective body similar
in powers to an English muncipal council might serve the
purpose. In any case, the actual creation of an assembly
was an act of royal grace and favor. The legislature so
established could have no power greater than was provided in the commission and instructions upon which it
was founded. Therefore the British officials vigorously
opposed the tendency of the assemblies to exercise freedom of action equal to that of parliament. These differing
views were never reconciled in the period before the
American Revolution.

Something can be said in support of each position. The
constitutional struggles in England during the seventeenth century and earlier show clearly how important
was the principle of taxation by the legislature alone. The
British authorities themselves were most reluctant to
allow any legislation or taxation in the colonies without
an assembly. The early royal governors and councils of
Virginia and Barbados exercised a limited ordinance
power but usually the governor's commission gave him
no authority, either singly or with the council, to make
laws for the province. The outstanding exceptions were
in the Dominion of New England from 1686 to 1689 and
in the province of New York at the same time. Governor
Andros of the former province, for example, had authority to make laws and statutes and to impose and collect taxes with the consent of the council.[2] But the exercise
of this power by Andros and his associates aroused opposition which undoubtedly contributed to his eventual
overthrow.[3] In New York, too, an assembly was finally set
up. These experiments were not repeated. In 1763, the

---

[2] Commission to Andros, New England, 1686, *N. H. Prov. Laws*, I, 144–
155; commission to same, 1688, *ibid.*, pp. 226–234; commission to Dongan,
New York, 1686, *N. Y. Col. Docs.*, III, 377–382.

[3] See V. F. Barnes, *The Dominion of New England*, pp. 80–100.

governors and councils of some of the newly conquered
provinces were given a somewhat restricted ordinance
power until there should be enough resident Englishmen
to warrant the summoning of assemblies. The instructions
in these cases provided, however, that such rules and
regulations as might be passed should not "anyways
tend to affect the life, limb, or property of the subject or
to imposing any duties or taxes."[4] But never during the
eighteenth century did the British government authorize a
governor by his commission to legislate without the assistance of an elective assembly in any province containing a substantial number of English inhabitants. When
in the middle of the century the home officials had their
attention called to the fact that the appointive council of
Nova Scotia was functioning as the sole legislative body,
they insisted that an assembly be called in spite of the
governor's protests that there were only enough Englishmen in the province to elect two representatives. The
Board of Trade admitted to Governor Lawrence that
legislative power had formerly been granted to a few governors and councils, but, they added, "it was a power of
very short duration and in later times, since the constitution of this country has been restored to its true principles
[that is, since the Revolution of 1689], has never been
thought advisable to be executed."[5] Thus by usage and

---

[4] Instructions to Grant, East Florida, 1763, art. 11, C.O. 5: 201, pp. 71–127
(L.C.); instructions to Johnstone, West Florida, 1763, art. 11, C.O. 5: 201,
pp. 131–181 (L.C.); instructions to Melville, Grenada, 1763, art. 11, C.O. 5:
201, pp. 183–231 (L.C.); instructions to Murray, Quebec, 1763, art. 11,
Report on Canadian Archives for 1904, p. 193; Shortt and Doughty, *Documents Relating to the Constitutional History of Canada*, I, 132–149. Following the passage of the Quebec Act of 1774 the legislative functions of the
council of that province were considerably extended. Instructions to Carleton,
Quebec, 1775, art. 9, *Can. Arch. Rept.*, 1904, pp. 229–247; *Docs. Rel. to Const.
Hist. of Canada*, I, 419–433.

[5] Board of Trade to Lawrence, March 25, 1756, *Nova Scotia Archives*,
I, 713. This volume contains (pp. 711–742) most of the documents relating
to this highly important case.

custom and by the actual admission of the home authorities, the right of the royal province to an elective assembly which would enact all local laws was clearly established.

There was much justice, therefore, in the colonists' contention that the existence of their assemblies was more than a mere matter of royal grace and favor and was, in fact, a right which the king could not destroy. More than that, as the bolder Americans eventually argued, if the assembly existed by virtue of a right not derived from the king, he could not legally limit its scope of legislative action except by the constitutional process of veto or disallowance. The assembly was founded on the same rights as parliament itself and its powers in local matters ought to be as great.

But, as the royal officials often pointed out, the assembly was actually created by virtue of the prerogative. The legislature could not create itself. Only the king or his governor, acting under his direction, could set in motion the machinery for calling such an assembly into being. The governor's commission and instructions contained the only legal authority for the purpose. These documents constituted, therefore, the real basis of the assembly and that body could have no power which was not specifically granted therein. If the king chose to limit the legislative power of the organ which he had created in this way, it was entirely legal and proper for him to do so. The limitations upon the assembly found in the commission and instructions had therefore as much weight as the original grant and ought to be as binding upon that body as upon the governor to whom they were directed.

These conflicting views of the origin and nature of the provincial assembly explain many of the constitutional struggles of the eighteenth century. Each party based its actions upon fundamentally differing principles. The British conception was that of government by "royal grace and favor,'' an expression often used. The colonial ideal, at first only dimly understood, was later defined by Jefferson as that of governments "deriving their just powers from the consent of the governed." Neither side appreciated fully the other's point of view. Few Englishmen were even aware of the fundamental issue. One man, Thomas Pownall, whose experience as a royal governor combined with his natural shrewdness gave him an unusual insight, caught at least the implications of the situation and the practical problem involved. In 1764 he declared in a wordy but significant sentence that the time had come when it ought to be definitely settled "how far the crown has or has not a right to direct or restrict the legislature of the colonies,—or if the crown has not this power, what department of government has, and how it ought to be exercised;—or whether in fact or deed, the people of the colonies, having every right to the full power of government and *to a whole legislative power,* are under this claim entitled, in the powers of legislature and the administration of government, to use and exercise in conformity to the laws of Great Britain, the same full, free, independent, unrestrained power and legislative will in their several corporations and under the king's commission and their respective charters, as the government and legislature of Great Britain holds by its constitution and under the great charter."[6] Perhaps Pownall was wrong. Perhaps by 1764 the time had already passed when this problem could be settled satisfactorily for the continental colonies. In any case, two generations were to pass for Great Britain and her other possessions before a Lord Durham arose to restate the question and, unchecked by the rigidity of eighteenth-century minds, to

6 Thomas Pownall, *The Administration of the Colonies,* pp. 42–43. The italics are in the original.

work out a solution which forms the constitutional basis of the modern British commonwealth of nations.

The conflict of British and American theories regarding the assembly was well illustrated in the quarrel over who had the right to extend representation to new districts. Whether the governor or the assembly ought to authorize the summoning of delegates from new communities would depend largely upon whether representative institutions existed by virtue of the royal prerogative or by natural right. At the first creation of the assembly in every colony the basis of representation was inevitably fixed by the executive, whatever the form of government then established. As the corporate and proprietary colonies came one after another under direct control of the crown, the royal authorities naturally tended to keep the same system of representation in the assemblies as had been in force under the former governments. The commissions to the governors usually directed them to summon assemblies "in manner and form according to the custom and usage" of the province.[7] Only rarely, therefore, did the instructions specify the towns or districts which were to send delegates.[8] Representation of the older settled regions was not usually a cause for serious disagreement between the assembly and the agents of the prerogative. But when settlement expanded into new sections and increase of population necessitated the setting up of local government there, or when a similar increase in an older county, town, or precinct made its division into two parts seem advisable, a dispute was

[7] The quotation is from the Barbados commissions. The phraseology differed slightly in the various provinces.

[8] The exceptions were New Jersey, Dominica, Grenada, and St. Vincent, where from the establishment of royal government the apportionment was indicated in the instructions; North Carolina, where it was given in the instructions of 1754 only; and the Bahamas, where it was indicated from 1728 on in the commission.

likely to arise. Both the governor and the assembly might claim the sole right of granting representation to the new district.

The British precedents in such cases were unsatisfactory. The Tudor monarchs had freely exercised the prerogative of granting representation to English boroughs but during the reigns of the first two Stuarts parliament had been active in the same direction. In the only case of its kind after the Restoration Charles II caused the admission of members from the borough of Newark, in 1677, though not without opposition in the House of Commons.[9] Three years earlier, the county and city of Durham had been granted representation by act of parliament,[10] but this incident also has no parallel during the next century or so. Englishmen of the eighteenth century viewed their political system so complacently that they were unwilling to extend the franchise and therefore they gave the colonies no new precedents to follow. The question of the right to extend representation was distinctly an American issue, created by the growth of population on the colonial frontier.

The most serious challenge to the prerogative in this matter came in New Hampshire. In 1745 the assembly refused to admit five delegates from new towns and districts to which Governor Benning Wentworth had ordered summonses to be sent. The representatives insisted that the initiative in such matters rested with themselves alone. When the governor said he knew of no method of summoning members but by royal writ, they replied by citing four cases in which votes of the lower house had been the basis for increase of membership and two others in which acts of assembly had brought about the same result. Since

9 *Journal of the House of Commons*, IX, 389, 403, 415; Anchitell Grey, *Debates of the House of Commons*, IV, 297–304.

10 25 Car. II, cap. 9.

war with France was then going on, Wentworth wisely submitted for the time being, but privately resolved on a fight to the finish when external peace was restored.[11] While waiting for this time to come he wrote the Board of Trade for directions and that body referred his inquiry to the attorney and solicitor general and to Francis Fane, standing counsel to the board. These three legal authorities agreed that ''the right of sending representatives to the assembly was founded originally on the commissions and instructions given by the crown to the governors of New Hampshire'' and that therefore his Majesty might ''extend the privilege of sending representatives to such new towns as he should judge worthy.''[12] In accordance with the recommendation of the law officers, additional instructions were sent to Wentworth in 1748 quoting *verbatim* from their opinions and positively directing him to exercise this prerogative.[13] The governor was now ready for the battle.

Wentworth made an ideal champion for the royal cause. Born in New Hampshire fifty-three years before, he was at this time the head of the most prominent family of the province. He understood thoroughly the workings of the provincial mind. His loyalty to the British government was matched only by his personal ambitions, and his stubbornness by his political cunning. When the first assembly after the peace met in January, 1749, new members from previously unrepresented towns again appeared and again were ejected before the naming of a speaker. But Wentworth declined to approve the assembly's nominee unless the new men were allowed to take part in the vot-

---

[11] *N. H. Prov. Paps.*, V, 260-264.

[12] Opinion of Attorney and Solicitor General Ryder and Murray, March 18, 1747, Chalmers, *Opinions of Eminent Lawyers*, I, 271-272; opinion of Francis Fane, *ibid.*, pp. 272-276.

[13] Additional instructions to Benning Wentworth, June 30, 1748, *N. H. Prov. Laws*, II, 653-654.

ing. The assembly denied his right to reject their speaker but the governor refused to be drawn aside from the original issue.[14] A month passed without result. Then two more new representatives offered themselves for admission bringing with them a copy of the royal instruction to Wentworth of the preceding year.[15] This paper demolished the assembly's contention that the governor was acting without authority. But the lower house resorted to delays, quibbles, and petty arguments which added heat but no light to the dispute. Finally the house voted to suspend the rights of the new men until the king's further pleasure should be known.[16] These tactics did not upset Wentworth for he was prepared, as few royal governors ever were, for a war of attrition.[17]

Adjournments and prorogations followed in steady series. Nothing was accomplished. In October, 1750, the assembly weakened and offered to admit representatives from the towns named in the additional instruction of 1748 if the governor would transmit that document in proper form. But Wentworth would not be content with anything less than complete admission of his right of sending writs to whatever towns he thought proper. It was not the assembly's privilege, he said, to "consider" an instruction; that belonged to the governor and council alone. The assembly's duty was simply to obey.[18] Again the deadlock was resumed. No laws could be passed, no bills, even, could be introduced, for the speaker was not yet approved. No fresh taxes could be laid, no fortifications repaired, no

[14] N. H. Prov. Paps., VI, 70–72.   [15] Ibid., pp. 81–82.

[16] Ibid., pp. 85–93; Wentworth to the Board of Trade, June 8, 1749, C.O. 5: 926, fos. 62–66.

[17] On June 12, 1749, Wentworth wrote the duke of Bedford: ''I think I can't dispense with my duty to his Majesty by dissolving this assembly until the minds of the people are better settled in this point, and a due obedience paid to the royal instruction.'' C.O. 5: 10, no. 126 (L.C.).

[18] N. H. Prov. Paps., VI, 120–124.

new expenses incurred. Most representatives did not even bother to attend the futile sessions.[19] For three wretched years this condition lasted and then, in January, 1752, the assembly expired under the terms of the local triennial act.[20] But Wentworth did not hurry matters. He gave the people eight months longer to reflect upon the sins of their representatives and then summoned a new assembly to meet in September.[21] At first a few sparks of opposition glowed in the new body but these soon disappeared. The new members who appeared were admitted to vote, a speaker was chosen and confirmed, and the struggle was over.[22] The governor's victory was complete. What was more, his victory was permanent. The New Hampshire assembly did not again challenge the governor's right of summons until the spring of 1775, after the battle of Lexington had opened a new form of hostilities in America.[23]

Few royal governors could boast of such an achievement. In one sense the contest was almost unique. Usually the assembly and not the governor profited by the colony's financial exhaustion. Wars and rumors of wars generally sent the governors scurrying to the assemblies for money at whatever sacrifice to the prerogative the occasion might demand. But Wentworth carefully picked the time for this contest when the province was at peace. He knew that an

[19] Wentworth to the Board of Trade, March 23, 1751, C.O. 5: 926, fo. 113. See also *Acts, Privy Coun., Col.*, 1745–1766, § 35.

[20] *N. H. Prov. Paps.*, VI, 125; *N. H. Prov. Laws*, II, 402; Wentworth to the Board of Trade, Nov. 25, 1751, C.O. 5: 926, fo. 130.

[21] Wentworth explained to the Board of Trade, June 9, 1752, that he had deferred summoning a new assembly in the hope of receiving fresh orders from England. C.O. 5: 926, fo. 171.

[22] *N. H. Prov. Paps.*, VI, 127–130; Wentworth to the Board of Trade, Nov. 18, 1752, C.O. 5: 926, fo. 197.

[23] *N. H. Prov. Paps.*, VII, 373, 378, 383–387. The fact that the assembly of New Hampshire thereafter admitted the governor's right to summon representatives from new towns did not prevent that body from occasionally enfranchising towns by act of assembly as had formerly been done.

empty treasury would harm the province far more than it would hurt himself, and he was willing that the assembly should learn this lesson. No doubt the poverty of New Hampshire and its exposed frontier position had an important bearing on its powers of resistance, but the fact remains that few other governors were willing to play the game out to its bitter end as Wentworth did. Had there been more Benning Wentworths in the provinces, colonial history might have taken a different course.[24]

Most controversies over the representation of new districts arose in a different way. While in New Hampshire the assembly began the quarrel by denying the governor's right to extend the franchise, generally the governor and royal ministers raised the issue by opposing any increase in representation by act of assembly. The agents of the prerogative adopted this course not only for constitutional reasons, but because they feared that an unlimited increase in the size of the lower house by additions from frontier regions would make that body more radical and, at the same time, would cause it to overshadow the governor and council by sheer force of numbers. These arguments were first advanced in Massachusetts about 1740 by the conservative merchants of the coastal towns at the time of the agitation for a land bank.[25] Two years later Governor Shirley pointed out that if the frontier towns then enfranchised were to take full advantage of their privileges—which they seldom did—they had it in their power "upon an extraordinary emergency to double and almost treble" the size of the lower house. He suggested

[24] Wentworth did not win without personal sacrifice. On Aug. 17, 1754, he wrote that anxiety of mind during the struggle had fixed so strongly on his spirits "that I fell into violent disorders, which with repeated relapses by entering too soon upon business has disabled me for upwards of two years of doing my duty in the common cause." C.O. 5: 926, fo. 214.

[25] The attitude of the conservatives in this matter is discussed in J. T. Adams, *Revolutionary New England*, p. 162.

that all the advantages of local administration might be
gained by erecting new settlements into "precincts, parishes, or villages with all the officers and privileges of a
township except that of sending representatives."[26] This
advice brought an additional instruction to Shirley commending his own policy to him and forbidding him to approve any bill for erecting a new town or dividing an old
one unless the measure contained a clause suspending its
operation until it received the king's approval.[27] The general instructions to the next two governors repeated this
injunction.[28] But this instruction clearly infringed upon
the rights of the assembly which was given full power
to apportion representation within the province by the
charter of 1691.[29] This fact may account for the failure of
the government rigidly to enforce the instruction and for
its omission from the general instructions in 1761.[30] At
that time the Board of Trade recommended to Governor
Bernard that all future acts for erecting townships be
"totally silent" on the question of representation.[31] The
issue in Massachusetts was thus left unsettled.

[26] Shirley to the Board of Trade, Oct. 18, 1742, C.O. 5: 883 (unpaged).

[27] Additional instructions to Shirley, submitted July 27, 1743, *Acts and
Resolves of Massachusetts Bay*, III, 72; C.O. 5: 918, p. 109 (Mass.).

[28] Instructions to Pownall, Mass., 1757, art. 40, C.O. 5: 918, p. 378 (Mass.);
instructions to Bernard, Mass., 1760, art. 40, C.O. 5: 920, pp. 54–133 (Mass.).

[29] Thorpe, *American Charters, Constitutions, and Other Organic Laws*,
III, 1878–1879.

[30] Shirley himself approved bills for the full incorporation of three towns
in 1754, without suspending clauses, thereby calling forth a formal though
mild rebuke from the Board of Trade. Board of Trade to Shirley, April 13,
1756, C.O. 5: 918, pp. 327–330 (Mass.). Later the board beat a hasty retreat
from its original position by declaring that "the instruction was in the
spirit and intention of it confined to the splitting townships in the old
settled counties"—a view utterly unsupported in the earlier correspondence
or the instruction itself. Board of Trade to Bernard, Nov. 20, 1760, C.O.
5: 920, pp. 1–3 (Mass.).

[31] Board of Trade to Bernard, Nov. 25, 1761, C.O. 5: 920, pp. 130–133
(Mass.).

In most of the other provinces where the assemblies had no such charter rights as did the Massachusetts general court, the question was not seriously raised until quite late. Sometimes the governors summoned representatives from new places on their own authority or with the advice of the council. As in New Hampshire, this method often led to opposition from the assembly. More generally, the assemblies passed acts or resolutions to the same purpose. But the ill effects of this latter system became apparent in other provinces as they had in Massachusetts. In 1767 a deluge of acts poured in to the Board of Trade from the assemblies of Nova Scotia, New Hampshire, Massachusetts, New York, and South Carolina, increasing the number of communities eligible to send representatives and rapidly expanding the size of the assemblies.[32] This situation was largely due to the settlements on the frontiers after the peace of 1763 and the collapse of the Pontiac Conspiracy. The privy council determined to check this movement toward enlargement of the legislatures and to prevent the assemblies from exercising the prerogative of granting representation. Therefore they ordered a circular instruction sent to the governors forbidding them to assent to any bills for altering the memberships in their assemblies.[33] This instruction was incorporated in most of the general instructions afterward issued, although in some cases it was modified in 1773 to permit the passage

[32] These acts were all recommended by the Board of Trade for disallowance, C.O. 324: 18, pp. 100–104, 109–115, 120, 133–144 (L.C.); *Acts, Privy Coun., Col.,* 1766–1783, pp. 29–30, 32–35, 40.

[33] Circular instructions to the governors of Nova Scotia, New York, New Jersey, Virginia, South Carolina, West Florida, Jamaica, Grenada, Bermuda, Leeward Islands, Barbados, and the Bahamas, approved Aug. 26, 1767, *N. J. Arch.,* IX, 637–638; C.O. 324: 18, pp. 175–177 (L.C.). Massachusetts had been the worst offender, with acts incorporating no less than eighteen towns, but the instruction was not sent to its governor, undoubtedly because it would conflict with the terms of the charter and acts of assembly already confirmed.

of the prohibited acts if they contained suspending clauses. Thus during the final years before the Revolution the British government took a definite position against the right of the assemblies to increase their membership.

Expediency dictated this attitude, but the British policy was based squarely upon the principle that the assemblies were inferior bodies, limited in powers, and constituted by royal grace and favor. Lord Hillsborough, secretary of state for the colonies, expressed this view clearly a year after the circular instruction was sent in a letter to Governor Moore of New York. "The division of the county of Albany," he wrote, "seems a very proper and necessary measure, and there can be no objection to a law for that purpose, provided it is silent as to the representation in the assembly, which, though it is certainly a privilege that ought not to be denied to the new county, yet his Majesty considers that they ought to derive it from his royal grace and favor and therefore consents that you should (in case the legislature think fit to create the new county) issue writs for the election of two members into the general assembly, but his Majesty does not approve of its being made a part of the law."[34] According to this view, representation was a privilege to be conferred by the king alone. It was in no sense a natural right.

But the colonists considered this attitude and its effect upon their frontier regions as the insufferable intrusion of an outworn theory upon the lives and liberties of a free people. The royal prerogative was interfering with the legitimate powers of the assembly and the rights of the inhabitants. Jefferson gave voice to this grievance against the king when he wrote in the Declaration of Independ-

[34] Hillsborough to Moore, Oct. 12, 1768, *N. Y. Col. Docs.*, VIII, 100. After the additional instruction of 1767, acts creating new counties, towns, or parishes in Virginia, South Carolina, and Jamaica were disallowed, as were also acts of West Florida and St. Christopher fixing the number of representatives.

ence: "He has refused to pass other laws for the accommodation of large districts of people, unless those people would relinquish the right of representation in the legislature, a right inestimable to them and formidable to tyrants only." In one sense the charge was hardly just. The instruction against which it was directed was not an expression of wilful tyranny. It was rather the outgrowth of a constitutional principle which seemed to the British officials both natural and right. The difficulty lay in the fact that the colonists had come to adopt a principle of government incompatible with the strict maintenance of the prerogative. Of this fact the responsible authorities in Great Britain seem hardly to have been aware. Or if they did perceive it, they failed entirely to admit its validity. In their instructions to the governors they continued to ignore it, emphasizing instead principles of the prerogative no longer workable in America and thus helping to widen the breach between the mother country and her colonies.

In spite of much which has been stated by political writers and speakers, the colonies were not democracies as the term is understood today. The principle of universal manhood suffrage seemed as undesirable to the great majority of colonial politicians as it did to the authorities in Great Britain. Nearly every one agreed that the right to vote or to sit in the assembly ought to be limited to freeholders—those who had a tangible stake in the community. For this reason the governor's instructions were usually silent on the qualifications necessary for voting or being elected. Those to the governors of some provinces—New Hampshire, Maryland, Virginia, the Carolinas, Bermuda, and Jamaica—required that the right to vote for members of the assembly should be extended to freeholders only. But the instructions for New Jersey alone specified the amount of property necessary for electors and elected.[35] At first the details of the suffrage franchise were usually left to the assembly.[36] British and American views on this question were in substantial agreement.

The home authorities were a little more strict in regard to laws establishing the qualifications of members of the assembly. Several such measures were permitted to stand, but a Jamaica act was disallowed in 1718 following an adverse report by Attorney General Northey. He condemned the law, partly because he considered that it fixed the minimum necessary estate too high, but chiefly "in regard that, as the assemblies subsist by her Majesty's commission and powers granted therein to the governor of that island, the qualifications of the assemblymen and also of their electors may be regulated in like manner by her Majesty as she shall think fit."[37] The Board of Trade and other British officials came to accept this view. Eventually additional instructions of 1767 to the governors of thirteen provinces forbade any acts fixing the qualifications of electors or elected.[38] In later years instructions modified the strictness of this rule in some prov-

[35] Instructions to Cornbury, New Jersey, 1702, art. 15, *N. J. Arch.*, II, 506. The provisions were modified by an additional instruction to Cornbury, Apr. 20, 1705, *ibid.*, III, 96. The clauses relating to the right to vote were dropped in 1708 in the instructions to Lovelace, art. 16, C.O. 5 : 994, pp. 355–406. On the general subject see A. E. McKinley, *The Suffrage Franchise in the Thirteen English Colonies in America* (Philadelphia, 1905).

[36] The Board of Trade went so far as to recommend the discontinuance in 1734 of the instructions to the governor of Jamaica requiring the limitation of the franchise to freeholders only, on the ground that this matter had been permanently provided for by provincial act. Representation on Cunningham's instructions, July 10, 1734, C.O. 138 : 17, pp. 420–421. This step was approved by order in council, Aug. 8, 1734, C.O. 5 : 196, p. 18 (L.C.); *Acts, Privy Coun., Col.*, 1720–1745, §303.

[37] Attorney General Northey's report on Jamaica acts of 1711–1712, July 22, 1714, C.O. 137 : 12, no. 63; Board of Trade representation, Oct. 23, 1717, C.O. 138 : 15, pp. 491–492; order in council disallowing the act, Feb. 9, 1718, C.O. 137 : 12, no. 119.

[38] Circular instruction, approved Aug. 26, 1767, *N. J. Arch.*, IX, 637–638.

inces by permitting measures which were approved by the king in draft form before passage or which contained suspending clauses. But in general during the last part of the period the home authorities took the position that the king ought to keep the control and regulation of the right to vote for assemblymen or to sit as a representative in his own hands as a part of his prerogative. As the assemblies grew in strength and importance, the British officials restricted more and more their control over their own organization.

Difficulties sometimes arose over the right of the governor to fix the place of meeting of the assembly. The commission and instructions rarely specified the town at which the legislature was to meet. The commission gave to the governor and council power to summon assemblies and to the chief executive alone full authority to adjourn, prorogue, and dissolve such bodies. From these clauses might be inferred the governor's right to fix not only the time of meeting but the place as well. On the other hand, the assembly could point to the clause which required the assembly to be summoned "in manner and form according to the custom and usage" of the province as prohibiting the governor from calling the assembly together at any but the customary spot. Contests took place over this matter in two provinces, New Jersey and Massachusetts, which deserve attention because each brought up a question of the greatest constitutional importance.

The instructions to the governors of New Jersey required the meeting of the assembly alternately at Perth Amboy in East Jersey and Burlington in West Jersey, although in cases of "extraordinary necessity" the governor might, with the advice of the council, select some other place.[39] Nothing appeared as to whether the as-

---

[39] Instructions to Cornbury, New Jersey, 1702, art. 14, *N. J. Arch.*, II, 506; instructions to Lovelace, New Jersey, 1708, art. 15, C.O. 5: 994, pp.

sembly might or might not legislate on the question. But in 1709 a political alliance between Lieutenant Governor Ingoldsby and the representatives of West Jersey resulted in an act requiring all future sessions to meet at Burlington.[40] When Governor Hunter arrived the next year he was perplexed over what to do. His instructions called for alternation between Perth Amboy and Burlington, but to obey them he would have to violate the act. Which was he to follow? His personal sympathies lay with the East Jersey faction, which fact was probably the real reason why he decided to obey the instruction. He called the next assembly to meet at Perth Amboy contrary to the provincial law. He explained his actions to the Board of Trade on the ground that the act in question clearly fell within that class of measures of "an unusual and extraordinary nature and importance" affecting the royal prerogative which all governors were forbidden to pass without suspending clauses or the previous consent of the crown. Since Ingoldsby had failed to comply with this rule in assenting to the measure, Hunter felt that the act was without force until confirmed.[41] As a matter of fact, the law had been approved and a copy of the order in council was on its way to Hunter at the very time.[42] The receipt of this order ended the difficulty for the time being and the governor gave way to the law. But Hunter was again placed in a dilemma in 1715 when the new instruc-

355–406. It will be noticed that the New Jersey instructions were unusually detailed in relation to the constitution of the assembly. This fact in general, and this instruction in particular, were due to an attempt to reconcile the two parts of the royal province which had formerly been distinct proprietary governments.

[40] S. Allinson, *Statutes of New Jersey*, p. 13; Tanner, *The Province of New Jersey, 1664–1738*, p. 325.

[41] Hunter to the Board of Trade, Oct. 3, 1710; May 7, 1711, *N. J. Arch.*, IV, 11–12, 67; *Cal. State Paps., Col.*, 1710–1711, §§ 414, 832.

[42] Board of Trade to Hunter, March 16, 1711, *Cal. State Paps., Col.*, 1710–1711, § 732.

tions issued by George I reached him containing the same old article requiring alternating sessions.[43] Could an instruction by a new monarch be considered as a valid suspension of a law confirmed by his predecessor? Hunter asked this question of the Board of Trade,[44] and then, without waiting for an answer, proceeded to act on the assumption that the instruction could suspend the act. He called the assembly to meet at Perth Amboy, but the West Jersey proprietors raised the cry, reminiscent of the days of James II in England, that the governor was dispensing with the laws. Hunter replied that the fixing of times and places for the meetings of parliaments and assemblies was "an undisputed part of the prerogative." Queen Anne had waived her rights in this case but she could not bind her successor to the same course.[45] But the Board of Trade could not support the governor. The act in question having been confirmed by the queen, they wrote, it could not legally be set aside by instructions, or, indeed, by any other agency than a new act of assembly expressly repealing the former law.[46] Hunter acted on this hint and secured the repeal of the obnoxious act in 1717.[47] The incident was thus satisfactorily closed. But the declaration of the Board of Trade that an act of a provincial assembly confirmed by the crown was superior to a royal instruction was of the utmost importance. This principle was the application to the provinces of the clauses in the Bill of Rights denying the right of the king to suspend or dispense with the laws. The recognition by

[43] Instructions to Hunter, New Jersey, 1717, art. 15, C.O. 5: 995, pp. 192–264.

[44] Hunter to the Board of Trade, Nov. 12, 1715, *N. J. Arch.*, IV, 222.

[45] Hunter to the Board of Trade, April 30, 1716, *ibid.*, pp. 230–232, 234.

[46] Board of Trade to Hunter, March 22, 1716, *ibid.*, p. 227.

[47] Hunter to the Board of Trade, Feb. 13, 1717, *ibid.*, p. 274; April 8, 1717, *ibid.*, p. 292; Allinson, *Statutes of New Jersey*, p. 41. The act was confirmed by the crown, Feb. 13, 1718, *Acts, Privy Coun., Col.*, 1680–1720, p. 849.

the royal authorities that colonial legislation confirmed by the king was entitled to the same immunity as an act of parliament, was perhaps the greatest single protection which the assemblies enjoyed against the king's prerogative.[48]

The controversy in Massachusetts over the meeting place of the legislature involved a different constitutional issue and grew out of different conditions. In contrast to the situation in New Jersey, no royal instrument—charter, commission, or instruction—specified where the Massachusetts general court, as the assembly was called, was to meet. A provincial act had been passed in 1698 governing the elections. This law prescribed the forms to be used in the writ of election, the sheriff's precept to the selectmen, and the constable's return of the results. In all these forms the words "Boston" or "Suffolk" had been used. The precept, for example, was headed "Suffolkshire," was to be signed by the sheriff of Suffolk, was addressed to the selectmen of Boston, and ordered them to warn the inhabitants of that town to elect their representatives. All these forms also referred to the assembly as summoned to meet in the townhouse of Boston.[49] When the controversy developed the representatives insisted that this mention of the townhouse of Boston obliged the governor to convene all assemblies there. The governor argued, however, that all the place-names were illustrative only,

---

[48] This principle of the validity of a colonial statute confirmed by the crown was more than once upheld by the law officers in England. Attorney General Northey informed the Board of Trade in 1703 that it would be impossible for Queen Anne to alter by proclamation a Massachusetts act for establishing the rates of foreign coins, "the passing of an act there with the absolute confirmation of her Majesty having the force of an act of parliament made in England." Northey to the Board of Trade, May 31, 1703, C.O. 324: 8, pp. 249–250 (L.C.). See also Attorney General Raymond's opinion on a Barbados case, Chalmers, *Opinions*, II, 1–2.

[49] *Mass. Acts and Res.*, I, 315–316.

and that the place of meeting mentioned in the precept might be as freely altered as the locality to which the document was addressed. The interpretation of this law was thus an important issue at the start.

The question arose in 1721 and again in 1728 but on neither occasion was a final settlement reached, although the attorney and solicitor general of Great Britain rendered an opinion supporting the governor's interpretation of the act in question.[50] But in 1769 a crisis developed. The presence of regular troops in Boston had led to such irritation that Governor Bernard deemed it wise to order the removal of the general court to Harvard College in Cambridge. A year before this Lord Hillsborough, secretary of state, had suggested that Bernard shift the assembly to Cambridge or Salem, in either of which places the representatives would be free from the "hazard of their lives" which threatened them in Boston so long as that town was "in the possession of a licentious and unrestrained mob."[51] But the assemblymen were evidently quite willing to take the risk for they objected strenuously to the removal. Bernard was firm, however, and on his departure for England, Lieutenant Governor Hutchinson loyally carried out his policy and Hillsborough's directions. Further orders from the secretary of state positively directed the lieutenant governor to hold the general court at Cambridge.[52] The Boston Massacre in the spring of 1770 and the general increase of opposition to the royal

[50] *Journal of Mass. House of Reps.*, III, 87; Hutchinson, *Hist. of Mass. Bay*, II (second edition), 266–267, 351–353; *Acts, Privy Coun., Col.*, 1720–1745, pp. 96–97.

[51] Hillsborough to Bernard, July 30, 1768, C.O. 5: 757, pp. 481–483 (Mass.).

[52] Hutchinson, *Hist. of Mass. Bay*, III, 280. The governor's own account of this controversy is given at length in this work (III, 236–357, *passim*). Naturally one must make allowances for the fact that the writer was one of the participants, yet his attempts to be fair are evident and his summaries of his opponents' arguments are reliable.

authority which marked the period destroyed the formerly conservative majority in the council and made that body distinctly hostile to the prerogative. Hutchinson and the two houses of the legislature carried on their dispute over the meeting place of the general court in a series of messages and addresses which soon passed far beyond the interpretation of the act of 1698.[53]

The arguments of both sides made it apparent that nothing less was at stake than the fundamental right of the king to instruct his governor and the latter's duty to obey the instructions. Hutchinson told the House of Representatives that he had convened them at Cambridge because he had been informed that such was the king's pleasure. He pointed out that his commission as lieutenant governor directed him to exercise all his powers "according to such instructions as are already sent, or hereafter shall from time to time be sent him" or such as he should receive from his Majesty.[54] A little later the council picked up the gauntlet. They called Hutchinson's attention to the wording of the charter which directed that the governor for the time being should have "full power and authority from time to time as he shall judge necessary, to adjourn, prorogue, and dissolve all great and general courts." This power was lodged wholly in the governor, to be exercised as he saw fit. It could not therefore be subject to instructions, said the council. This limitation was actually a privilege granted to the people of the province by the charter, for it assured them that

[53] Most of these messages and addresses are printed in appendices P-U, Hutchinson, *Hist. of Mass. Bay,* III, 502–544, and in Alden Bradford, *Speeches of the Governors of Massachusetts, from 1765–1775; and the Answers of the House of Representatives, to the Same* . . . (hereafter cited as Bradford, *Mass. State Paps.*).

[54] Hutchinson to the House of Representatives, April 26, 1770, Hutchinson, *Hist. of Mass. Bay,* III, 507; see his commission as lieutenant governor, 1761, Mass. Col. Soc., *Publ.,* II, 305–306.

the power would be exercised by a person already in the province and not by one three thousand miles away.[55] Hutchinson replied that, in any case, he had been merely using the power lodged in him by the charter when he summoned the assembly to meet at Cambridge, whether he was obeying instructions or not. He added that he had "not the least doubt of the right of the crown to control the governor by instructions or other signification of the royal pleasure."[56] Later he told both houses that regardless of the provision in the charter for a governor, his own power to exercise that office was derived from his commission, by the terms of which, as he said, "instructions relative to any matter not unconstitutional must be obligatory" upon him.[57]

In reply to this speech the House of Representatives presented a lengthy address undoubtedly the work of Samuel Adams. The most significant parts of this paper dealt with the right of the people and their representatives "to withstand the abusive exercise of a legal and constitutional prerogative of the crown." The author quoted Locke to show that a body of people have the right to "appeal to heaven" against the authorities in power should the latter "design or go about to enslave or destroy them." In spite of this implied threat of revolution, the paper added that the representatives did not wish to be "understood to suggest that this people have occasion at present to proceed to such extremity." Yet they held "that whenever instructions cannot be complied with, without injuring the people, they cease to be binding."

[55] Council to Hutchinson, June 12, 1770, Hutchinson, *Hist. of Mass. Bay*, III, 517–521; Bradford, *Mass. State Paps.*, pp. 223–226.

[56] Hutchinson to the council, June 15, 1770, Hutchinson, *Hist. of Mass. Bay*, III, 521–522; Bradford, *Mass. State Paps.*, pp. 227–228.

[57] Hutchinson to the council and House of Representatives, July 25, 1770, Hutchinson, *Hist. of Mass. Bay*, III, 522–525; Bradford, *Mass. State Paps.*, pp. 237–240.

The governor should have no fear that the representatives would "except to the proper use of the prerogative," which they deemed as sacred as the liberty of the subject. But they would always take exception to every abuse of it "so long as the love of liberty or any public virtue remains."[58] The protestations of loyalty which appear now and then throughout this paper detract nothing from the fact that it represents on the whole one of the most daring attacks upon the prerogative before the outbreak of the Revolution.

The speeches and letters which followed added nothing to the arguments of either side, but the controversy continued for three years. Hillsborough appreciated the governor's difficulty in fighting the assembly without local support. He wrote to Hutchinson that the situation was one "which among many others shows the necessity for an interposition of the authority of parliament."[59] All through these years the British officials were realizing more and more clearly that the prerogative was losing ground and could be maintained only with the help of the British legislature. In 1772 Hutchinson effected a compromise and returned the general court to Boston in response to a resolution which did not directly call in question the king's right to instruct his governor about the meeting place of the legislature.[60] But when parliament interposed two years later and passed the Boston Port Act and the Massachusetts Government Act, Secretary of State Dartmouth ordered the removal of the general court to Salem in keeping with the intent of the former meas-

[58] House of Representatives to Hutchinson, July 31, 1770, Hutchinson, *Hist. of Mass. Bay*, III, 525–534; Bradford, *Mass. State Paps.*, pp. 240–248. The latter gives the date as August 1.

[59] Hillsborough to Hutchinson, July 31, 1770, C.O. 5: 765, pp. 178–181 (Mass.).

[60] Hutchinson, *Hist. of Mass. Bay*, III, 348, 356–357.

ure.[61] The representatives protested again but without result. This dispute, along with many others, was soon made the subject of that "appeal to heaven" which Samuel Adams and the House of Representatives had hinted at a few years before.

The position taken by the general court in this contest marks the high point of colonial opposition to the prerogative as expressed in the governor's commission and instructions. The threat of revolution was important, but at least equally significant was a further point which Samuel Adams implied in his argument. Hitherto no one had ventured to deny the right of the king to instruct his governor within the limits of the constitution or to question the governor's duty to obey such instructions. But Adams dared to enter upon this forbidden ground. Instructions which were injurious to the people were not binding, he said, adding, in effect, that it made no difference whether such orders were legal and constitutional or not. Therefore the governor must not be permitted to obey them. From this position the conclusion seems inescapable, although Adams avoided its frank declaration, that the assembly and not the governor must be the interpreters of such documents and the judges of whether or not they constituted an "abusive exercise" of the prerogative. To have permitted such a privilege to the assembly would have meant that the British government had abandoned its fundamental claim to authority in America and had delegated to the assembly the sole right of controlling the provincial executive. No more sweeping challenge than this was made to the system of royal government in the provinces before the actual expulsion of the governors upon the outbreak of the Revolution. And so, though the meeting-place of the assembly was not in itself a vital point in the colonial system, it gave rise to contro-

[61] Dartmouth to Gage, April 9, 1774, C.O. 5: 765, pp. 298–307 (Mass.).

versies which went to the heart of the provincial constitution.

A further series of disputes between governors and assemblies grew out of the selection of the speaker. Here again the instructions rarely prescribed the exact procedure to be followed. In accordance with the practice of the House of Commons, the representatives regularly chose a speaker at the first organization of a new assembly and presented him to the governor for approval. Here came the difficulty. The lower house often contended that this approval was a mere formality and that the chief executive had no right to negative the choice of the house. The governor, however, maintained that his discretion was very real and that no speaker was legally elected until admitted as such by the king's representative. Such an opinion was based on the words of the commission which gave the governor a negative voice ''in the making and passing of all laws, statutes, and ordinances,'' and on the analogous prerogative of the king to approve or disapprove of the speaker selected by the House of Commons. Neither of these arguments can stand very close inspection. To infer that the vote of the lower house of assembly in choosing a speaker constituted a law, statute, or ordinance within the literal meaning of the commission would require a considerable stretch of language. As regards the British precedent, the colonists were not slow to point out that the royal approval had actually become a mere formality. So far as the records show, only once, in 1679 had a speaker duly elected by the House of Commons been rejected by the crown.[62] The rejection of an assembly's choice of a speaker by a governor was clearly an attempt

[62] Cobbett, *Parliamentary History*, IV, 1092–1113, Anchitell Grey, *Debates in the House of Commons*, VI, 402–439. See Josef Redlich, *The Procedure of the House of Commons*, II, 162–163. True, the privy council always told the Commons whom to choose and the members always obeyed, but with this one exception the king never personally interfered on his authority alone.

to retain in American affairs a prerogative which had remained practically unused in the mother country. But this method of controlling the legislature was widely employed in the colonies. After a controversy in Massachusetts in 1705 the Board of Trade formally approved Governor Dudley's persistence in using this prerogative.[63] The renewal of the dispute in Shute's administration brought about the passage of a new or "explanatory" charter in 1725, specifically asserting the governor's right to disapprove of the speaker presented to him by the House of Representatives.[64] Similar contests in other provinces arose from time to time, in all of which the home officials upheld the governors. The British government insisted on the rights of the king in this matter.

The Bermuda and Barbados assemblies developed customs relative to the choice of the speaker which differed widely from the practice of the House of Commons. In Bermuda, instead of naming a presiding officer to serve throughout the life of the assembly, the lower house chose a new speaker at the beginning of every fourth session. The votes of a majority of the whole number of representatives were necessary for a choice and when illness or absence from the island kept several members away, business was reduced to a standstill for want of a speaker.[65] For this reason and because the custom differed so radically from that of the House of Commons, Governor Popple received an instruction in 1755 directing that a speaker was to be elected at the first meeting of each new assembly and was to hold office during all its sessions unless his death or legal incapacity necessitated another

[63] Board of Trade to Dudley, Feb. 4, 1706, C.O. 5: 912, pp. 114–124 (Mass.).

[64] Thorpe, *American Charters, Constitutions, and Other Organic Laws*, III, 1886–1888; *Acts, Privy Coun., Col.*, 1720–1745, pp. 94–95, 103.

[65] Francis Jones, president of the Bermuda council, to the Board of Trade, Nov. 13, 1754, C.O. 37: 18 (unpaged).

choice.[66] Although the governor's right to approve or disapprove of the assembly's candidate did not enter into the question, the incident is striking because it illustrates the demand of the home authorities that the provincial assemblies follow the procedure of the "mother of parliaments" at the same time that they were supporting the governors in maintaining a prerogative control over the speakership which was not exercised by the king over the House of Commons.

The Barbados assembly also elected its speaker every three months or at every fourth sitting. They presented him to the governor at the beginning of a new assembly but did not bother to do so on subsequent occasions when the same man was usually reelected. By 1727 the assembly had found a way occasionally to avoid submitting the choice of a new man to the governor. Their method was simply to name a speaker *pro tempore* for one meeting at a time without consulting the governor, whenever the regular speaker was absent.[67] No governor seems to have objected to this procedure until 1727 when Governor Worsley told the assembly that they must present their temporary choice for his approval. The lower house demurred but complied with the governor's directions, since the point he insisted on was "rather a matter of form and ceremony than any real substance."[68] Worsley's report on this matter led the Board of Trade to introduce an article into his general instructions the following year which characterized the assembly's former procedure as "very derogatory to our royal prerogative." The instruction prohibited the assembly from entering upon any

[66] Instructions to William Popple, Bermuda, 1755, art. 12, C.O. 38: 9, pp. 52–144.

[67] Henry Worsley to the Board of Trade, Aug. 4, 1727, C.O. 28: 19, fos. 5–9.

[68] Worsley to the Board of Trade, Aug. 15, 1727, *ibid.*, fos. 15–17; assembly minutes, Aug. 8, 1727, *ibid.*, fos. 21–23, 117–120.

business until the governor had approved of their presiding officer.[69] In 1746, eighteen years later, the assembly discovered that the governor's approval was more than "a matter of form and ceremony" when Sir Thomas Robinson rejected the choice of one of his worst enemies as speaker.[70] Following this incident the governor and council had two articles of the general instructions dealing with the assembly's privileges and the approval of the speaker printed in the *Barbados Gazette*. These were followed by a half-column account of the rejection by Charles II of Sir Edward Seymour as speaker of the Commons in 1679.[71]

An anonymous newspaper discussion followed. One writer cited historical authority to prove that the Seymour incident had actually established the mere formality of the king's approval of the speaker.[72] Another correspondent declared: "I should be sorry to hear that any man under the present administration could publicly declare to commend the popish and arbitrary advice which was given King Charles in those days, since it ought rather and will no doubt be mentioned with abhorrence by all that love the Protestant religion and wish well to the just liberties of their country."[73] No doubt the recent Jacobite uprising in Scotland accounts for the fact that nearly every writer extolled Seymour as the champion of Protestantism against the Roman Catholic supporters of

[69] Instructions to Worsley, Barbados, 1728, art. 22, C.O. 5: 191, pp. 374–431 (L.C.). The instruction was repeated to all subsequent governors of the island.

[70] Sir Thomas Robinson to the Board of Trade, Oct. 7, 1746, Dec. 4, 1746, C.O. 28: 27 (unpaged).

[71] *Barbados Gazette*, Oct. 1–4, 1746 (no. 517). Copies of this issue and those for Oct. 4–11 (no. 518), Nov. 5–8 (no. 524), and Nov. 12–15 (no. 526) were sent home by Worsley and are preserved as appendices C, D, E, and F to the letter of Dec. 4, 1746, cited in the last note above (C.O. 28: 27).

[72] *Barbados Gazette*, Oct. 4–11 (no. 518).

[73] *Ibid.*, Nov. 5–8 (no. 524).

the prerogative. The general opinion was perhaps best summed up by the contributor who pointed out that no speaker of the House of Commons had been rejected since the Revolution of 1689 and added: "I hope Revolution principles will always prevail and be strictly adhered to, which will preserve our excellent constitution."[74] These letters show most clearly the general belief in the colonies that parliament's victories over the royal prerogative in the last part of the seventeenth century ought of right to be shared by the assemblies. "Revolution principles"— freedom of the legislature from royal dictation—ought to dominate the provincial constitution as they did that of Great Britain herself. The home authorities were willing to apply this theory to a few matters such as the right of the colonists to be taxed by a legislative body only, and the illegality of the suspending and dispensing power. But in most questions, such as the extension of representation to new places and the approval of the speaker, the officials in England, themselves descendants of the leaders in 1689, insisted that the royal prerogative ought to continue in full force in the colonies. And so the constitutional struggles of the mother country were repeated in the royal provinces, each assembly striving against governors and ministers to gain that same supremacy over the prerogative which parliament had won in England.

When the speaker of the assembly had received the approval of the governor, he regularly asked that he and the assembly might have the usual privileges. These normally included such points as freedom of access to the governor's person, freedom of debate and vote in assembly, and freedom from arrest during term-time. This procedure, reflecting as it did the practice of the speaker of the House of Commons, illustrates again the extent to which the assemblies asserted the same rights as parliament. The

[74] *Ibid.*, Oct. 4–11 (no. 518).

Massachusetts assembly once expressed the common attitude when they declared, although in connection with another matter, that "this house has the same inherent rights in this province, as the House of Commons has in Great Britain."[75] In granting the speaker's request for privileges the governor sometimes had instructions to guide him. Such directions usually dealt only with the exemption of the assemblymen from arrest and from suits at law during the time the legislature was in session. The British officials recognized that the members of a legislative body ought not to be hindered in their attendance if that body was to do its work efficiently. They insisted, however, that such freedom as the assemblymen might have was a privilege granted by the king and not an inherent right, and further that it should not be permitted to defeat the ends of justice.

During the latter part of the seventeenth century and the first part of the eighteenth, the assemblymen of several provinces showed a disposition to abuse the privilege of freedom from suits at law. The situation became particularly serious in Jamaica. In 1713 Robert Saunders, an inhabitant of that island, petitioned the king for redress against Gersham Elye, a member of the assembly. According to Saunders, his wife inherited a plantation in 1708 at a time when the couple were in England. Before they could return Elye took possession, entirely without right. While Saunders was preparing to bring suit the usurper had himself elected to the assembly, and by his claim of parliamentary privilege prevented the case from coming to trial. Saunders was forced to leave the island to make a living and before he could return his wife and child

[75] Massachusetts House of Representatives to Hutchinson, July 31, 1770, Hutchinson, *Hist. of Mass. Bay*, III, 532; Bradford, *Mass. State Paps.*, pp. 246–247.

died of want.[76] The privy council committee referred this
pitiful case to the Board of Trade for report upon the
privileges of the Jamaica assembly. The board examined
the Jamaica planters then in London who informed them
that no court in the island would take cognizance of any
suit where the defendant claimed parliamentary privilege.
Apparently, such privilege was not limited to the periods
when the assembly was actually in session, but was construed as protecting the representatives during the entire
life of the assembly. Since the present body had been in
existence for five years, the grievances of the merchants
and other creditors were real and serious.[77] In reporting
on the matter the Board of Trade declared: ''The members of the assembly not only of Jamaica, but of the other
plantations also, do assume pretended rights and privileges (for which we cannot find the least grounds) tending
to an independency on the crown of Great Britain. . . .
Most of the assemblies in the plantations claim all the
privileges the House of Commons here does, and some of
them, others that the House of Commons never pretended
to.'' In the particular case before them, the board continued, they saw no reason for Elye's avoiding suit by
pretence of privilege, nor could they find by examination
of their books that the governors had any authority by
their commissions or instructions to allow such privilege.[78]
This report led to an order in council authorizing Saunders to bring suit against Elye without obstruction and

[76] Petition of Robert Saunders to the king, annexed to an order of reference by the privy council committee to the Board of Trade, May 22, 1713,
C.O. 138: 13, pp. 424–427; *Cal. State Paps., Col.*, 1712–1714, § 348.

[77] *Board of Trade Journal*, 1708/9–1714/5, p. 431. The last assembly had
been dissolved by Governor Handasyd in 1708. Handasyd to the Board of
Trade, March 31, 1708, C.O. 137: 8, no. 9; *Cal. State Paps., Col.*, 1706–1708,
§ 1423.

[78] Board of Trade to privy council committee, May 28, 1713, C.O. 138: 13,
pp. 428–430; *Cal. State Paps., Col.*, 1712–1714, § 352.

directing that no such claim of privilege as had delayed this case be admitted in the future.[79] Further information on the outcome of Saunders' suit would be welcome, but the record is silent.

However, the question of privilege in Jamaica was not yet settled. Disputes continued so that an instruction on the matter became necessary in 1718. This forbade Governor Lawes to allow the members of the council and assembly any "pretended privilege" of protection from suits at law or freedom from other judicial process except exemption from personal arrest.[80] The governor told the assembly of this rule in his first speech after assuming office, whereupon the lower house dutifully resolved "that no member of this assembly ought to insist on any privilege against suits."[81] The instruction was continued without change to the governors of Jamaica for many years. A somewhat similar instruction was sent to the governors of many other provinces.[82] But in Jamaica neither the royal orders nor the assembly's self-denying resolution were strictly enforced. As in England, the members asserted that the protection of their persons from arrest should be extended to include their servants and belongings. In 1766, after a bitter dispute over the attachment of the coach horses of one assemblyman, the governor received an additional instruction which authorized him

[79] *Acts, Privy Coun., Col.*, 1680–1720, § 1184.

[80] Instructions to Lawes, Jamaica, 1718, art. 100, C.O. 5: 189, pp. 334–375 (L.C.).

[81] Jamaica assembly minutes, Aug. 19, 1718, C.O. 137: 13, no. 16 ii.

[82] The provinces to which the instruction was sent, together with the date when the articles first appeared in the instructions, are: South Carolina, 1720; Virginia, 1727; Bahamas, 1729; North Carolina, 1730; New Hampshire, 1761; East Florida, West Florida, Grenada, Quebec, 1763; Dominica, 1770; St. Vincent, 1776. It was also given to the governor of Nova Scotia in 1756 but was not repeated. In the instructions for all these provinces, except Virginia prior to 1756 and the Bahamas, the exemption from personal arrest was limited to the actual sessions of the assembly.

to grant exemption from seizure for six days before and after each session of the assembly for such servants and equipage as were "absolutely necessary for the personal accommodation" of the members, provided that each member should deposit with the provost marshal general a list of the persons and property for which he claimed exemption.[83] A fair compromise seems thus to have been finally reached.

The subject of parliamentary privilege is vital to the study of the development of self-government in America. The claims put forward by the assemblies show more clearly than anything else the growing self-consciousness of these legislative bodies and their feeling of equality with the parliament of Great Britain.[84] But for the study of royal government in America, the major interest lies in the attitude of the home officials. They recognized the necessity of granting some immunities to the provincial assemblymen, but they rejected utterly the idea that these belonged to the representatives by natural right. They could not agree that the assemblies were parliaments in miniature. The legislatures had been created by act of the prerogative and their members held their privileges only by royal grace and favor. Whatever the concessions which the British officials were willing to make, they failed to satisfy the American point of view.

Through most of the eighteenth century the instructions were as emphatic upon the question of self-adjournment by the assemblies as they were upon that of personal privilege. Nearly every governor of the eighteenth century received by his commission the sole right of adjourn-

[83] Additional instructions to Lyttelton, Jamaica, submitted June 3, 1766, C.O. 138: 22, pp. 334–336.

[84] Miss Mary P. Clarke is now engaged upon an extensive treatise dealing with parliamentary privilege in the colonies. The anticipated publication of her work in the near future makes unnecessary any further discussion here.

ing the assembly.[85] But common sense dictated that in the case of day-to-day adjournments the assembly should act on its own initiative. No one objected to this practice. But inevitably the assemblies of some provinces came to assert the right to adjourn themselves for as long a time as they pleased. Again Jamaica was the scene of the critical struggle. Although some earlier governors had complained, the Board of Trade did not seriously investigate the situation until 1716. Then, in response to a memorial from Thomas Pitt, recently appointed governor, asking for certain instructions, the board prepared a long report giving many extracts from the council minutes and assembly journals on the points involved. These quotations showed that until 1705 the assembly had never asserted the right to adjourn themselves for longer than over Sunday without first asking the governor's permission. But in 1706, after Governor Handasyd had refused to allow them to adjourn for a month, they had declared that it was "the privilege of the assembly to adjourn itself." The governor replied denying their assertion. He added that he remembered "some passages of the like being attempted in the year 1641 or thereabouts by a party of barbarous people who took off the head of Charles the Martyr of ever blessed memory, to the great disgrace of the English nation." The question came up again now and then during the next seven years but without becoming a serious issue. In February, 1714, the assembly asked leave to adjourn for a month but Governor Hamilton refused permission since the legislation they had been summoned to pass remained unfinished. The assembly thereupon resolved that in their opinion it was "the undoubted right of this house to adjourn themselves when and as

[85] The very early commissions gave the governors only the right to "dissolve" assemblies; later the word "prorogue" was added; and from about 1702 on the word "adjourn" was almost always included as well.

often as they think fitting'' and promptly adjourned for a
month. Then Hamilton as promptly dissolved the assembly. Such was the state of affairs when the Board of
Trade rendered its report.[86] Eleven men, apparently merchants and planters then in London, presented a memorial
in defence of the assembly. They offered various arguments in favor of the assembly's action, including the importance of the season to the sugar industry and the alleged precedents of forty years before. They hoped the
assembly's action would not be styled undutiful, ''and the
less so that it is humbly apprehended to be warranted by
their charters of government, whose constant language
has successively directed that the laws and usage of the
assemblies of that island are to be assimilated to the laws
and usage in England; and if it be the right of the Commons of Great Britain to adjourn longer than from day
to day, it seems to be the original intent of the crown as
well to grant such a liberty to that little body of freemen,
as it does in general to institute the legislative power of
the island in the nature of an epitome of the English
parliament. For should it be the misfortune of the island
to be lopped of that privilege they become subject to the
pleasure of a governor and in consequence are deprived
of the freedom of Englishmen.''[87]

But the argument that the assembly ought to be ''in the
nature of an epitome of the English parliament'' ap-
pealed not at all to the Board of Trade. When they pre-

[86] This report, dated, Dec. 19, 1716, is given in C.O. 138: 15, 59–60, 67–130.
Letters from the governors referring to this dispute include: Handasyd to
the Board of Trade, Dec. 27, 1706; March 8, 1707; March 31, 1708; July 16,
1711; C.O. 137: 7, nos. 36, 42; C.O. 137: 8, no. 9; C.O. 137: 9, no. 44; *Cal.
State Paps., Col.*, 1706–1708, §§ 678, 794, 1423; 1711–1712, § 18; Hamilton
to the Board of Trade, Aug. 29, 1711; March 22, 1714; C.O. 137: 9, no. 48;
C.O. 137: 10, no. 51; *Cal. State Paps., Col.*, 1711–1712, § 82; 1712–1714,
§ 615.

[87] ''Memorial in vindication of the island of Jamaica and the assembly
thereof'' [1715?], C.O. 137: 11, no. 12.

pared instructions for Sir Nicholas Lawes, appointed governor on Pitt's resignation, they added an article forbidding the assembly to adjourn for longer than from day to day or over Sundays and holidays without first getting the governor's consent.[88] This instruction was repeated to all subsequent governors and was later extended to most of the other royal provinces.[89] The same result was obtained in Massachusetts by the addition of a clause in the explanatory charter of 1725. Both Lawes in Jamaica and other governors elsewhere had some difficulty in forcing the assemblies to accept this limitation upon their self-regulation, but complaints on this score tended to subside as other more important issues arose.[90]

Following English precedent, the lower house could lay some claim to the right of self-adjournment, but they could never successfully challenge the governor's sole right to dissolve the assembly. This power, granted in the commission, was one of the most important weapons which the king's representative retained over the popular body. Again and again in all the provinces the governors exercised this prerogative in order to punish an unyielding opposition. Now and then, a governor would dissolve a new assembly almost upon its first meeting if the administration party was in a small minority. The attitude which the colonies took toward this practice is shown in the Declaration of Independence. Among the charges against the royal master of the later governors are these:

[88] Instructions to Lawes, Jamaica, 1718, art. 95, C.O. 5: 189, pp. 334–375 (L.C.).

[89] Instructions to this effect were first sent in the following years: South Carolina, 1720; Virginia, 1727; Barbados, 1728; Bahamas, 1729; North Carolina, 1730; New Hampshire, 1761; East and West Florida, Grenada, Quebec, 1763; Dominica, 1770; St. Vincent, 1776.

[90] Lawes to the Board of Trade, Jan. 31, 1719, C.O. 137: 13, no. 29; Worsley, Barbados, to the Board of Trade, Dec. 10, 16, 1728, C.O. 28: 20, fos. 124, 127.

"He has dissolved representative houses repeatedly for opposing with manly firmness his invasions of the rights of the people. He has refused for a long time after such dissolutions to cause others to be elected; whereby the legislative powers, incapable of annihilation, have returned to the people at large for their exercise; the state remaining in the meantime exposed to all the dangers of invasion from without and convulsions within." That the governors had repeatedly dissolved the assemblies and had occasionally failed to summon new ones for some time afterward was a fact which the British authorities would readily have admitted. But to their minds the representatives had not shown "manly firmness" in opposing the king's "invasions" of the people's rights, but a "spirit of faction" and undutiful opposition to the rightful prerogative of the crown. And the idea that legislative powers could ever legally "have returned to the people at large for their exercise" was so utterly at variance with the principle of government by royal grace and favor as to be quite beyond discussion. To the minds of the British officials, the improper acts had been those of the assemblies themselves and not those of the king or his governors.

The governor's right to dissolve the assembly had another aspect. Just as he was often ready to end the life of a body of men hostile to himself and the interests which he served, so was he ready and anxious to prolong the life of a legislature willing to cooperate with him. Here again the power of extending or terminating the existence of an assembly rested in his hands alone. But the assemblies had before them the example of the British parliament in passing the Triennial Act of 1694 and the Septennial Act of 1716.[91] The representatives did not care to permit an American counterpart of the seventeen-year-

91 6 & 7 William and Mary, c. 2; 1 George I, stat. 2, c. 38.

long Cavalier Parliament of Charles II. Consequently, a
number of assemblies passed acts requiring automatic
dissolution, usually at the end of three years. But any
such limitation of the governor's discretion was a clear
encroachment upon the prerogative and was not to be
tolerated for a moment. There were three exceptions.
Barbados passed an act for annual assemblies in 1660
which the Board of Trade later termed "a good and useful law to the island." Because this law was in force a
triennial act of 1706 was disallowed.[92] In South Carolina
the situation was reversed and an act of 1745 which provided for annual assemblies was disallowed, partly because it repealed a clause in an act of 1721 establishing the
triennial system.[93] Both the original measures of Barbados and South Carolina were passed at times when
royal government had not been fully established in those
provinces. But a New Hampshire triennial act passed in
1728 after almost half a century of royal government
there was allowed to stand for unknown reasons.[94] On the
other hand, the British officials showed their more usual
attitude by disallowing acts limiting the duration of the
assemblies of New Jersey, North Carolina, New York,
and Jamaica between the years 1731 and 1752,[95] and by
issuing an additional instruction in 1767 in which they
forbade such measures in any of the thirteen provinces
to which it was sent.[96] Later, Nova Scotia and Bermuda

[92] Board of Trade to the queen, Nov. 22, 1706, C.O. 29: 10, pp. 354–355;
Cal. State Paps., Col., 1706–1708, § 624. The act of 1706 was disallowed by
order in council, Jan 2, 1707, C.O. 29: 10, pp. 390–391; Acts, Privy Coun.,
Col., 1680–1720, p. 829.

[93] Board of Trade to the king, Aug. 13, 1747, C.O. 5: 402, pp. 136–138;
Acts, Privy Coun., Col., 1745–1766, § 67.

[94] N. H. Prov. Paps., IV, 288, 294, 489, 492; N. H. Prov. Laws, II, 402.

[95] Acts, Privy Coun., Col., 1720–1745, §§ 242, 410, 449; 1745–1766, § 114.

[96] Circular instruction to the governors of Nova Scotia, New Hampshire,
New York, New Jersey, Virginia, West Florida, Jamaica, Grenada, Bermuda,
Leeward Islands, Barbados, Bahamas, South Carolina, approved Aug. 26,

passed acts regulating the life of the assemblies, both of
which the privy council emphatically rejected.[97] The
reason advanced for all these disallowances was the usual
one, that the assembly had no right to regulate itself in
this way. As the privy council committee reported in the
New Jersey case, such an act "appears to be of a very
extraordinary nature, for assemblies being thereby made
triennial, a very great change is created in the constitution of the province of New Jersey, which, if it should
have been thought proper to be made, ought to have taken
its rise from the royal authority, which first gave being
to the form of government established there, and not from
the assembly of that province."[98] To similar arguments
the Board of Trade added in the Jamaica case the extraordinary statement that "the limiting the duration of
assemblies to short periods and fixing their determination
by law, manifestly tends to the discouragement of industry and the prejudice of trade, destroys good neighbor-
hood, keeps up ill blood, nourishes a spirit of party divisions, and gives faction an opportunity to act with better
concert and to greater effect." The board was convinced
from "the experience of the bad effects of such acts" in
the few provinces where they were in force, that "a law
for fixing one invariable rule for the determination of
assemblies" was wholly undesirable.[99] But parliament
had passed laws "fixing one invariable rule" for its own
termination in exactly the same way that the assemblies
proposed, and the Board of Trade and privy council
would hardly have admitted that their effects were equally
disastrous. Nothing shows better how firmly convinced

1767, *N. J. Arch.*, IX, 637–638. This instruction also forbade the assemblies
to increase their numbers or to fix the qualifications of electors or elected.
See above, pp. 186, 189.

[97] *Acts, Privy Coun., Col.*, 1766–1783, §§ 397, 441.

[98] *Ibid.*, 1720–1745, § 242.   [99] *Ibid.*, 1745–1766, § 114.

these officials were that the assemblies could not safely be permitted to enjoy the same privileges as parliament. The British policy toward the assembly was inconsistent. The commissions and instructions provided for a legislature built on the pattern of parliament. Governor, council, and elective house took the place of king, lords, and commons. In form of organization and procedure the British officials strove, both consciously and unconsciously, to recreate the parliamentary system in America. They so far succeeded that as early as 1683 Governor Lynch of Jamaica could truthfully write that the king had "constituted assemblies that are umbras of an English parliament."[100] In form the provincial assembly was not an English municipal council but a parliament. But here the British policy stopped. The assembly was to have the form of parliament but not its powers. The authorities would not permit the provincial legislature to exercise the same control over its own constitution or the same law-making powers which parliament exercised in Great Britain. In such matters it was to be deemed not a parliament but merely a municipal council. So when the St. Christopher assembly passed a resolution affecting its own composition, the British officials declared that the House of Representatives had "corrupted its own constitution by affecting a power which they have not, analogous and coequal to that of the House of Commons in Great Britain."[101] The Board of Trade and privy council could not forget that the assembly had "no right to meet or debate upon any matters whatsoever but by virtue of a clause in [the royal] commission under the great seal of this kingdom, without which they could not be elected or sit

[100] "The State of Jamaica under Sir Thomas Lynch, His Majesty's Present Captain General and Chief Governor," Sept. 20, 1683, C.O. 138: 4, pp. 215–216.

[101] *Acts, Privy Coun., Col.*, 1766–1783, p. 278; additional instructions to Payne, Leeward Islands, July 1, 1772, C.O. 5: 27, pp. 251–252 (L.C.).

as an assembly.''[102] The legislature was created by the king's prerogative. Its membership, its place of meeting, its speaker, its privileges, its adjournment, and its final dissolution should be regulated by the prerogative alone. Whatever position the assembly held in the provincial constitution came from the king's grace and favor and need bear no relation to the position of the House of Commons in Great Britain.

The assemblymen failed to appreciate this reasoning. If the legislature was modeled on parliament and was required to follow parliamentary precedent in details of organization and procedure, they felt that it ought to have the same freedom from restriction. If, contrary to local custom, the speaker in Bermuda and Barbados must hold office throughout an assembly's life because such was the British practice, then the speaker's confirmation by the king's representative ought to follow his election as a matter of course, as it did in the House of Commons. If the provinces were at all entitled to representative institutions, as the British officials admitted they were, and if those institutions were copied from the forms of parliament rather than from those of a municipal council, the colonists felt that they were entitled to the same rights as parliament, which in the eighteenth century were no longer dependent on the royal grace and favor. The fact that their assemblies were ''umbras of an English parliament'' strengthened enormously the colonists' claim to legislative independence.

The British policy brought about its own undoing. By insisting that the assembly adopt the forms of parliament, the authorities taught the colonists to look upon it as a miniature parliament. But by asserting and reasserting

---

[102] Instructions to Lawes, Jamaica, 1718, art. 96, C.O. 5: 189, pp. 344–375 (L.C.). The instruction containing this clause was repeated to all subsequent Jamaica governors.

that the assembly's privileges and powers were dependent upon the king's prerogative, they led the representatives to feel that the prerogative was the great enemy of their rights. Everyone knew the attitude which parliament had repeatedly taken toward the royal authority during the seventeenth century. Nothing, then, could be more natural and inevitable than that the assembly, following the example of the House of Commons, should use every occasion to strengthen its own position at the expense of the crown. Good precedent the colonists had for such a policy —precedent by which the very officials they opposed in England had benefited. Nor were occasions lacking. Every phase of assembly organization and nearly every subject of legislation gave opportunity for attack upon the prerogative. But the British authorities could not afford to let the prerogative be weakened. They realized that the authority of the king was the basis of their political control over the colonies. If the prerogative should be abridged in America as it had been in England, then the whole colonial system would be endangered unless, as a last resort, parliament should interfere. Yet in spite of all that the Board of Trade and the ministers in England and the governors in America could do, they had to admit that the royal power was seriously threatened in the provinces. They declared that each fresh advance of the assemblies was "an innovation and encroachment upon his Majesty's prerogative and derogatory of the authority of the crown, the securing and supporting which in his Majesty's colonies and plantations is become every day the more necessary by frequent unwarrantable attempts made to diminish it."[103] Their policy, therefore, became one of increasing severity as the assemblies grew steadily stronger.

[103] Board of Trade representation on the Jamaica triennial act of 1741, June 16, 1752, *Acts, Privy Coun., Col.*, 1745–1766, p. 90.

Under these conditions no agreement could be reached as to the status of the assembly. The contest went on, becoming more and more serious and bitter, until after 1763, the British officials felt that parliament must be called upon to intervene on behalf of the royal authority. But by that time the assemblies had come to consider themselves so entirely as local parliaments, coordinate in status with the parliament of Great Britain, that interference in their affairs by a so-called supreme legislature was intolerable to them. Thereafter, the final crisis could not be long postponed.

CHAPTER VI

LEGISLATION

ACCORDING to the British theory the representatives had no "inherent right" to engage in the business of making laws. The assembly's legislative powers came entirely from the king and were conferred through that all-important document, the governor's commission. This instrument made the original grant of legislative power and briefly outlined the process by which a bill might become a law. The commission empowered the governor, by and with the advice and consent of the council and assembly, "to make, constitute, and ordain laws, statutes, and ordinances for the public peace, welfare, and good government" of the province. The governor's signature turned the bill into law, and he had an absolute veto over all measures which passed the other two branches of the legislature. He was required to transmit all acts to the king within three months after passage. If the king in council should reject any measure, previously unconfirmed, it became null and void immediately after the governor had received notice of the disallowance. But until the king did so reject the measure, or after it had received his formal approval, the British officials recognized it as valid. In the brief clauses of the commission which outlined these points lay the authority for all provincial legislation.

But British interest in the matter did not stop with the mere drafting of the commission. Since the crown made its contacts with the assembly through the person of the governor, that official had to see to the passing of such laws, and such laws only, as the king's advisors might desire. So the instructions on this subject were also of the greatest importance. The Lords of Trade and their successors, the Board of Trade, spent much time and thought in preparing and revising these instructions and then insisted that the governors observe them literally. No parts of the general instructions were more important to British minds than the articles which dealt with legislation.

But the attempt to control the assembly by means of instructions to the governor had one serious drawback. In spite of the phraseology of the commission, it was the governor who consented to the bills which the other two houses proposed, and not the council and assembly who advised and consented to the governor's measures. The very nature of a representative assembly, popularly elected, made impossible any direct coercion of the legislature by the executive. As the king's representative, the governor was an important part of the legislature, but, after all, he had very little to do with bills until they had been passed by the council and assembly and then he could only accept or reject them as they stood. So the instructions could be, on the one hand, only recommendatory, or on the other, purely negative. That is, the governor might be told to urge the assembly to pass certain laws, using his power to prorogue or dissolve that body if it disobeyed, or he might be directed to refuse his assent to objectionable bills. But, in either case, the real initiative rested with the assembly. From the British point of view, this fact was one of the greatest weaknesses of the provincial legislative system.

At one time the Lords of Trade tried to remedy this weakness. Before 1677 the legislative system of Jamaica had been in an experimental stage and all laws passed by the assembly had been allowed to remain in force for two years only. But in that year the Lords of Trade, having become thoroughly dissatisfied with the way in which the assembly had conducted itself, proposed to take away from that body the initiative in legislation and to establish for the island a system modeled directly on the celebrated Poynings' Act in force in Ireland.[1] Accordingly, the new governor, Lord Carlisle, carried with him to Jamaica in 1678 a series of bills under the great seal drafted by the Lords of Trade with the help of the law officers of the crown, to which the governor was directed to secure the assent of the assembly. His commission and instructions provided that for the future all necessary bills were to be framed by the governor and council and sent to England for revision and approval by the privy council. They were then to be returned to the island under the great seal and the assembly was to be called together to give its consent to their final enactment. Only in case of invasion or other dire emergency might the assembly meet on the governor's sole authority, and then only for the purpose of granting money.[2] Similar directions were given to Lord Culpeper as governor of Virginia in 1679,[3] and had the system proven successful in these two provinces, the Lords of Trade would probably have extended it to the other royal provinces, thereby permanently placing the American provincial assembly on the same inferior plane as the parliament of Ireland. Such a result would have been momentous for it would have gone far to destroy the power of the assembly to oppose the prerogative in pro-

---

[1] C.O. 138: 3, pp. 143–153, 157, 161–164; *Cal. State Paps., Col.*, 1677–1680, §§ 412, 423, 457, 480; *Acts, Privy Coun., Col.*, 1613–1680, § 1177.

[2] Commission to Carlisle, Jamaica, 1678, C.O. 138: 3, pp. 198–214; instructions to Carlisle, Jamaica, 1678, arts. 14–16, C.O. 138: 3, pp. 216–241.

[3] Commission to Culpeper, Virginia, 1679, C.O. 5: 1355, pp. 313–326 (L.C.); instructions to Culpeper, Virginia, 1679, art. 23, C.O. 5: 1355, pp. 326–356 (L.C.).

vincial government. That the effectiveness of the most important colonial institution—the assembly with its right of initiative—was not thus impaired in its very infancy is due almost entirely to the opposition of the Jamaican representatives. The burgesses of Virginia apparently failed to appreciate the significance of the innovation, for they passed with only a few amendments the three measures which Culpeper brought with him.[4] But in Jamaica the opposition was intense. The most important bill that Carlisle brought was one for a perpetual revenue, which the representatives realized would result in the less frequent summoning of assemblies. They also pointed out that the long delay which would inevitably take place between the first drafting of a necessary bill by the governor and council and its final approval by the assembly would often be most harmful to the island's welfare. No comparison was possible between the situation of Ireland, so near to England, and that of Jamaica, so distant. Carlisle inclined to agree with this view although he did his best to win the submission of the assembly. But the representatives refused to surrender. They would pass no bills which they did not themselves initiate. The Lords of Trade insisted for a time upon the establishment of their system, but finally came to realize what Carlisle had known from the start, that the plan could not be enforced.[5] With the understanding that the assembly would pass a revenue bill for at least seven years, they prepared, late in 1680, powers and instructions to the governor, authoriz-

[4] *Cal. State Paps., Col.*, 1677–1680, § 1433; Hening, *Statutes at Large*, II, 458–469.

[5] On this controversy see: C.O. 138: 3, pp. 179–188, 249–251, 270–274, 277–285, 293–305, 313–316, 327–328, 342–343, 363–373, 389–396, 400–403, 405–412, 418–422, 442–443; *Cal. State Paps., Col.*, 1677–1680, §§ 596, 600, 601, 786, 794, 814, 815, 827, 961, 1001, 1117, 1188, 1265, 1361, and index under "Jamaica, constitution"; *Acts, Privy Coun., Col.*, 1613–1680, §§ 1201, 1202, 1257, 1274.

ing him to restore the initiative to the assembly.[6] Corresponding changes were made in the next commission and instructions for Virginia, and the threat to the assembly's powers was ended. Thus to the Jamaica assembly goes the credit for one of the very earliest victories over the prerogative and one of the most important for the development of the colonial constitution.[7]

But the fact that the assembly was to keep the initiative in legislative matters led the Lords of Trade to introduce into the governor's instructions explicit directions as to the forms and methods to be used in framing laws. The instructions given to nearly all the governors of royal provinces from this time forward provided that the style of enactment was to be "by the governor, council, and assembly"; that different topics were to be treated in separate bills; that no "riders" were to be permitted; and that no perpetual clause was to be made part of any temporary law. All acts repealing, continuing, or altering laws already passed must mention in their enacting clauses the title and date of the act or acts to which they referred. All revenue laws, except those laying imposts on liquors and those passed for some purely temporary service, were to be perpetual and without limitation of time. The governor was not to approve any other sort of measure unless it was to be in effect for at least two years. Before a private act might be passed, publication of intent to introduce such a measure was to be made in the churches of the parishes where the property in question lay, and the bill was to contain clauses saving the rights

[6] "Powers to the Earl of Carlisle for making laws," Nov. 3, 1680, C.O. 138:3, pp. 444–447; instructions to Carlisle, Jamaica, Nov. 3, 1680, *ibid.*, pp. 447–453.

[7] Accounts of the struggle in Jamaica are given at considerable length in Bryan Edwards, *History of the West Indies* (2d ed.), I, 175–178; Edward Long, *History of Jamaica*, I, 14–16, 194–213, and Agnes M. Whitson, *The Constitutional Development of Jamaica, 1660 to 1729*, chap. IV.

of the crown and of all persons and bodies except those mentioned therein, and suspending the execution of the act until the royal consent had been obtained. Appropriation bills or those imposing fines and penalties must say expressly that the sums raised were granted to his Majesty for the public uses of the province and the support of its government as directed in the act. These and other regulations were introduced into the instructions from time to time and modified or elaborated as circumstances seemed to warrant. In some cases they simply reflected the long years of legislative experience of parliament itself. In others they represented efforts to prevent the assembly from evading the governor's veto and the royal disallowance. But in all cases they introduced from outside definite restrictions upon the assembly's freedom.

By means of the veto the governor was often able to prevent the passage of undesirable legislation. But he yielded all too frequently to pressure from the assembly and assented to bills prohibited by his instructions. For just such occasions the privy council held the royal disallowance in reserve. By this means the home government might nullify an act which expressed the will of a majority of both houses of the assembly and which had been consented to by the king's own representative, the governor. Furthermore, this power did not have to be exercised immediately upon receipt of the act in England, nor, in the case of any royal province except Massachusetts, within any certain time limit. The laws of the Bay Colony could not be disallowed more than three years after their presentation to the privy council, but acts from other provinces were sometimes rejected half a dozen or more years after they had been passed.[8] All acts went first to the Board of Trade for consideration and the

8 Perhaps the outstanding case of delay in disallowing acts had to do with North Carolina, twenty-six of whose acts were disallowed in 1754. The

members of that body took full advantage of the fact that they need not report at once. Sometimes their delays in recommending approval or disapproval were the result of sheer inefficiency. But on other occasions they had a definite purpose in mind. As they explained once to the duke of Newcastle, they generally divided colonial acts into three groups: "Such as, for the service of the colonies or the security of private property, demand an immediate confirmation; such as in their own nature are so pernicious as to demand an immediate repeal; and lastly, such of whose effect being doubtful, we think it necessary to let them lie by probational, till we shall have been fully informed what effect they may have in their execution." They added as a further observation, which speaks for itself, that "the fewer acts there are confirmed, the greater will be the dependence of the colonies upon the crown."[9]

Normally an act was in force from the time of the governor's signature until its disallowance was notified to the colony. In order to prevent the enforcement of undesirable legislation pending its disallowance, the British government required a "suspending clause" in certain types of bills. This was a clause postponing the operation of a law until it had received the royal consent

first five of these acts were dated 2 George I, and consequently were thirty-eight years old. Nineteen of the acts had been passed under the royal government, the first of them being twenty-four years old and the last three years old at the time of disallowance. *Acts, Privy Coun., Col.*, 1745–1766, p. 807. The privy council had only six months in which to reject Pennsylvania laws, but in both the Massachusetts and Pennsylvania cases the law officers declared that the time was to be counted from the actual presentation to the privy council and not from the receipt of the acts by the Board of Trade to whom they were regularly first sent. Chalmers, *Opinions*, I, 348, 349.

[9] Board of Trade to Newcastle, July 1, 1724, C.O. 138: 16, pp. 476–477. This letter was in reply to one from Newcastle of the same date asking the board to expedite their representations on all colonial laws "to the end that his Majesty's pleasure may be signified upon them in due time." C.O. 137: 14, fo. 323.

by order in council. The bill still needed the assent of the governor before it could be sent to England and in all other respects it followed the usual procedure. What the suspending clause really did was to change the royal allowance or disallowance from an act of executive prerogative to a direct participation in the process of legislation itself. The king in council became, in such cases, a part of the colonial legislature and not merely an external reviewing authority.

In ordinary cases disallowance did not go into effect until notice thereof had been received in the province by the governor. This notice usually took the form of an order in council signed by the clerk and sealed with the privy council seal, or occasionally that of an instruction or warrant to the governor under the signet and sign manual. In 1718 the fees which had to be paid in the privy council office before the order in council would be sealed and delivered, amounted to £3 2s. 6d.[10] The fees for private acts had to be paid by the beneficiaries, but in all other cases the province itself was responsible through its agent. The frequent failure of the provincial agents to take out orders in council for the repeal or confirmation of acts caused some difficulty during the first part of the eighteenth century and the colonists were often for a long time ignorant of the fate of their laws. The Board of Trade reported in 1724 that the island of Bermuda "was very little informed what acts of their assemblies were in force till we sent them a collection of their laws lately revised and printed by our direction," upon which the

10 Governor Lawes of Jamaica wrote to William Popple, March 7, 1718, just before sailing, expressing his fear that he would be expected to pay "14 times £3 2s. 6d." for fourteen acts, some of them confirmed and some disallowed, which had recently been passed upon. C.O. 138: 16, pp. 98–102. Popple replied, April 4, 1718, that "the council office will expect their legal fees from the island" and that an agent should be appointed to transact such business. C.O. 138: 15, pp. 109–110.

islanders discovered that they had "long been governed by laws which had been repealed many years by the crown."[11] But such cases became increasingly rare as the details of colonial administration became better systematized.

Although the share of the crown in colonial legislation was largely a negative one, the officials of the government were able to prescribe fairly effectively the method by which laws should be passed. From the regulations to be followed in drafting bills, through the passage in both houses and the approval of the governor, to the confirmation or disallowance by the privy council and the final notification of such action to the colony, the commission and instructions indicated the processes of legislation and reserved to the prerogative as complete a check as possible upon the initiative which the government had been unable to deny to the assembly.

But the Board of Trade and privy council did not stop with instructions which prescribed the machinery and process of legislation. The absolute veto granted to the governor would be valueless if it did not give him an important voice in determining what kinds of bills should become law and what kinds should be kept from passage. The instructions went on, therefore, to lay down rules by which the governor was to determine his attitude toward the various sorts of measures which came to him from the two houses. Some classes of bills might not be approved unless the king had given his consent before their introduction into the assembly; others must contain clauses suspending their execution until the royal ap-

[11] Board of Trade to the lord president of the council, May 19, 1724, C.O. 324: 11, pp. 15–16 (L.C.). They added a request that all orders in council in confirmation or disallowance of acts of assembly be sent immediately on passage to the board that they might be forwarded without loss of time to the province, but the board failed to suggest how the fees were to be paid in such cases.

proval had been received; and still others might not be
signed by the governor under any circumstances whatsoever. As the assemblies slowly gained more and more control over their own organization and as they became more
and more adept in the legislative art, the instructions
restricting legislation increased correspondingly. More
and more the agents of the prerogative had to depend
upon the veto and the disallowance or the threat of these
to keep the assemblies within the bounds set for their
legislative freedom. Unfortunately for the royal authority, this movement was coincident with the weakening of American respect for the prerogative. As the assemblies showed more and more independence of spirit
and impatience at restraint, the home authorities felt
more and more the necessity of imposing restrictions upon
the scope of their legislative powers. But the increase in
instructions limiting the governor's discretion in approving bills merely added to the colonial discontent and to the
grievances which the Americans felt toward the British
government.[12] From all points of view the situation became increasingly unsatisfactory.

These instructions were by no means intended as mere

[12] The following table indicates how far the instructions went in restrain-
ing the governors from approving bills, and shows the steady increase in
these instructions throughout the period. Only those instructions which went
to all or nearly all provinces are included, although there were several others
sent to only one or two colonies. In each case, the date, actual or approximate,
when the instruction became general is indicated:

I. The previous consent of the crown was required for:
   Laws reenacting those previously disallowed (1682)
   Laws lessening or impairing the royal revenue (1682)
   Laws altering the value of foreign coins (in force from 1690 to 1727; see
      group IV)
II. Suspending clauses were necessary in:
   Laws for issuing bills of credit (1720) (Some special exceptions were
      made)
   Private acts (1723)
   Laws repealing other laws, whether previously confirmed or not (1728)

expressions of advice which the governor could safely ignore at his pleasure. They were fundamental parts of British policy and were upheld with all the vigor which the Board of Trade, the secretary of state, and the privy council could command. Failure on the part of the governor to veto bills which did not meet the terms of these regulations was seldom allowed to pass unnoticed. Such disobedience of his instructions usually brought him a sharp rebuke from the Board of Trade and sometimes from the privy council itself. It was almost invariably followed by prompt disallowance of the act in question, however harmless the latter might really be. The significance attached to these regulations in British minds was well expressed by the privy council committee in

III. Either the previous consent of the crown or a suspending clause was required for:
 Laws ''of an unusual or extraordinary nature and importance'':
  Affecting the prerogative or the property of subjects (1706)
  Affecting the trade and shipping of Great Britain (1717)
IV. The following were absolutely prohibited:
 Laws levying money which was not made liable to be accounted for in England to the Treasury (1702) and audited by the auditor general of the plantation revenues (1732)
 Laws placing imposts on liquors for less than one year at a time (1702)
 Other revenue laws of a temporary nature (1702)
 All other laws of less than two years' duration (1720)
 Laws laying duties on:
  European goods imported in English vessels (1724)
  Negroes imported, if the tax were to be payable by the importer (1731)
  Felons imported (1731)
  The produce or manufacture of Great Britain (1732)
 Laws whereby natives or inhabitants of the province were placed on a more advantageous footing than those of Great Britain (1732)
 Laws violating the act of 6 Anne for ascertaining the value of foreign coins in the plantations (1740)
 Laws altering the constitution of the assembly (1767) (Transferred to group III for some colonies after 1773)
 Laws for naturalization of aliens (1773)
 Private acts of divorce (1773)
 Laws granting title to lands which had previously been granted to aliens antecedent to their naturalization (1773).

1760 when three private acts of Virginia lay before them. Although these measures were unobjectionable in themselves and were later allowed to be repassed in proper form, they were recommended for disallowance because they contained neither suspending clauses nor clauses saving the rights of the crown, bodies politic and corporate, and private persons, and because the lieutenant governor had failed to attach the necessary certificates of due publication in the parish churches. These regulations, declared the committee, "are coeval with the constitution of the British colonies, . . . form an essential part of that constitution, and cannot be set aside without subverting a fundamental principle of it."[13] This statement is thoroughly typical of the British attitude toward the instructions.

The instructions against acts which interfered with the interests of British merchants were among the most important of them all and received the most watchful attention. Emphasis has been laid in a previous chapter on the important part played by the mercantile classes in drafting instructions of this character.[14] Each violation of either the letter or the spirit of these instructions called forth memorials from the merchants which often led not only to the disallowance of the offending act but to the issuance of still more stringent regulations. One might almost think that the instructions as a whole were prepared for the benefit of the merchants.

The most comprehensive of the instructions which were intended to safeguard the interests of the traders to America was one forbidding the governor to give his assent to any bill "of an unusual and extraordinary nature and importance" wherein the royal prerogative or the property of British subjects might be prejudiced or the

---

[13] *Acts, Privy Coun., Col.*, 1745–1766, § 421.   [14] See above, pp. 60–63.

trade or shipping of the kingdom "any ways affected," unless the bill contained a suspending clause or had been previously approved by the king. The origin and development of this instruction will illustrate the way in which many of these regulations were adopted. An act was passed in Barbados in 1706 making paper bills of credit legal tender for all debts.[15] The Board of Trade entertained strong doubts of the desirability of the measure and asked the Royal African Company for their opinion. That organization sent back a representation sharply condemning the act.[16] A group of eighteen "merchants and others trading to and interested in the island of Barbados" also memorialized the board setting forth in great detail their objections.[17] Thereupon the board laid a long representation before the queen, as a result of which the privy council disallowed the act as being "very prejudicial to our subjects in the course of their trade."[18] On the same day, "taking notice of the ill consequences that might happen by passing of acts of like unusual and extraordinary nature and importance in her Majesty's plantations, which will remain in force there until her Majesty's pleasure be signified to the contrary," the council ordered the board to prepare a royal circular letter for all the governors forbidding them to pass such bills in the future without first receiving the queen's pleasure.[19] Two

---

[15] Governor Granville to the Board of Trade, July 1, 1706, C.O. 28: 9, no. 51; *Cal. State Paps., Col.*, 1706–1708, § 405.

[16] C.O. 28: 9, no. 55; *Cal. State Paps., Col.*, 1706–1708, § 529.

[17] C.O. 28: 9, no. 56; *Cal. State Paps., Col.*, 1706–1708, § 540.

[18] Board of Trade to the queen, Oct. 17, 1706, C.O. 29: 10, pp. 143–152; *Cal. State Paps., Col.*, 1706–1708, § 542 (i); order in council, Oct. 21, 1706, C.O. 28: 9, no. 57; *Cal. State Paps., Col.*, 1706–1708, § 545.

[19] Order in council, Oct. 21, 1706, C.O. 28: 9, no. 58; *Cal. State Paps., Col.*, 1706–1708, § 546; *Acts, Privy Coun., Col.*, 1680–1720, § 1007; royal letter to the governor of Barbados, Nov. 8, 1706, C.O. 324: 30, pp. 111–113; *Cal. State Paps., Col.*, 1706–1708, § 582; royal circular letter to the governors of New Hampshire, New York, New Jersey, Jamaica, Maryland, Virginia, Massachu-

weeks later the secretary of state instructed the Board of
Trade to include a similar restriction in all general instructions.[20] Thus appeared the first general regulation
on this subject.

The prohibition at this time extended merely to unusual and extraordinary bills "wherein our prerogative
or property of our subjects may be prejudiced," but a
few years later a more inclusive phraseology became necessary. In 1717 a number of merchants complained to the
Board of Trade against several Virginia acts, among them
one of 1713 relating to the tobacco trade. At a subsequent
hearing one of the most prominent of these merchants,
Micajah Perry, the elder, told the board that this act
meant "not less than £300 per annum out of his pocket
in his particular trade, in loss of time and payment of
seamen's wages." Although the act was designed to improve the quality of tobacco shipped from the colony, he
said that the crop continued as bad as before. One witness
hinted that the act had been obtained by the governor and
his friends for personal advantage and was not desired
by the majority of the planters. One of the other objectionable acts related to the Indian trade of the province
and gave certain privileges to a monopoly called the Indian Company. For thirty years, Perry said, he had been
engaged in selling goods for use in the Indian trade but
now the company employed factors of their own, greatly
to Perry's disadvantage. The merchants begged that no
law of such sweeping effect be permitted to go into force
without the lapse of considerable time.[21] The upshot of

setts Bay, Bermuda, and the Leeward Islands, Nov. 8, 1706, C.O. 324: 30, pp.
113–115; *Cal. State Paps., Col.*, 1706–1708, § 583. In these letters, as also in
the subsequent instructions, a suspending clause was allowed as an alternative
to the previous consent of the queen for passing such laws.

[20] Secretary of State Hedges to the Board of Trade, Nov. 6, 1706, C.O.
28: 9, no. 62; *Cal. State Paps., Col.*, 1706–1708, § 566.

[21] *Board of Trade Journal*, 1714/5–1718, pp. 229–230.

the matter was that the Board of Trade sent a representation to the privy council recommending the disallowance of the acts in question and proposing an additional instruction to all governors which would forbid them to pass any law interfering with the trade or shipping of Great Britain without a suspending clause.[22] The circular instruction which resulted was an amendment to that already in the hands of the governors, and added to the group of laws "of an unusual and extraordinary nature and importance" previously restricted, a further class of acts affecting trade and shipping of Great Britain.[23]

The instruction was next expanded in 1724, this time because of a New York act. For eighteen years, beginning in 1691, that province had levied an *ad valorem* duty on all European goods imported, the rate at times running as high as ten percent. But the measure had not been renewed in 1709 chiefly because the unscrupulous governor, Lord Cornbury, had misused the funds. In 1720, when a more trustworthy governor, William Burnet, was in office, the assembly proposed to renew the levy but at a rate of only two percent. In accordance with his instructions Burnet had a suspending clause added before he gave his consent. Again and again he urged upon the Board of Trade the confirmation of the act, on the ground that the money was to be used for the building of much-needed fortifications.[24] The board was averse to any act affect-

[22] Board of Trade to the queen (in the absence of the king), June 29, 1717, C.O. 5: 1364, pp. 474–476 (L.C.); *Acts, Privy Coun., Col.*, 1680–1720, § 1271. In a report to the Board of Trade, June 19, 1717, on these Virginia acts, the solicitor general gave his opinion that the act relating to the tobacco trade violated the instruction against extraordinary bills already given to the governor. C.O. 5: 1318, p. 41 (L.C.).

[23] Circular instruction, Sept. 27, 1717, *N. H. Prov. Laws*, II, 237.

[24] Burnet to the Board of Trade, Nov. 26, 1720; Dec. 14, 1720; Oct. 16, 1721; Nov. 3, 1721; May 29, 1723; June 25, 1723, *N. Y. Col. Docs.*, V, 576–581, 582, 631, 634, 643, 684, 685.

ing trade, but in 1723 they decided, in view of the governor's pleas, to recommend the confirmation of the law.[25] Their report was, as usual, referred to the privy council committee. There it met opposition. The merchants of London were up in arms. At a hearing before the committee, counsel for both sides spoke, but the victory rested completely with the merchants. Not only was the act recommended for disallowance, but a circular instruction was proposed forbidding all governors to assent to any act—whether containing a suspending clause or not—which laid duties on European goods imported in English vessels. The privy council approved this report as a matter of course and ordered the instruction prepared.[26] The new order was more drastic than any of its predecessors since it absolutely forbade the bills in question, while the former instructions had simply required the previous consent of the king or the inclusion of a suspending clause before the governor might approve the measure affected.[27]

For some unknown reason the new instruction was not included in the next sets of general instructions. But in 1731 the merchants of London complained of various obstacles to their trade in the colonies, including among other things, the practice of several provinces of laying lesser import duties upon the ships and goods of their own inhabitants than upon those belonging to other British subjects. Upon the recommendation of the Board of Trade, which conducted a hearing on this petition, a further circular instruction was sent in 1732, forbidding the governors, upon pain of the king's highest displeasure, to assent to any law whereby the inhabitants of the prov-

[25] Board of Trade to Burnet, June 6, 1722, *N. Y. Col. Docs.*, V, 647.
[26] Order in council, April 30, 1724, *ibid.*, p. 706; *Acts, Privy Coun., Col.*, 1720–1745, p. 849.
[27] Circular instruction, Aug. 31, 1724, C.O. 324: 35, pp. 82–83 (Mass.).

ince were put "upon a more advantageous footing" than
those of Great Britain. The instruction also cautioned
the governors not to approve any bill laying duties upon
British shipping or the products or manufactures of Great
Britain.[28] In subsequent general instructions to the governors of the various provinces the phraseology of the
rule was slightly changed from time to time but the general restrictions were the same. The governor might assent to a bill of an unusual and extraordinary nature and
importance affecting the royal prerogative, the property
of British subjects, or the trade and shipping of Great
Britain, only if the bill had previously been approved by
the king or if it contained a suspending clause; while the
governor was absolutely forbidden to assent to any measure which discriminated in favor of the inhabitants of
his province or which specifically laid duties on British
shipping or on the products or manufactures of Great
Britain.

These instructions represented the efforts of the governmental officials, influenced by the merchants, to prevent colonial legislation which might be harmful to British
trade. According to the political and economic philosophy
of the eighteenth century, such prevention was part of
the duty of government. The colonies did not exist primarily for their own benefit, but rather for that of the
mother country which fostered and protected them. The
colonial system of the mercantilists required both affirmative and negative action. Affirmative action took the form
of legislation by the parliament in Westminster which
guided and protected colonial trade. All those measures
which are classed under the general title of the Navigation

[28] *Board of Trade Journal*, 1728/9–1734, pp. 229, 233, 245, 246, 248, 265,
268–269, 270; Board of Trade to the king, Jan. 21, 1732, C.O. 324: 11, pp.
248–253 (L.C.); circular instruction, May 5, 1732, *N. H. Prov. Laws*, II,
491–492.

Acts belong to this category. Negative action took the form of restrictions upon the powers of the subordinate legislatures in the colonies, in order that the trade of the British merchants, protected by the Navigation Acts, might develop fully, freely, and most profitably. Such restriction was a function of the prerogative and was carried out through the instructions to the governors.

The instructions which have just been described were the most far-reaching and all-inclusive of the entire group sent for this purpose, but they were by no means the only ones. The crown sent a number of other instructions to one or more provinces to check the tendency which appeared among the assemblies to pass laws harmful to particular branches of British trade. Among such prohibitory regulations that against the levying of duties on the slave trade had perhaps the most interesting development and provoked the most bitter controversy. In 1716 the Jamaica assembly passed an act laying a duty on every negro exported from that island in a vessel belonging in Jamaica or to the South Sea Company. Jamaica had served for many years as a clearing house for the slave trade to the Spanish colonies as well as to other British plantations, and the masters of slave ships coming from Africa had become accustomed to stopping at the island for wood and water and "refreshment" even when the negroes were not to be disposed of there. The levying of a duty upon slaves shipped into or out of the territorial waters of Jamaica had seemed unobjectionable as long as the export trade had been in the main in the hands of others than Englishmen. But now that the South Sea Company had secured the asiento contract for supplying the Spanish colonies with slaves, the duty took on a very different complexion. The passage of the act and its renewal in 1717 raised protests from the company which were referred to the Board of Trade for report. The company asserted that the duty placed such a burden upon their trade that, if it were not discontinued, they would be forced to abandon their "factory" in Jamaica. Such a result would be harmful not only to the company but to the island as well, which, they declared, derived great benefit from the company's activities there.[29] Nicholas Lawes, a Jamaica planter and merchant, who had just been named governor, prepared a memorandum in reply to the company. He asserted, as did the islanders generally, that the asiento was actually harmful, rather than beneficial, to Jamaica, since the company made it their practice to carry "all the able stout, and young negroes, or such as they called 'piec'd India,' to the Spaniards, and sell none to the planters but old, sickly, and decrepit, or what are called 'refuse.' " Lawes argued that negroes were necessary to the prosperity of Jamaica and added, in an appeal for mercantilist sympathy, that "planting is the mother of trade, and negroes the support of planting." The South Sea Company had insisted that the asiento contract was making the nation rich and would bring in mountains of gold. If so, said Lawes, the company could well afford the "easy duty" of twenty shillings per head. "But if the case be so that the company cannot afford to pay that duty out of the profits of the asiento, then it may be supposed the negroes employed in our plantations are of greater advantage to this kingdom than selling them to the Spaniard."[30] In such fashion did the long controversy begin.

[29] South Sea Company to Secretary of State Stanhope, Feb. 28, 1716, C.O. 137: 11, no. 6 (i); order in council, Oct. 31, 1717, referring to the Board of Trade the enclosed petition from the South Sea Co., C.O. 137: 12, nos. 92, 92 (i); Daniel Wescomb, secretary of the South Sea Co., to William Popple, Nov. 15, 1717, *ibid.*, no. 100.

[30] Nicholas Lawes's memorandum on the negro duty [Nov. 21, 1717], C.O. 137: 12, no. 99; *Board of Trade Journal*, 1714/5–1718, pp. 285, 288, 296, 297, 300, 303–304, 306–307, 318, 319, 320–321.

LEGISLATION 237

In its representation the Board of Trade summarized the arguments for and against the act. They added their opinion that, however just a tax on negroes purchased in Jamaica might be, any duty placed upon negroes landed for refreshment only would be unreasonable, for it "would be an oppression upon the South Sea Company and consequently support Jamaica at the expense of British trade."[31] The privy council disallowed the act of 1717 and ordered the secretary of state to prepare an additional instruction for Governor Lawes, forbidding any tax upon negroes landed for refreshment only, but permitting one upon negroes actually bought in the island and exported thence. At the same time Lawes was cautioned to obey his general instructions against bills affecting the prerogative or British trade.[32] There the matter rested for a time.

A little later the question of duties on negroes was raised in a new quarter. In 1723 Lieutenant Governor Drysdale of Virginia reported the passage of an act there laying a duty of forty shillings per head on slaves imported into the province. Since the tax was three pounds less than that imposed by acts in force from 1710 to 1718, he did not feel that the law was contrary to his instructions.[33] But as soon as word of this new act reached Eng-

[31] Board of Trade to the king, Dec. 21, 1717, C.O. 138: 16, pp. 32–43; Board of Trade to Lord Sunderland, Jan. 3, 1718, *ibid.*, p. 48; *Acts, Privy Coun., Col.*, 1680–1720, pp. 728–729.

[32] Two Orders in council, Jan. 9, 1718, C.O. 137: 12, nos. 109, 113; *Acts, Privy Coun., Col.*, 1680–1720, p. 729; additional instructions to Lawes, Jan. 16, 1718, C.O. 137: 16, fos. 12–14. Sunderland, who prepared this instruction, failed to send a copy to the Board of Trade so that when they prepared general instructions for the duke of Portland in 1722 they were unable to add this article. William Popple to Daniel Wescomb, March 6, 1722, C.O. 138: 16, pp. 409–410; Board of Trade to Newcastle, March 12, 1725, C.O. 138: 17, pp. 24–26.

[33] Drysdale to the Board of Trade, June 29, 1723, C.O. 5: 1319, pp. 222–223 (L.C.).

land, protests began to pour in from the merchants. The Royal African Company, "divers merchants trading to Africa," the "Mayor, Aldermen, and Merchants of the ancient and loyal Corporation of Liverpool," and others expressed their opinions in no uncertain terms.[34] Richard Hill, a former commissioner of the Admiralty, declared that England ought "to prevent in the beginning our colonies from laying their duties either directly or indirectly on the trade or navigation of Great Britain" by the protection of whose fleet and power they existed.[35] In contrast to these protests was a petition signed by Micajah Perry, the elder, and fourteen other merchants trading in Virginia tobacco, who urged that the act be confirmed.[36] But in view of the preponderance of opinion against the act, the Board of Trade could hardly do otherwise than recommend its disallowance. In their representation they pointed out that since the act required the duty to be paid by the importer it would directly affect trade and should not therefore have been passed without a suspending clause.[37] The privy council concurred in this opinion and disallowed the act. The order in council which followed forbade the governor to give his consent to any similar act in the future without a suspending clause.[38] The merchants won against Virginia as they had against Jamaica.

During this period the South Sea Company and other slave traders began also to complain against the duties which the Jamaica assembly annually levied upon negroes bought in Jamaica and exported, and upon negroes im-

---

[34] C.O. 5: 1319, pp. 251, 259–261, 279, 315 (L.C.).

[35] Richard Hill to Secretary Popple, Sept. 23, 1723, *ibid.*, pp. 255–256 (L.C.).

[36] *Ibid.*, p. 283 (L.C.).

[37] Board of Trade to the king, Jan. 29, 1724, *ibid.*, p. 325 (L.C.).

[38] *Acts, Privy Coun., Col.*, 1720–1745, § 59. A similar act passed in 1728 in spite of this injunction was repealed on petition of the merchants for the same reasons. *Ibid.*, 1720–1745, pp. 64–65, § 156.

ported and sold there. The former tax, they said, seriously injured the asiento and ate up the profits of the slave trade to the continental English colonies. The latter tax placed an intolerable burden upon the British importer. Richard Harris, an independent trader, explained why the incidence of the import duty could not be shifted to the purchaser: "As duties on metals and unperishable goods which may be kept for a market are chiefly borne by the consumer, so, on the contrary, all duties on perishable goods as cattle, fish, negro slaves, flesh, fruits, etc., are wholly borne by the importer or owner thereof; for instance, when fish decays, or when 20 or 30 negroes die and other[s], growing sickly, weak, or lame, become unmerchantable, which too often is the case after the duty is paid, for God['s] sake, who reimburses the importer for the duty he was forced to pay on their arrival? And in case the market being glutted, what buyer regards what duty was payable on merchandise which must perish or be very chargeable to keep if not sold out of hand?"[39] Such complaints came frequently to the Board of Trade. The South Sea Company also charged that duties were again being laid upon negroes landed simply for refreshment contrary to the former instruction.[40] But the board

[39] Richard Harris to William Popple, Nov. 13, 1727, C.O. 137: 17, fos. 25–26.

[40] The South Sea Company to the king, Aug. 3, 1724, C.O. 137: 16, fos. 4–5; four "merchants trading to his Majesty's island of Jamaica" to the king [1724], *ibid.*, fo. 18; D. Wescomb to Popple, March 3, 1725, *ibid.*, fo. 21; D. Harris to Popple, March 20, 1725, *ibid.*, fos. 34–35; court of directors of the South Sea Company to the Board of Trade, Oct. 6, 1726, *ibid.*, fos. 278–280. The Board also received a memorial, March 11, 1725, from fifteen "gentlemen concerned in Jamaica as traders and planters now residing in Great Britain" in defence of the acts, *ibid.*, fos. 23–26. The governor, the duke of Portland, also wrote, Feb. 8, 1725, explaining that "common prejudice" demanded the tax upon negroes landed for refreshment, since along with other disadvantages these negroes "infected the inhabitants with all their malignant fevers, small pox, and other dangerous distempers," *ibid.*, fo. 63.

failed to take action at once, because, as they later explained, they lacked accurate information from the island.[41] When instructions were prepared for Governor
Hunter in 1727, the Board of Trade, the privy council
committee, and the merchants each made proposals, the
final result of which was an additional instruction, forbidding any duty on negroes "brought into or landed in
our island for refreshment only" but permitting a tax
"upon the negroes of our said island bought there."[42]
The merchants gained part, though not all, of what they
wanted.

During the first years of his administration Hunter
adhered strictly to this instruction. But the act of 1731,
which he approved, increased by fifty percent the import
and export duties on negroes. The slave traders were
apparently made liable for the import duty on all negroes
landed, for whatever purpose, although they were exempted from the export tax for negroes who did not
change ownership while there. This violation of the additional instruction brought the usual series of protests
from the merchants, to which the Board of Trade listened
with sympathy.[43] Another clause in the act which aroused

[41] Board of Trade to the king, May 31, 1727, C.O. 138: 17, pp. 136–145.

[42] Board of Trade to the king, June 8, July 25, Nov. 7, 1727, *ibid.*,
pp. 148–149, 233, 238–239; order in council, Nov. 13, 1727, C.O. 137: 17, fo.
38; *Acts, Privy Coun., Col.*, 1720–1745, pp. 159–161; additional instruction
to Hunter, Nov. 13, 1727, C.O. 138: 17, pp. 239–240.

[43] On July 7, 1731, the privy council committee referred petitions from the
following groups to the Board of Trade for report: "The merchants trading
to his Majesty's island of Jamaica" (17 names); "Master, wardens, assistants, and commonalty of the Society of Merchant Adventurers within the
City of Bristol"; and "Merchants and owners of ships of and in the port
of Liverpool, in the County Palatine of Lancaster, trading in his Majesty's
island of Jamaica" (40 names), C.O. 137: 19 (unpaged). From the similarity
of wording of the first and third petitions, the probability is great that both
were drafted by the same solicitor, William Wood. For the Board of Trade's
proceedings on these petitions see, *Board of Trade Journal*, 1728/9–1734,
pp. 219, 228–229, 247.

the ire of the board laid a duty of £100 per head on the importation of convicts sent to the island from British law courts and prisons. This prohibitive duty directly violated an act of parliament providing for the transportation of felons to the colonies and ordering the provincial governments not to interfere with the practice.[44] The Board of Trade and privy council now took a decided stand. They sent an additional instruction to Hunter, severely reprimanding him for this violation of his orders and warning him to adhere to them more closely in the future on pain of incurring the king's highest displeasure. They absolutely forbade him to assent to any act laying an import duty on slaves which was payable by the importer or any export duty on slaves who remained in the island for less than twelve months without changing ownership during that time.[45] At the same time, the British authorities sent a circular instruction to the governors of all other colonies, forbidding them to pass any acts imposing duties on negroes imported, if payable by the importer, or on negroes exported without sale in the colony, or on felons brought in.[46] The merchants had completely gained their point. No provincial assembly was

[44] 4 Geo. I, c. 11.

[45] Board of Trade to privy council committee, Aug. 25, 1731, C.O. 138: 17, pp. 344–349; order of privy council committee, Nov. 23, 1731, C.O. 137: 19; Board of Trade to privy council committee, Nov. 30, 1731, C.O. 138: 17, pp. 350–351; Acts, Privy Coun., Col., 1720–1745, pp. 161–162; additional instruction to Hunter, Dec. 10, 1731, C.O. 5: 195, pp. 247–248 (L.C.).

[46] Circular instruction to the governors of fifteen colonies, Dec. 10, 1731, C.O. 5: 195, pp. 249–250 (L.C.). The article was repeated in the general instructions to all succeeding governors of royal provinces. Both the circular instruction and the additional instruction to Hunter were based in part upon an article of the general instructions to Robert Johnson of South Carolina in 1730 (art. 114, C.O. 5: 192, pp. 65–118, L.C.) which had been sent in consequence of duties laid on slaves there. With these instructions the merchants expressed themselves as satisfied, Board of Trade Journal, 1728/9–1734, pp. 229, 249.

to be allowed to interfere with the slave trade as the Jamaica legislature had done.

But just one week before he received his new instruction, Hunter gave his assent to a bill for the year 1732.[47] This act was less harmful to the merchants' interests than its predecessor, for the duties imposed were lower; nevertheless, it provoked a similar storm of protest.[48] Hunter joined the council and assembly in support of the principle of this taxation. The additional instruction, he said, had struck the islanders "all of a heap" and had cast "such a damp upon public credit that we know not where to find money for immediate exigencies, not to mention the expense of the government and contingencies." The government needed the money very badly, and for his part, Hunter, who usually could see the colonial point of view as well as the British, could not "think that the merchants at home have any just ground to complain of the additional duty on negroes, for if they are sold here the planter pays it; if carried abroad, the Spaniard."[49] But in spite of such arguments from the king's own governor, the merchants held their advantage, the additional instruction, "founded on the principles of reason and justice," was continued, and the act was disallowed.[50]

On Hunter's death in 1734 the governorship was given to Henry Cunningham, a Scot who had served in parlia-

[47] Hunter to the Board of Trade, Feb. 29, 1732, C.O. 137: 20 (unpaged).

[48] C.O. 137: 20 (unpaged) contains no less than seven letters and petitions against the act of 1732 and the defense of Hunter and the assembly.

[49] Hunter to the Board of Trade, Nov. 13, 1731, C.O. 137: 19; address and representation of the Jamaica council and assembly, Feb. 10, 1732; Hunter to Newcastle, Feb. 19, 1732; Hunter to the Board of Trade, March 16, 1732; Hunter to A. Popple, April 14, 1732, C.O. 137: 20 (unpaged).

[50] Board of Trade to queen guardian, Aug. 3, 1732, C.O. 138: 17, pp. 364–369; Board of Trade to privy council committee, Sept. 6, 1732, *ibid.*, pp. 374–378; two orders in council, Oct. 13, 1732, C.O. 137: 20; *Acts, Privy Coun., Col.*, 1720–1745, pp. 162–164.

ment continuously since 1708. His instructions contained an article against duties on slaves in the same words as the circular instruction of 1731 to the governors of other provinces.[51] But before sailing Cunningham sent a memorial to the privy council which dwelt upon the heavy expenses incurred in fighting runaway and rebellious negroes—the maroons—who were menacing the safety of the island. In view of the situation he begged that the assembly might be allowed to lay a small import and export duty on slaves, as they had done continuously from 1693 until stopped by the additional instruction of 1731.[52] The merchants protested again and the Board of Trade and privy council committee conducted hearings. In spite of the confident assertions of the merchants that Jamaica was as prosperous as ever, Cunningham produced witnesses who established conclusively that the island had suffered heavily in recent years. The rebellious negroes had become more numerous and bold until now five negroes could frighten fifteen whites. Internal taxes were heavy, there was little currency on the island, the receiver general often was unable to borrow money even at twelve-and-a-half percent interest, and general desertion of the island was feared. In view of these circumstances the British authorities agreed to permit, during the "present exigencies," a reasonable duty on negroes bought in the island, to be paid by the purchaser, provided that the South Sea Company should in no way be discriminated against.[53] This permission was incorporated in an addi-

[51] Instructions to Cunningham, Jamaica, 1734, art. 80, C.O. 5: 196, pp. 21–70 (L.C.).

[52] Cunningham's memorial enclosed with privy council committee order, Nov. 1, 1734, C.O. 137: 21 (unpaged).

[53] William Wood, agent for the merchants, to the Board of Trade, Nov. 25, 1734; memorial from "Governor and Company of Merchants of Great Britain trading to the South Seas and other parts of America and for encouraging the fishery," Nov. 22, 1734; Wood to Popple, Nov. 29, 1734,

tional instruction to Cunningham and was repeated to all his successors through Keith in 1773.[54]

For once the islanders had won from the merchants. But it was not an easy victory. In spite of the fact that every royal governor from Lawes in 1717 to Cunningham in 1734 had expressed to the home authorities his sympathy with the provincial point of view and his belief that the unrestricted slave trade was harmful to the island, the merchants had gained increasing protection for their traffic on the plea that it was "not agreeable to the rules of reason or policy that the trade of Great Britain, the mother country, should be burdened with taxes to ease the weight thereof on a colony."[55] Only a desperate crisis in Jamaica convinced the British officials that the island's welfare demanded some slight sacrifice of the merchants' interests.

During the years that followed, the instruction against the duties on negroes produced some difficulties in other provinces, notably in South Carolina, New York, and Virginia.[56] But nowhere did the situation become as acute as it had in Jamaica, and in no other case did the home authorities relax the regulation. The sequel in that island is, however, illuminating. In conformity with the instruction of 1735, acts had been passed from time to time laying relatively light duties upon negroes purchased in

ibid. For the Board of Trade hearings see *Board of Trade Journal,* 1728/9–1734, pp. 417–427, *passim.* Board of Trade to privy council committee, Dec. 12, 1734, C.O. 138: 18, pp. 3–12; order of privy council committee, May 10, 1735, C.O. 137: 21; order of queen guardian in council, July 9, 1735, C.O. 137: 22; *Acts, Privy Coun., Col.,* 1720–1745, pp. 165–167.

[54] Additional instruction to Cunningham, July 10, 1735, C.O. 5: 196, pp. 121–122 (L.C.).

[55] This quotation is from the memorial of the "Governor and Company of Merchants of Great Britain trading to the South Seas and other parts of America and for encouraging the fishery," Nov. 22, 1734, in answer to Cunningham's memorial, C.O. 137: 21.

[56] *Acts, Privy Coun., Col.,* 1720–1745, §§ 285, 313; *N. Y. Col. Docs.,* VI, 32–34, 37–38; and see above, pp. 62–63.

Jamaica. But the taxes had come to be payable by the importer and not by the purchaser as required by the instruction.[57] As Richard Harris had vehemently explained in 1727, the slave traders did not believe that the duty on such "perishable goods" as negro slaves could be shifted to the purchaser by the importer if the latter made the actual payment.[58] The Board of Trade took no action, however; until by an act of 1774 the assembly imposed a greatly increased duty upon the importation of slaves, the tax to be paid by the importer. The merchants of London, Bristol, and Liverpool, engaged in the slave trade, presented memorials against the act. At a hearing before the board the merchants testified that the additional duty had already cost them £15,000 and that without relief they could no longer carry on the trade to Jamaica with profit. The Jamaica agent, Stephen Fuller, countered with the assertion that the island legislature had "an unquestionable right to judge of the ways and means of raising supplies for the public service of that island." He added, in opposition to the economic theories of the merchants, "that in fact the burden of the duty must fall upon the consumer and not the importer, who doubtless has been paid an advanced price for his slaves in proportion to the advance of the duty." This statement, the Board of Trade declared in its report, was "controvertible even as a general argument," and certainly did not apply in this case where the act expressly made the duty payable by the importer! More fundamental than this economic discussion was the board's contention that "the legislative authority of the assemblies in your Majesty's colonies in America in point of taxation does not extend beyond the imposing taxes and duties upon the inhabit-

---

[57] Mathew Lamb, standing council to the Board of Trade, objected to Jamaica acts of 1746, 1747, 1748, and 1749 on this ground but it does not appear that any further action was taken. C.O. 137: 25, *passim*.

[58] See above, p. 239.

ants of those colonies; that all laws enacted by the legislatures that operate to the imposition of duties upon ships
and goods of the merchants of this kingdom or to prejudice or obstruct its commerce are not warranted by the
constitution.'' Therefore the board recommended and
prepared an additional instruction for the governor of
Jamaica requiring a return to the duties in force before
the passage of the act of 1774.[59] Again the merchants won
the day.

This episode, occurring as it did such a short time before the outbreak of the American Revolution, has particular significance. The Board of Trade, even at this
late date, insisted upon the right and duty of the prerogative to defend the interests of the British merchants
against the adverse legislation of a provincial assembly.
But Stephen Fuller, as agent for a province which remained loyal during the succeeding revolution, stood
forth as champion of the right of an assembly to complete
legislative independence. By this time the issue was
clearly joined throughout the British colonial world.
Within a few months after this hearing took place in
Whitehall, those colonies best situated for revolt were
destined to rise in arms in assertion of their ''unquestionable right'' to control their own affairs.

The struggle over the duties on the slave trade in
Jamaica was unique only in that it lasted for so long a
time and that during its course the home authorities made
some concession to the interests of the island. In all other
respects it was entirely typical of the conflicts which took

[59] Board of Trade representation to the king, Dec. 19, 1774, C.O. 138: 23,
pp. 342–350; *Acts, Privy Coun., Col.*, 1766–1783, § 313; additional instruction to Keith, submitted Feb. 23, 1775, C.O. 138: 23, pp. 352–354. The
struggle over the duties on negroes in Jamaica is described, especially on its
economic side, in F. W. Pitman, *The Development of the British West Indies,
1700–1763*, pp. 79–85.

place again and again over instructions designed to protect British trade against the legislation of the assemblies. In general, these instructions, representing the negative activities of the crown in maintaining the mercantile system, aroused more opposition than did the enforcement of the Navigation Acts themselves. By the first quarter of the eighteenth century the trade of the colonies had generally become adjusted to the channels laid down in the acts of parliament. In cases where the laws were too strict, evasion and subterfuge could and did give relief. But such methods were not possible against the ever increasing instructions which prohibited colonial legislation. From its very nature, an act of assembly was a public matter. It could not be smuggled through as could a pipe of French wine. Each act was sent to the Board of Trade by the governor and scrutinized by them and by their legal counsel. Any hardship which it might impose upon British merchants was certain to be reported to the home government by the traders, sometimes even before the act itself had arrived. With very few exceptions, based upon the strongest evidence of necessity, the home officials upheld the instructions and disallowed these acts. The satisfaction with which the merchants viewed such support of their interests and the wrath with which the assemblies learned of such denials of their legislative freedom can easily be imagined.

There was one way in which an assembly, under a compliant governor, might sometimes evade these instructions and the almost inevitable disallowance of prohibited acts. They might pass a bill for so short a time that it would have expired before its disallowance could be signified to the governor, and then they might renew the measure for a similar term under plea of necessity. The king would be unable to make void any of these short-lived acts during the period when it was in force. Several of the

Jamaica slave duties were laid in this way and nearly all the provinces found the method convenient at one time or another, especially in the case of revenue laws. That instructions were given to the governors against this practice is, therefore, not surprising. Even before the reign of James II an article was included in the general instructions of several governors requiring that every law for the support of government be made to run for an unlimited time, unless the act was "for a temporary service" and should have its full effect within a definite period. In the special case of laws raising impositions on wines and liquors, a minimum duration of one year was required.[60] By 1697 the Board of Trade had realized the necessity of extending this instruction to every royal province, a result which they accomplished within the next few years.[61] Thus, except in special cases, the provinces were not supposed to pass short-term revenue laws. Every such measure was to be passed for an indefinite period so that the king might exercise his right of review.

For some time this order affected only revenue laws. But that other measures were subject to similar abuses gradually became apparent. The matter was brought to the attention of the British officials by the special conditions existing in the proprietary province of Pennsylvania. By the charter, the proprietor was allowed five years in which to submit to the privy council every law passed in his province. Consequently many acts of a tem-

[60] The instruction was first given to Governor Dutton, Barbados, 1680, art. 18, C.O. 29: 3, pp. 37–53 and to Carlisle, Jamaica, 1680, art. 7, C.O. 138: 3, pp. 447–453. Before the Revolution of 1689 it was being regularly sent to the governors of Virginia, New Hampshire, and the Leeward Islands, as well as to those of Barbados and Jamaica.

[61] In a representation to the Lords Justices, prepared but not sent, Aug. 26, 1697, the Board of Trade suggested that this instruction be given to all royal governors, C.O. 324: 6, pp. 176–178; *Cal. State Paps., Col.*, 1696–1697, §§ 1281, 1305. The article was sent to the remaining provinces after the accession of Anne.

porary nature had long expired before the council could consider them. In 1709 and again in 1714 the Board of Trade complained of this situation.[62] A general investigation of the possibility of preventing temporary laws in all the colonies followed in the latter year. The discussion produced no results at the time,[63] but four years later the Board of Trade determined to tighten the regulations in the royal provinces. While leaving the article on the duration of revenue laws as it already stood, they introduced a new clause into the instructions for Governor Lawes of Jamaica, requiring him to withhold his consent from any other measure enacted for a shorter period than two years.[64] The new instruction had been extended to all other royal provinces by 1728. The rule now stood that, with the exception of revenue bills for purely temporary purposes, and of bills for impositions on liquors, which latter must run for at least one year, all revenue bills must be indefinite and without limitation, and that all non-revenue acts must run for at least two years. These regulations continued until after 1770, when the government introduced a modification in some provinces by permitting all revenue laws to be passed for a year at a time. With the exception of South Carolina, none of the provinces thus favored were among those which revolted in 1775.[65]

[62] *Cal. State Paps., Col.,* 1708–1709, §§ 717, 791, 809; 1712–1714, § 553; *Acts, Privy Coun., Col.,* 1680–1720, § 1108.

[63] The attorney general gave his opinion that conditions growing out of the charters of proprietary or corporate colonies could be remedied only by act of parliament. As to the royal provinces, a strict adherence to the instructions by the governors would improve the situation. *Cal. State Paps., Col.,* 1712–1714, §§ 689, 692, 728; *Board of Trade Journal,* 1708/9–1714/5, pp. 540, 553, 565, 567; C.O. 324: 10, pp. 42–48, 58–60 (L.C.).

[64] Instructions to Lawes, Jamaica, 1718, art. 30, C.O. 5: 189, pp. 334–375 (L.C.). Most provinces had received this instruction by 1720 but it did not reach all until after the accession of George II.

[65] In addition to South Carolina the provinces for which this change was

However necessary these restrictions upon temporary legislation seemed to the Board of Trade and privy council, they worked considerable hardship upon the colonies. Even the Board of Trade was willing to admit this fact. In commenting in 1761 upon an address from the Virginia council and House of Burgesses to the king, asking for the withdrawal of this and one other instruction, the board conceded that there were "particular cases of emergency" especially in time of war, in which the rules as to the duration of acts could not be strictly enforced. In such cases the governor "must of necessity be left to use his own discretion, remembering that if he transgresses the instruction, he can only be justified by the nature of the case." Yet the Board remained of the opinion that the instruction was "founded on the true principles of a provincial constitution" and appeared to be "indispensably necessary for preserving that constitution within its just limits and for maintaining the supreme authority of the Crown."[66] The Virginia request for the withdrawal of the instruction was therefore turned down.

A mere restriction upon temporary laws was not enough to prevent evasion of the royal disallowance. Experience showed that some restriction upon the power of the assembly to reenact disallowed laws or to modify or repeal laws already passed was necessary if the review of colonial legislation was to be effective. During the same period that the British officials were working out the regulations about temporary laws they were also framing other rules to limit the passage of laws on subjects with which the

made were East Florida, the Bahamas, Barbados, Jamaica, Dominica, Grenada, the Leeward Islands, St. Vincent, and Nova Scotia. Some indication will be given in the following two chapters of the extent to which the general rule against temporary revenue laws was violated in all the provinces before 1770.

[66] Board of Trade to privy council committee, May 20, 1761, C.O. 5: 1368, pp. 183–185 (L.C.).

assembly had once dealt. As early as 1680 the governors of some provinces were forbidden to reenact any law once passed "except upon very urgent occasions" and in no case more than once without the king's express consent.[67] Together with the prohibition of temporary laws this rule went far to check the practice of passing annual revenue laws, each one of which would expire before the royal disallowance could be received. The regulation was continued for about forty years without change, but it eventually proved inadequate. What constituted "very urgent occasions" was not defined. The term might mean one thing to the Board of Trade and quite another to a governor harassed by his assembly. A more precise rule about the reenactment of laws became necessary. Accordingly the Board of Trade sent a new instruction on this point to the various provinces between 1718 and 1728 which varied slightly at first but had become standardized by the accession of George II. In the first place, this instruction told the governor to refuse his consent to the reenactment of any law which had previously been disallowed unless he first obtained the king's "express leave." The governor could get this permission only after explaining fully the reason and necessity for passing such a law. In the second place, he was to refuse his consent to any bill repealing an act already passed in the province, whether or not that act had been confirmed by the king, unless the new measure contained a suspending clause.[68] In effect then, once an assembly had passed a law on a

[67] First given in instructions to Dutton, Barbados, 1680, art. 19, C.O. 29: 3, pp. 37–53, and instructions to Carlisle, Jamaica, 1680, art. 8, C.O. 138: 3, pp. 447–453. But similar orders had once before been given to the governors of each of these islands; additional instructions to Atkins, Barbados, May 11, 1674, art. 1, C.O. 29: 1, pp. 172–173; instructions to Vaughan, Jamaica, 1674, art. 18, C.O. 1: 31, no. 83.

[68] This change was made at the same time that the change was being made in the instruction about temporary laws. The rules on both points were gen-

given subject the governor might not allow them to make a second attempt to enact the measure if it should be disallowed, or to repeal it or change its terms if it had not been disallowed, unless the king gave his express consent. By this rule the disallowance was protected and the king kept the final decision on all measures which came up for approval or disapproval.

On its face the latter part of this rule applied only to bills which actually repealed former laws. But in practice the Board of Trade interpreted the word "repeal" to include partial as well as entire repeal, so that the instruction really prohibited revision or amendment, as well as entire repeal, of any act once passed unless the new bill should be suspended until the king gave his consent. In another respect, however, the board interpreted the instruction more liberally than the words implied. Since either the securing of the king's approval before the passage of a bill or the including of a suspending clause would insure consideration of a measure in Great Britain before it could go into effect in the province, the board was generally indifferent as to which method the governor followed in any case which arose under the instruction. The suspending clause, being more convenient, was generally adopted both for reenacting disallowed laws and for repealing or altering laws once passed. These interpretations, not apparent in the phraseology of the instruction, were actually a part of the instruction as it was applied to the legislation of the various provinces.

Judging from the number of violations of these rules and the frequent attempts of the assemblies to have them withdrawn, this instruction seems to have formed the

erally included in the same article although Lawes of Jamaica, the first governor to receive the instruction, was given only the first part of the rule about reenactment of laws already passed. Instructions to Lawes, Jamaica, 1718, art. 30, C.O. 5: 189, pp. 334–375 (L.C.).

most burdensome restriction upon colonial legislation to
be found in the history of the period. Probably not a single
royal province escaped having at least one of its laws
disallowed because it reenacted a disallowed law or repealed or amended some former act but did not at the
same time contain a suspending clause. And in addition
to the times when the privy council actually voided provincial acts on these grounds, there were many occasions
when the governors vetoed bills which failed to conform
to the instruction, and countless times when the assemblies
felt the need of passing laws to go into immediate effect
but did not do so because the instruction stood in their
way. But the British government placed itself firmly
against the violation of the instruction. As early as 1724,
three years after it was first given to Lieutenant Governor Hope of Bermuda, the assembly of that island passed
an act, with the governor's approval, levying a duty on
imports. The bill was much like a measure which had been
disallowed the previous year, except that it lowered the
rate of the duty. When the new act reached the privy
council committee with the Board of Trade's recommendation for disallowance, the committee investigated
and reported to the council that the governor's action
in approving the bill had constituted a "willful and notorious breach" of his instructions. Although the disallowance of the former act had not been signified to the
province in form, the preamble of the new act made clear
that the disallowance was known in the island. This fact
aggravated Governor Hope's "crime" and the new act
was, of course, disallowed.[69] Similar instances, almost
without number, might be cited to show the British attitude toward such violations of the instruction. Obviously
the disallowance would be worthless if the colony might
freely repass any law which had met with the royal dis-

[69] *Acts, Privy Coun., Col.*, 1720–1745, § 66.

approval. The assembly was to be made to understand that a disallowance was a final settlement of the matter and one which they must learn to respect.

More burdensome to the assembly was the other part of the instruction which required the king's consent for any bill altering or repealing an act previously passed, whether confirmed or not. Many of the governors recognized the hardship caused by this rule. Some of them, such as Belcher of Massachusetts, asked the Board of Trade for the withdrawal of the instruction, only to be met with a rebuff.[70] Belcher's successor, William Shirley, reduced the proceeding almost to a farce. He meticulously asked the king's consent before approving even such a petty measure as a bill withdrawing the bounty formerly granted for the killing of crows and blackbirds.[71] The Board of Trade solemnly commended his action but expressed a wish that he had followed the more usual method of including a suspending clause.[72] The instruction, they explained to a later governor of the same province who had violated it, was "founded upon just constitutional principles of government" and "ought never to be departed from, but in cases of real exigency, not admitting of the loss of so much time as would necessarily intervene between the passing of the act and the notification of the crown's assent to it.'"[73] The home authorities believed thoroughly in the value of the instruction.

The official position was based upon the British theory of the part played by the crown in colonial legislation. The normal legislative prerogatives of the king were

[70] Board of Trade to Belcher, Sept. 27, 1733 [1738?], C.O. 5: 917, pp. 83–90 (Mass.).

[71] Shirley to the Board of Trade, July —, 1743, C.O. 5: 884, p. 208.

[72] Board of Trade to Shirley, Aug. 9, 1743, C.O. 5: 918, pp. 129–132 (Mass.).

[73] Board of Trade to Bernard, Feb. 4, 1762, C.O. 5: 920, pp. 134–138 (Mass.).

delegated to the governor in his commission. But the king specifically reserved to himself the important executive prerogative of confirming or disallowing every law which passed a provincial assembly. If the assembly should repeal an act before the king had confirmed or disallowed it, they would thereby deprive him of his right of final action upon the original measure. Such an infringement of his prerogative as the repeal would involve could not be tolerated. Hence the assembly ought to suspend the repealing measure until the king could pass upon it along with the earlier law.[74] For the assembly to repeal a law actually confirmed by the king was an even more serious infringement upon his prerogative, unless they suspended the repeal until the king's pleasure should be known. Every confirmed act had received the sanction of the assembly, the council, the governor, and the king. Each of these four parties had a right to be consulted before the act thus unanimously agreed upon was altered or repealed. The repeal of such a measure by the assembly without a suspending clause was just as unconstitutional as would be the exercise of a dispensing power by the king. "Every act so passed," declared the Board of Trade in 1761, "is a violation of the just and lawful authority of the crown, and so dangerous a deviation from the true principles of the constitution of the colony that it is of the highest importance that a practice so subversive of both should be constantly checked in every instance."[75]

But in America the assemblies raised objections to the instruction on both practical and theoretical grounds. Experience showed that the inclusion of a suspending clause

[74] "This [rule] we think the more necessary because acts for repealing others have had their effect before your Majesty's pleasure could be known thereupon." Board of Trade representation on the instructions for Governor Montgomerie of New Jersey, Sept. 28, 1727, *N. J. Arch.*, V, 170.

[75] Board of Trade to the privy council committee, May 20, 1761, C.O. 5: 1368, pp. 180-182 (L.C.).

usually resulted in an inordinately long delay before the desired act went into force. The usefulness of a bill repealing or altering a former law often depended almost entirely upon the promptness with which it could be carried out. Even if the Board of Trade and privy council were to make their decision immediately upon receipt of a suspended act, the best part of a year would elapse between the passage of the act in the province and the governor's proclamation of its confirmation. And during a large part of the eighteenth century the Board of Trade was notorious for its delays and procrastination.[76] Any system which prevented the local legislature from making immediate changes in the laws when necessity arose, was bound to create dissatisfaction and occasionally to cause real hardship. By the very nature of the instruction, it was certain to produce more and more distress the longer it was in force. By the middle of the eighteenth century the natural process of legislation had provided all the provinces with laws on nearly every important subject. As time went on it became increasingly difficult to pass any new act without in some way altering a previous law on the same subject. So the suspending clause became more and more frequently necessary, even for what might be called ordinary legislation.[77] The assembly found it

[76] The Board of Trade wrote President Dottin of Barbados, Oct. 6, 1736, authorizing the repeal of five undesirable laws if suspending clauses were included in the acts of repeal. C.O. 29: 16, p. 54. Dottin replied, May 14, 1737, promising to comply. He added: ''But your Lordships will allow me the liberty most humbly to remark that the assembly here seldom care to make an act wherein this clause is inserted, because it has generally happened to lie by a long while without being confirmed or disallowed, an instance of which is the Church Wardens' Act transmitted with this clause about four years since.'' C.O. 28: 25 (unpaged). But the Board of Trade was actually no more dilatory than other governmental offices during the same period.

[77] In *The Royal Government in Virginia, 1624–1775*, pp. 200–201, Dr. P. S. Flippin presents an analysis of the volumes of Hening's *Statutes at Large of Virginia* to show the increasing use of the suspending clause in that province. In the first three volumes, covering the period to 1711, the

harder each year to take effective and prompt action on matters of local concern.

Nearly all the assemblies complained of the burdens which the suspending clause imposed, but none took such a determined stand for what they called their "rights" as did the assembly of Jamaica. This body absolutely refused to put suspending clauses in any measures except private acts. In 1752 they passed a bill appointing commissioners of *nisi prius*, which not only encroached upon the governor's appointing power, but materially changed the laws relating to the administration of justice. Governor Edward Trelawney asked for a suspending clause, but the most he could get was a clause postponing the operation of the act for a period of about fourteen months.[78] The privy council disallowed the law, of course, but not until nearly two years after it was passed.[79] In the meantime, Charles Knowles, a high-spirited and impetuous naval officer, had been appointed governor and had plunged at once into a controversy with the assembly. One subject of dispute had been his refusal to pass certain bills unless suspending clauses were added. Thereupon the assembly adopted a striking series of resolutions. The first two dealt with the right of the assembly to raise money and with the legislative process as laid down in every gover-

suspending clause does not once appear. In volume IV (1711–1736) it is used 6 times—for the first time in Nov., 1720; in volume V (1738–1748), 15 times; in volume VI (1748–1755), 19 times; in volume VII (1756–1763), 26 times; and in volume VIII (1764–1773), 77 times. This count shows that the increase was gradual until 1764 and rapid thereafter. In this connection, attention may be called to the fact that Lieutenant Governor Fauquier (1758–1768) was very lax in enforcing the requirement during the first six years of his administration but very facile in explaining his misconduct. He was repeatedly censured by the Board of Trade and apparently became more obedient in 1764. See C.O. 5: 1330 and 1331, *passim*.

78 Edward Trelawney to the Board of Trade, March 25, 1752, C.O. 137: 25.

79 Attorney General Ryder and Solicitor General Murray to the Board of Trade, June 22, 1753, *ibid.; Acts, Privy Coun., Col.,* 1745–1766, pp. 215, 218–219.

nor's commission since 1681, which was "as nearly agreeable to the prerogative of the Crown of England, and of [*sic*] the rights and privileges of the people of that kingdom, to which the people of this island are undoubtedly entitled, as the distant situation of this island can admit of." The assembly then further

Resolved, that it doth appear that no clause hath been inserted in any act of a public nature passed by the legislature of this island suspending the execution thereof until his Majesty's pleasure should be known.

Resolved, that if such clause had been inserted in acts heretofore passed by the legislature of this island, this island could not have been preserved and defended from its foreign and intestine enemies.

Resolved, that if such clause should be inserted in acts to be hereafter passed in this island, and the legislature should be thereby delayed upon emergent occasions from exerting the utmost force of the whole island as well of money as men to defend and preserve themselves and their fellow subjects, his Majesty may be in danger of losing this colony and his people their lives, liberty, and property.

Resolved, that the inserting such a clause in acts to be passed by the legislature of this island may be attended with this manifest inconvenience to the inhabitants thereof, in as much as such acts after they shall pass may lie for many years without being offered to his Majesty for his royal pleasure thereupon, as many heretofore have done, and now do, which if it should happen would be of much worse consequence than the disallowance of them by his Majesty could be; . . . [for in case of disallowance, the assembly would have an opportunity to repass the acts with the objectionable features removed] whereas in the other case, let the evils or inconveniencies be ever so great which the legislature should be desirous of redressing or preventing by their acts, they must patiently bear them and wait the event of the remedies they had provided without having it in their power either to present them to his Majesty to know his pleasure thereupon, or to take any new methods to help themselves whilst the former should be in suspense.

Resolved, that as the inserting such suspending clauses in bills of a public nature to be passed by the legislature of this island will not be for his Majesty's service or the peace, welfare, good government, and security of this island, but on the contrary, will endanger the former and be prejudicial to the crown, and as such insertion will be a very great alteration of the known and established constitution of this island, and as the same is derogatory to the undoubted right of the subject hath [sic] of proposing laws to the crown, this house cannot consent to the insertion of such clauses in public bills without giving up the rights of the people, their own liberties, and the happy constitution which they have enjoyed under his present most gracious Majesty and his royal predecessors for above seventy years.[80]

In commenting on this bold indictment of the suspending clause, the Board of Trade declared that the assembly's resolutions rested upon "a total misapprehension" of the instructions, which did not direct how the assembly was to frame bills, but in what manner the governor was to approve or veto the measures laid before him. The inclusion of a suspending clause actually permitted the governor to assent to a bill which otherwise he must have vetoed according to one or another of his instructions and his own private judgment. With the clause he could pass the measure on to the king for final decision instead of killing it out of hand. "The instruction, therefore, is in favor of the assembly, whose bills of the nature described in it could not otherwise have had their existence as acts and consequently could not have been laid before his Majesty in so short and so easy a manner."[81] How far the

[80] Resolutions of Oct. 29, 1753, quoted in the Board of Trade representation to the king, Oct. 15, 1754, C.O. 138: 20, pp. 47–50.

[81] Board of Trade to Governor Knowles, Oct. 15, 1754, ibid., pp. 89–91. This letter repeated nearly verbatim the appropriate passages from their representation to the king of the same date, ibid., pp. 41–75.

Jamaica assembly profited by this little homily and how far they appreciated in the future the benefits which the suspending clause conferred upon them, may be judged from the fact that only seven months later they passed four acts, one of which repealed parts of several earlier laws, and three of which were "of an unusual and extraordinary nature" affecting the property of subjects, but none of which contained a suspending clause.[82]

None of the provinces which revolted in 1775 ever dared to oppose officially the suspending clause with as much vigor as did Jamaica. But the clause played a leading part in one of the most famous of controversies in Virginia and led to one of the boldest attacks upon the king which took place in the entire pre-revolutionary period. In 1748 the Virginia council and assembly felt the need of a new edition of the provincial laws, codified and revised. The task was completed by the end of 1749 and the sixty-seven acts which composed the work were passed and transmitted to the Board of Trade as usual. In its report to the privy council the board praised this undertaking highly and

[82] These acts all related to the removal of the provincial capital from San Jago de la Vega to Kingston. The Board of Trade and privy council committee recommended the measures for disallowance because they lacked suspending clauses, but action was postponed until Lieut. Gov. Moore could report the dispassionate judgment of the assembly as to where the capital ought to be. In June, 1758, these four acts were disallowed and Kingston was deprived of the position of capital which it had occupied for three years. Board of Trade to privy council committee, Feb. 12, 1756, C.O. 138: 20, pp. 160–165; additional instruction to Moore, submitted March 9, 1756, *ibid.*, pp. 173–176; *Acts, Privy Coun., Col.,* 1745–1766, § 236. The Jamaica attitude toward the suspending clause was soon afterward brought to the attention of the House of Commons, who, after several sittings in committee of the whole, resolved that the Jamaica resolutions of 1753 on the subject proceeded "upon a manifest misapprehension of his Majesty's instruction" and "that such instruction is just and necessary, and no alteration of the constitution of that island, nor anyways derogatory to the rights of his subjects there." But the Commons took no further action. *Journal of the House of Commons,* XXVII, 399–400, 468–469, 530, 833, 837, 838–839, 883, 889, 910–911.

recommended that it be used as a model by all the other provinces for a revision of their own enactments. Unfortunately, however, all of these sixty-seven acts took the place of, and so repealed, amended, or altered former acts, but without the use of a suspending clause in a single instance. The Board of Trade magnanimously agreed to waive the rule in relation to fifty-seven of these laws and recommended their confirmation since the changes they made were unimportant and their speedy enactment seemed necessary. But the remaining ten measures definitely repealed laws which had been previously confirmed, "a deviation and departing from your Majesty's instructions which no circumstance or necessity can justify." Some of these laws also were objectionable on other grounds.[83] The privy council approved the board's report, confirmed the fifty-seven acts, and disallowed the remaining ten.[84]

This action proved most disturbing to the Virginians. The council and assembly sent an address to the king on the subject. The document begins with a temperate review of the clauses in the governor's commission regarding the legislative power, and rehearses the facts connected with the recent revision of the provincial laws. According to the Virginians' conception of the "ancient constitution and usages" of the colony, all laws not repugnant to those of England had full force until their disallowance had been proclaimed in the province, and such laws might be re-

[83] Board of Trade to the king, Aug. 6, 1751, C.O. 5: 1366, pp. 479–504 (L.C.) ; *Acts, Privy Coun., Col.*, 1745–1766, § 155.

[84] *Acts, Privy Coun., Col.*, 1745–1766, § 155. The privy council adopted the suggestion of the Board that all other provinces be required to codify their laws as Virginia had done. But profiting by the Virginia experience they required that every act in the revised series contain a suspending clause and be transmitted separately under the provincial seal for the royal allowance or disallowance. *Ibid.*, § 167; circular instruction, March 12, 1752, C.O. 324: 15, pp. 294–297 (Mass.).

vised, altered, and amended as the exigencies of the case might require until their confirmation by order in council. Thereafter, the address admitted, the suspending clause was necessary for amendment. But this very fact filled the petitioners with concern. For had not his Majesty just confirmed and ratified in a "solemn manner" fifty-seven of their revised laws? These acts could no longer be altered in the colony without suspending clauses, "which, if understood in a strict sense, will subject us to great hardships and inconveniences since it is not within the reach of human foresight to form any laws but what may from experience be found to want necessary and speedy amendments." They begged his Majesty to consider their "unhappy case" and instruct his lieutenant governor that his intention was not "to fix those confirmed laws so unalterably" upon the province but that they might be amended when necessary, provided the changes did not require suspending clauses for other reasons. In conclusion, the address admitted the wisdom of two of the ten disallowances, but explained why the assembly wished to repass the eight other laws.[85]

In reporting their opinion of this address the Board of Trade declared that to allow the assembly to repeal, alter, or amend laws once confirmed, without suspending clauses "would be to take away, or at least render useless and ineffectual, that power which the crown has so wisely and properly reserved to itself" of disallowing improper laws "and would destroy that check which was established, not only to preserve the just and proper influence and authority which the crown ought to have in the direction and government of the colonies in America, but also to secure to its subjects their just liberties and privi-

[85] Council and Burgesses of Virginia to the king, July 12, 1752, C.O. 5: 1327, pp. 509–514 (L.C.).

leges.'' With this opinion the privy council agreed and the Virginia request was refused.[86]

Only a few years passed before each side could point to an incident in Virginia as justifying its arguments on the amendment of confirmed laws. One of the fifty-seven acts of 1748 and 1749 confirmed by the king provided for the payment of salaries to the clergy in a fixed quantity of tobacco. In some of the years which followed the crops were poor and the clergy anticipated a handsome advance in the value of their salaries due to the increased market price of tobacco. But in 1758, the assembly passed an act, to be in force for one year only, authorizing the payment of all dues in paper money at a rate well below the current high price of tobacco. The bill amended the act of 1748, so that Lieutenant Governor Fauquier, who had just taken office, should have required a suspending clause. But he realized that to insist upon such a clause in an act of this short duration would be the equivalent of rejecting it. Similar measures, passed in 1753 and 1755, had not yet been examined by the Board of Trade so that the previous governor had not been censured. Fauquier felt that in view of these precedents he could not veto this highly popular measure without destroying all possibility of future influence with the council and House of Burgesses. Hence he passed the bill as it stood.[87]

But the Virginia clergy were up in arms against this seemingly unfair pruning of their salaries. The situation gave rise to the celebrated ''Parsons' Cause.'' They held a convention, subscribed a fund to send an agent to Eng-

[86] Two of the formerly disallowed acts were permitted to be repassed. Board of Trade to privy council committee, Feb. 14, 1753, C.O. 5: 1367, pp. 13–19 (L.C.); order in council, March 7, 1753, C.O. 5: 1327, pp. 605–609 (L.C.); *Acts, Privy Coun., Col.,* 1745–1766, § 186; additional instruction to Albemarle, Va., May 10, 1753, C.O. 5: 200, pp. 851–852 (L.C.).

[87] Fauquier to the Board of Trade, Jan. 5, 1759, C.O. 5: 1329, pp. 229–235 (L.C.).

land, and prepared memorials to the king and Board of Trade against the law.[88] The merchants trading to the province were willing allies of the clergymen, for they also felt the burden of the law, which permitted the planters who had contracted for the delivery of fixed quantities of tobacco to evade their pledges by paying in depreciated paper currency at less than market rates. In order to complete their cargoes the factors of the merchants had to buy tobacco at a sixty percent advance over the contract price.[89] Roused by the clamor of the parsons and the traders, the home officials took prompt action. The act of 1758 and its similarly offending predecessors were at once disallowed, and a strongly worded additional instruction was sent to Fauquier reprimanding him for his action, both because the act of 1758 was a temporary law of less than two years' duration and because it modified the act of 1748 without a suspending clause.[90]

The disallowance was keenly felt in the colony. The council and House of Burgesses united in another address to the king, protesting against the decision and begging for withdrawal of the instructions which required suspending clauses in temporary laws or in acts to repeal or amend other laws, particularly those which had not already been confirmed. They asked especially for relief in cases of emergency which related only to the people of the colony and did not affect the prerogative or the trade of Great Britain. Their argument was summed up in the statement that "the limiting the legislative power in such cases must necessarily involve the colony in the most insuperable difficulties, since many unavoidable changes in our cir-

[88] C.O. 5: 1329, pp. 268, 271–273 (L.C.).

[89] See G. L. Beer, *British Colonial Policy, 1754–1765*, pp. 183–185.

[90] C.O. 5: 1329, pp. 315–316, 431, 439 (L.C.); *Acts, Privy Coun., Col., 1745–1766*, § 394; additional instruction to Fauquier, Aug. 30, 1759, C.O. 5: 1367, pp. 486–489 (L.C.).

cumstances do frequently happen which require the immediate assistance of the legislature before it is possible for us at so great a distance to make any application to your Majesty.'"[91] In the minds of the Virginians, the law which had just been disallowed was an excellent illustration of the necessity of prompt action in time of emergency. But in the minds of the British officials, the case illustrated perfectly the harm which might befall British subjects, and especially the merchants, from permitting an assembly to alter at will laws which had previously been passed. The Virginia petition was therefore promptly rejected in accordance with "the true principles of a provincial constitution.'"[92]

But before the incident was entirely closed, it led to an attack upon the crown more violent than any in which the assembly had dared to engage. Several of the ministers brought suit to recover the sums lost by the operation of the act of 1758. In one such suit, brought by the Reverend James Maury, Patrick Henry was attorney for the defense. He rested his case largely upon the utility of the act which the king had recently disallowed. According to Maury's account, Henry had the audacity to suggest in his address "that a king, by disallowing acts of this salutary nature, from being the father of his people, degenerated into a tyrant, and forfeits all right to his subjects' obedience.'"[93] The word "tyrant" was strong language, and was hardly approved by the more sober-minded colonists. Yet the popularity which Henry won for himself by his remarks might have warned the British officials that a considerable group in America was beginning to

[91] Council and House of Burgesses to the king, Oct. 20, 1760, C.O. 5: 1330, pp. 105–110 (L.C.).

[92] Board of Trade to the privy council committee, May 20, 1761, C.O. 5: 1368, pp. 179–185 (L.C.).

[93] James Maury to a friend, Dec. 12, 1763, Ann Maury (ed.), *Memoirs of a Huguenot Family*, pp. 418–424.

identify the royal notions of "the true principles of a provincial constitution" with nothing less than tyranny.

Certainly the colonists were becoming more and more restive under the restrictions imposed upon their legislative freedom by the instructions. But from the British point of view these limitations were entirely justifiable. They were based upon two principles, one economic and the other constitutional. Believers in the mercantile system of colonial organization held that the rights and interests of the mother country and her merchants transcended those of the colonists themselves. Colonies did not exist as ends in themselves but only as means for increasing the might and wealth of the mother country. Only in the rarest cases of dire emergency might conditions in a colony be said to warrant interference by the assembly with the free course of British trade and shipping. In all other cases provincial legislation which threatened British interests should be checked in every possible way. The home officials also believed that the subordination of the assembly was a fundamental principle of the constitution. The assembly was not a sovereign parliament either in origin or in authority. It was created by the king through his royal grace and favor and its lawmaking powers were only such as the king chose to confer upon it. At all times the king reserved a voice in colonial legislation. If in his wisdom he instructed his governor to reject certain types of measures, the colonists could not justly complain of invaded "rights." Or if he generously allowed the governor to approve certain bills of doubtful propriety, provided their execution were suspended until the king himself could pass upon them, then the assemblymen should be grateful for his condescension rather than impatient at the resulting delay. Or, lastly, if the king disallowed certain laws when laid before him either because the governor had violated his instructions in passing them or because they might be harmful to British subjects, then the Americans ought to submit dutifully to this just and constitutional exercise of the royal prerogative.

But the trend of opinion in the colonies ran directly against these British principles. As the Americans increased in numbers, wealth, and political experience, they opposed more and more strongly the notion that the colonies were only means to a British end, a notion which they had never willingly accepted. They insisted that their rights as Englishmen were equally as great as those of British merchants and that within each province the interests of the inhabitants should receive consideration ahead of those of individuals or corporations in the mother country. Constitutionally also, the Americans came to deny the British theory. The assemblies had been created in the image of parliament. In the raising of revenues and the passing of local laws for the colonies, the parliament at Westminster had never taken a part. These legislative functions had been exercised by the assemblies which had thereby become, in fact as well as in appearance, miniature parliaments. Both expediency and sound policy dictated that the assemblies should have within their respective provinces the same legislative independence as parliament had at home. Royal interference with colonial legislation was as contrary to the spirit of the constitution as would be such interference with the measures of parliament itself.

When such differing views were held on either side of the Atlantic compromise was difficult at any time. By the close of the last intercolonial war the situation had become tense. When the representatives of the prerogative charged the colonists with "undutiful behavior" and began to talk seriously of the "interposition of parliament," and when the American radicals countered with the cry of "Tyranny!" and began to threaten an "appeal to heaven," conditions were serious indeed. But most of the British leaders were unable to understand the need for compromise. They could not or would not realize that the assemblies had grown to maturity and now required different treatment from that which they had received in the past. The royal officials saw no reason even to discuss the foremost question of their day: whether the assemblies should be allowed to exercise—in Thomas Pownall's words—"the same full, free, independent, unrestrained power and legislative will" as parliament exercised in Great Britain. Instead of facing this question openly and attempting to find a mutually satisfactory answer, the officials on whom the responsibility lay, continued the old policy of prerogative control of colonial legislation, supplemented by the new policy of parliamentary interference and coercion. So long as such an unenlightened attitude persisted, peaceful compromise was impossible.

CHAPTER VII

PROVINCIAL FINANCE

"MONEY is the very vitals of government" observed Governor Nicholas Lawes during a trying dispute with the Jamaica assembly.[1] The history of royal administration in the colonies illustrates the truth behind this statement. The British officials tried to check the growth of the assemblies in power and importance by means of the instructions dealing with their composition and legislative competency. But in spite of the limitations which these instructions placed upon their powers the assemblies continued to grow in strength and to acquire control of the more important functions of government. The chief weapon which they used in their contests for supremacy was their power to control finance. Money was indeed "the very vitals" of provincial government.

In an opinion written in 1724 the attorney and solicitor general of Great Britain laid down the rule that a colony of English subjects "cannot be taxed but by the parliament of Great Britain or by and with the consent of some representative body of the people of the [province], properly assembled by the authority of the crown."[2] Parliament never undertook to lay taxes adequate to the support of government in any royal province during the seventeenth or eighteenth centuries. In accordance, there-

---

[1] Lawes to the Board of Trade, April 27, 1722, C.O. 137: 14, pp. 149–150.

[2] Attorney General Yorke and Solicitor General Wearg to the Board of Trade, May 18, 1724, C.O. 137: 14, fos. 341–342; Chalmers, *Opinions*, I, 222–224. The question involved was as to what would be the constitutional status of Jamaica if the 21-year revenue act, due to expire in that year, should not

fore, with the constitutional principle as stated by the law officers of the crown, the task devolved upon the local assemblies. The financial dependence which the government was thus forced to place upon the legislative body in each province was the greatest weakness of the royal administration and the greatest source of power to the popular body.

In general, the assembly's control over finance tended toward greatest effectiveness through three main channels, here named in the order of their importance: first, their sole right to initiate legislation for raising revenue, the importance of which the royal officials tried to minimize by getting permanent revenues ample for the support of government; secondly, their control over appropriations and the actual disposition of the money so appropriated, against the exercise of which numerous instructions were issued to the governors; and thirdly, the granting of salaries to the governors and other officers, the importance of which—especially in the cases of the governors—can be overemphasized, but which raised serious controversies, particularly in the two New England provinces, in New York, and in New Jersey. These were the issues in which the assemblies won their chief victories and through which they forced the governors to give up the prerogative in many other points. The British officials recognized this fact and did all in their power to keep control of the financial affairs of the provinces. The measures which the Board of Trade, the privy council, and the governors took to restrict the assemblies'

be renewed. The law officers declared that the raising of a new revenue would depend on whether Jamaica was to be deemed a conquered country or a colony of English subjects; if the former, then taxes might be laid by the crown, if the latter, then only by parliament or a local assembly. The evidence before them did not warrant a decision as to which term more accurately described Jamaica. As a matter of fact, the island was always treated as a colony of English subjects.

control of the purse were among the most important parts
of British colonial policy.

At a very early date the home authorities recognized
the desirability of having in each province a fund which
would be adequate for the support of government and at
the same time free from control by the assembly. The
most general source of independent royal revenue was
found in the quit-rents, collected with greater or less
efficiency in all provinces in which the king claimed immediate title to the soil. Massachusetts and New Jersey
were the two royal provinces on the continent in which
no quit-rents were ever paid to the crown.[3] But in none of
the royal provinces were the quit-rents actually collected
in sufficient amount to provide for more than a fraction of
the cost of government.[4] Consequently the royal authorities tried to persuade the assemblies to grant certain
taxes in perpetuity and subject to the king's sole right
of disposal. Success met these efforts irf Barbados and
the Leeward Islands soon after the establishment of royal
government in these islands following the Restoration.
In 1663, Francis, Lord Willoughby of Parham, governor
of the Caribbee Islands, persuaded the Barbados assembly
to lay a perpetual duty of four-and-a-half percent upon
all "dead commodities" exported, in return for the confirmation of land titles and the surrender of the proprietary dues paid before the transfer of the island to the

[3] To these two must be added Maryland during its period of royal government. In some cases, such as New Hampshire and South Carolina, the
crown received quit-rents during only part of the period of royal government. See B. W. Bond, jr., *The Quit-Rent System in the American Colonies.*

[4] In most of the provinces the king was also entitled to receive various
other miscellaneous revenues from such sources as escheats, fines, wrecks,
and prizes of war. Such income was naturally irregular and usually insignificant in amount. These "casual revenues" could play no large part in the
fiscal system of the provinces. For a discussion of this subject, see G. L.
Beer, *The Old Colonial System,* Part I, I, 168–171.

king. Similar acts were passed in the next year in each of the Leeward Islands—St. Christopher, Nevis, Montserrat, and Antigua.[5] Although the colonists insisted that this revenue ought to be used solely for the public services of their provincial governments, there was in fact no such limitation, the money being spent for many other purposes, such as private pensions, and even for the salaries of the governors of several other provinces. Attempts to secure a similar revenue in Jamaica at the same time failed and the further extension of the scheme was temporarily abandoned.

But even in those provinces in which the royally controlled revenue was greatest, it never for any length of time proved adequate for the entire support of local government. In every colony the governors were forced sooner or later to appeal to the assemblies for money with which to carry on the administration. The crown was never able to win free from financial dependence upon the representatives of the people. In recognition of this fact and in an endeavor to minimize the importance of the taxing power of the assemblies, the home authorities adopted certain principles which they embodied in the commissions and instructions to the governors. The movement began in the latter part of the reign of Charles II after the creation of the privy council committee known as the Lords of Trade. Late in 1677 this body submitted a report to the king in council on "the present state and government of Jamaica" with particular reference to the commission and instructions about to be prepared for the earl of Carlisle, recently appointed governor. The document shows that the Lords of Trade were awake to

[5] The history of these acts is given in G. L. Beer, *The Old Colonial System*, Part I, I, 171–192; J. A. Williamson, *The Caribbee Islands under the Proprietary Patents*, pp. 198–214; and V. T. Harlow, *A History of Barbados, 1625–1685*, pp. 145–147.

the dangers inherent in the freedom then exercised by
the assembly. Among other things the report criticized the
loose way in which money was appropriated in Jamaica.
The failure of the assembly to grant money specifically
to the king was deemed "derogatory to your majesty's
right of sovereignty."[6] Consequently the instructions
issued to Carlisle in the following spring and those
prepared for all subsequent governors of royal provinces
required that every act imposing a tax, fine, or forfeiture,
appropriate the money thereby raised to the king for the
public uses of the province.[7] At the same time the disposition of the funds so raised was safeguarded by a
clause in Carlisle's commission which prescribed that
money was to be issued out only on warrants from the
governor.[8] Although the assembly was allowed to inspect
the accounts of expenditures from funds raised by provincial acts, a further check upon the governors was soon
considered necessary. From 1680 on, the commissions and
instructions regularly provided that money warrants
were to be issued, not by the governor alone, but by the
governor with the advice and consent of the council.[9]
These instructions were a fundamental part of the colonial system.

Two other financial regulations found their way into
the instructions at about the same time. One of these
related to the right of the English Treasury officials to
receive accounts of the provincial revenues. After the
instructions on this subject became standardized all gov-

---

[6] *Cal. State Paps., Col.*, 1677–1680, § 480; *Acts, Privy Coun., Col.*, 1613–
1680, § 1177. This was the report which contained the first proposal to institute a method of legislation for the island modeled on the system in force in
Ireland.

[7] Instructions to Carlisle, Jamaica, 1678, art. 49, C.O. 138: 3, pp. 216–241.

[8] Commission to Carlisle, Jamaica, 1678, *ibid.*, pp. 198–214.

[9] Instructions to Dutton, Barbados, 1680, art. 16, C.O. 29: 3, pp. 37–53.
The change was not made in the Virginia instructions until 1702.

ernors were required to see that "fair books of accounts" of all receipts and expenditures were kept in detailed manner and that they were certified under oath and sent to England to the Commissioners of the Treasury and the Board of Trade at least semiannually. The governors were forbidden to approve any revenue-producing measures in which the money to be raised was not made accountable to England.[10] The other instruction forbade the passage of any act lessening or impairing the revenue in the province.

Had these instructions been fully enforced, they would have provided what, from the British point of view, would be a very nearly ideal system of colonial finance. In principle, they contemplated a fiscal scheme in which the sole vital function of the assembly would be the granting of money. Within broad lines, the disposition of the funds so raised would remain in the discretion of the executive branch of government. General oversight and the audit of accounts would be assured to the home government. Although the assembly might inspect the accounts to see that no embezzlement was taking place, the popular body was to have no voice in the details of expenditure and was to be powerless to coerce the governor by reducing the revenue. Under such a system the advantages which the assembly might otherwise gain in provincial affairs by their right to lay taxes would be largely prevented. In some provinces the system worked successfully for a few years. But as the assemblies came to identify their functions more and more with those of the House of Commons, they tended naturally to demand the same control over finance which the lower house exercised at Westminster. A scheme which reduced the elective body to a

[10] The two instructions relating to English supervision of provincial accounts went through many verbal changes prior to about 1730 but without change in principle from the articles first given in the reign of Charles II.

mere money-granting agency could meet with no more permanent success among Englishmen on one side of the Atlantic than among those on the other. Consequently the assemblies began to make the same encroachments upon the executive control of finance in the colonies that the seventeenth-century House of Commons made in England.

The royal officials realized the danger in this situation. They appreciated that the only certain guarantee of freedom from interference by the assembly lay in the establishment of a permanent, independent, and adequate revenue in each province. Hence at the very time that they were drafting instructions on financial matters they renewed their attempts to get permanent grants from the assemblies of Jamaica and Virginia—the two provinces then in royal control which had not followed the example of Barbados and the Leeward Islands—and they made similar attempts in other provinces when these in turn were royalized. The Virginia assembly complied almost at once. In 1679 Lord Culpeper persuaded them to pass an act which he had brought with him from England granting to the king a perpetual duty of two shillings per hogshead on all tobacco exported. Certain other taxes were included in the measure but the fund was always known as the "two shillings per hogshead" revenue.[11] The income from this source together with the quit-rents of the province gave the crown a considerable revenue, permanent in its continuance and independent of the assembly's control. Even these funds proved inadequate, especially during time of war, but the Virginia arrangements were more satisfactory to the British than those of most provinces.

The Jamaica assembly proved less tractable and the

---

[11] Hening, *Statutes at Large*, II, 466–469. Such a law had previously been in force but it had not been perpetual.

controversy over a perpetual revenue in that province continued off and on for fifty years. At first the struggle was complicated by the dispute over the procedure in legislation required in Carlisle's commission and instructions. But in 1683, when the home government had abandoned the attempt to apply Poynings' Act to Jamaica, the assembly passed a revenue act for a period of twenty-one years.[12] When this law was approved by the privy council, a number of other important laws were also confirmed but only for a similar period and not in perpetuity.[13] In 1688 the duke of Albemarle, an intimate of James II and governor of the island, secured the passage of a perpetual revenue act to take the place of the former measure of limited duration. But because of charges that Albemarle's assembly had been fraudulently elected, the privy council of William and Mary declined either to confirm or disallow the acts it had passed.[14] The revenue question did not again come prominently to the front until the twenty-one-year period named in the act of 1683 was drawing to a close. Various attempts were made between 1699 and 1702 to get the assembly to pass a permanent revenue act but with uniform lack of success.

[12] A revenue act for seven years had been passed in 1682 and in the next year was extended to twenty-one years, largely through the influence of the able governor, Thomas Lynch. Lynch to the Lords of Trade, Oct. 8, 1682, Nov. 2, 1683, C.O. 138: 4, pp. 96–98, 180–181; *Cal. State Paps., Col.*, 1681–1685, §§ 745, 1348. The account of the contest in Jamaica over the permanent revenue law here given must necessarily be comparatively brief. For a full and detailed discussion see Agnes M. Whitson, *The Constitutional Development of Jamaica—1660 to 1729*, chaps. V–VII.

[13] Order in council, April 17, 1684, C.O. 137: 14, fos. 345–346; *Acts, Privy Coun., Col.*, 1680–1720, p. 833.

[14] *Cal. State Paps., Col.*, 1685–1688, §§ 1858, 1941; 1689–1692, §§ 7, 50, 54. The decision of the privy council not to confirm these acts was not entirely due to a desire to show abstract justice to the island. The chief opponent of confirmation was the Royal African Co. who asserted that the legislation of Albemarle's assembly was harmful to their interests and that a majority of the assemblymen were debtors of the company. C.O. 138: 6, pp. 300–302.

Finally in the early months of 1703 two instructions were sent to Lieutenant Governor Handasyd. One of these, a public instruction, told him to direct the council and assembly to pass a perpetual act before the next November. If they should comply, the king would confirm in perpetuity the other measures due to expire with the twenty-one-year revenue law. If they should refuse, however, the king would confirm the objectionable permanent revenue law of Albemarle.[15] The other and "private" instruction told Handasyd that he might consent to another twenty-one-year revenue act if a perpetual law should prove impossible.[16]

Handasyd went energetically to work to overcome a discouraging opposition. He confessed that "though an old soldier, I'm but a young politician,"[17] and painted a gloomy picture of the assembly: "The greater part of their time is spent in heats and divisions; they, being this sessions most of them Creolians, are at as great variance with those born in England as if they themselves were not descended from English parents, and are so obstinate in their humors that they will neither lead nor drive, and if they go on in the methods they are now in, they will teach me what I never expected to learn, that is, either to be a conjurer or a philosopher, but I shall use my utmost endeavors by fair means to make them sensible of their errors and bring them to reason.'"[18] Whether conjury, philosophy, or politics proved most successful in accom-

[15] Additional instruction to Handasyd, submitted Feb. 23, 1703, C.O. 138: 10, pp. 406–408.

[16] Private instruction to Handasyd, submitted Feb. 25, 1703, *ibid.*, pp. 415–417.

[17] Handasyd to the Board of Trade, Aug. 27, 1703, C.O. 137: 6, no. 1 (*Cal. State Paps., Col.*, 1702–1703, § 1055, omits this statement from the letter).

[18] Handasyd to the Board of Trade, Aug. 27, 1703, C.O. 137: 6, no. 1; C.O. 138: 11, pp. 51–52; *Cal. State Paps., Col.*, 1702–1703, § 1055.

plishing his ends, Handasyd does not inform us, but in any case he was able to report before the end of November, 1703, the passage of a revenue act for twenty-one years, in conformity with his private instruction.[19] Probably the assembly was induced to make this concession chiefly through fear of the confirmation of Albemarle's revenue measure and through a desire to prevent the lapse of the other expiring laws. At any rate Handasyd could justly feel proud of his success.

Although unable at this time to get the desired perpetual revenue, the home authorities did not entirely give up hope. As early as 1718 they renewed the campaign although the revenue would not expire until 1724. Governor Lawes was instructed to move the assembly "in the most pressing manner" to pass a perpetual revenue act.[20] But Lawes was so discouraged by the "stupidity, ignorance, and want of duty to the best of sovereigns" which he found in the assembly, that he repeatedly urged the passage of an act of parliament to provide an independent revenue for Jamaica.[21] The home officials did not adopt the suggestion. Instead, in the instructions of 1722 to the duke of Portland they repeated the order given to Lawes and a few months later gave the new governor an additional instruction which provided that, if the assembly would not grant a perpetual revenue, he was to get an act taking care of all the regular expenses of the island for a definite period of not less than twenty-one years. In such case the king would again confirm the other expiring laws

19 Handasyd to Nottingham, Nov. 27, 1703, C.O. 137: 6, no. 24 i; *Cal. State Paps., Col.,* 1702–1703, § 1326; Handasyd to the Board of Trade, Nov. 27, 1703, C.O. 137: 6, no. 24; *Cal. State Paps., Col.,* 1702–1703, § 1327.

20 Instructions to Lawes, Jamaica, 1718, art. 99, C.O. 5: 189, pp. 334–375 (L.C.).

21 Lawes to the Board of Trade, Nov. 13, 1720, April 20, 1721, C.O. 137: 13, nos. 45, 53; June 12, Aug. 28, Oct. 30. 1721; April 27, 1722, C.O. 137: 14, pp. 6–7, 63, 96, 149–150.

for a like period.[22] The situation of 1703 was thus largely reproduced.

The duke of Portland was the eldest son of William Bentinck, earl of Portland, the trusted Dutch friend of William III. His appointment to the governorship of Jamaica, the most lucrative post in the colonial service, was undoubtedly inspired by the hope that he might there repair a fortune damaged in the South Sea Bubble.[23] He had had four years' experience in the House of Commons before inheriting his father's earldom and he achieved some personal popularity in Jamaica, but he never displayed that political ability which has so often appeared in other generations of his family.[24] The one advantage which Portland had in the ensuing controversy with the assembly lay in the fact that a series of important and highly desired laws would expire with the revenue act and that the king had promised to confirm these in perpetuity upon the passage of an adequate perpetual revenue law. But the assembly had no intention of passing any measure which would establish the complete financial independence of the administration. Three times during the three and a half years of Portland's residence in Jamaica the two houses passed permanent revenue bills. Two of these Portland signed and the other he sent to England in draft form. But in each case the Board of

[22] Instructions to Portland, Jamaica, 1722, art. 46, C.O. 5: 191, pp. 222–271 (L.C.); additional instruction to Portland, submitted April 13, 1722, C.O. 138: 16, pp. 418–419.

[23] As late as April 8, 1726, Lady Portland wrote the duke of Newcastle that "the difficulties he lies under in relation to his private affairs makes the thoughts of his coming back into England terrifying." Newcastle Papers, II, Add. MS., 32,687, fo. 190. Three months later Portland died in Jamaica.

[24] In spite of the disputes which marked Portland's administration, an address is said to have been sent to England from Jamaica after his death in which he was described as "the finest person and most accomplished gentleman that ever adorned the British court." Cokayne, Peerage, VI, 273.

Trade, the law officers of the crown, and the Treasury officials pointed out grave defects which the governor had ignored. The bills either failed to provide adequate revenue or else they contained provisions contrary to Portland's instructions. Consequently, the privy council refused to approve any of the measures.[25] In the meantime the term of the revenue act and the other laws had ended and the island's affairs were only saved from chaos by additional instructions to the governor permitting the assembly to extend the expiring laws for a year at a time.[26] In this crisis the home authorities resorted to an unfortunate expedient. On the recommendation of the Board of Trade, the attorney and solicitor general of Great Britain prepared the draft of such a revenue bill as would be acceptable to the crown. This document was dispatched to Portland in the summer of 1726 with a royal letter directing him to urge its passage in the council and assembly.[27] But three days before this letter was signed Portland died, leaving a rich heritage of discord to his successor.[28]

[25] The documents relating to these bills and their disposition in Great Britain are too numerous to cite individually. They are scattered throughout C.O. 137: 14 and 16 and C.O. 138: 16. See also *Acts, Privy Coun., Col.*, 1720–1745, §§ 45, 68.

[26] Additional instruction to Portland, July 30, 1724, C.O. 138: 16, pp. 486–490; additional instruction to Portland, June 1, 1725, C.O. 137: 16, fos. 165–166.

[27] Royal letter to Portland, July 7, 1726, C.O. 137: 16, fos. 372–373.

[28] John Ayscough, president of the council, to the Board of Trade, July 14, 1726, *ibid.*, fo. 272. The date of Portland's death is erroneously given as 1724 in Cokayne, *Peerage*, VI, 273. A poem which appeared in the *Weekly Jamaica Courant* for Nov. 2, 1726, four months after the governor's death, paints a surprisingly attractive picture of the state of the island during Portland's administration, in view of the continuous controversy which took place. The verses "inscribed to the Goddess Liberty and her champions" were dated Nov. 4, 1725, the anniversary of William III's landing in England, and were accompanied by a note addressed to the duchess which explained that the poem had not been presented during the duke's lifetime lest "an ill-natured construction" of a design to compliment

When the draft bill arrived in the island the assembly would have none of it. The preparation of a bill in England and its transmission to the colony for enactment there smacked too much of the hated Poynings' Act system which the island had successfully resisted nearly fifty years before. But when the British officials learned from the acting governor that the assembly had "in a violent and disrespectful manner rejected the draft with disdain," the privy council committee hastened to explain that they had no intention of reintroducing the Irish legislative system, but that they had caused the draft to be sent over only to indicate the terms on which the king would be willing to confirm in perpetuity the laws which had previously been in force only for limited periods.[29] Consequently they introduced an article into the instructions prepared for the next governor authorizing him to give his consent to any revenue bill which agreed in substance with the draft prepared by the law officers of the crown. They directed him to meet in a conciliatory spirit any specific objections to the terms of the draft bill.[30]

The British authorities could hardly have selected as governor a man better fitted than Robert Hunter to meet

him be placed upon it. The four stanzas eulogized in turn Liberty, the duke of Portland, William III, and George I. The second stanza reads:

> At either Pole with Thee [Liberty] on Rocks of Ice;
> Or in the burning Zone all's Paradise:
> No Lion, Bear or Bajazet we fear,
> Thy Noble, Gen'rous PORTLAND governs here:
> Sad Widows Sighs, or injur'd Orphans Cries;
> Ascend not hence to move the pittying Skies;
> Melodious soothing notes we only hear,
> Sweet Philomels, or the Italian Air:
> Eternal Spring of Halcion Days delight,
> And Glittering Nymphs outshine the Stars at Night.

[29] Ayscough to the Board of Trade, Jan. 26, 1727, C.O. 137: 16, fos. 349–352; *Acts, Privy Coun., Col.*, 1720–1745, pp. 79–80.

[30] Instructions to Hunter, Jamaica, 1727, art. 21, C.O. 5: 193, pp. 377–427 (L.C.).

the difficult situation. A member of an old Scottish family, he had served under Marlborough on the continent, and had been promoted to brevet lieutenant colonel on the field. He was a fellow of the Royal Society and a friend of Addison and Swift. He had gained colonial experience through nine years' service as governor of New York and New Jersey where his personal popularity was marked. Such a man was able to succeed in Jamaica where the noble duke, his predecessor, had failed. In May, 1728, less than four months after his arrival in Jamaica, Hunter reported that the assembly had "behaved with moderation and calmness" and had passed a permanent revenue act which agreed with the bill transmitted from England "in most things literally, but in everything as to its material substance," except where his instructions had permitted a variation.[31] The British officials found some minor objections to the measure, but wisely decided to overlook these rather than jeopardize the fruits of a half century's struggle by requiring further change. The privy council, therefore, confirmed the law.[32]

The political skill of an able governor and the desire of the assemblymen to secure permanent confirmation of their laws combined to produce what seemed to be a notable victory for the British policy. At last the Jamaica assembly had granted an acceptable permanent revenue. But to a large degree the victory proved barren. The revenue act was estimated to yield approximately £8000 a year, all of which was appropriated to cover the specific items of ordinary governmental expenditure. In some years the taxes produced more than this sum, and occasionally a surplus appeared in the treasury. But gen-

[31] Hunter to the Board of Trade, May 16, 1728, C.O. 137: 17, fos. 49–50.

[32] Attorney General Yorke and Solicitor General Talbot to the Board of Trade, March 25, 1729, *ibid.*, fos. 139–141; Board of Trade to the king, May 4, 1729, C.O. 138: 17, pp. 261–268; order in council, May 22, 1729, C.O. 137: 18 (unpaged).

erally, expenditures for extraordinary purposes, such as the numerous expeditions against the revolting maroons and the support of the independent military companies, made additional revenues necessary. The administration found itself again dependent upon the assembly for all outlays not included in the schedule of ordinary expenses. Even during Hunter's own administration, the assembly quite effectively asserted that financial dictatorship which the royal policy had tried to destroy.

But although the permanent revenue act of Jamaica did not bring entire financial independence to the executive, that island was the only province in which the British policy met with even nominal success during the eighteenth century. No other assembly granted a perpetual revenue after 1700, although the royal officials constantly urged the passage of such measures in every royal province. The question provoked bitter contests which resulted not only in defeat for the representatives of the prerogative, but in increased stubbornness and independence on the part of the assemblies. The issue went to the very heart of the colonial problem.

The struggle which took place nearly everywhere can perhaps be best illustrated by the case of New York, where the dispute was most prolonged and heated, and where the British policy suffered its most ignominious defeat. From the collapse of the Dominion of New England until 1709 the financial structure of New York was based upon a series of revenue acts running for periods of five or six years each.[33] The assembly refused all proposals for a permanent revenue, in large part because of well-

[33] Benjamin Fletcher to William Blathwayt, Aug. 15, 1693, *N. Y. Col. Docs.*, IV, 37; Fletcher to the Lords of Trade, Oct. 9, 1693, *ibid.*, p. 57; Lord Bellomont to the Board of Trade, May 29, 1699, *ibid.*, p. 528; Chief Justice Mompesson's account of maladministration in New York, *ibid.*, V, 407; *Colonial Laws of New York*, I, 248–253, 287–293, 325–326, 419–425, 517–518.

grounded fears that the less scrupulous governors, such as Benjamin Fletcher and Lord Cornbury, would convert the money so raised to their private uses. Robert Hunter, the man who later put an end to the permanent revenue controversy in Jamaica, arrived in New York as governor in 1710. The last revenue act had expired the year before and Hunter found that the assembly would grant no more money unless that money was kept under their control rather than under that of the governor and council as required in the instructions. The representatives demanded that all funds raised by their enactments be placed in the custody of a treasurer appointed by themselves and that the money be expended only in accordance with directions contained in the revenue bills. They further refused to permit the council to amend the provisions of their money bills in any particular. This position infringed upon the prerogative control of finance and grossly violated the terms of the governor's instructions. In despair of getting an adequate revenue law without surrendering all these contested points, Hunter made the same proposal to the Board of Trade that Nicholas Lawes later made in connection with Jamaica, that is, that parliament pass an act establishing a permanent revenue for New York.[34] The suggestion met with approval in Great Britain to the extent that the Board of Trade, at the order of the privy council, prepared the heads of such a bill, but it was never introduced into parliament.[35] Probably the home authorities never intended anything more than a threat to the assembly.[36]

[34] Hunter to the Board of Trade, Nov. 14, 1710, *N. Y. Col. Docs.*, V, 177–182. See also *ibid.*, pp. 183, 263, 293.

[35] Board of Trade to the queen, Feb. 16, 1711, *ibid.*, pp. 190–192; order in council, March 1, 1711, *ibid.*, pp. 192–193; Board of Trade to the queen, March 15, 1711, *ibid.*, p. 197; Hunter to the earl of Stair, Oct. 18, 1714, *ibid.*, pp. 451–453; *Acts, Privy Coun., Col.*, 1680–1720, pp. 641–642.

[36] On July 20, 1713, the Board of Trade informed Governor Lowther of

In the meantime, the province suffered from the lack of an adequate revenue. In 1711 Hunter reported that "the officers of the government are starving, the forts on the frontier are in ruin, the French and Indians threatening us every day, no public money nor credit for five pounds on the public account."[37] These conditions naturally grew worse as the deadlock continued. Finally, the clamors of the public creditors, the fear of parliamentary intervention, and the confidence which Hunter inspired in his own integrity, combined to produce a conciliatory spirit in the assembly. After some preliminary palliative measures, they passed a five-year revenue act in 1715 which permitted the expenditure of all money by warrant of the governor and council, as the commission and instructions required, in return for a pledge on Hunter's part that he would issue no money not indicated in the votes of the lower house.[38] For about twenty years after this compromise, the revenue question dropped into the background of New York politics. Although the instructions to the governors of the province continued to require all supply bills to be "indefinite and without limitation," both Hunter and his successors were satisfied with acts which imposed taxes for not more than five years at a time. But the administration of the last governor of this group, William Cosby, aroused so much factional bitter-

Barbados, who was having trouble with his own assembly, of the proposed parliamentary bill for New York. They declared that they had received the queen's orders to introduce the bill "but the parliament rising so soon after, there was not time to do it. However it is ready against the next session." *Cal. State Paps., Col.*, 1712–1714, § 412. But the fact that the bill was not introduced in the next session tends to confirm Hunter's own view when he wrote to Secretary Popple, Nov. 8, 1714: "You know well that the revenue bill was never intended to be passed in parliament, though prepared by the Lords." *N. Y. Col. Docs.*, V, 389.

37 Hunter to the Board of Trade, May 7, 1711, *N. Y. Col. Docs.*, V, 209.

38 Hunter to the Board of Trade, Nov. 8, 1714, July 25, 1715, *ibid.*, pp. 381–382, 416–417; *Col. Laws of New York*, I, 815–826, 847–857.

ness that when the last revenue act expired in 1738, two years after his death, the assembly absolutely refused to continue the taxes except on their own terms. They demanded a triennial act, which would limit the governor's discretion over the life of the legislature; complete control over appropriations by the lower house; and the issuance of paper bills of credit in violation of the instructions. Even when Lieutenant Governor Clarke, alarmed by the defenseless condition of the province, gave in to these conditions in 1739, the assembly was willing to pass a revenue act for only one year at a time.[39] Clarke's submission marked the end of the royal control of finance in New York. Struggle as they might, the later governors were unable to check the system of annual revenue acts and minutely detailed appropriations which the assembly now established and which enabled that body to dominate the provincial government.

The next governor, George Clinton, was an officer of the navy who was totally unfitted either by temperament or by previous experience to cope with the situation. He had sought the office in the hope of escaping from financial difficulties at home, apparently without realizing the problems which he would face in the province. His utter lack of political foresight or skill led him to place full reliance in the advice of one or two men without stopping to consider the motives which might lie behind their suggestions. His first confidant and political advisor was James DeLancey, chief justice of the province and leader of a powerful faction in the assembly. Later he broke with DeLancey and accepted the guidance of Cadwallader Colden, a mortal enemy of the chief justice. On his first arrival in 1743, Clinton made no effort to check the assembly's usurpation of financial power, because, as he

[39] Clarke to the Board of Trade, Nov. 30, 1739, *N. Y. Col. Docs.*, VI, 150–151.

later declared, DeLancey advised him to build up confidence in himself by showing a conciliatory spirit at the start.[40] By the time Colden had convinced the governor that such a policy was unsound, the opportunity for a determined stand had passed. Great Britain was then at war with France, and New York was in danger of attack by the Indians and Canadians. In view of the exposed position of the province and its great need for military defense, Clinton had no choice but to allow the assembly to continue making annual grants and controlling all expenditures. He complained bitterly of his plight to the home authorities, but received no effective support from Great Britain. The efficiency of the Board of Trade was at a low ebb, the secretary of state was concerned with other matters, and the governor was left to shift for himself.

By the fall of 1748 the assembly had secured practically complete control over the most important branches of the administrative department. The chief methods by which they had accomplished this result were, as Clinton described them: refusal to accept any amendments to money bills as originally passed in the lower house; appropriation of salaries to officials by name and not by office—an effective limitation upon the governor's power of appointment and removal; attachment of these salary bills as riders to bills for the payment of the forces on the frontier, which latter measures the governor could not afford to veto; and provision in appropriation bills for the issuance of money without the governor's warrant.[41] In each case

[40] Clinton to the Board of Trade, June 22, 1747, *ibid.*, pp. 352–357. The entire history of the revenue controversy during the years 1743–1751 is given in ''An Abstract of the Evidence in the Office Books of the Lords Commissioners for Trade and Plantations relating to the State of New York,'' printed in *ibid.*, pp. 639–703. Only the more important documents and communications will be cited individually.

[41] Clinton to the Board of Trade, Oct. 20, 1748, *ibid.*, pp. 456–457.

Clinton had to submit to the will of the assembly in order to get the money necessary for the military service. The control of finance had enabled the assembly to become supreme. In these years the authority of the crown and of the governor sank to the lowest ebb in the history of colonial New York. Only a large revenue granted for a long term of years, if not in perpetuity, could have restored the governor's office to the position of importance and influence it was intended to occupy.

What made Clinton's situation the more trying was the fact that he was not receiving adequate support from home. During two years the Board of Trade, slothful and incompetent, though in part concerned with other affairs, failed to write him a single line of encouragement or advice. At the end of this time they chided him for the incompleteness of the papers he had forwarded and recommended him to pursue "such moderate and prudent measures" as might reconcile the differences existing between the three branches of the legislature.[42] In sharp contrast to this fatuous advice was the counsel which Clinton received from William Shirley, governor of Massachusetts, who visited New York during the summer of 1748. Clinton, always more dependent upon the suggestions of others than upon his own judgement, was anxious to get the help of another governor upon the problems of his administration. Shirley examined the papers which were laid before him and advised that Clinton should lose no time in insisting upon the assembly's surrender of its usurped authority. Vigorous measures by the governor who had suffered these encroachments would, he felt, be more effective than postponement of the controversy until a successor should be appointed.[43] Heartened by Shirley's

42 Board of Trade to Clinton, June 29, 1748, *N. Y. Col. Docs.*, VI, 427–428.

43 Shirley to Clinton, Aug. 13, 1748, *ibid.*, pp. 432–437.

words and by the prospect of the end of the war, Clinton abandoned "moderate and prudent measures" and embarked upon a policy of starving the opposition into surrender. In the fall of 1748 he signed a bill continuing the last year's taxes but he vetoed all appropriation bills except those for the forces on the frontier. The province might suffer but the assembly must be taught a lesson.

For two years Clinton followed this policy, refusing to sign any appropriation bills unless the assembly would restore to him his rightful control of finance. He begged the home government for an additional instruction which would fortify him in his position, but with the exception of a few words of encouragement from the duke of Bedford, secretary of state, he received no help from home. The Board of Trade again let two years pass by in silence.[44] Clinton held out as long as possible without support but the situation became impossible. The French were sending emissaries among the Iroquois, the British governor could not make the customary presents to these tribes, the garrison at Oswego was unprovided with supplies, and the British hold on the northern and western frontiers was in danger of being entirely lost. Alarmed by this situation and discouraged by the lack of support from home, Clinton surrendered to the assembly in December, 1750. He agreed to pass all bills in the form used since the death of Governor Cosby. But he informed the secretary of state and the Board of Trade that the responsibility for his failure did not rest upon his shoulders alone. "My duty therefore obliges me," he wrote, "to tell your Grace my humble opinion that the king must enforce the authority of his own commission or else resolve to give up

[44] The first letter which the Board of Trade wrote Clinton at the end of this period was dated Sept. 1, 1750, and acknowledged the receipt of nineteen letters from him since their last letter of June 29, 1748. *Ibid.*, pp. 586–587.

the government of this province into the hands of the assembly.''[45]

One can hardly fail to sympathize with Clinton, incompetent though he was. The home authorities had set for him a difficult task of maintaining the prerogative in the face of increasingly powerful opposition from the assembly. Because of their failure to appreciate the true conditions in the province, they insisted upon his carrying out the policies embodied in his instructions but failed at the same time to give him the necessary support from Great Britain. They left him to fight his battle unaided, although they were ready to censure and even to remove him if he failed to assert and maintain the prerogative. His failure, therefore, is not surprising.

The injustice of the Board of Trade's attitude toward Clinton and their misunderstanding of the condition of affairs in the province are apparent in their recommendations when they were finally induced to take action. Although an order in council of February 2, 1750, called upon the board for information on the disturbed conditions in New York and New Jersey, their report on the former province was not signed until exactly fourteen months later.[46] This lengthy document contained a detailed review of the financial history of the province, especially since the beginning of Clinton's administration. The board criticized Clinton for having submitted to the assembly on money matters at his first arrival and they especially deplored his surrender in 1750, after he had taken a stand in support of the prerogative. They declared that such a retreat would only confirm the assembly in its opposition, but they said not a word about

[45] Clinton to the duke of Bedford, Dec. 13, 1750, *N. Y. Col. Docs.*, VI, 602–603. Clinton wrote the Board of Trade in almost identical words on Dec. 2, 1750. *Ibid.*, pp. 598–599.

[46] *Acts, Privy Coun., Col.*, 1745–1766, § 123.

the governor's appeals to Great Britain for help. In the opinion of the board, the constitution of the province could be restored to its proper balance only through the appointment of a new governor who would not be hampered by the personal animosity that Clinton had aroused. When the new governor had restored peace and cooperation he should be instructed to get an act granting a perpetual revenue, or one for a long term of years, on the model of the act in force in Jamaica.[47] In almost every line this long report displayed a total misunderstanding of the spirit which moved the assembly and the condition of affairs in the province. The primary cause of Clinton's defeat lay in the growing self-reliance of the assembly and the natural desire of that body to hold in local affairs a position similar to that which parliament held in Great Britain. As events were soon to reveal, the mere removal of one unfortunate governor and the appointment of another man, would not result in a change in the situation, for it could not alter the assembly's conception of its own importance.

Nevertheless, the British officials decided to make the attempt. According to the terms by which the Board of Trade's powers were expanded in 1752, that body, under the presidency of the earl of Halifax, was given the right to nominate provincial officials. Halifax soon named as governor of New York his brother-in-law, Sir Danvers Osborn, not because of his special fitness for the post but for purely personal reasons. The recent death of his wife had produced in Osborn a brooding melancholy, which Halifax hoped the strenuous duties of the New York governorship would help him to overcome. But the hope was

[47] Board of Trade to the privy council committee, April 2, 1751, *N. Y. Col. Docs.*, VI, 614–639; *Acts, Privy Coun., Col., The Unbound Papers*, § 488. The board also presented an "Abstract of the Evidence," *N. Y. Col. Docs.*, VI, pp. 639–703.

vain, for two days after his arrival in the province, Osborn committed suicide. His place was taken by Clinton's former friend but recent enemy, James DeLancey, now lieutenant governor of the province. When the new chief executive examined Osborn's instructions, one article must have given him some searchings of the heart, in view of his leadership of the anti-Clinton faction in the assembly. This article began by expressing indignation at the "most unwarrantable and illegal manner" in which the royal authority and prerogative had been "trampled upon and invaded," whereby the assembly had acquired control of many "executive parts of government." The king was determined, said the instruction, not to permit his "authority and prerogative to be in any degree violated or lessened by any encroachments whatever." The governor was therefore to inform the assembly of the king's displeasure at their actions and to enjoin them to pay due obedience to the commission and instructions in the future. The governor was to recommend in the strongest possible manner the passing of a perpetual revenue law which would make provision for all the fixed charges of government. Other revenue laws might be passed but only for temporary and emergency purposes, but in any case, all money was to be expended solely on the warrant of the governor and council. Lastly, if any councillor or other officer joined the assembly in opposition to such measures, the governor should remove or suspend him at once and report the facts to the Board of Trade.[48] Whether wise or not, the British officials were at least clear as to what they wanted the governor to do.

Such orders as these must have moderated DeLancey's satisfaction at succeeding to the government before his enemy, Clinton, had even left the province. But to his

[48] Instructions to Osborn, New York, 1753, art. 39, C.O. 5: 200, pp. 875–964 (L.C.).

credit be it said, that the lieutenant governor was loyal to his oath of office and that he made a reasonably strenuous effort to persuade the assembly to obey the instruction. But even with a chief executive who had recently been one of the assemblymen's own leaders, success for the British policy was out of the question. The assembly did finally consent to make appropriations payable on warrant by the governor and council, but they absolutely refused to raise a revenue for more than one year at a time.[49] In the meantime, troubles with the French were again impending. Washington suffered his defeat at Great Meadows and the Albany Congress was held. Faced with an imperative need for funds, DeLancey abandoned the attempt to carry out the instructions.[50]

In the critical year 1755, Charles Hardy, another naval officer, was named governor and almost immediately knighted. In preparing instructions for him the Board of Trade modified the tone of the article on the revenue situation, thereby tacitly admitting the impossibility of waging war successfully upon both the French and the colonial assembly at the same time. They omitted the sharp criticisms of the assembly which they had drawn up two years before and retained only the clauses which insisted upon the warrant of governor and council for every expenditure and upon the passage of a perpetual revenue act. They even modified the latter requirement to permit the passage of a temporary act in an emergency to supply funds for such services as should seem to the governor "immediately and absolutely necessary to be undertaken

[49] DeLancey to the Board of Trade, Jan. 3, May 21, 1754, *N. Y. Col. Docs.*, VI, 819 821, 838–840. The assembly went so far as to send an address to the king asking for the withdrawal of the instruction but the address was flatly rejected. *Ibid.*, pp. 831–832, 899–900; *Acts, Privy Coun., Col.*, 1745–1766, § 235.

[50] DeLancey to the Board of Trade, March 18, 1755, *N. Y. Col. Docs.*, VI, 940–941.

for the security of his Majesty's said province or for assisting the neighboring provinces in cases of like exigency or emergency.''[51] Almost certainly such permission would mean the postponement of a permanent revenue until the end of the approaching war with France, a fact which became clear to Hardy soon after he reached the province. He reported that the assembly had at its first session declared its unwillingness to grant a permanent revenue and he begged to be excused from pressing a dispute at a time when the most perfect harmony was necessary in the legislature.[52] To this request the officials in Great Britain reluctantly agreed. In the spring of 1756 the Board of Trade told the governor on the authority of the king that, although the pretences of the assembly were ''not to be supported upon any principles of reason or justice,'' he might refrain for the present from insisting upon a permanent revenue act. He might consent instead to temporary money bills according to the practice of the governors for the past twenty years.[53] When Robert Monckton was named governor in 1761 he was not required to insist on a perpetual act and the instruction as given to him was repeated to Sir Henry Moore in 1765 without change.[54] Although the war was now over and the danger of French attack was removed, the time was certainly not propitious for a renewed attempt to get a permanent revenue. The British officials had backed down completely from their earlier position.

[51] Board of Trade to the lords justices, April 22, 1755, *N. Y. Col. Docs.*, VI, 947–950; instructions to Hardy, New York, 1755, art. 17, C.O. 5: 1128, pp. 383–531. The article also forbade the nomination of executive officers by act of assembly.

[52] Hardy to the Board of Trade, Dec. 18, 1755, *N. Y. Col. Docs.*, VI, 1022–1023.

[53] Board of Trade to Hardy, March 4, 1756, *ibid.*, VII, 39–40.

[54] Instructions to Monckton, N. Y., 1761, art. 16, C.O. 5: 1130, pp. 62–159; instructions to Moore, N. Y., 1765, art. 16, C.O. 5: 201, pp. 361–436 (L.C.).

Finally the instructions to the last two governors of New York before the Revolution, the earl of Dunmore and William Tryon, appointed in 1770 and 1771 respectively, omitted all references to the proposed permanent revenue law.[55] This omission was due, the Board of Trade explained, to the plan for paying the salaries of all royal officials in the province out of the revenues provided by act of parliament.[56] The administrative and judicial officers of the province would now be able to function without reference to the grants of the assembly. The government would be restored to the hands of the king's representatives. The ultimate purpose of a perpetual revenue act was thus to be secured in another way.

More than half a century before this time a far-sighted governor, Robert Hunter, had recommended the raising of a revenue for New York by act of parliament. But the home authorities had given only lukewarm support to his proposal and although they had prepared the necessary bill, they had actually failed to introduce it into the House of Commons. During the years when parliamentary taxation of the province might have been imposed with some hope of success, they had been content with half-measures and with short-term revenue acts which left the assembly free at almost any time to throw down a challenge on the issue of financial supremacy. When the contest finally developed, the British officials were even more short-sighted. During the period of Clinton's struggles with the assembly they gave him absolutely no support but contented themselves with criticizing his failure to maintain the prerogative. Then, at one of the

[55] Instructions to Dunmore, N. Y., 1770, art. 17, C.O. 5: 203, pp. 189–242 (L.C.); instructions to Tryon, N. Y., 1771, art. 17, C. Z. Lincoln, *Constitutional History of New York*, III, 710–756.

[56] Board of Trade representation on Dunmore's instructions, May 21, 1769, *Acts, Privy Coun., Col.*, 1766–1783, § 134.

least opportune moments of the entire century, when the assembly had gained confidence by its victory over Clinton and when the final death struggle with France for the control of the North American continent was impending, the British government demanded that the assembly surrender all that it had won and grant a permanent revenue. Only disappointment and defeat could come from such a policy, as the Board of Trade and ministry soon learned. At last, when all other solutions of the problem failed, the government turned back and adopted in modified form the proposal of Hunter for a parliamentary revenue. But that which might at one time have been peacefully accepted by the people was now certain to arouse the bitterest opposition. Quite aside from the question of taxation without representation, the creation of colonial revenues by act of parliament was an attack upon the financial supremacy which the assembly had won by years of constant struggle. The blundering program of parliamentary taxation was the climax to a series of mistakes and failures which had characterized the British policy toward provincial finance for generations. The disasters which followed were well deserved.

Although the question of a permanent revenue was the central issue in the financial controversies in New York as well as in other provinces, there were many disputes over other matters of only slightly less importance. In all such cases the aims of the contending forces were clear. The assembly desired to gain the same financial influence which the House of Commons exercised, while the British officials hoped to limit the power of the assembly and keep control and regulation in the hands of the royal appointees. One of the most common subjects of dispute was the right of the council to amend money bills. The council considered itself a coordinate branch of the legislature with powers derived from the same clause in the governor's commission as that upon which the existence of the elective house was based. Neither the commission nor the instructions restricted in any way the council's share in legislation, hence that body demanded the right to amend money bills as freely as other measures. But the assembly, looking upon itself as a replica of the House of Commons, insisted that the council had no more right to amend a money bill than had the House of Lords. Controversies arose over this point in nearly every province. Uniformly the governors and the authorities in Great Britain tended to support the contention of the council, partly on the ground of constitutional theory, and partly because they wanted the royally appointed councillors to act as a check upon the assembly's initiative in financial matters. If every bill dealing with money had to be accepted or rejected by the supporters of the prerogative in exactly the form proposed by the elective house, the only possible result would be a weakening of the authority of the crown. According to British theory the council had and ought to have "as much to do in the forming of bills for the granting and raising of money as the assembly."[57]

Consequently, the Board of Trade and the privy council brought all their influence to bear in support of the provincial council. The Board of Trade informed Lord Archibald Hamilton of Jamaica in 1714 that the assembly's claim to the sole right of framing money bills was groundless and would not be supported in Great Britain. The members of the lower house sat as an assembly and formed a part of the legislature, as did also the council, only "by virtue of a clause in her Majesty's commission" to Governor Hamilton, and "their assuming a pretended right no ways inherent in them is a violation of the con-

[57] Board of Trade to Lord Cornbury, governor of New York, Feb. 4, 1706, *N. Y. Col. Docs.*, IV, 1171.

stitution of Jamaica and is derogatory to her Majesty's royal prerogative.'' If the assembly persisted in their claim, the governor might tell them ''that, as they must not assume to themselves the rights and privileges of the House of Commons of Great Britain, so such measures will be taken here as may be effectual to assert her Majesty's undoubted prerogative in that island.''[58] But the assemblymen were unimpressed. Four years later an article on this subject was added to the instructions for Governor Lawes, repeating the substance of the earlier letter and calling attention to the fact that the ''council, as such, are a more ancient part of, and still have at least an equal share in the legislative with the assembly.''[59] This instruction was repeated to all subsequent governors of Jamaica down to the end of the period but it produced not the slightest change in the attitude of the assembly. As late as 1766 the lieutenant governor sent to England an address from the council asking that the assembly be forced to share with them the power of framing and amending money bills.[60] But neither pleas, commands, nor threats could force the assembly to abandon its position.

Instructions relating to the same matter were sent to the governors of the Carolinas from the first establishment of royal government in these two provinces, but they failed to produce any permanent results.[61] A similar

[58] Board of Trade to Lord Archibald Hamilton, June 21, 1714, *Cal. State Paps., Col.*, 1712–1714, § 701; C.O. 138: 14, pp. 134–135.

[59] Instructions to Lawes, Jamaica, 1718, art. 96, C.O. 5: 189, pp. 334–375 (L.C.).

[60] Lieutenant Governor Elletson to the secretary of state, Sept. 30, 1766 (abstract), C.O. 5: 218, p. 158 (L.C.).

[61] Instructions to Nicholson, South Carolina, 1720, art. 35, C.O. 5: 189, pp. 630–661 (L.C.); instructions to Burrington, North Carolina, 1730, art. 14, C.O. 5: 192, pp. 167–217 (L.C.). The controversy in South Carolina is discussed at length in W. R. Smith, *South Carolina as a Royal Province*, pp. 289–290, 294–295, 306–312, 317–319, 321–329.

article was sent to the first governors of the provinces
acquired by the Treaty of 1763, even before the establishment of assemblies there. In other colonies where the
same question was raised, such as New York, New Jersey,
St. Christopher, and Barbados, no instructions were sent,
but the governors and British officials carried on the same
losing fight in other ways. In Barbados, it is true, the
lower house accepted some of the council's amendments
as late as 1728, but by 1740 the assembly was taking the
same high ground that its sister bodies had already assumed in the other provinces.[62] Whenever disputes arose
the members of the lower house always had the advantage,
for they could refuse to concur in the council's amendments and could return the bill to the upper house in its
original form. The latter body was then faced with the
alternatives of passing the measure without amendment
or of accepting responsibility for its failure. If the supply
were not to be lost entirely, the council would have to
give way. In this manner the assembly was able to create
precedents in support of its position. By the middle of
the eighteenth century the assemblies of all the royal
provinces seem to have successfully established the principle, already well recognized in the British parliament,
that the upper house must accept or reject all money bills
in the exact form in which they came from the representative chamber. Thus the members of the lower house gained
a control over financial arrangements which could not be
thwarted and, by the use of "riders" in their money bills,
were able to force the adoption of many other proposals
which the council and governor would otherwise have rejected.

The assembly also extended its control over finance at

[62] Governor Henry Worsley to the Board of Trade, Dec. 10, 1728, C.O.
28: 20, fos. 124–125; President James Dottin to the Board of Trade, Dec.
30, 1740, C.O. 28: 25.

the expense of the prerogative by its attitude on the custody and expenditure of funds raised by local act. The British officials wished to have all money lodged in the hands of receivers or treasurers appointed by the king or by the governor and to have payments made solely on the authority of warrants of the governor and council. But very early the representatives began to insist that, in special cases, certain funds should be lodged in the hands of officials named by themselves and should be paid out according to their directions. In 1691 Lord Inchiquin expressed his vexation at a plan of the Jamaica assembly whereby the funds for soliciting the island's affairs in England were to be placed in the hands of eleven commissioners, four from the council and seven from the assembly, leaving out the governor entirely, "as if he were a Judas, not fit to be trusted among the other seven [eleven?] apostles."[63] In several provinces the British government allowed the assemblies to appoint their own treasurers to take charge of "extraordinary supplies for particular purposes (which is no part of her Majesty's standing revenue)," as the Board of Trade phrased it in a New York case.[64] The home officials undoubtedly made this concession largely because they realized that some of the early governors had betrayed their trusts. Later, when outright dishonesty on the part of the governors was rare and when the assemblies were using their treasurers to deprive the royal officials of all financial supervision, the Board of Trade and the governors tried to check the practice, but with little success. Precedents for the appointment of financial officers by the representatives were too firmly established. In Barbados in 1710

[63] Inchiquin to the Lords of Trade, Aug. 12, 1691, *Cal. State Paps., Col.*, 1689–1692, p. 523.

[64] Board of Trade to Lord Cornbury, Feb. 4, 1706, *N. Y. Col. Docs.*, IV, 1172.

the council demanded that they be allowed to join with the assembly in naming a treasurer for the excise, but the assembly refused to agree and the dispute was carried to England. When the attorney and solicitor general of England reported that the precedents of the past forty years were all in favor of the choice of the treasurer by the lower house, the home authorities felt unable to help the council in its dispute.[65] In Virginia the receiver general of the province and the officials charged with the collection of the quit-rents and the two shillings per hogshead revenue were appointed either by the king directly or by the governor, but after 1691 the treasurer of the colony, who had custody of funds arising from such taxes as those on land, slaves, and liquor, was chosen by the House of Burgesses.[66] For the sixty-seven years between 1699 and 1766, the Virginia offices of treasurer and speaker of the House of Burgesses were always held by the same person, in spite of the frequently expressed wish of the lieutenant governors to separate them. In nearly all the provinces money granted for special purposes, such as the payment of troops, was often lodged in the hands of commissioners named in the appropriation act, which could not be amended by the council. Thus the appointment of financial officials by the assemblies became a well-established custom.

The worst feature of this situation, from the British point of view, was that a treasurer appointed by the assembly would be more likely to take orders from that body than from the governor and council in case of conflict. The commission and instructions always required that money should be paid out solely on the warrant of the governor with the advice and consent of the council, but the as-

[65] *Cal. State Paps., Col.*, 1710–1711, §§ 296, 377, 402, 403, 406, 407.
[66] *Ibid.*, 1689–1692, § 1476; Hening, *Statutes at Large*, III, 92–94.

sembly was by no means always willing to agree to this arrangement. The lower house of nearly every royal province worked out some substitute for the executive money warrant which would give the representatives actual control of all expenditures. Such devices were naturally more effective against the opposition of the royal officials when the custodians of the money were named by the assembly rather than by the crown. The British officials realized this fact but often found themselves unable to do anything about it.

Disputes over the issuing of money took place in nearly every province and throughout the eighteenth century. In St. Christopher, for example, an act creating a public stock, passed as early as 1704, provided that the treasurer was to make payments on an order signed by the governor or lieutenant governor, two councillors, the speaker, and two other assemblymen. The representatives could block any payments desired by the executive officers. The act was therefore disallowed.[67] But by the middle of the century the question was again opened in the Leeward Islands by the insistence of the assemblies of St. Christopher and Antigua that the treasurers should make no payments except to persons whose claims had previously been approved by both council and assembly. When the lower house of Antigua was ordered in 1752 to obey the instructions, they pointed out that from 1693 until 1718 all money orders had been countersigned by the speaker and one councillor. In the latter year they had waived the privilege of countersignature at the demand of the governor but had kept the right of approving all accounts before payments were made.[68] In spite of the opposition of the Board of Trade and the governor, the assembly in-

[67] *Cal. State Paps., Col.*, 1710–1711, §§ 690, 691.
[68] Lieutenant Governor Fleming to the Board of Trade, April 10, July 9, 1751; Antigua council minutes, May 9, 1751; order of privy council com-

sisted on having this check over expenditures.[69] Governor
William Popple encountered similar trouble in Bermuda
about the same time. When he tried to exclude the assembly from a voice in the issuing of money in 1753, he
discovered that a liquor excise act of 1698 required all
payments from this source to be made on the joint authority of the governor, five councillors, and ten men
named by the assembly. The fact that this act had been
confirmed in 1704 made the governor and the Board of
Trade helpless. An additional instruction was therefore
sent to Popple requiring him to observe the terms of this
act but to refuse the assembly a voice in the disposition of
money arising from any other source.[70]

The assembly of Massachusetts tried to get financial
control by appropriating money by votes and resolves of
the lower house alone, thus eliminating the governor and
council entirely from the disposition of money. In addition they insisted upon approving all accounts before the
treasurer might make payments on the governor's warrant as the charter required. Lieutenant Governor Dummer received an additional instruction in 1730 to stop this
practice and a long controversy followed.[71] The people of
this province seem to have believed most sincerely in the

mittee referring to the Board of Trade a petition of the council and assembly
of Antigua, C.O. 152: 27 (unpaged); Board of Trade to Fleming, Aug. 6,
1751, C.O. 153: 17, pp. 133–134.

[69] Governor George Thomas to the Board of Trade, Oct. 8, 1753, C.O. 152:
27; Board of Trade to Governor Thomas, Dec. 18, 1753, C.O. 153: 17, pp.
440–441.

[70] Order of privy council committee, Dec. 18, 1753, referring to the Board
of Trade, William Popple's memorial to the king, C.O. 37: 18 (unpaged);
Board of Trade report to the privy council committee, C.O. 38: 9, pp. 22–26;
order in council, April 9, 1754, C.O. 37: 18; *Acts, Privy Coun., Col.*, 1745–
1766, § 225; additional instruction to William Popple, April 9, 1754, C.O.
5: 200, pp. 977–980 (L.C.).

[71] Additional instruction to Dummer, Jan. 2, 1730, C.O. 5: 192, pp. 431–
432 (Mass.); *Acts, Privy Coun., Col.*, 1720–1745, §§ 190, 240.

justice of their position, for the council and House of Representatives petitioned the privy council twice for the withdrawal of the instruction and in 1733 they had the presumption to appeal to the House of Commons to "become intercessors with his Majesty that he would be graciously pleased to withdraw the said instructions as contrary to their charter and tending, in their own nature, to distress, if not ruin, them." But the House of Commons was no more sympathetic than the privy council had been, for they rejected the petition out of hand, resolving that it was "frivolous and groundless, an high insult upon his Majesty's government, and tending to shake off the dependency of the said colony upon this kingdom, to which by law and right they are, and ought to be, subject."[72] Massachusetts got cold comfort from that appeal.

The Jamaica assembly also called down upon itself the wrath of the House of Commons. The controversy over the disposition of money was one of long standing in that island and aroused frequent unfavorable comment in England. Finally in 1753, during the administration of Governor Knowles, the assembly resolved "that it is the inherent and undoubted right of the representatives of the people to raise and apply moneys for the service and exigencies of government and to appoint such person or persons for the receiving and issuing thereof as they shall think proper, which rights this house hath exerted and will always exert in such manner as they shall judge most conducive to the service of his Majesty and the interest of his people."[73] When the matter came to the attention of the House of Commons three years later, that body voted that in so far as the resolution of the assembly imported "a claim of right in the said assembly to raise and

[72] *Journal of the House of Commons* (May 10, 1733), XXII, 145.

[73] Resolutions of the Jamaica assembly, Oct. 29, 1753, quoted in the Board of Trade representation, Oct. 15, 1754, C.O. 138: 20, pp. 41–75.

apply public money without the consent of the governor
and council," this claim was "illegal, repugnant to the
terms of his Majesty's commission to his governor of the
said island, and derogatory of the rights of the crown and
people of Great Britain." The Commons characterized
in the same way the assembly's assertion of a right to
appoint officers to receive and expend money.[74] Although
the Commons never would do anything to increase the
prerogative control over the colonies, they regularly opposed any provincial attacks upon the existing authority
of the crown.

One of the most interesting controversies over the expenditure of money took place in South Carolina just
before the Revolution. During the first fifty years of royal
government in the province the assembly had encroached
so gradually and imperceptibly upon the executive control of finance that the Board of Trade was never able to
decide just when the most important changes in procedure had taken place. They had simply been part of a
general movement to which Lieutenant Governor Bull
referred when he wrote: "From the great religious and
civil indulgences granted by the crown to encourage adventurers to settle in America, the government in the
colonies had gradually inclined more to the democratical
than the regal side."[75] At any rate, the Board of Trade
suddenly discovered that the governors of the province
had of late years "improvidently acquiesced" in a method
of authorizing expenditures which deprived the executive
of any voice in the matter. When the Commons House of
Assembly wished a payment made to which the governor
and council might object, they simply ordered the treasurer to advance the money from any funds in his care and

[74] *Journal of the House of Commons* (May 23, 1757), XXVII, 910–911.
[75] Lieut. Gov. Bull to Lord Hillsborough, Dec. 12, 1769, C.O. 5: 379, pp.
203–206.

later included an item reimbursing him in the annual finance act. Nothing but the rejection of this act by the council or the governor, with the consequent loss of all supplies, could check this procedure.

This situation did not come to the attention of the authorities until 1770 when Lieutenant Governor Bull wrote that the lower house had ordered the treasurer to pay £10,500 local currency (£1,500 sterling) to a committee of seven representatives to be remitted to England ''for the support of the just and constitutional rights and liberties of the people of Great Britain and America.'' Actually the money was sent to the Bill of Rights Society for the assistance of John Wilkes, that thorn in the flesh of the ministry.[76] Naturally the proceeding created a furor among the officials in Great Britain. After a careful investigation the Board of Trade and attorney general concurred in denouncing the South Carolina practice as repugnant to the commission and instructions and in declaring the payment in question to be illegal. An additional instruction to this effect reached the province while the assembly and council were deadlocked over the reimbursement of the treasurer. The lower house petitioned for the withdrawal of the instruction and asked ''that a constitutional branch of legislature might be appointed by his Majesty independent of the council.''[77] Later a committee of the representatives adopted a series of strongly worded resolutions, among which was one which asserted that the original vote for the payment in behalf of Wilkes could not ''be deemed dangerous or unwarrantable, that the same would not have been so represented or the power of this house upon that point drawn into question, if the

[76] Lieut. Gov. Bull to Hillsborough, Dec. 12, 1769, C.O. 5: 379, pp. 203–206. The proceedings in Great Britain on this case are fully given in *Acts, Privy Coun., Col.*, 1766–1783, § 140.

[77] Bull to Hillsborough, April 15, 1770, C.O. 5: 379, pp. 231–233.

money borrowed had not been applied toward frustrating the unjust and unconstitutional measures of an arbitrary and oppressive ministry.'"[78] The Commons House insisted on reimbursing the treasurer and the council refused to concur, so that no money bills were passed during the rest of the period. In 1774 a new instruction was given to Lord William Campbell, recently appointed governor, forbidding him to assent to any appropriation bill which replaced in the hands of the treasurer any money expended on the authority of the lower house alone.[79] Had this instruction been put into effect it would have restored the authority of the governor and council in money matters. But Campbell did not arrive in the province until the day on which the British regiments stormed Bunker Hill far to the north. The local controversy was ended by more serious events which soon involved an entire continent.

Incidents such as these in South Carolina and elsewhere indicate the lengths to which the dispute over the expenditure of money went in the colonies. Both royal officials and provincial leaders realized that whichever group settled how money was to be spent would greatly increase its power in provincial affairs. Consequently, neither party was willing to give way to the other. The British officials did their best to enforce the clauses in the governor's commission and instructions which forbade any payments except on the warrant of the governor and council. The assembly leaders insisted on the adoption of other forms of authorization which would give them a voice in the disposal of money. Neither party was entirely

---

[78] Resolves of committee of Commons House of Assembly [Aug., 1770], C.O. 5: 379, pp. 284–285.

[79] Instructions to Lord William Campbell, So. Car., 1774, art. 24, C.O. 5: 206, no. 1 (L.C.). A full discussion of this controversy is given in W. R. Smith, *South Carolina as a Royal Province*, pp. 369–387.

successful, but at least the members of the lower houses, where the all-important initiative in financial legislation lay, were generally able to destroy the executive monopoly over expenditures.

Before the outbreak of the American Revolution the assemblies of most of the provinces were exercising much the same control over finance that the House of Commons exercised in Great Britain. They framed all bills for laying taxes and making appropriations and refused to permit the upper houses to amend such measures. Although they did not establish the same intimate relationship between the executive officials and the legislature which existed between the ministry and parliament, they gained a generally compensating advantage through their attitude on the custody and disposal of funds. They were able in many cases to dictate appointments to local offices through control of the salary appropriations. The governors gave abundant testimony to the degree in which the assemblies had usurped the powers of the royally appointed executives through their domination of provincial finance. The limits to which the New York assembly went in this direction, as described in 1746 by Governor Clinton, illustrate the general tendency. He wrote in part:

From such like instances and the apparent influence of the assembly in these cases, the ruling faction has obtained in effect the nomination to all offices; and they have become even so insolent that they have in the bill for payment of the salaries, &c., removed one officer's name and put in another without consulting me, and the speaker, in the presence of the council and assembly, had the assurance to tell me that they had thought fit to remove such an officer and put another in his place, and thereupon added "Please to order the secretary to make out a commission accordingly."

By these means all the officers of the government are become dependent on the assembly, and the king's prerogative of judging of the merit of his servants and of appointing such persons as he may think most proper is wrested out of the hands of his governor of this province, and the king himself (as far as in their power) deprived of it. The assembly carries matters in this case to such a length that they call these bills for payment of salaries and other contingencies "money bills," to which they will not allow the council to make any amendments and a governor must either take it as it comes from them, or he and all the officers of the government must remain without support. The effect of this influence of the assembly and the officers of government are [sic] on all occasions very remarkable and every man in this place is sensible of it.[80]

When an assembly could accomplish such results through the control of finance, a "responsible" government in the modern sense was hardly necessary from the provincial point of view, though its establishment would have gone far to prevent that bitterness and distrust which helped to precipitate the Revolution when the final crisis came.

In military as well as in civil affairs the governors found their authority greatly limited by their lack of financial independence. When Lieutenant Governor Dinwiddie of Virginia applied to the assembly for an appropriation to make possible Washington's expedition to the Ohio country in 1754, he was unable to get a penny until he consented, in violation of his instructions, to the appointment of a committee of four councillors and ten assemblymen to have full oversight over the expenditure of the £10,000 granted.[81] Benning Wentworth of New Hampshire summed up this situation when he declared that military power was "rather vested in the assemblies than in the king; the governors by virtue of his Majesty's

80 "The Present State of the Province of New York," Dec. 12, 1746, *N. Y. Col. Docs.*, VI, 460–463.

81 Dinwiddie to the Board of Trade, May 10, 1754, *Dinwiddie Papers*, I, 160–161.

commission can cause one or more regiments to appear on a certain date and at any place [t]he[y] shall order within the limits of the regiment, but they have no power to cause them to be subsisted one day, let the emergency be never so great, unless there is a vote of assembly for it."[82] The intercolonial wars, with their necessarily increased expenditures for military services, proved to be golden opportunities for the assemblies. The governors were generally endowed with a greater sense of responsibility for the safety of the inhabitants than were the assemblymen and with a far greater appreciation of the importance of effective cooperation with the British and with other provinces. Consequently, they were often willing to make great sacrifices in order to induce the assemblies to grant the necessary supplies. The greater the need for military appropriations, the more the assemblies were likely to gain by pursuing a dilatory policy. By the end of the period of intercolonial conflict the assemblies of the continental colonies, in which the emergency had been greatest, had reached a position of almost complete control of finance and were thereby able to direct in large measure the activities of their governments along lines most agreeable to themselves.

In the years that followed, the hand of parliament was felt for the first time in matters of colonial taxation and appropriation, fields which by that time the assemblies had come to look upon as their own exclusive preserves, and from which they had so painstakingly and successfully excluded the crown. There is little reason to wonder, therefore, that they objected and that they resisted these new efforts to oust them from their hard-won position of financial supremacy. In spite of the attempts of the governors to enforce the royal policy as laid down in the

[82] Wentworth to Newcastle, Nov. 14, 1746, C.O. 5: 10, no. 89 (L.C.).

commissions and instructions, the assemblies had gained a control over local money matters similar to that which the House of Commons exercised in Great Britain. For the British parliament to enter the field of provincial finance, to which it had formerly been an entire stranger and from which the agents of the prerogative had largely been excluded, was intolerable to the colonial leaders. The earlier defeat of the governors made the later opposition to parliament inevitable.

CHAPTER VIII

THE GOVERNOR'S SALARY

ACCORDING to the mercantilist view, the colonies were expected to bear the entire expense of their own civil government. The only outlay of money on the part of the mother country should be for those things which would directly benefit British trade. The colonies ought to be a help to England and not a drain upon her resources. Consequently, although some financial help might be necessary in the early years, each province was expected to provide at the first possible moment adequate salaries for all local officials and especially for the royal governor. If one were to judge solely by the heat of the controversies raised over this question in a few provinces, one might believe that in this matter the assemblies were able to make their greatest gains, and that their control over salaries was their most effective check upon the exercise of royal authority in America. But the bitter quarrels over the governor's salary were limited to a very few of the royal provinces, in particular to New York, New Jersey, New Hampshire, and Massachusetts Bay. Elsewhere the matter was adjusted with much less friction and a solution of the problem was reached which at least approximated the ideal of British policy.

The home authorities wanted a fixed and permanent salary to be settled within each province, payable out of a permanent fund over which the assembly should have no control. If the governor was then barred from accepting any gifts to increase his income, he would be free from personal dependence on the assembly. Only by such an arrangement could he avoid any direct financial interest in local legislation; only thus, argued the British officials, could he administer the royal government without fear or favor. The home authorities did not work out methods to apply their ideas all at once. Nor were they uniformly successful in their efforts. But after about half a century of experimentation with one plan and another, they managed to reach some solution of the salary problem in nearly every province that assured the practical independence of the governor. An analysis of the successes and failures of this important part of British policy is the aim of this chapter.

As was true of many other matters relating to colonial administration, no general survey of the salary question was undertaken until 1679. Before that time the salary arrangements in the few royal provinces had developed independently of each other. In Virginia between 1628 and the outbreak of the Civil War the governors were allowed £1000 a year "for entertainment" out of the customs duties of goods imported into England from the colony.[1] In 1662 the Council for Foreign Plantations decided that the colony should hereafter bear its own charge "and no longer be burthensome to the crown."[2] Governor Berkeley was thereupon instructed to take £1000 a year from the proceeds of the local export duty of two shillings per hogshead of tobacco.[3] In the Leeward Islands and Barbados no specific sum was allowed to the governors until 1671 and 1672, respectively, because of the semi-

[1] During the first years after the dissolution of the company in 1624, the governors had received no fixed salary but had been allowed occasionally to bring a vessel or two into England without paying the normal customs charges. In later years the £1,000 salary was often in arrears. *Acts, Privy Coun., Col.*, 1613–1680, §§ 171, 212; *Cal. State Paps., Col.*, 1574–1660, pp. 116, 136, 184, 276, 285; 1675–1676, § 152.

[2] *Cal. State Paps., Col.*, 1661–1668, § 345.

[3] Instructions to Berkeley, Va., 1662, art. 4, *Va. Mag.*, III, 15.

proprietary nature of the governorship.[4] But when Sir Charles Wheler was named first separate governor of the Leeward Islands in the former year, he received an allowance of £700 a year out of the four-and-a-half percent export duty of those islands.[5] In the following year the governor of Barbados, William, Lord Willoughby of Parham, was granted an annual salary of £800 from the similar duty in that island.[6] Jamaica had no such revenue fund as did the three other royal provinces and the local finances were as yet unable to bear the charge of a governor's salary. Consequently, the chief executives there were permitted to draw from the English Exchequer the sum of £1000 annually.[7] These early arrangements were the best that could be made at the time, unsatisfactory as they proved to be.

[4] The first governor after the Restoration, Francis, Lord Willoughby of Parham, and after his death his brother, William, were permitted to take half the profits of the islands during the term of their 21-year lease, which expired in 1670. For the next two years, William, Lord Willoughby, was allowed ''for entertainment'' whatever was left over from the impost on liquors after the other expenses of civil government had been met. *Cal. State Paps., Col.*, 1661–1668, §§ 80, 180, 309, 359, 380, 387, 1820.

[5] This sum was made subject to reduction if the assembly of St. Christopher should make an allowance to Wheler, but no such reduction seems to have taken place. *Ibid.*, 1669–1674, §§ 410, 412, 446, 448, 925. A special gift of £400 as ''royal bounty'' was made to Wheler which was ordered to be paid out of the queen's dowry. *Cal. Treas. Books*, 1669–1672, pp. 797, 802–803.

[6] *Cal. State Paps., Col.*, 1669–1674, § 845; *Cal. Treas. Books*, 1669–1672, pp. 707, 1059–1060.

[7] Lord Windsor, the first regularly appointed royal governor, was authorized by his commission of 1661 to receive £2000 from this source. C.O. 138: 1, pp. 9–12. But in 1663 the amount was reduced to £1000 at which figure it remained until 1678, when the earl of Carlisle was directed to take £2000 from the revenue to be raised by the bill which was drawn up in England and given to him to be carried to Jamaica, in the vain expectation of approval by the assembly. ''An establishment allowed by his Majesty for the island of Jamaica beginning from the 25th of December, 1663,'' C.O. 138: 1, p. 35; instructions to Carlisle, Jamaica, 1678 art. 47, C.O. 138: 3, pp. 216–241.

In June, 1679, the newly reorganized privy council tried to bring about a retrenchment of the expenses of colonial administration and defence. To this end the Lords of Trade prepared a schedule showing the salaries of the governors and the cost of maintaining the troops and fortifications in the royal colonies. A special establishment was created, for the payment of which the paymaster general of the forces was to be responsible. The governors' salaries remained unchanged in this estimate.[8] But relief to the Exchequer was to come, not through reduction of salaries, but rather through their entire transference to funds raised by colonial taxation. In the same year the new governor of Virginia, Lord Culpeper, was instructed to take £2000 a year from the local revenue of two shillings per hogshead in addition to one third of all escheats, fines, and forfeitures.[9] So, although the nominal salary was in this case doubled, the increased burden fell entirely upon the fund raised in the colony itself. In 1683, when new instructions were issued to Culpeper, he received the same salary but without the addition from the escheats, fines, and forfeitures.[10] This arrangement was never changed throughout the entire colonial period. The

[8] *Acts, Privy Coun., Col.*, 1613–1680, §§ 1277, 1288; C.O. 324: 4, pp. 63–66 (L.C.); *Cal. State Paps., Col.*, 1677–1680, §§ 1036–1038.

[9] Instructions to Culpeper, Va., 1679, art. 66, C.O. 5: 1355, pp. 326–356 (L.C.). The actual payments were for a time much complicated by the conflicting claims of the representatives of Governor Berkeley, Lieutenant Governor Jeffreys, and Governor Culpeper. These three men each asserted with some justice their rights to priority of payment. The incident does not, however, affect the general statement of the salary arrangements of the province. See the instructions to Jeffreys, Nov. 11, 1676, C.O. 5: 1355, pp. 122–124 (L.C.); also *Cal. Treas. Books*, 1676–1679, pp. 946, 1450, 1453, 1460; 1679–1680, pp. 212–213, 215, 263, 596–597, 618; 1681–1685, pp. 319, 545, 1067, 1133, 1175–1177, 1492, 1498; 1685–1689, pp. 399, 474–475, 1294–1296; *Cal. State Paps., Col.*, 1675–1677, § 599; 1677–1680, §§ 539, 1037–1038; *Acts, Privy Coun., Col.*, 1613–1680, pp. 847–848.

[10] Instructions to Culpeper, Va., 1682, art. 75, *Va. Mag.*, XXVII, 41–52; C.O. 324: 4, pp. 63–66 (L.C.).

sum of £2000, payable from the two shillings per hogshead revenue, over which the assembly had no control, continued to be the regular salary of all Virginia governors. Although gifts were apparently sometimes received from the assemblies, they never seem to have had any real influence in Virginia affairs and were severely censured by the home authorities when brought to their attention.[11] The salary system in Virginia was from the British point of view very nearly ideal. Any arrangement which required no alteration from 1682 to the outbreak of the Revolution and which worked smoothly throughout is an extraordinary thing in our colonial history. Not only was the salary the largest of any in the continental colonies, but it was absolutely free from control by the assembly. The removal of this question from the realm of politics meant that a potential source of friction between the legislature and the executive was permanently eliminated. Virginia was the first colony to have its governor's salary definitely and satisfactorily arranged.

Meanwhile, changes were being made in the arrangements for the other provinces. In 1680, the new governor of Barbados, Sir Richard Dutton, likewise received an increase in salary from £800 to £1200 payable from the

[11] The governors of Virginia, like those of other provinces, were forbidden from 1703 on to receive any gifts from their assemblies. But in 1728 Lieutenant Governor Gooch wrote asking permission to accept £500 voted him by the assembly. Gooch to Newcastle, June 9, 1728, C.O. 5: 1337, no. 69 (L.C.). Both Newcastle and the Board of Trade severely reprimanded him for this request, the former declaring that it would constitute "a very ill precedent" to make an exception to the rule which had been framed to prevent "the many inconveniencies formerly arising in the plantations on that account." Newcastle to Gooch, Dec. —, 1728, C.O. 5: 1337 (loose paper between nos. 70 and 71) (L.C.). To the board Gooch replied that other governors usually received such gifts upon their arrival and he "had reason to hope the same indulgence would be allowed to him." But the board reported adversely to the privy council. This body postponed action and we are left in doubt as to the final disposition of the gift. Acts, Privy Coun., Col., 1720–1745, § 180.

four-and-a-half percent duty, since the former allowance was clearly insufficient for the requirements of the office.[12] Here again the burden fell upon a revenue raised in America and not upon the English taxpayer. An even more important change soon followed in Jamaica when Sir Thomas Lynch, appointed governor in 1681, was able to secure the passage of a revenue act for seven years from the proceeds of which he was instructed to take a salary of £2000 a year.[13] The allowance remained the same for many years and was made permanent by the twenty-one-year revenue acts of 1683 and 1703 and the perpetual revenue act of 1728.[14] In the Leeward Islands the salary remained fixed at £700 until 1703, but the fact that it was drawn from the four-and-a-half percent duty relieved the English Treasury officials from any anxiety on its behalf.[15] Thus by 1682 all four royal provinces had provided revenues from which the governors' salaries could be paid without annual recourse to the assemblies and without drain upon the English Exchequer.

But any idea that the salary problem had been finally settled was premature. A governor might yet receive gifts from the assembly which would look much like bribes to the authorities at home. In early years the governors of

[12] *Cal. Treas. Books*, 1679–1680, p. 741. No mention was made of the salary in the instructions to Dutton, but authority for receiving the £1200 from the sub-commissioners for collecting the duty in Barbados was given in the instructions to his successor, James Kendall, 1689, art. 64, C.O. 29: 4, pp. 82–103.

[13] *Cal. State Paps., Col.*, 1681–1685, § 227; 1685–1688, § 1374; 1689–1692, §§ 587, 2497; 1701, § 647; *Acts, Privy Coun., Col.*, 1680–1720, § 772.

[14] See above, pp. 276–282.

[15] Governor Stapleton, appointed in 1672, was in arrears from two to five years during most of his administration. One cannot read his letters without a feeling of admiration for the patience and modesty with which he made his requests for payment. *Cal. State Paps., Col.*, 1669–1674, §§ 1297, 1360, 1365; 1675–1676, §§ 592, 595, 895; 1677–1680, §§ 233, 254, 636; *Acts, Privy Coun., Col.*, 1613–1680, §§ 1028, 1052, 1076.

Barbados had received many such presents but these were apparently expected to cease with the fifty percent increase in salary granted to Dutton in 1680.[16] But at this time the four-and-a-half percent revenue was most inefficiently farmed and the governor seems to have received no more than a third of the amount due him during his first two years in office. He was finally able to persuade the assembly to add a clause to the liquor tax bill whereby £1500 was presented to him from the proceeds of the tax.[17] When word of this act reached England the Lords of Trade awoke to the fact that Dutton had become what he himself had once termed "a precarious governor," dependent on the island assembly and not on the royal bounty. To prevent such gifts in the future the privy council issued an order forbidding the governors of all provinces to receive any presents from their assemblies unless they should first obtain the king's consent.[18] Circular instructions to this effect were issued and the essential parts were included in the general instructions to all royal governors until 1703 when more drastic regulations were adopted.[19] With the exception of a few men, including Dutton himself, who coolly ignored the order and was recalled for this and other reasons,[20] the governors seem

[16] *Cal. State Paps., Col.*, 1669–1674, §§ 1395, 1396; 1675–1676, §§ 411, 682, 946, 1164; 1677–1680, §§ 319, 517.

[17] *Ibid.*, 1681–1685, §§ 646, 666.   [18] *Ibid.*, §§ 820, 822, 827, 832.

[19] Circular instructions, Dec. 15, 1682, C.O. 324: 4, pp. 114–115 (L.C.). These instructions directed that if the king should not approve of the grant to the governor, the money should be applied to some other use mentioned in the act itself. Until royal confirmation should be received, the money was to be lodged with the receiver or treasurer and not paid out. The instruction was to be entered in the registers of the council and assembly "for the better information of all such whom it may concern."

[20] Dutton declared that he had never received the order as all his mail had been lost at sea, but after his recall to England he was confronted with evidence that the instruction had been delivered to him, whereupon he confessed its receipt and begged the king's pardon. When his accounts were

generally to have obeyed their instructions and to have secured the royal approval before accepting gifts from the assemblies. An important principle was thus laid down.

In the meantime, the establishment of royal government in other colonies considerably increased the difficulty of the salary problem. The cases of New York, New Hampshire, Massachusetts, and New Jersey will be separately discussed. But the situation in Bermuda and in Maryland may be briefly mentioned. The island of Bermuda was so lacking in resources that no single fund could provide even a meager salary, hence several had to be used. Twelve shares of land, formerly belonging to the company and now made crown land, estimated to be worth a total of £60 a year, were put at the lieutenant governor's disposal. To this was added the profits from the licenses for the whale fishery, bringing £100 a year. The remaining £240 of the £400 salary was paid directly from the English Exchequer.[21] This arrangement violated the principle of independence of English financial support so successfully established elsewhere, but the rule was eventually vindicated to the satisfaction of the Treasury officials by selecting the four-and-a-half percent revenue of Barbados and the Leeward Islands as the fund from which the payments of this part of the Bermuda salary should be made. The makeshift character of this whole scheme was far from satisfactory, yet it shows the determination of the English officials to work out a solution of the problem.

In Maryland a permanent revenue independent of the

finally adjusted with the lord high treasurer, it was found that the amount owed him by the crown was approximately the same as that he owed in return. He was therefore discharged from his obligations and allowed to keep the illegally granted presents of the assembly. *Cal. State Paps., Col.,* 1681–1685, §§ 855, 2044, 2048–2049; 1685–1688, §§ 98, 209, 245, 400, 448, 455; *Cal. Treas. Books,* 1685–1689, pp. 444, 450, 611.

21 *Cal. State Paps., Col.,* 1685–1688, § 919.

assembly existed in a duty of two shillings per hogshead on tobacco exported, similar to that of Virginia. One half the fund belonged to the proprietor, but of the other half a part, variously estimated at £1000 or £1200 a year, was available for the royal governor.[22] Hence the salary question was easily solved. From 1699 on, acts were passed with the royal consent at the beginning of each administration granting to the governor during his term the proceeds of an additional tax of threepence per hogshead, which increased his income by about £500 a year.[23] This system continued as long as Maryland remained a royal province. Like Virginia, this colony had a thoroughly satisfactory arrangement.

During the period from 1682 to 1703 the governors of all the colonies with which we are now dealing were entitled to regular salaries, quite independent of the assemblies. But the situation at large was still far from satisfactory. Many of these men had accepted colonial office with the expectation of enriching themselves. All of them felt that they must live on a far higher scale than their salaries would permit. Sir William Beeston, for many years a resident of Jamaica, was appointed lieutenant governor of the island in 1692, rather than governor, as a measure of economy, since his salary would be only £1000 instead of £2000.[24] But he complained that his expenses were £2500 a year above his official salary "which

[22] Instructions to Copley, Maryland, 1691, art. 19, *Maryland Archives,* VII, 271; *Cal. State Paps., Col.,* 1689–1692, § 1839.

[23] *Acts, Privy Coun., Col.,* 1680–1720, pp. 430–431.

[24] By an order in council, Nov. 3, 1682, and a royal warrant, Dec. 10, 1682, the substance of which was repeated in a declaration at the Treasury, June 24, 1698, and in all general instructions, a lieutenant governor was entitled to one half of the salary and of the perquisites due a governor in the absence of the latter from the province. C.O. 324: 4, p. 87 (L.C.); *Va. Mag.,* XVIII, 353–354; C.O. 324: 6, pp. 293–294 (L.C.); *Cal. State Paps., Col.,* 1681–1685, §§ 794, 836–838.

does not pay for the meat on my table.''[25] He pleaded ill
health as his reason for wishing to resign, but when he
was promoted to governor in 1699 at the full salary, his
health was enough restored for him to remain in office for
two years more.[26] From Barbados Lord Grey wrote in
1701 begging for an increase in salary "that, as others
have been sent hither to improve their fortunes, so I may
not come this far to ruin my own.''[27] Edward Randolph,
surveyor general of the customs, told the Board of Trade
after a visit to Bermuda in 1700 that the governors there
were forced to work all sorts of injustice upon the inhabitants to increase the perquisites of their unprofitable
office. Among other things, ships which barely touched
the rocks were seized as wrecks in order that the governors might extort the royal share.[28] Under such conditions,
gifts from the assemblies were more than welcome, and
even though the king's consent was necessary before the
governors might receive such presents, they probably
found it easy to conceal from the home authorities the
bargains they may have had to make with their assemblies. The inadequacy of the salaries was dangerous to
the independence of the governors.

[25] Beeston to the Board of Trade, Aug. 7, 1694, C.O. 138: 7, p. 404; *Cal.
State Paps., Col.*, 1693–1696, § 1194; Beeston to William Blathwayt, June
12, 1697, C.O. 138: 9, p. 132; *Cal. State Paps., Col.*, 1696–1697, § 1080.

[26] Memorial of Lord Lucas on behalf of Beeston [1699], C.O. 138: 9, p.
386; Board of Trade to Secretary Vernon, Oct. 27, 1699, *ibid.*, pp. 387–389;
Board of Trade to Beeston, Nov. 9, 1699, *ibid.*, pp. 396–398; instruction to
Beeston on salary, submitted Dec. 14, 1699, *ibid.*, p. 410; Beeston to the
Board of Trade, Feb. 1, 1700, C.O. 137: 5, no. 15; *Cal. State Paps., Col.*,
1699, §§ 882, 901, 941, 1055; 1700, § 71.

[27] Lord Grey to the Board of Trade, Sept. 13, 1701, C.O. 28: 6, no. 16;
C.O. 29: 7, p. 440. *Cal. State Paps., Col.*, 1701, § 856. In this letter Grey
gives some information on prices in Barbados at this time: beef and mutton
were 12d. a pound; veal, 15d.; turkeys and capons, 21d.; "all manner of
horse grain," 8s. 3d. a bushel.

[28] Edward Randolph to the Board of Trade, Nov. 15, 1700, *Cal. State
Paps., Col.*, 1700, § 936.

But the Board of Trade was aware that all was not well. In 1701 they sent a representation to the king explaining that the receiving of presents by the governors tended "to render them precarious and dependent on the people." They recommended therefore that additions be made to the salaries where necessary and that all gifts be prohibited for the future.[29] The privy council read this representation but did nothing further.[30] Again in 1702 the Board of Trade called attention to the situation, making specific recommendations for increases in several provinces.[31] But not until a year later did the privy council become interested. An act was passed in the Leeward Islands appropriating £1200 sterling to be spent by Governor Codrington in the purchase of plate for himself as a gift from the assembly and as "a testimonial of their respect." The Board of Trade recommended the approval of this act in 1703 since the governor's salary was clearly insufficient.[32] The privy council confirmed the act, but, realizing for the first time the seriousness of the situation, ordered the board to lay before the queen an account of all salaries assigned or paid to the various governors, in order that she might check the practice of giving and receiving presents.[33] Thereupon the Board of Trade submitted a long representation stating the salaries paid to all governors, recommending an increase in many of them, and proposing a royal order which would prohibit the governors from receiving any presents from the as-

[29] Board of Trade to the king, April 29, 1701, C.O. 324: 7, pp. 454–455 (L.C.); *Cal. State Paps., Col.,* 1701, § 383.

[30] *Acts, Privy Coun., Col.,* 1680–1720, § 824.

[31] Board of Trade to the queen, April 17, 1702, C.O. 29: 7, pp. 507–517; *Cal. State Paps., Col.,* 1702, § 349.

[32] *Cal. State Paps., Col.,* 1702–1703, § 407; *Acts, Privy Coun. Col., The Unbound Papers,* § 107.

[33] *Cal. State Paps., Col.,* 1702–1703, §§ 408, 409; *Acts, Privy Coun., Col.,* 1680–1720, § 896.

semblies for the future, with the exception of house-rent where this was necessary. The Barbados salary was to be raised from £1200 to £2000 sterling; that of the Leeward Islands from £700 to £1200, with an addition of £200 to each of the four lieutenant governors who had been unpaid up to this time; the Bermuda salary was to be increased from £400 to £500 by an added grant from the Exchequer; and the Jamaica salary, which in recent years had been paid in the depreciated local currency, was to be brought back to a sterling value of £2000 by the addition of £500 current money from the twenty-one-year revenue. The salaries in Virginia and Maryland were considered adequate and were left alone.[34] The privy council approved these recommendations and ordered royal letters to be written the governors accordingly.[35] Each of these letters authorized the increase which had been made for the particular colony and all added a strict injunction to the governors not to receive any gifts or presents from their assemblies in the future on any pretext whatsoever, except that in those provinces which were without established residences for the governors, the assemblies might grant limited amounts in lieu of house-rent until permanent homes should be provided.[36] These letters were later incorporated as articles in the general instructions to the succeeding governors. By the substantial increase in most of the salaries and the absolute prohibition of all gifts from the assemblies, the British policy of independence for the governors was advanced another step toward its final form.

The Board of Trade felt that the troublesome salary

---

[34] Board of Trade to the queen, April 2, 1703, C.O. 324: 8, pp. 229–240 (L.C.); *Cal. State Paps., Col.*, 1702–1703, § 536; *Acts, Privy Coun., Col.*, 1680–1720, pp. 427–433.

[35] *Cal. State Paps., Col.*, 1702–1703, § 566.

[36] *Ibid.*, §§ 593–602.

question had now been put upon a permanent and satisfactory basis in these provinces. Reasonably adequate
salaries were provided from funds over which the assemblies had no control and the governors were prevented
from looking to the assemblies for further grants. The
provisions for house-rent were only temporary and were
to be made at the first session of each legislature so that
continual bargaining would be impossible. The board
proposed to keep a sharp watch over the governors to
prevent evasion of the new rules. Only recently they
had censured Lieutenant Governor Handasyd for what
seemed to be an improper grant. The Jamaica council
had directed the receiver general of the island to buy for
the governor's house two pipes of Madeira, two hogs-
heads of ale, glasses, pipes, tobacco, candles, and "a
handsome bed and bedstead with all other furniture suitable for a lodging room." The board was suspicious and
wrote warningly: "These are matters not fitly treated of
in council."[37] To complaints from governors or assemblies
that the increased salaries were still inadequate, the
board turned a deaf ear. "It is not for us," they told
Governor Granville of Barbados, "to propose anything
to her Majesty against a settlement so solemnly made."[38]
The Board of Trade felt well satisfied with their work.

For some years all seems to have gone along smoothly in
spite of some mutterings from the governors about the
high cost of living. But in 1718 the Board of Trade discovered that Governor Lowther of Barbados had eluded
their watchfulness and had violated the prohibition of
gifts from the assembly. They wrote with a touch of sar-

[37] Board of Trade to Handasyd, March 23, 1703, C.O. 138: 10, pp. 430–
431; *Cal. State Paps., Col.*, 1702–1703, § 496.

[38] Board of Trade to Granville, Oct. 28, 1703, C.O. 29: 8, p. 336; *Cal.
State Paps., Col.*, 1702–1703, § 1205. Granville had written, June 16, 1703,
that £600 in England would go as far as his £0,000 salary in Barbados, C.O.
28: 6, no. 98; *Cal. State Paps., Col.*, 1702–1703, § 831.

casm: "We observe with much satisfaction from the minutes of your council and assembly the great harmony and
good understanding there is between you and his Majesty's subjects in Barbados, of which the great presents the
assembly have made you for the last two years are convincing proofs, but they are proofs of such a nature as are
directly contrary to your instructions and therefore we
must admonish you not to break in upon his Majesty's
orders in this particular for the future."[39] In spite of this
warning Lowther continued to violate his instructions and
by 1720 he had received gifts which the Board of Trade
estimated at a total of £23,290 on various pretexts which
neither he nor his agents had been able to explain away.[40]
In the following year Lord Belhaven, a Scottish courtier,
was appointed in his place. Belhaven petitioned the king
for relief from the financial difficulties which he anticipated. The income of former Barbados governors had not
equalled their expenses, he said, consequently they had
violated their instructions by receiving gifts from the assembly. He himself intended loyally to obey the king's
orders, but that he might not suffer for his obedience he
asked that the assembly be allowed to make him a permanent grant under proper safeguards.[41] When asked their
opinion of this request, the Board of Trade answered that
if the salary was not enough they had no objection to an
addition by the assembly provided it was made at Belhaven's arrival and for the entire time he should remain
in office.[42] An instruction was consequently prepared au-

[39] Board of Trade to Lowther, March 28, 1718, C.O. 29: 13, p. 457.

[40] Answer of the Barbados agents to the complaints against Lowther,
Jan. —, 1720, C.O. 28: 15, fo. 66; C.O. 29: 14, pp. 44–52; Board of Trade
to Secretary of State Craggs, Feb. 25, 1720, C.O. 29: 14, pp. 62–66.

[41] Memorial of Lord Belhaven to the king, enclosed in Secretary Carteret's
letter to the Board of Trade, June 24, 1721, C.O. 28: 17, fo. 148.

[42] Board of Trade to the king, June 30, 1721, C.O. 29: 14, pp. 124–128.

thorizing the governor to approve an act granting him an additional salary provided it was passed by the first assembly after his arrival and was to remain in force as long as he continued governor.[43] Belhaven was drowned while on his way to Barbados, but the instruction was repeated to his successor, Henry Worsley, in 1722, with a further safeguard added by the privy council to the effect that the act for additional salary must contain a suspending clause.[44] The instructions to Governors Hart of the Leeward Islands and Hope of Bermuda in 1721 and to the duke of Portland of Jamaica in 1722 included the same privilege of receiving additional salaries from the assemblies.[45] The instruction was repeated without substantial change to all later governors of these four island provinces. The salaries could now be made adequate, the pretext for gifts was removed, and the governors' complaints of poverty would be stopped.

This arrangement represents the final stage in the development of royal policy regarding the governors' salaries. During the rest of the colonial period the governors of these provinces received their salaries in two parts: one, fixed in amount by the instructions and drawn from a fund over which the assembly had no control; the other,

[43] Instructions to Belhaven, Barbados, 1721, art. 26, C.O. 5: 191, pp. 14–74 (L.C.).

[44] Order in council, Aug. 7, 1722, C.O. 28: 17, fos. 284–285; instructions to Worsley, Barbados, 1722, arts. 22 and 28, C.O. 5: 191, pp. 374–431 (L.C.).

[45] Instructions to Hart, Leeward Islands, 1721, art. 32, C.O. 5: 191, pp. 126–183 (L.C.); instructions to Hope, Bermuda, 1721, art. 29, C.O. 5: 191, pp. 308–340 (L.C.); instructions to Portland, Jamaica, 1722, art. 31, C.O. 5: 191, pp. 222–271 (L.C.). The addition in the case of Bermuda was to be an appropriation ''for keeping up and repairing'' the house allotted to the chief executive. That in the case of Jamaica had to be provided not only by the governor's first assembly, but within a year after his arrival, since the sitting of the assembly there was not limited as in some other provinces. Board of Trade report on Portland's instructions, Oct. 13, 1721, C.O. 138: 16, pp. 341–342.

granted by the assembly, it is true, but granted at the beginning of the administration and for its entire term, so that both governor and assembly were committed at the very start to whatever amount they had agreed upon and were deprived of further bargaining power. On the whole, the system worked satisfactorily. There were some cases of friction, but the general attitude of the assemblies when the salary question was under discussion was one of a desire to abolish their contributions entirely rather than to make the governors more dependent upon themselves. Trouble appeared in Barbados after the death of George I, when some members of the assembly insisted that the act laying taxes for Worsley's additional salary had automatically expired. An opinion of the attorney and solicitor general of Great Britain, a new instruction to Worsley, and several suits in the Barbados courts were necessary before the taxes could be collected.[46] The assembly complained bitterly in later years of the burden of the additional salary and after the death of Governor Byng in 1740 they declared that they would make no such grant to future governors, preferring that the additional salary should be taken from the four-and-a-half percent.[47] Nevertheless, on the arrival two years later of Sir Thomas Robinson, a man said to have had a great talent for flattery, they voted him a salary fifty percent higher than

[46] Worsley to the Board of Trade, April 20, 1729, C.O. 28: 20, fos. 186–188; June 1, Sept. 27, Dec. 1, 1729; April 23, 1730; Jan. 16, 1731, C.O. 28: 21 (unpaged); instructions to Worsley, Barbados, 1728, art. 28, C.O. 5: 194, pp. 303–367 (L.C.); order of council, Aug. 18, 1729, C.O. 28: 21. The proceedings of the privy council on the Barbados salary from 1729 to 1741 are given in *Acts, Privy Coun., Col.*, 1720–1745, § 179.

[47] Barbados assembly to the Board of Trade, Oct. 28, 1740, C.O. 28: 25. Worsley had been granted the extraordinary sum of £6000 local currency; his successor, Howe had received £4000, and Byng, £2000. Worsley reported in 1730 that the Barbados currency was thirty percent lower than sterling, that is, that £130 currency was worth £100 sterling. Worsley to the Board of Trade, Dec. 23, 1730, C.O. 28: 22.

they had given Byng.[48] Corrupt agreements were, of course, not impossible, but the available evidence points quite the other way.

In Bermuda, the opening of the whale fishery to all subjects and a circular instruction of 1730 forbidding the governors to give "any manner of discouragement" to this industry, deprived the governor of that part of his salary based on the whale licenses.[49] Similarly, the twelve shares of crown land, from which another part of the salary had been derived, were sold in 1758.[50] Both these events made changes in the system of paying the governors necessary. A further loss followed in 1763 when the independent company of foot in Bermuda was disbanded, the governor, who had always been captain of the company, thereby losing the profits of that command with which he had eked out his slender salary.[51] But in each case some adjustment was made which preserved the independence of the governor, although it did not always meet with full satisfaction on his part.[52] Throughout our period the royal officials found means, even in this poverty-

[48] Cokayne, *Baronetage*, V, 68–69; *Dictionary of National Biography;* Robinson to the Board of Trade, Nov. 27, 1742, April 22, June 25, 1743, C.O. 28: 26. He had expressed a hope that he could live on the salary granted by the assembly and put away part of his royal salary for himself and his family. "This is what I understand all former governors have expected as the price and reward of their coming abroad and have been hitherto so supported from the people as to effect it." But on arriving he had found the cost of living so high that the £2600 first offered (£2000 sterling) was inadequate. The assembly thereupon raised the salary to £3000 Barbados currency.

[49] *Acts, Privy Coun., Col.,* 1720–1745, § 197; circular instructions, March 6, 1730, C.O. 5: 192, pp. 441–473 (L.C.); C.O. 324: 11, pp. 161–162 (L.C.).

[50] *Acts, Privy Coun., Col.,* 1745–1766, § 553.

[51] Memorial of Governor Bruere to the Board of Trade [June 1, 1764], C.O. 37: 19.

[52] From 1730 to 1748 the governor was authorized to receive from the assembly an additional salary of £100 in lieu of the whale licenses, but in the latter year, at the assembly's own request, the system of licenses was

stricken island, to support the governors without introducing the system of annual grants or presents. No evidence has been found to show that the assemblies' share in providing salaries in any of these provinces was used as a means of controlling the policies of the governors.

The main element in the success of the salary arrangements of the six provinces which we have considered was the fact that in each case a fund existed or was created from which expenditures might be made, independently of the assembly. The four-and-a-half percent duty in Barbados and the Leeward Islands, the two shillings per hogshead duty in Virginia and Maryland, the twenty-one-year revenue and later the perpetual revenue in Jamaica, and even the crown lands and whale licenses in Bermuda, provided funds from which the governors could be paid the greater parts of their salaries. For the rest, the British government relied on the assemblies but so arranged matters that continual bargaining between the governors and their legislatures was impossible. In these six provinces the British policy of protecting the salaries met with nearly complete success.

But soon after the home authorities had evolved their final policy in regard to these colonies, they were confronted with the same problem in other provinces which had come under the crown so late that there was little or

restored for Bermuda alone, as less burdensome to the people than the additional salary. *Acts, Privy Coun., Col.*, 1720–1745, § 197; C.O. 324: 11, pp. 349–350 (L.C.); Board of Trade to privy council committee, Feb. 5, 1730, C.O. 324: 11, pp. 160–161 (L.C.); additional instruction to William Popple, Bermuda, submitted June 29, 1748, C.O. 5: 200, pp. 508–509 (L.C.). In 1764 with the consent of the Treasury the sum of £250 a year was granted Bruere out of the revenue from the sale of the crown lands. The assembly also voted him an additional salary of £400 currency (equalling £265 10s sterling). *Acts, Privy Coun., Col.*, 1745–1766, § 553; instructions to Bruere, Bermuda, 1764, art. 87, C.O. 5: 201, pp. 301–355 (L.C.); Bruere to John Pownall, Sept. 10, 1764, C.O. 37: 19.

no hope that similar independent and permanent revenues could be procured. If efforts to induce the assemblies to grant such revenues failed—as in every case they did fail —and if the system of annual grants of salaries by the assemblies was to be avoided, then only three methods remained. Royal quit-rents, where these were collected in sufficient amounts, might be used; drafts might be made on the permanent revenues of other provinces, as had been done when part of the Bermuda salary was paid from the four-and-a-half percent duty of Barbados and the Leeward Islands; or the principle of independence of British support might be entirely abandoned, and the governors' salaries be paid from the British Exchequer.

During the first twenty years of royal government in South Carolina the third method was used. Although the first royal governor, Francis Nicholson, was instructed in 1720 to get a permanent revenue act passed with a specific provision for a salary for himself and his successors,[53] such an act was never passed in the province. Instead, an establishment was created in England for the independent company of foot in the province, containing an item of £1000 a year for the governor, payable by the paymaster general of the forces.[54] But after the creation of the frontier province of Georgia, this establishment was diverted to the military commander of both provinces, James Oglethorpe. So in 1739 the newly appointed governor of South Carolina, James Glen, petitioned for a new allowance for his salary.[55] The Treasury Board hesitated for nearly two years but finally consented to a salary of £800. They decided to follow the Bermuda precedent and ordered the

[53] Instructions to Nicholson, South Carolina, 1720, art. 25, C.O. 5: 189, pp. 630–661 (L.C.); Rivers, *Chapter in the History of South Carolina*, p. 68.

[54] *Cal. Treas. Books and Paps.*, 1729–1730, pp. 135–136, 432–433, 441; 1735–1738, pp. 252, 582.

[55] *Ibid.*, 1739–1741, p. 47; Board of Trade to the Commissioners of the Treasury, Aug. 7, 1740, C.O. 5: 402, pp. 24–26.

sum to be paid from the four-and-a-half percent duty of Barbados and the Leeward Islands.[56] This arrangement was continued throughout the colonial period, although the allowance was eventually raised to £1000 a year.[57] Glen was instructed to secure a permanent revenue and thereafter to assent to no act for making a gift to himself or any other officer except for house-rent.[58] But the assembly never created a permanent revenue. So both Glen and his successors took advantage of the indefiniteness of this instruction and accepted from the assembly annual grants which became fixed at £3500 local currency, or £500 sterling, in addition to smaller sums for house-rent.[59] This system continued in force until the Revolution.

Toward the close of the period an incident took place in South Carolina illustrating the danger that might lie in the system of yearly grants by the assembly to the governor. Thomas Boone, appointed governor in 1761, soon quarrelled with the assembly over the right of judging elections. To show their feeling, the assembly voted him no salary and only half the usual sum for house-rent during the remaining two and a half years he was in office.[60] After his recall Boone laid the matter before the home officials. The Board of Trade reported that since the point in dispute was "merely relative to matter of privilege," the assembly ought not to withhold the salary. Such a precedent would be prejudicial to the crown by "awing and deter-

[56] *Cal. Treas. Books and Paps.*, 1739–1741, pp. 260, 263, 325, 462, 463, 580, 584, 585.

[57] Board of Trade report on salary establishments in the North American (continental) colonies, April 16, 1767, C.O. 5: 67, p. 588 (L.C.).

[58] Instructions to Glen, South Carolina, 1739, art. 26, C.O. 5: 198, pp. 101–158 (L.C.).

[59] See the schedules appended to the annual revenue acts in *Statutes of South Carolina*, III and IV. The home authorities never seem to have objected to these grants.

[60] *Stat. of So. Car.*, IV, 199, 223, 224; *Acts, Privy Coun.*, *Col.*, 1745–1766, § 529.

ring'' the governors from the full performance of their duty. An additional instruction was given to Boone's successor directing him to ''recommend it earnestly'' to the assembly to make good the salary.[61] The assembly never complied but neither Boone nor the governors who came after him seem to have been awed or deterred by the incident. Yet a weak man might have given way, as the Board of Trade well knew, hence they were always opposed to a system by which the assembly could bring financial pressure to bear upon the governor. But the significant feature of the controversy to the student of the times is not that the assembly withheld the salary, but that the home authorities showed so little understanding of colonial prejudices as to speak of a contest over election to the assembly as ''merely'' relating to privilege. In view of the pride and self-importance of the assemblies and their claim to equality with parliament, the Board of Trade should have realized that the dispute over privilege touched the colonists at a most sensitive point and was not to be dismissed so lightly. This British indifference to colonial sentiments did more to break down royal authority in America than the entire control of salaries by the assemblies could ever do.

Although the regular salaries of the South Carolina governors were paid from British or West Indian revenues, the government made a valiant effort to provide for the salaries in North Carolina from the local quit-rents. The first royal governor, George Burrington, was authorized in 1730 to take £700 a year out of the quit-rents of the province, a sum which was increased for Gabriel Johnston three years later to £1000.[62] But the money was most inefficiently collected, and at Johnston's death in 1752,

[61] *Acts, Privy Coun., Col.*, 1745–1766, § 637.
[62] *Cal. Treas. Books and Paps.*, 1729–1730, p. 498; 1731–1734, pp. 5, 397, 410; *No. Car. Col. Recs.*, V, 19–20, 97.

arrears of over £13,000 were due his estate.[63] Since this sum constituted a first charge upon the fund, the next governor, Arthur Dobbs, despaired of ever being paid. He asked for some other provision for his salary and the Board of Trade and the auditor general of the plantation revenues supported his petition.[64] Clearly the quit-rents would not do. Again the Treasury found the Barbados four-and-a-half percent duty nicely suited to the purpose and ordered Dobbs's salary of £1000 paid from this convenient fund.[65] This arrangement was continued throughout the period and the governors seem to have obeyed their instruction forbidding gifts from the assemblies.

The instructions to Governor Woodes Rogers of the Bahamas in 1729 suggested the reasonableness of having each plantation settle a fixed salary out of the produce of that province and permitted the assembly to levy an export duty for this purpose.[66] But an adequate revenue from this source or from quit-rents in these sparsely settled islands was out of the question. Here again the presence of a military company helped somewhat, but once more the four-and-a-half percent duty was drawn upon to the extent of £400 a year for the salary of Rogers and his successors.[67] Thus for the Bahamas as for the

[63] *No. Car. Col. Recs.*, V, 21–23, 77; *Acts, Privy Coun., Col.*, 1745–1766, § 230. A large part of these arrears were eventually paid from the quit-rents of South Carolina, but the claims of the various Johnston heirs were not entirely settled until 1798. See E. W. and C. M. Andrews, *Journal of a Lady of Quality*, pp. 294–295, 308, 310–312.

[64] *No. Car. Col. Recs.*, V, 21–22, 77–78, 114, 167–169; *Acts, Privy Coun., Col.*, 1745–1766, § 230.

[65] Treasury minutes, April 10, May 1, June 19, 1754, Treas. 29: 32, pp. 187, 190, 207; docquet of sign manual warrant for a privy seal for Dobbs's salary from the 4½ percent, May, 1754, Signet Office Docquet Books, Public Record Office Index 6825.

[66] Instructions to Rogers, Bahamas, 1729, art. 30, C.O. 5: 194, pp. 516–568 (L.C.).

[67] *Cal. Treas. Books and Paps.*, 1729–1730, pp. 57, 65.

Carolinas, where no adequate and independent funds existed from which the governor might be paid, the government eventually fell back upon the revenues of another part of the colonial world and freed the British taxpayer from additional burdens.

It would have been pleasant if the authorities could have done the same in the cases of all colonies later brought under the British crown. But that was clearly impossible. By the middle of the eighteenth century the theory of colonial self-support was breaking down under the burden of nascent empire. Civil administration in frontier provinces, as well as general defence, involved expenditures which only the mother country was able to make. Parliament gave tacit recognition to the fact in 1749 by voting an estimate for "supporting, maintaining, and enlarging" the settlement of Nova Scotia, in which provision was made for the salaries of the civil officers.[68] Similar estimates were first voted for the royal province of Georgia in 1753,[69] and for East and West Florida in 1764.[70] Parliament made no such provision, however, for the other colonies acquired by the Treaty of 1763,[71] since other arrangements were possible. For a time the taxes

[68] *Journal of the House of Commons*, XXV, 1037, 1059 (March 7 and 19, 1749).

[69] *Ibid.*, XXVI, 628, 678 (March 2 and 16, 1753). It should be pointed out that parliament had periodically granted financial aid to the Georgia trustees ever since 1733, *ibid.*, XXII, 152 (May 17, 1733).

[70] *Ibid.*, XXIX, 877–878, 892 (Feb. 24 and March 1, 1764). The governor of Nova Scotia regularly received £500 "additional salary"; the governor of Georgia, £1000; and the governors of East and West Florida, £1200 each.

[71] Among the secretary of state's papers of 1764 is an account, apparently meant for parliament, of the salaries to be allowed the governors in Quebec and the Ceded Islands. They include: governor general of Quebec, £1200; governor general of Grenada, £2500; lieutenant general and [lieutenant] governor of Grenada, £400; and the lieutenant governors of Dominica, St. Vincent, and Tobago, £400 each. C.O. 5: 65, p. 385 (L.C.). But the *Journals of the House of Commons* contain no evidence that this estimate was ever laid before parliament.

levied by the former French government of Quebec were continued and probably the civil officers were paid from this source.[72] In Grenada and the lesser islands the four-and-a-half percent duty was imposed by letters patent until the establishment of legislative bodies in 1766.[73] Thereafter the salary arrangements were similar to those in Barbados and the Leeward Islands.[74] The instructions to the governor of Quebec in 1775 after the passage of the Quebec Act contained a long schedule of salaries to be paid from the provincial revenues.[75] Lastly, upon the establishment of independent royal government in the island of St. John (Prince Edward Island) in 1769 the governor was authorized to take £500 sterling from the quit-rents collected there.[76] In none of these provinces was the governor's salary left to the annual determination of an assembly.

In the end, the British policy with regard to the salary question was applied in one form or another to eighteen royal provinces with considerable success. The underlying principle in each case was the creation of a fund in-

[72] *Acts, Privy Coun., Col.*, 1745–1766, § 611. In a report on salaries in the continental colonies in 1767, the Board of Trade declared that they had no information as to the amount, origin, or terms of the salaries paid the civil officers of Quebec. C.O. 5: 67, p. 576 (L.C.).

[73] *Acts, Privy Coun., Col.*, 1745–1766, § 534; 1766–1783, p. 9, § 443. Quite possibly the early governors and lieutenant governors received only the pay allowed them on the military establishment as commanders of garrisons. This usually came to one pound a day for governors of garrisons and ten shillings for lieutenant governors.

[74] *Ibid.*, 1766–1783, p. 14, §§ 183, 450. Upon the establishment of independent government in each of these islands the salaries of the governors were: Grenada, £1200; Dominica, £1200; St. Vincent, £1300. Additional grants were permitted from the assembly of each island on the same terms as were in force in Barbados.

[75] Instructions to Carleton, Quebec, 1775, art. 56, *Report on Canadian Archives*, 1904, pp. 229–247; Shortt and Doughty, *Docs. Rel. to Const. Hist. of Canada*, I, 419–433.

[76] Instructions to Patterson, St. John, 1769, art. 22, Warburton, *A History of Prince Edward Island*, p. 459.

dependent of the assembly's control. In about half of these provinces the fund was drawn from local revenues. These were either originally granted by the assembly, as in Barbados, Jamaica, Virginia, and elsewhere, or else were collected by virtue of the prerogative, as was the case with the North Carolina quit-rents and the Bermuda whale licenses. But in the latter instances the funds were seldom sufficient. For those provinces where no adequate fund existed, outside help was necessary. The four-and-a-half percent duty was most often drawn upon for this purpose, although parliament voted sums in a few special cases. In all eighteen provinces the governors were assured of at least moderate salaries no matter how much they might quarrel with their assemblies. Many of the legislatures, indeed, came to have a share in providing the governors' incomes. But, with one exception, their action was so safeguarded that after the additional salary had once been granted it ceased to be under the control of the assembly during the rest of the governor's term. The one exception was South Carolina, where the legislature made annual grants amounting to about a third of the total salary. Once the assembly withheld this grant to punish a governor, but neither he nor his successors ever gave way as a result. It is hard to see where the salary question played or could play a part of any significance in the maintenance of royal authority in these eighteen provinces.

But in four royal provinces—New York, New Jersey, New Hampshire, and Massachusetts—there were no permanent, independent revenues and, until just before the Revolution, the British authorities did not see fit to make use of funds from outside sources to pay any of their governors' salaries. In these four colonies, therefore, the salary question had a very different history. The salaries were always on the same precarious footing as the rest of the expenses of government, a situation which was directly contrary to the British policy. A few incidents in these provinces give color to the charge that the assemblies used their control of salaries to coerce the governors. But the assemblies' failure to make grants for other purposes of a general or special nature was far more often a cause of concession by the governors. The salaries were but part of the larger problem of colonial finance, through the control of which the assemblies made their greatest advances.

The close connection between the method of paying the governors and the agitation over permanent revenues is particularly clear in New York. Until 1709 the governors of this province received their salaries, according to their instructions, from the local revenues granted for a few years at a time. Before 1703 the annual allowance was fixed at £600 but at the time of the general revision of salaries in that year the amount was doubled and the governor was forbidden at the same time to receive any gifts from the assembly.[77] The failure of the legislature to continue the revenue beyond 1709 prevented Governor Hunter, who arrived the next year, from carrying out his instruction which authorized him to take a salary of £1200 a year from the provincial revenue. He laid his instruction before the assembly, stating that he presumed they would

[77] *N. Y. Col. Docs.*, III, 367; instructions to Dongan, N. Y., 1686, art. 63, *ibid.*, p. 374. When New York was joined to the Dominion of New England in 1688, Governor Andros was given £200 and the remaining £400 went to Lieut. Gov. Nicholson, *ibid.*, IV, 263; *Cal. Treas. Books*, 1685–1689, p. 1941. During the administration of Bellomont, who was also governor of Massachusetts and New Hampshire, this arrangement was reversed, he receiving £400 and the lieutenant governor £200. Bellomont complained that his was a "mean and insufficient" salary and that he had to borrow money to get along. *N. Y. Col. Docs.*, IV, 263; instructions to Bellomont, N. Y., 1697, art. 58, *ibid.*, p. 290. For the increase of 1703, see *Cal. State Paps., Col.*, 1702–1703, § 536; *Acts, Privy Coun., Col.*, 1680–1720, p. 431; *N. Y. Col. Docs.*, IV, 1040–1041.

not dispute her Majesty's right to appoint a salary for her governor. But that is exactly what some of the assemblymen did do. They emphatically denied that the queen had a right to grant a salary out of the revenue raised by the provincial assembly and added that if she could authorize her governor to take £1200 she could authorize him to take £12,000 as well.[78] Such remarks were not to be taken too seriously, although they did show the attitude of some of the more extreme colonials. During the next few years Hunter received no pay for his services, but when a settlement of the revenue question was reached in 1714 and 1715, the governor, against whom the assembly bore no personal grudge, received his arrears of salary for the full amount authorized by his instructions.[79]

From this time until 1737 there was no particular difficulty, for the five-year revenue acts passed during this period made regular provision for the governor's salary at the rate of £1560 currency. This sum was supposed to equal £1200 sterling, but later governors complained that the currency had depreciated until they were receiving no more than £900 sterling.[80] The instructions to Governor Montgomerie in 1727 authorized him to accept an additional salary from the assembly on terms similar to those in force in the West Indies.[81] But there was no occasion to fear that this concession would be abused, for the assembly entirely failed to act upon it.[82]

[78] N. Y. Col. Docs., V, 177–178, 179, 190–193.

[79] Ibid., pp. 379–380, 765.   [80] Ibid., VI, 433; VII, 163.

[81] Instructions to Montgomerie, N. Y., 1727, art. 25, C.O. 5: 193, pp. 141–195 (L.C.). See also N. Y. Col. Docs., V, 833.

[82] A gift of £1000 to Governor Cosby, Montgomerie's successor, for services performed before leaving England in opposing the Molasses Act, called forth the criticism of the chief justice, Lewis Morris, who wrote to the Board of Trade, Aug. 27, 1733, objecting to ''that smuggling trade of presents from an assembly to a governor'' which he declared would subsist ''until some way is found to make the governors believe that the king's in-

The expiration of the last five-year revenue act in 1737 and the refusal of the assembly to renew it for more than a year at a time, reopened the salary question. Enough has been said in a previous chapter to show how utterly dependent upon the assembly Lieutenant Governor Clarke and Governor Clinton were in financing the governmental services.[83] The salary was an important item in the usual list of appropriations. One may, perhaps, believe that the concessions which both these men made to the assembly were largely brought about by anxiety to receive their salaries. Clinton himself wrote the Board of Trade in 1745 that while the assembly was at the charge of maintaining a governor he had little hope of seeing the proper dispatch of public business. "Nothing but governor's independence can bring them to a just sense of their duty to his Majesty and his service."[84] Two years later he vainly urged the passage of an act of parliament to establish and regulate the quit-rents of the province so as to create an independent fund from which the salaries of the governor and other officers might be paid.[85] But after all, the salary was only one of the items appropriated by the assembly over which that body secured complete control during these years. A study of the struggle leaves the strong impression that Clinton's loss of executive independence was caused far more directly by the assembly's control of appropriations in general than by his dependence on them for his salary.

But while the home authorities were unwilling to go to the length of an act of parliament to create an independent fund for the governor's salary, they had not yet aban-

structions prohibiting any presents really mean what the words seem to import." *N. Y. Col. Docs.*, V, 953–954. But the British officials seemed to consider the gift legitimate, for they allowed Cosby to keep it without criticism.

[83] See above, pp. 286–290, 308–309.

[84] Clinton to the Board of Trade, Nov. 30, 1745, *N. Y. Col. Docs.*, VI, 287.

[85] Clinton to the Board of Trade, Sept. 27, 1747, *ibid.*, p. 379.

doned hope of a perpetual revenue by act of assembly, which would have met the difficulty equally well. The instructions to Osborn in 1753, directing him to secure a permanent revenue, stated that provision was to be made in the act for the salaries of the governor and other officers. As matters turned out, no such act was passed. The chief members of the assembly told Lieutenant Governor DeLancey that he might dissolve that body as often as he pleased but they would not grant his salary for more than a year at a time. So he asked permission to receive an annual grant.[86] Such permission was given to Governor Hardy, who was appointed in 1755, and with this date the home authorities abandoned their attempt to get a perpetual salary by act of assembly.[87] A report of the Board of Trade on the salaries of governors, judges, and other officials in the continental colonies, which was submitted while the Townshend Duty Bill was before parliament, mentioned New York as one of the four provinces in which the salaries were paid by annual appropriations of the assemblies.[88] As a direct result of this statement, orders were given to the customs officers in America to pay the earl of Dunmore, appointed governor in 1770, his salary of £2000 out of the revenue arising from the tea duty. The governor was at the same time directed not to accept any gift or salary from the assembly.[89] Both Dunmore and his successor, Tryon, refused offers of the assembly of annual

[86] DeLancey to the Board of Trade, Jan. 3, 1754, *N. Y. Col. Docs.*, VI, 820.

[87] Instructions to Hardy, N. Y., 1755, art. 17, C.O. 5: 1128, pp. 383–531. Hardy persuaded the assembly to raise the usual grant from £1560 to £1800 currency which he estimated to equal £1000 sterling. Hardy to the Board of Trade, Oct. 13, Dec. 2, 1756, *N. Y. Docs.*, VII, 163, 203; *Col. Laws of N. Y.*, IV, 149, 150. In 1762 the sum was raised to £2000 currency, *Col. Laws of N. Y.*, IV, 627. See also Governor Moore to Lord Shelburne, Dec. 7, 1767, *N. Y. Col. Docs.*, VII, 1004.

[88] Board of Trade report, April 16, 1767, C.O. 5: 67, pp. 582–583 (L.C.).

[89] Hillsborough to Dunmore, July 16, 1770, *N. Y. Col. Docs.*, VIII, 223.

grants of £2000.[90] At last the government had created a fund, raised partly in New York and partly outside, from which they could pay the governors without the assembly's interference. At last an important object of British policy, the independent support of the governor, was secured, but not until the province had gone through a long period of controversy and mutual distrust. The salary question was, after all, only one phase, and not the most important one at that, of the permanent revenue problem of New York. When the assembly was dictating the expenditure of almost the last penny of the funds which they raised and were holding up appropriations for military defence and for all branches of civil government to get their demands, the fact that they controlled the governor's salary loses most of the significance which has been attached to it.

The struggle over the governor's salary in New Jersey was in many respects similar to that in New York. But in this case nothing remotely approaching a permanent revenue was granted until the time of Governor Burnet, appointed in 1720, during whose administration the first five-year act was passed. This measure gave £500 for salary and £100 for expenses to the governor during the life of the act.[91] Before this time the grants were irregular and uncertain, ranging from £500 to £800 a year with an additional £100 for house-rent, firewood, candles, and other expenses.[92] From 1720 until 1738 the regular passage of revenue acts for short periods of years allowed the salary question to drop into the background. It played

[90] Tryon to Hillsborough, June 4, 1772, *ibid.*, pp. 299–300. Lieutenant Governor Colden accepted a grant by the assembly of £2000 in 1775 for his administration of the colony for something over a year during Tryon's absence. *Col. Laws of N. Y.*, V, 725.

[91] Burnet to the Board of Trade, Oct. 3, 1722, *N. J. Arch.*, V, 53.

[92] *Ibid.*, II, 506; III, 352–353; IV, 21–22, 57, 185, 201, 292, 368, 369, 371; V, 82; XIII, 528, 548; XIV, 67, 79, 83, 107, 128, 129, 140, 143, 144.

no part in the political disputes which occasionally took place.[93]

The appointment of Lewis Morris as the first separate governor brought a change in the situation with an increase in the allowance from £500 to £1000 and with £60 additional for house-rent. But the assembly made the grant for a period of three years only.[94] Until 1744 the salary was continued at the same rate.[95] During this period the relations of governor and assembly were becoming more and more strained. The insistence of the lower house upon the passage of a bill for £40,000 in bills of credit, contrary to the instructions, their refusal to pass a satisfactory militia bill, the occurrence of riotous demonstrations against the proprietors in East Jersey, and other causes of friction completely nullified the advantages which had been expected from the appointment of a separate governor. The blame for this situation must be divided equally among the assembly, the council, and the governor, the first for its self-assertiveness, the second for its domination by the landed interests, and the last for his irascible and undiplomatic temper. Matters reached the point where the assembly leaders informed Morris that they would vote him no support unless he passed the £40,000 currency bill and other desired measures, in spite

[93] Warrants for the governor's salary were regularly signed at the quarterly executive meetings of the council. Occasionally, warrants for two or three quarters were signed at the same time, but never after 1722 was the salary more than 12 months in arrears. The initiative in passing the warrant, of course, always rested with the governor. *N. J. Arch.*, XIV, *passim.*

[94] Morris to Sir Charles Wager, May 10, 1739, *ibid.*, VI, 68; *Morris Papers*, pp. 45–46; Morris to the Board of Trade, May 26, 1739, *Morris Paps.*, p. 49.

[95] *N. J. Arch.*, VI, 150. No act covering the fiscal year, Sept., 1743, to Sept., 1744, has been found and the warrants mentioned in the council journal run only to March 23, 1743. *Ibid.*, XV, 243, 244. But numerous references point to the fact that Morris's salary was paid to Sept. 23, 1744, *ibid.*, VI, 421–422; VII, 171–172; XVI, 101–102.

of the fact that sufficient funds for the usual salary lay unappropriated in the treasury. The House of Representatives directed a deputation to inform the governor that the people would always exert themselves in keeping up the salaries when "his Majesty's salutary intentions" for the province were answered by the officers, but that with "the addition of new and unheard-of perplexities, then they will make use of their known rights and privileges allowed them by their happy constitution, in judging according to Scripture and right reason, that every man ought to be rewarded according to his works."[96] Lest bribery with biblical sanction should not be appreciated by the governor, the speaker and other members of the house later told him frankly that they would willingly support the government with the usual salaries on condition that they could obtain the acts they wanted.[97] Shortly before Morris's death, the assembly again proposed "that they would willingly support the government by giving his Excellency £1000 out of the first interest money which should arise by the new bills for making £40,000, provided he would sign the few bills which were then passed both houses for his assent."[98] But the stubborn old governor, on his deathbed as he was, refused to be influenced. The salary for the last twenty months of his administration was never paid.

This incident is the only clear case in New Jersey, and one of four such cases in the entire British colonial world in the eighteenth century, in which the assembly definitely refused to grant a salary to a royal governor unless he

[96] Minutes of the House of Representatives, Oct. 3, 1745, *N. J. Arch.*, VI, 249.

[97] Minutes of the House of Representatives, Oct. 18, 1745, *ibid.*, p. 259.

[98] House of Representatives to Governor Belcher, referring to their message of May 7, 1746, *ibid.*, VII, 335–353; XVI, 100–106; *Morris Paps.*, pp. 315–320, especially p. 318.

would assent to certain measures desired by them and not
directly connected with the salary itself. There were instances in New York and New Hampshire as well as in
New Jersey when the governor's salary was not paid because of his refusal to accept a revenue bill which made
the salary possible. But in each case the governor's attitude was influenced as much by his fear of the consequences to the civil government as a whole or to the military situation from a failure of the revenue bill as by
anxiety as to his own support. In some cases, it is true,
governors vetoed salary grants directly because these
grants failed to comply with the terms of the instructions.
But in no instance aside from the one in South Carolina
already mentioned, two in Massachusetts to be discussed
later, and this one in New Jersey, did the members of the
lower house definitely withhold a royal governor's support until he should assent to other bills which lay before
him. And it should be pointed out that both in South
Carolina and in New Jersey the governors refused to
yield and accept the proffered bribes. Certainly the dependence of a governor upon his assembly for support
was undesirable from the British point of view, but that
it resulted in weak surrender by the royal appointee to
the wishes of the assembly cannot be argued from the
cases of Boone and Morris.

The New Jersey crisis of 1744–1746 made future efforts
to get a permanent salary grant quite hopeless. All later
governors had to content themselves with yearly appropriations. The annual support act became a regular
feature of the legislative program.[99] The situation did

[99] Belcher, who succeeded Morris, had been instructed, as had his last
three predecessors, not to assent to any bill for payment to himself or any
other person unless the bill contained a suspending clause. He petitioned for
exemption from this rule, and although no final action on the petition is
recorded, both Belcher and his successors assented to annual salary bills
without suspending clauses. Instructions to Belcher, N. J., 1747, art. 19,

not entirely satisfy the Board of Trade, who felt that Belcher's inaction during the land riots that marred his administration was largely due to his dependence on the assembly for support.[100] How far this charge is true cannot be stated. But probably the old man's weariness with controversy after his decade and more of troubled administration in Massachusetts and New Hampshire, his recognition of the impossibility of getting effective support from the anti-proprietary assembly in putting down the disturbances, and his lack of agreement with the proprietor-controlled council were equally important factors. In general the salary question in New Jersey was never as important an element in the policies and actions of the governors as were other phases of local politics. With jealousies between East and West Jersey, with a council usually dominated by the proprietary group, and with an assembly generally supporting the popular interests, the province was a particularly difficult one to govern. That the governor was unduly influenced by financial considerations was easy to charge, but conclusive evidence of such a fact is entirely wanting.

C.O. 5: 200, pp. 385–419 (L.C.); *N. J. Arch.*, VI, 443–445; *Acts, Privy Coun., Col.*, 1745–1766, § 53. On one occasion after the arrival of Governor Boone in 1760, a support act was passed for two years. Governors Bernard, Boone, and Hardy each received £500 additional allowance for the first year. Governor Franklin was able to get his salary raised from £1000 to £1200 (about £750 sterling). *N. J. Arch.*, IX, 248, 388–389; XVII, 199, 274; S. Neville, *Statutes of New Jersey*, II, 307–310; Franklin's account of standing salaries, Dec. 28, 1766, *N. J. Arch.*, IX, 579–580.

100 "That his dependence upon the assembly has been the motive of his conduct may be hard to say, but very easy to believe, when considered that he has readily come into every favorable measure proposed by them; out, however this may be, the fact is that by the obstinacy of the assembly on the one hand, in whose power it was to have suppressed the means of riots in their infancy, and the want of power in the governor and council on the other, his Majesty's province of New Jersey is at present in open rebellion. . . ." Board of Trade representation on New Jersey affairs, June 1, 1750, *N. J. Arch.*, VII, 517–518.

Failure to establish a permanent method of paying the New Hampshire governors was due far more to the poverty of this frontier province and to the example of near-by Massachusetts than to inherent opposition in New Hampshire itself. Until the appointment of Joseph Dudley in 1702 there can hardly be said to have been a salary problem at all. Lieutenant Governor Cranfield had been voted £100 a year by the council in 1685,[101] but the first royal governor after the downfall of the Dominion of New England, Samuel Allen, claimant to the proprietorship of the province, and his son-in-law and lieutenant governor, John Usher, had received nothing from the antagonistic assembly. The popular earl of Bellomont, who visited the provinces in 1699, was presented with £500, which the privy council allowed him to accept.[102] But after the general revision of salaries in 1703 Dudley was ordered to reject all gifts and to press for a permanent salary.[103] The assembly gave way to this demand to the extent of voting him a salary of £160 a year during his incumbency.[104] When Dudley was succeeded by the untactful Samuel Shute in 1716, the New Hampshire assembly, taking a leaf from the Massachusetts book, refused to do more than make semiannual grants to the governor, and later to the lieutenant governor, John Wentworth. The usual sum

[101] *N. H. Prov. Paps.*, I, 555; *N. H. Prov. Laws*, I, 91–92. By the terms of Cranfield's commission such grants of money were within the power of the council.

[102] *N. H. Prov. Paps.*, III, 86; *N. H. Prov. Laws*, I, 659–660; *Acts, Privy Coun., Col.*, 1680–1720, p. 846.

[103] Royal letter to Dudley, April 20, 1703, *N. H. Prov. Paps.*, III, 251–252; *N. H. Prov. Laws*, II, 29–30. Dudley had previously received a gift of £250 from the assembly which had been approved by order in council, *N. H. Prov. Laws*, II, 45–46; *Acts, Privy Coun., Col.*, 1680–1720, p. 847.

[104] Because of a dispute between the council and assembly over the method of collecting the necessary tax, the bill did not become law until 1705. *N. H. Prov. Paps.*, III, 255, 260, 308; *N. H. Prov. Laws*, II, 57, 64–65.

voted was £100 every six months, although during the period of Râle's War the amount was often increased.[105]

Two things were clear in the New Hampshire situation when Burnet came into office in 1728: first, that after a fairly promising start under Dudley, the assembly had failed completely to provide that permanent salary which was such an important part of British policy; and secondly, that the province was so small and poor that a salary even equal to that of Bermuda was hardly to be expected. In view of these conditions, Burnet's instructions contained an entirely new clause relating to salary. It called attention to the fact that in spite of former instructions and the repeated urgings of the governor, the legislature had not settled a fixed salary upon the chief executive. Continuation of such undutiful behavior might require the attention of parliament. The assembly was to settle a salary of £200 sterling upon the governor if they hoped "to recommend themselves to the continuance of our royal grace and favor."[106] This phraseology was too much for the farmer-legislators of the little province. After some debate they voted an annual salary of £200

[105] Upon his first arrival Shute was voted a sum for expenses which was finally fixed at £250. *N. H. Prov. Paps.*, III, 667–668, 670, 691. He was then given an allowance of 30 shillings a day for one year during the sessions of the assembly "for the defraying his entertainments and expense," but only through the insistence of the council was the grant made as large as this. *Ibid.*, pp. 687, 688. Finally, in October, 1717, the first semiannual grant was passed for £160. The next two grants were for £140 and £90 respectively and thereafter the sum of £100 was regular. *Ibid.*, pp. 717, 735, 748, 768, 777, 794, 808, 838; IV, *passim.* There is no evidence that the fluctuations which occasionally took place were affected by the relations between governor or lieutenant governor and assembly.

[106] Instructions to Burnet, N. H., 1728, art. 30, *N. H. Prov. Laws*, II, 418–441. Shute had been unpaid during his absence in England since 1722, and an instruction in much the same terms had been proposed for him before the death of George I and the appointment of Burnet. Less opposition was expected from New Hampshire than from Massachusetts, the former province "more immediately depending upon his Majesty's pleasure." *Acts, Privy Coun., Col.*, 1720–1745, p. 104; *ibid., The Unbound Paps.*, § 349.

sterling or £600 currency to Burnet for three years or during his incumbency.[107] The death of Burnet within four months of the passage of this act and the appointment of Jonathan Belcher in his place led to the renewal of the act to continue in force during the latter's administration.[108] Apparently the British officials had gained their point, if not entirely, at least to the extent of making the individual governor independent of the assembly during his term in office.[109]

Benning Wentworth, the first separate governor of New Hampshire, who assumed the administration late in 1741, was told to get a public revenue sufficient to provide all official salaries. In order to avoid loss through depreciation, the allowances were to be paid in sterling, proclamation money, or bills of credit at current rates of exchange. No gifts from the assembly were to be per-

[107] Out of this sum any allowance to the lieutenant governor was to be made by the governor himself. Burnet permitted Lieut. Gov. Wentworth, who resided in New Hampshire while he lived in Massachusetts, to draw one third of the salary. *N. H. Prov. Paps.*, IV, 511, 535–536, 539, 546, 550; *N. H. Prov. Laws*, II, 442–444.

[108] Instructions to Belcher, N. H., 1730, art. 32, *N. H. Prov. Laws*, II, 467–490; salary grant of 1730, *N. H. Prov. Paps.*, IV, 569–570, 760–761; *N. H. Prov. Laws*, II, 517–518.

[109] Belcher actually lost by the semi-permanency of the grant because the currency depreciated though the nominal value of the allowance remained unchanged in spite of his protests. In 1741 he declared that over £600 sterling was actually due him on the basis of his instructions. *N. H. Prov. Paps.*, V, 84–85. One cannot escape the feeling, however, that he suffered just retribution for his ungenerous attitude toward his lieutenant governors, with whom he refused to share the salary as Burnet had done. To Lieut. Gov. Dunbar, for example, he wrote in 1733: "Indeed I always thought it mean, and considering there is no provision made here [in Massachusetts] or at New Hampshire for a lieutenant governor, I think a governor (in honor to the commission he bears) ought to let him enjoy all the perquisites he fairly can; nor do I, I assure you, desire to interfere with these things at New Hampshire. But as they are my right, they must be enjoyed under me." *Belcher Papers*, I, 336–337. This quotation gives somewhat the measure of the man.

mitted.[110] Such a revenue was a serious problem for the frontier province. After much dispute two acts were passed for the governor's salary. One granted him £250 a year in proclamation money during his incumbency payable from the excise, and if this fund fell short, from the general treasury. The other provided £25,000 in bills of credit to remain outstanding for twelve years, from the interest of which Wentworth was to receive £250 in bills during his administration or the life of the act.[111] This arrangement might have worked well for a short time, but for a long administration such as Wentworth's, lasting as it did until 1767, the plan was anything but ideal. The excise failed, other treasury funds were needed for military purposes, the bills of credit depreciated, and then the act for issuing them expired. Fortunately for the governor, he was a man of independent means, for his salary was well in arrears most of the time.[112] All these facts proved fruitful grounds for dissatisfaction and controversy. In the end the system of annual grants was almost inevitably restored.[113] To his credit be it said that Wentworth always seems to have put the welfare of the province above his personal interest when it came to the drawing of his salary from a depleted treasury. On one occasion, for example, he deliberately refrained from taking £2000 voted him for arrears, because he found that

[110] Instructions to B. Wentworth, N. H., 1741, art. 29, *N. H. Prov. Laws,* II, 608–636. Permission for payment in bills of credit at current rates instead of sterling or proclamation money was reinserted in the instruction by order in council after having once been omitted.

[111] *N. H. Prov. Paps.,* V, 142–155, 609, 611, 623; *N. H. Prov. Laws,* II, 691, 695–701. In 1748 Wentworth declared that these two grants together brought him only £200 sterling a year. Wentworth to the duke of Bedford, Oct. 24, 1748, C.O. 5: 10, nos. 100, 101 (L.C.).

[112] *N. H. Prov. Paps.,* VI, 692.

[113] *Ibid.,* V–VII, *passim.* For a more complete account of the difficulties resulting from the salary question in Wentworth's administration see W. H. Fry, *New Hampshire as a Royal Province,* pp. 93–119.

to do so would not leave enough in the treasury to pay the salaries of other officials and provide for the troops and military defences.[114] Although Wentworth was often at odds with his assembly in connection with both his salary and other provincial affairs, he never seems to have allowed his own interests to interfere with his duty.

The last royal governor, John Wentworth, who succeeded his uncle in 1767, called the attention of his first assembly to his instruction requiring the payment of an "adequate, honorable, and permanent salary" in sterling or proclamation money.[115] The assembly's reply recognized "the propriety and reasonableness" of making at an early date "an adequate and honorable support for his Majesty's governor" but failed to say anything about a "permanent" salary.[116] They explained to the council their unwillingness to do this on the ground that the governor would soon be paid from the customs duties levied by parliament. Or if no such arrangement should be made and the responsibility should fall back on the assembly, they hoped that the circumstances of the province would soon be enough improved to warrant a larger grant than they could make now.[117] Presumably they did not wish their more generous impulses hampered by a fixed allowance! Eventually, however, the lower house consented to the establishment of a salary of £700 a year during Wentworth's continuation in office.[118] But a dispute arose at once over the appointment of officials to manage the excise from which the allowance was to be paid and the assembly took a position which directly infringed upon the appointive power of the governor and council. Too wise to

[114] *N. H. Prov. Paps.*, VI, 187, 328.

[115] *Ibid.*, VII, 125; instructions to J. Wentworth, N. H., 1767, art. 24, *N. H. Prov. Laws*, III, 421-453.

[116] *N. H. Prov. Paps.*, VII, 126-127.

[117] *Ibid.*, pp. 130, 132, 133.   [118] *Ibid.*, pp. 146-147.

endanger his popularity by pressing the point, Wentworth let the bill drop and received the proffered £700 by annual grants during his administration.[119] Although this arrangement flagrantly violated his instructions, the governor was undoubtedly wise in his decision, because he was able to keep control of the appointing power without sacrificing his popularity and to administer the government until the outbreak of the Revolution with the full confidence of both the inhabitants and the home authorities.[120]

Examination of the salary question in New Hampshire shows that the assembly's control of the grants was never an effective check upon the governors. In only two administrations after 1703—those of Samuel Shute and John Wentworth—did the assembly fail to provide at the outset an allowance for the full term of incumbency. In one other—that of Benning Wentworth—provision for the full term failed primarily because of the governor's unusually long tenure of office. In none of these cases did the salary question effectively hamper the activities of the governor in carrying out the royal policies. Even in John Wentworth's struggles over the appointing power within

119 *Ibid.*, pp. 147, 177, 179, 227, 246, 279, 303, 324, 368. Wentworth also received grants for house-rent which increased his total allowance by ten to fourteen percent.

120 Additional grants of £100 and £500 in 1771 and 1772 respectively for ''sundry extra services rendered the province'' and ''in consideration of the eminent services his Excellency our governor has done this province and in grateful acknowledgement of which,'' although in violation of his instructions, attest the good will of the assembly during these critical years before the Revolution. *Ibid.*, pp. 257, 276, 294. On the other hand, British confidence in him was shown by his reappointment as surveyor general of the king's woods in America in 1783 and his appointment as lieutenant governor of Nova Scotia in 1792 when Lord Dorchester was governor of all the North American provinces. In 1795 Wentworth was made a baronet and the next year he was given the privilege of wearing two keys in the chevron of his arms in token of his fidelity. See A. S. Mayo, *John Wentworth, passim,* and *Dictionary of National Biography.*

a decade of the Revolution, the assembly made no attempt to decrease the income of this popular executive. The salary controversies of New Hampshire must be considered as inevitable incidents in the life of a poverty-stricken frontier province and not as deliberate efforts on the part of a popular body to win control over the actions of a representative of the crown.

Similar in result but quite different in meaning was the salary controversy in Massachusetts. Here the struggle took the form of a pitched battle between the royal administration and the popular assembly, with a decisive and important victory for the latter. Accustomed as the people were in the years before 1684 to governors of their own choice, elected for a short term only, and given but nominal compensation, the question of a permanent salary for a royal governor naturally proved a troublesome one to all concerned. During the administration of the Dominion of New England by Andros the inhabitants had no voice in the matter, for the governor's salary was at first provided from the royal Exchequer and later from the proceeds of the taxes which Andros had been authorized to continue as established before the introduction of royal government.[121] But when Sir William Phips arrived as governor under the charter of 1691 the long controversy began. Phips asked the Lords of Trade for instructions on the subject and for a royal order to the assembly, but failed to get either.[122] The assembly considered itself most gen-

[121] Andros received £1200 for his first year and £1200 additional as "royal bounty," both paid from the Exchequer. *Cal. Treas. Books*, 1685–1689, pp. 768, 821, 864; *Acts, Privy Coun., Col.*, 1680–1720, § 244. See also Board of Trade representation, 1697, on the state of the salaries in New England and New York, *N. Y. Col. Docs.*, IV, 263; instructions to Andros, Dom. of N. E., 1686, art. 15, *N. H. Prov. Laws*, I, 155–167; commission to Andros, 1688, *ibid.*, pp. 226–234; instructions to Andros, 1688, art. 15, *ibid.*, pp. 234–244; *Cal. Treas. Books*, 1685–1689, pp. 1583, 1941.

[122] *Massachusetts Acts and Resolves*, VIII, 292.

erous in voting him £500 during each of the three years he remained in the colony.[123] After his departure for England in 1694 the assembly discontinued these grants on the not unreasonable ground that a governor who was no longer governing was entitled to no pay. The precedent thus established caused much sorrow to later governors, especially to Shute and Bernard, who felt entitled to their salaries until the revocation of their commissions.

Upon the arrival of the earl of Bellomont in 1699, the general court, complimented by the appointment of a peer, granted him £1000, a gift which they repeated in the following year.[124] But it remained for Joseph Dudley to call their attention to the desirability of a permanent and regular salary in accordance with his instructions. In his first address he told the council and assembly that the queen ordered him to say "that there is no other province or government belonging to the crown of England, except this, where there is not provided a fit and convenient house for the reception of the governor, and a settled salary for the governor, lieutenant governor, secretary, judges, and all other officers, which therefore is recommended to you."[125] A committee of the lower house appointed to draft a reply reported that the subject was "altogether new" to them (a common form of evasion in Massachusetts) but that they would be ready to do according to their

[123] *Ibid.*, I, 109, 174, 188.

[124] For the first year Bellomont's house-rent was also paid by the assembly. *Ibid.*, pp. 395, 437; VII, 230.

[125] *A Collection of the Proceedings of the Great and General Court . . . of the Massachusetts Bay in New England, Containing Several Instructions from the Crown to the Council and Assembly of That Province for Fixing a Salary on the Governor and Their Determination Thereupon* . . ., p. 5. This pamphlet was printed by order of the House of Representatives in 1729 at the time of the dispute with Burnet, and contains extracts from journals no longer extant. It contains practically all the Massachusetts proceedings on the salary question to its date of publication. (Cited hereafter as *Mass. Proc. on Sal.*)

ability "what may be proper on our part for the support of the government.'"[126] A present of £500 was all that Dudley received at this time.[127] The subject came up again at the next session but the committee reported: "It is not convenient (the circumstances of the province considered) to state salaries, but to allow as the Great and General Court shall from time to time see necessary.'"[128] The principle here expressed continued to be the guiding policy of the lower house, against which the royal authorities struggled for years without success.

While words were being bandied back and forth in Boston in this fruitless manner, the Board of Trade was preparing its general report on salaries for the privy council. The board took the occasion to criticize the Massachusetts assembly sharply. On their recommendation a royal letter was sent to Dudley. He was to acquaint the assembly at their next meeting that, "in regard of the great privileges our loving subjects of that our province do enjoy," they should "forthwith settle a constant and fixed allowance upon the governor suitable to the character and dignity of that government," together with a fitting provision for the lieutenant governor, both to be made without limitation of time. No gifts to the governor were to be permitted after the establishment of such salaries.[129] Dudley presented this letter to the general court. A little later the lower house replied: "It hath been the privilege from Henry the Third and confirmed by Edward the First, and

[126] *Mass. Proc. on Sal.*, p. 6.

[127] *Mass. Acts and Res.*, I, 498; VII, 343, 717.

[128] A resolve embodying this statement was sent to the council but there rejected. Dudley was finally forced to accept £200 for his house-rent and services for the year. The next spring £300 was added. *Mass. Proc. on Sal.*, pp. 9–10; *Mass. Acts and Res.*, VII, 358–359, 733–734; VIII, 23.

[129] *Acts, Privy Coun., Col.*, 1680–1720, pp. 431–432; *Cal. State Paps., Col.*, 1702–1703, §§ 536, 597; C.O. 324: 8, pp. 238–239 (L.C.); royal letter to Dudley, April 20, 1703, C.O. 5: 190, pp. 467–469 (Mass.).

in all reigns until this day granted, and now is allowed to be the just and unquestionable right of the subject to raise and dispose how they see cause, any sum of money by consent of parliament: the which privilege we, her Majesty's loyal and dutiful subjects here, have lived in the enjoyment of and do hope to enjoy the same under our most gracious Queen Anne and successors, and shall ever endeavor to discharge the duty incumbent on us; but humbly conceive the settling perpetual salaries not agreeable with her Majesty's interest in this province but prejudicial to her Majesty's good subjects.'"[130] The significance of this address is apparent. In words reminiscent of Hampden, Pym, and Eliot, the assembly was drawing a close analogy between itself and parliament and was claiming for itself all those authorities and powers which the legislature of the mother country had won for itself through generations of conflict with the crown. Furthermore, it shows that the representatives considered themselves in no way bound to obey a royal order addressed to the governor which did not agree with their ideas of the interests of the province. Both of these views were to become of increasing importance as the century advanced and as the assemblies of all the provinces gained in self-consciousness and power. The failure of the British authorities to appreciate these conditions, or if they did so, to take effective steps to meet the situation constitutes one of the great reasons for the eventual break between the colonies and the mother country.

On this statement the assembly stood its ground and Dudley finally had to give way. In reply to his reports of ill-success, the Board of Trade wrote expressing a wish that he could suggest to them "any method for rendering this affair more easy to you." They pointed out that his instructions did not forbid him to accept gifts prior to

[130] *Mass. Proc. on Sal.*, p. 13; *Mass. Acts and Res.*, VIII, 341.

the settlement of a permanent salary, but they cautioned him to report such gifts immediately for the queen's eventual approval.[131] The debate ended by the establishment of a system of semiannual grants by which Dudley received £500 each year during his administration.[132] The sum was small, but life in Puritan Massachusetts was on a comparatively simple scale, and during most of the term the colony was waging war with the French and Indians. The grants were usually made among the first measures of each session and, once established, the system caused little dissatisfaction. But the assembly had clearly won the first round of the contest.

The instructions prepared for Burges in 1715 and for Shute in 1716 contained the same article as that given to Dudley. It met, however, with no greater success. The semiannual grants made to Shute were raised to double those voted to Dudley, but the increase was largely offset by continued depreciation of the bills in which they were paid. "In consideration of the dearness of all necessaries of housekeeping," of which Shute complained to the assembly, the latter raised his allowance from £1000 to £1200 for the years 1717–1719, but this generosity was not long continued.[133] In 1720, after a bitter quarrel over the governor's right to approve the choice of a speaker, the house voted the semiannual salary at the old rate of £500.[134] Shute's feelings can be imagined, but he was forced to accept the grant with the best grace he could muster or go entirely without. At the next session he had his salary instructions read to the house, in order, as he said, that

[131] Board of Trade to Dudley, May 26, 1704, C.O. 5: 911, pp. 330–334 (Mass.); *Cal. State Paps., Col.*, 1704–1705, § 349.

[132] *Mass. Acts and Res.*, VIII and IX, *passim*. Dudley declared that the £500 currency did not amount to more than £350 sterling.

[133] *Ibid.*, IX, 581, 611, 636, 674, 698.

[134] *Ibid.*, X, 22; *Journal of the House of Representatives*, II, 263.

they might consider how far they had complied with his Majesty's directions. That august assemblage coolly replied that they deemed £500 to be "an honorable allowance," that the affair of settling salaries was a matter "of great weight and wholly new to this house," and that it was unwise to enter into the subject so late in the session as many members had gone home.[135] Again £500 was all the governor received.[136]

The assembly's attitude was now taking a more sinister turn. Not only had they reduced the governor's salary because of a quarrel, but, before considering his allowance at all, they had sent a committee to the council to inquire whether Shute had signed all bills which had passed the two houses. Not until they had been assured of such action did they grant the reduced salary.[137] The situation which the Board of Trade so greatly dreaded in all the colonies had now definitely arrived in Massachusetts. The grant of salary was to be made conditional upon favorable action by the governor. The test came in June, 1721. Before acting on the salary the assembly inquired whether the governor had yet approved the list of civil officers. Shute untactfully replied that "he would take his own time for it."[138] The messages which followed showed that the governor would not approve the assembly's choice of excise commissioners until the salary vote was passed. He was evidently trying to use his veto power as a means to get his £600 salary restored. Both sides were playing the same game. Other factors entered into the controversy and not until the close of a special session in September, 1721, did the assembly vote Shute £500. But they apparently held back the resolve until informed that all

[135] *Mass. Proc. on Sal.*, pp. 30–31; *Jour. of H. of R.*, II, 347, 350, 353; *Mass. Acts and Res.*, II, 632.

[136] *Mass. Acts and Res.*, X, 65. [137] *Jour. of H. of R.*, II, 263.

[138] *Ibid.*, III, 46.

transactions of the two houses had been approved by the governor.[139] The same method was followed in the November session.[140] But the assembly failed to press its advantage in the spring of 1722. For in spite of a bitter dispute with the governor relating to the fellows of Harvard College, the assembly voted the customary allowance of £500 without waiting for the governor's final action.[141] Before the salary question came up in the session of December, 1722, Shute had quietly slipped away to England to pour his troubles into the ears of the royal ministers and the Board of Trade. The contest had ended in a stalemate. The governor had been unable to prevent a decrease in his salary, but the assembly had failed to coerce him in the Harvard case. Both contestants had found their weapons ineffective.

Upon arriving in England, Shute presented a series of charges against the assembly, which resulted in the "explanatory charter" of 1725.[142] Curiously enough, neither the governor's complaint nor the charter made any mention of the salary question. The omission from the charter is probably explained by the fact that that document was intended to remedy defects in the original charter of 1691 and not to deal with matters of administrative policy. Nevertheless, the failure of the British authorities to seize the opportunity of forcing a favorable settlement of the salary dispute may be an indication that they thought it less important than has sometimes been supposed. In any case, Shute brought the matter up again in 1726 with a petition asking for the "arrears" of salary due him from his two provinces since his departure. He

---

[139] *Jour. of H. of R.*, III, 53, 64–69, 74–81, 127, 130.

[140] *Ibid.*, pp. 156, 159.   [141] *Ibid.*, IV, 69, 73, 116, 147, 207.

[142] *Acts, Privy Coun., Col.*, 1720–1745, pp. 92–104; Thorpe, *Charters, Constitutions, etc.*, III, 1886–1888; *Board of Trade Journal*, 1722/3–1728, pp. 41–42, 197.

urged that the assemblies be required to settle a permanent salary upon him. After hearings before the Board of Trade and the privy council committee, the latter recommended that an order under the sign manual be given to Shute to carry back to America requiring an immediate compliance with what had so often been recommended to the assemblies. If there should be further disobedience, the committee advised that the whole matter be laid before parliament.[143] A royal order was accordingly issued. But Shute's failure to leave England before the death of George I, and the appointment of Burnet to the governorship prevented the document from being delivered to the assemblies.[144] A new governor was to take up the struggle.

While these questions were being considered in England the House of Representatives showed again the possible danger in the system of annual grants. Early in 1728 Lieutenant Governor Dummer vetoed a bill for repairing the fortifications because it provided for an issue of bills of credit contrary to the instructions. The lower house refused to vote salaries or allowances to any provincial officers because, as they said, the people could not pay the necessary taxes without the increased currency. Dummer finally gave way and signed a new measure for bills of credit, whereupon the lower house promptly voted the allowances of the lieutenant governor and all other officers.[145] Later the supporters of the crown seized upon this incident as evidence of the assembly's determination

---

[143] *Board of Trade Journal*, 1722/3–1728, pp. 225, 227, 229, 230, 282, 283, 284; *Acts, Privy Coun., Col.*, 1720–1745, pp. 104–106; Historical Manuscripts Commission, *Report*, XI, app. 4, pp. 272–273.

[144] Royal letter to Shute, April 10, 1727, C.O. 5: 870 (unpaged) (Mass.). It need hardly be said that Shute never received any "arrears" of salary from New England, but in 1739 the home government allowed him £400 as "royal bounty" for his services in Massachusetts, to be paid from the four-and-a-half percent of Barbados and the Leeward Islands. *Cal. Treas. Books and Paps.*, 1739–1741, p. 152.

[145] *Jour. of H. of R.*, VIII, 124–169, *passim*.

to destroy the governor's independence by controlling his salary. The representatives disclaimed any such intention but the charge was probably well founded.

By 1728 the salary dispute in Massachusetts was rapidly approaching a crisis. The House of Representatives had definitely taken the ground that they were the sole judges of when and how the governor should be paid. They had even gone to the point of reducing the salary of a weak, inefficient, and domineering governor and had actually forced another chief executive's hand by withholding his pay. The British government, however, had taken an equally strong stand for obedience to the royal order with a threat of intervention by parliament. The importance of the situation transcended the mere question of who should control the governor's salary. The real issue now was the ability of the British government to enforce its orders upon a provincial assembly. Victory for the crown would go a long way toward insuring that "balance" in the constitution of the province to which the Board of Trade was constantly referring; defeat would mean an irreparable blow to the prestige of royal government in New England.

The issue was soon joined. Governor Burnet, son of the famous bishop of Salisbury, with a record of considerable success in the administration of New York and New Jersey, arrived in Boston in July, 1728, amid a demonstration of enthusiasm seldom exceeded in provincial America. But the warmth of his welcome was turned to coolness by his first address to the assembly. He began by dilating on the glories of the British constitution, among the greatest of which was the mutual independence of the three branches of the legislature: king, lords, and commons. If one should become weak, "the whole must inevitably suffer by the alteration." And so in the provincial system, where the king was actually the head of the legislature and the governor merely his officer, the same held true. Burnet continued in much the same vein, discussing the civil list in England, granted to the king for life. He hoped the Massachusetts assembly would follow this excellent example. In conclusion, he laid before them the twenty-third article of his instructions demanding a perpetual salary for the royal governors.[146] This instruction reviewed the situation for many years back, declared that the attitude of the assembly must be looked upon as "a neglect of their duty" to the king, and directed the assembly to pass an act granting a "fixed and honorable salary" of at least £1000 sterling upon the governor. Failure of the council and assembly to comply, said the instruction, would be looked upon by the king "as a manifest mark of their undutiful behavior to us, and such as may require the consideration of the legislature in what manner the honor and dignity of our governor ought to be supported in our said province for the future.[147] With this demand and with this threat the supporters of the crown launched their attack.

The assembly's response was simple. They voted Burnet £1700 "to enable him to manage the public affairs of the government" and to defray his expenses in coming to the government, but they made no move toward a permanent salary.[148] The governor immediately rejected this grant as contrary to his instructions.[149] Fruitless mes-

[146] *Jour. of H. of R.*, VIII, 245–246; *Mass. Proc. on Sal.*, p. 40.

[147] Instructions to Burnet, Mass., 1728, art. 23, C.O. 5: 916, pp. 67–109 (Mass.); *Jour. of H. of R.*, VIII, 246–247.

[148] *Jour. of H. of R.*, VIII, 251; *Mass. Proc. on Sal.*, p. 42.

[149] *Jour. of H. of R.*, VIII, 255–256; *Mass. Proc. on Sal.*, p. 43. The assembly thereupon split the grant into two parts, voting £300 for Burnet's charges in coming to the province and £1400 for "managing the public affairs." Burnet eventually accepted the smaller amount but rejected the larger. £1400 in local currency was at this time worth about £1000 sterling. Only to this extent did the assembly obey the instruction. *Jour. of H. of R.*, VIII, 267–268; *Mass. Acts and Res.*, XI, 355.

sages, resolutions, and replies filled the days that followed. Much was said about the liberties of Englishmen, the privileges conferred by the charter, obedience to the king, the precedent of parliament, the dignity of the governor—and of the assembly as well.[150] Neither side would give way, other issues became involved as the argument became more bitter, and the whole dispute was eventually carried to England. Burnet's letters home were matched by the activity of the representatives in employing agents to present their case at Whitehall. After hearings given the agents by the Board of Trade and the committee of the privy council, the latter body reported in April, 1729, that Burnet "had acted with the utmost duty to your Majesty and just regard to the trust reposed in him." Since the assembly had shown so little regard for the instruction, only one remedy was left—the whole matter must be laid before parliament.[151] But that anything should come of this proposal was not to be expected in Great Britain at this time. Parliamentary action was often threatened, but except in a few matters immediately affecting trade and industry, was never carried out during this period.[152]

Signs of weakening on the part of the British officials were already apparent. In a "private" letter to Burnet in June, 1729, Newcastle expressed a wish to avoid the

[150] These messages and votes are printed in *Jour. of H. of R.*, VIII, *passim*; and *Mass. Proc. on Sal.*, *passim*. A useful account of the controversy is to be found in J. F. Burns, *Controversies Between Royal Governors and Their Assemblies*, pp. 78–91.

[151] *Board of Trade Journal*, 1728/9–1734, pp. 6–7, 16–18; *Acts, Privy Coun., Col.*, 1720–1745, pp. 107–111; Hist. MSS. Comm. *Report*, XI, app. 4, pp. 273–274.

[152] The provincial agents, Francis Wilks and Jonathan Belcher, in a letter to the speaker, June 7, 1729, advised the assembly that the submission of the question to parliament was "very unlikely ever to be the case." But if this eventuality should develop the only question raised would be whether Massachusetts should settle £1000 a year on Burnet during his administration. "It will be the first question of the kind that was ever moved in the House

extremity of parliamentary action. The assembly would have a chance to reconsider during the months that would intervene before the next session of parliament. He called attention to the wording of a more public letter which he wrote to Burnet on the same day, in which the salary was required to be settled only during Burnet's administration, and not in perpetuity. He relied on Burnet's "skill and prudence in making a proper use of these hints," but whatever the governor did in this connection was to be in his private capacity "and not to let it look like any new overture to them on the part of the crown, as if it were not really intended to lay the matter before parliament." In case the assembly voluntarily complied with the new requirement, the governor might let them know that he would use his "best endeavors that a stop may be put to any parliamentary enquiry."[153] But anyone who knew the temper of the representatives would realize that such signs of weakening would only serve to strengthen them in their own position. Burnet's sudden death in September of 1729 put a temporary stop to the controversy in the colony, but left the assembly clearly in the more advantageous position.

One of the agents appointed by the assembly to handle their case was Jonathan Belcher, to whose name belongs more space than glory in the annals of the province. He and the other agent, Francis Wilks, now gave the Board of Trade to believe that the dispute had become almost entirely personal between the assembly and Burnet, and that with the death of the latter, favorable action might be

of Commons; but should it pass into a law, it will be a much better and safer foundation for your doing it than any instruction can be." *Jour. of H. of R.,* IX, 54–55. This statement hardly helped one of its authors, Belcher, when, as governor a little later, he had instructions to threaten parliamentary action if the assembly did not give way.

153 Newcastle to Burnet, June 26, 1729 (two letters), C.O. 5: 10, ff. 42–43 (Mass.); C.O. 5: 871, pp. 15–16 (Mass.).

secured, especially as Belcher had gained for himself the vacant governorship.[154] The board consequently wrote a conciliatory letter to the speaker of the assembly and prepared instructions for Belcher offering a suspension of the king's "just resentment" if the assembly would grant the required salary. Belcher was forbidden to assent to any act or order for a gift to himself as governor, and in case the assembly failed to comply with this "last signification" of the royal pleasure, he should immediately come to England or appoint an agent to lay the matter before the king in order that it might be reported to parliament.[155] These were brave words, but as the governor and the home authorities must have known, the threat of parliament's intervention was nothing but a colossal bluff.

The assembly was undeceived. They knew the strength of their hand and the weakness of their opponents'. When Belcher reached the province, much the same procedure took place as during the first part of Burnet's administration. The assembly made him several grants for his services as agent, in accepting which he violated the spirit, though not the letter, of his instructions.[156] But he rejected a bill for £2400 allowance for one year, although both houses offered to address the crown in favor of its passage. Yet in his letters to the Board of Trade and Newcastle, Belcher recommended that this measure "be taken as a settlement during the present governor's administration," a proposition that the board quite naturally ex-

[154] *Board of Trade Journal*, 1728/9–1734, pp. 70–72.

[155] *Acts, Privy Coun., Col.*, 1720–1745, pp. 255–256; *ibid., The Unbound Papers*, § 418; Hist. MSS. Comm. *Report*, XI, app. 4, p. 274; instructions to Belcher, 1730, arts. 26, 27, C.O. 5: 916, pp. 276–327 (Mass.); *Jour. of H. of R.*, IX, 243–245.

[156] *Jour. of H. of R.*, IX, 238–245, 252–253, 261, 284; *Mass. Acts and Res.*, II, 633; XI, 487.

pressed themselves as unable to understand.[157] In the session which met in June, 1731, a bill passed the two houses granting Belcher £5400 in the depreciated currency of the province, which the governor, now heartily sick of the fruitless quarrel, asked permission to accept. He professed to deplore a retreat by the king but found consolation in reflecting that "to take the people's money must be a punishment upon them, for they really smile at the late governor serving them and spending £1000 sterling of his own estate without receiving a farthing from them." He saw no reason for the governor's starving until the royal orders should be put into effect.[158] Thus valiantly did the governor support the crown.

Partly through the solicitations of Belcher's son, then in England, whom he had named agent in his behalf, but no doubt largely through a realization of the hopelessness of the struggle, the home authorities consented. They granted the necessary power by an additional instruction which expressly declared that it was not the royal purpose "to enervate or in any way invalidate or take from the force" of the former instruction which the governor was again to press upon the assembly.[159] But however much the home government might reaffirm its old position, it should have been clear to all that the battle was now lost.

Belcher asked for and received similar permission to accept the allowances voted in the next three years, even though the sums involved fell short of the stipulated £1000 sterling according to his calculations.[160] Finally, in ap-

---

[157] *Jour. of H. of R.*, IX, 259, 264, 297, 300, 302–306, 351, 382, 387–388; *Mass. Acts and Res.*, II, 633; Board of Trade to Belcher, Feb. 12, 1731, C.O. 5: 916, p. 401 (Mass.).

[158] *Mass. Acts and Res.*, II, 613; Belcher to the Board of Trade, June 12, 1731, *ibid.*, II, 633–634.

[159] *Acts, Privy Coun., Col.*, 1720–1745, pp. 261–262; additional instructions to Belcher, Aug. 13, 1731, C.O. 324: 36, pp. 282–284 (Mass.).

[160] *Mass. Acts and Res.*, II, 661, 668–669, 700, 701–703, 741, 746; *Acts,*

proving the bill passed in 1735, the crown acceded to the
governor's repeatedly expressed desire for permission to
accept these annual grants without waiting for authority
from England in each case. The additional instruction
then sent stipulated that Belcher might in the future assent to annual bills for salary to the amount of £1000 sterling or its equivalent, provided they be the first passed
by the assembly before proceeding to any other business
of the session.[161] This time the home government made no
attempt to conceal their defeat but tried only to salvage
what they could in the *débâcle*.

During the years that followed, Belcher was skillful in
securing grants in addition to the regular allowances of
salary for "extraordinary services," for Indian confer-
ences, or for increased household expenses on account of
"the dearness of provisions." To charges by his enemies
that these grants were merely bribes, he hotly retorted
that the accusations "could spring from nothing but the
dregs of malice, and an attempt to make something out of
nothing."[162] He was clearly trying to feather his own nest,
but the detailed story of his relations with the assembly
shows that he was not tamely submitting to bribery. In the
two major contests which took place aside from that over
his salary, the one relating to the passage of provincial

Privy Coun., Col., 1720–1745, pp. 262–263; Board of Trade to Belcher, Oct.
10, 1732, C.O. 5: 917, pp. 72–75 (Mass.); additional instructions to Belcher,
Feb. 21, 1733; Jan. 11, 1734; Nov. 8, 1734; C.O. 324: 36, pp. 395–396,
431–432, 487–488 (Mass.). The grants for these years were for £3000 currency each, but in several letters of the time Belcher declared that exchange
was 35 to 10 which would have made these grants worth a little less than
£860 sterling each. *Belcher Paps.*, I, 36, 160.

161 Belcher to the Board of Trade, June 28, 1733, *Belcher Paps.*, I, 308–
309; *Mass. Acts and Res.*, II, 789, 790; *Acts, Privy Coun., Col.*, 1720–1745,
pp. 263–264; additional instruction to Belcher, Nov. 7, 1735, C.O. 5: 917, pp.
149–150 (Mass.).

162 Belcher to Lord Wilmington, May 13, 1737; Mar. 7, 1739, Hist. MSS.
Comm. *Report*, XI, app. 4, pp. 278, 283–284.

accounts, and the other over the land bank, his stand was unshaken, even though some representatives vainly suggested the withholding of his salary on that account.[163]

But the real struggle over the governor's salary in Massachusetts was now at an end and the victory of the assembly was as complete as they could desire. Echoes of the contest were heard now and then but with decreasing volume. William Shirley, Belcher's successor, pressed for a permanent salary but finally fell back on his instruction which said that if the assembly would not "readily comply with his Majesty's reasonable recommendation," he might assent to annual acts until the royal pleasure should be signified to the contrary.[164] Thereafter he received his annual grants without difficulty. Later governors, similarly instructed, raised little or no objection to the assembly's method of paying them.[165] The only restriction enforced was the one requiring the vote to be passed at the beginning of the session before the assembly proceeded to other business. But nothing more was heard of references to parliament for many a year. Royal demands for a permanent salary were forgotten. In the entire range of colonial history the officials of the crown were never so thoroughly put to rout. As a matter of fact, the submission of the crown seems to have ended for the time the importance of the salary question. The later grants were made without dispute. Even in May, 1768, at the height of the quarrel over the Massachusetts Circular Letter, the assembly voted the usual salary with unexampled

[163] Belcher to the Board of Trade, June 28, 1733, *Belcher Paps.*, I, 308–309.

[164] Instructions to Shirley, Mass., 1741, art. 23, Lincoln, *Shirley Correspondence*, I, 43–72; Shirley to the Board of Trade, June 23, 1742, *ibid.*, pp. 87–89.

[165] The acts and votes are to be found in *Mass. Acts and Res.*, III–IV, XIII–XVII, *passim*. The amounts fluctuated with the currency in an effort to approximate £1000 sterling.

promptitude.[166] From these facts alone could the British officials gather any crumbs of comfort as they surveyed the loss of prestige which the royal instructions had suffered by their defeat.

That this loss of prestige was real there can be no doubt. It was shown in many ways but never so clearly as when Governor Bernard was leaving for England in 1769 for what he planned to be a short absence. He asked that his salary be voted for the coming year and that half the sum be paid to Lieutenant Governor Hutchinson and half to himself as his instructions provided. But the assembly, which had unanimously agreed to petition for Bernard's removal, were in no frame of mind to violate an old precedent by granting a salary to an absent and unpopular governor. When a new governor arrived, they said, they would provide an ample salary. As to the instruction, it was a rule for the governor, "but as we conceive, it was never intended for the House of Representatives."[167] Postponements and evasions, such as had earlier been used, were no longer necessary. Royal instructions about the salary, or any other instructions for that matter, could be ignored with impunity. Why believe that they were even intended to be obeyed by the assembly?

The final chapter of the story in Massachusetts was written soon after Hutchinson assumed the government. As in the case of New York, the British officials remained dissatisfied with the system of annual grants in Massachu-

[166] *Mass. Acts and Res.*, IV, 1011. Hillsborough had written Bernard to get the Circular Letter rescinded or to dissolve the assembly, promising the governor that he would not suffer financially by his actions, since proper care would be taken ''for the support of the dignity of the government.'' But the assembly's grant of salary made such provision unnecessary. Hillsborough to Bernard, April 22, 1768, C.O. 5: 757, pp. 113–117 (Mass.).

[167] Hutchinson, *Hist. of Mass. Bay*, III, 239–241; *Mass. Acts and Res.*, IV, 1032–1033; House of Representatives to Bernard, July 4, 1769, Bradford, *Mass. State Paps.*, pp. 181–182.

setts, however well it might be working. Hutchinson was ordered to draw his salary from the proceeds of the tea tax collected by the American Board of Customs Commissioners and to take nothing from the assembly. But the representatives insisted on their right, according to the charter, to raise all taxes and make all appropriations for the support of government. Hutchinson stood firmly upon the right of the king to compensate his governor as he saw fit, and ignored the assembly's proffered grants. From 1770 until the Revolution, the governors of Massachusetts, like those of New York, were paid from funds raised by parliament and controlled by the crown.[168] The old threat of parliamentary intervention, offered so insincerely in Burnet and Belcher's time, was at last made good.

He who laughs last does not necessarily laugh best. The British government did eventually deprive the Massachusetts assembly of control over the governor's salary. But the antagonism aroused by the tea tax from which the last governors were paid cost far more than was gained by the victory. Final success in the salary dispute was as expensive to the crown as earlier defeat had been. And the game was certainly not worth the candle. For in all the long history of the salary question in Massachusetts there is little evidence that the assembly gained much advantage over the governors by controlling their salaries. There was, of course, the case of 1721, when Shute's

168 Hutchinson's own account of this dispute is in *Hist. of Mass. Bay*, III, pp. 357–361. Most of the messages, resolutions, and reports dealing with it are printed in *ibid.*, III, appendices V and W, in *Mass. Acts and Res.*, V, 34, 58–60, and in Bradford, *Mass. State Paps.*, pp. 298–299, 324–331. See also Dartmouth to the Lords of the Treasury, Dec. —, 1774, C.O. 5: 145, no. 10 (L.C.). Governor William Franklin of New Jersey declared that this controversy in Massachusetts had been continued by the discontented faction merely to keep their party alive. Franklin to Dartmouth, Jan. 5, 1773, *N. J. Arch.*, X, 389–393.

salary was first reduced by an antagonistic assembly and then withheld until he should pass a desired measure. There was Dummer's concession on the Currency Act in 1728. There were occasional threats to withhold the salaries of other governors, but they were never carried out. The weapon was always potentially available, it is true, but its importance and effectiveness never corresponded to the heat of the disputes raised over its mere possession. If control of the salary had been as valuable a weapon as has been supposed, it seems incredible that the assembly should not have used it during the years of Bernard's administration, when Otis, Hancock, and Samuel Adams were busily engaged in extending the assembly's power at the expense of the executive. The truth is that the assemblies and their leaders had other means of accomplishing their ends, some of which we have reviewed in preceding chapters. The British government suffered needless anxiety and loss of prestige over what they feared might happen but which in reality almost never did take place.

Nevertheless, the controversy stands out as one of the most important that occurred in provincial America. First, it demonstrated the inability of the home government to force upon an assembly a policy which the latter was determined to oppose. Secondly, it proved the futility of treating the legislature in the province as if that body were subject to dictation from above, ignoring thereby the power of independent deliberative action which the representatives actually exercised.[169] Thirdly, the quarrel exposed to the colonial world the weakness of government by instruction. Lastly, the defeat of the crown in Belcher's administration seriously lowered the prestige of the home

[169] The truth of these first two points was already apparent to Governor Shute in 1726. When considering the matter of fresh instructions for him, the Board of Trade called Shute before them and asked "whether he knew of any method to oblige the people of New England to pay their governor a

government in American eyes, making easier local opposition to instructions on other and more weighty matters.

The extent to which the control of the governors' salaries by the assemblies of the royal provinces in general helped to weaken the administration is, by the very nature of the case, hard to determine. Undoubtedly some improper gifts were made to influence the governors, especially in the West Indies before the salary arrangements there were fully worked out. But neither the journals of the assemblies nor the governors' letters home would be likely to give much evidence of outright bribery. Without question the morale of some of the less strong-minded governors on the continent, especially in New York and Massachusetts, suffered from their dependence on the assemblies for support. Their own letters bear testimony to the fact. But if they ever gave way to the assemblies for fear of losing their salary grants they were careful to prevent the true facts from reaching England and thus coming down in the records. Concealment in such cases was important for all concerned, making difficult the task of the historian.

In view of these conditions any attempt to deny that the salary question was ever the cause of an executive defeat would be highly dangerous. But even if we allow for the possible omissions from the records, the evidence is ample that, in the colonial world as a whole, the personal dependence of the governors on the assemblies has been greatly exaggerated both by contemporary British officials and by later historians. Outright bribery of the gov-

fixed salary, to which he answered he knew no other way than by an act of parliament.'' *Board of Trade Journal*, 1722/3–1728, p. 283. Had the British authorities accepted this statement, decided definitely whether or not to invoke the aid of parliament, and then abode by that decision, much time and energy would have been saved in settling the whole question.

ernors by the assemblies disappeared pretty completely
early in the eighteenth century. In only a few continental
provinces did the legislatures have opportunities to withhold the governors' salaries after each administration had
well begun. On the other hand, the governors of all the
provinces had to look regularly to the assemblies for
money with which to carry on the government, provide
for military defence, and meet extraordinary emergencies. In general, the governors' salaries were more assured than almost any other matter of public expense.
Even where the reverse was true, the governor's salary
was only one item in the annual list of appropriations
through the making or withholding of which the assemblies learned to dominate the government. It would be
difficult to say that the failure of the four northern colonies to provide permanent salaries was responsible in any
significant degree for a lessening of royal power there as
compared with the rest of the provinces. Other factors
and other conditions, more generally prevalent, brought
about this result in all colonies, regardless of who paid the
governors' salaries.

CHAPTER IX

THE ADMINISTRATION OF JUSTICE

ONE of the most important agencies for the centralization of the English government during the Middle Ages was the royal administration of justice. And when the dominions of the king were extended beyond the seas and royal government was set up in America, the officers of the crown took care that the provincial judicial system should remain within the control of the king and that his prerogative of justice should help in binding the local governments to that of the mother country. Although the commissions and instructions to the governors did admit the assemblies to a voice in some matters connected with judicial organization, they generally reflected the principle that the establishment and maintenance of the courts and the regulation of the appellate system should be determined in the first instance by royally appointed officials, either in England or in America.

As early as 1661 the commission to Colonel Edward D'Oyley as governor of Jamaica empowered him to erect such "civil judicatories" as he and his council should think necessary.[1] Similar authority was given to later governors and councils of all the royal provinces, in accordance with the principle that the erection of courts was a function of the prerogative. Before long the discretion

---

[1] Commission to D'Oyley, Jamaica, 1661, C.O. 138: 1, pp. 3–5. Governor Wyatt of Virginia and his council were given authority by instruction in 1639 to erect inferior courts for the trial of suits up to £10, and the same article was repeated in 1641 to Sir William Berkeley (*Va. Mag.*, II, 281; XI, 54–57) but the general power to erect courts was not given in a commission for that colony until 1679.

of the governor and council was limited by instructions which forbade them to establish any new courts or offices of judicature or to dissolve any which might already be in existence, without express leave from the home government.[2] In all cases, the governors were to transmit to England full accounts of "all establishments of jurisdictions, courts, offices and officers, powers, authorities, fees, and privileges" which were granted or settled within the province. They were also often required to send to England reports on the actions which had been tried or were pending in the local courts. Thus the home authorities hoped to keep in close touch with the judicial machinery operating in America and to prevent any undesirable practices from gaining a foothold within the royal provinces.

In a few provinces the principle that courts of justice ought to be erected by prerogative action was successfully maintained. New Jersey furnishes the best example of such procedure. During the first quarter century of royal government in this province the governors issued no less than five successive ordinances establishing or modifying the system of courts, without permitting the assembly to share in the decisions reached.[3] Elsewhere the governors occasionally issued ordinances to similar effect, but in the majority of royal provinces the courts of common law were established by act of assembly. The representatives naturally preferred that a royal governor should be disabled from altering or abolishing the regular

[2] This rule first appeared in the instructions to Sir Richard Dutton, Barbados, 1680, art. 24, C.O. 29: 3, pp. 37–53.

[3] The texts of the ordinances of 1704, 1714, 1724, 1725, and 1728 are given in R. S. Field, *The Provincial Courts of New Jersey*, appendices C-G (in *Collections* of the New Jersey Historical Society, III). Field's work quite amply covers the judicial system of New Jersey as do E. P. Tanner, *The Province of New Jersey, 1664–1738*, chap. XXIII, and E. J. Fisher, *New Jersey as a Royal Province*, chap. VIII.

tribunals without their consent. The British officials were sufficiently tolerant of this attitude to permit the confirmation of many of the acts establishing courts, and even went so far as to instruct the governors of several provinces to get laws passed creating certain special courts.[4] Toward the close of the period, when they became alarmed at the general decline of the prerogative in America, the home authorities insisted more strongly upon the use of the executive ordinance and gave to the governors of the newer provinces more specific instructions as to what courts they were to erect.[5] But until about 1750, acts of assembly for the establishment of courts were seldom disallowed unless they seemed to conflict with the terms of the instructions or interfered in some other way with the royal authority. The Board of Trade, indeed, criti-

[4] The most important case of this sort is found in a letter from the Board of Trade to all the royal governors, April 20, 1703, directing each of them to recommend to his assembly the passage of an act creating a court for the trial of small causes. C.O. 324: 8, pp. 244–246 (L.C.); *Cal. State Paps., Col.*, 1702–1703, §§ 578, 590. The substance of this letter was included in the general instructions to the subsequent governors of Barbados, the Leeward Islands, New York, and New Jersey, throughout the period, to the governors of North Carolina from 1754 until the Revolution, and to the governors of New York and Jamaica through 1715.

[5] The Board of Trade summed up the case in a representation dated Aug. 31, 1759: ''The governors of every [royal province] is impowered by his commission under the great seal, to erect courts of judicature; and accordingly, in the infancy of the colonies, courts of judicature were established under that authority, which courts have in most of them been confirmed and their proceedings regulated by provincial laws ratified by the royal approbation. But in colonies of a later establishment, as Nova Scotia and Georgia, the courts of judicature exist and act under the appointment of the governor in virtue of his commission.'' *Acts, Privy Coun., Col.*, 1745–1766, pp. 430–431. For an example of the later trend see the instructions to Hopson, Nova Scotia, 1752, arts. 10, 11, C.O. 218: 4, pp. 177–326. Governor Murray of Quebec issued a detailed ordinance, Sept. 17, 1764 (Newcastle Paps., cccxlv, fos. 21–26, Add. MS., 33,030), but the passage of the Quebec Act with its provision for French civil law, required new articles relating to the courts totaling 1,200 words in the instructions to Carleton in 1775 (arts. 12–15), *Report on Canadian Archives*, 1904, pp. 229–247.

cized a Virginia act of 1705 on the ground that its very passage implied an infringement of the prerogative.[6] But after the assembly had passed an explanatory act, at the suggestion of Lieutenant Governor Spotswood, in which the burgesses disclaimed any desire to infringe upon the queen's prerogative of establishing courts or of hearing appeals, the home officials were satisfied.[7] Subsequent Virginia acts relating to the courts were not objected to on the same ground and the case stands without any exact parallel among the royal provinces.

Nevertheless, the Board of Trade and other officials scrutinized provincial acts relating to the courts with some care in order to prevent any departure from the general arrangements which they had made for the colonies. The commissions and instructions to the governors of Massachusetts omitted most of the usual clauses relating to the judicial machinery of the province, since the charter of 1691 had given control over such matters to the general court rather than to the governor and council alone. But an act passed in 1692 was disallowed because it prohibited appeals to the king in council in cases involving £300 or less, whereas the charter merely permitted appeals in cases involving more than £300 without barring the smaller cases.[8] Again, the privy council disallowed an act of 1697 from the same province because it required all suits to be tried before juries, although a statute of parliament of the previous year had provided for trials of breaches of the Navigation Acts in admiralty courts in which no juries were used.[9] The general court

---

[6] Hening, *Statutes at Large*, III, 287–302; Board of Trade to the president and council of Virginia, March 26, 1707, C.O. 5: 1362, p. 112 (L.C.); *Cal. State Paps., Col.*, 1706–1708, § 824.

[7] Hening, *Statutes at Large*, III, 489–490; Spotswood to the Board of Trade, March 6, 1711, *Spotswood Letters*, I, 49–50.

[8] *Mass. Acts and Res.*, I, 72–76; *Acts, Privy Coun., Col.*, 1680–1720, p. 842.

[9] *Mass. Acts and Res.*, I, 283–287; *Acts, Privy Coun., Col.*, 1680–1720, p. 843.

did not succeed in passing a series of judiciary acts satisfactory to the home officials until 1699.[10] The royal authorities took care that the assembly should not abuse the privileges which the charter conferred.

In New Hampshire the situation was more complicated. In 1706 the privy council disallowed two acts passed in 1699 and 1701 respectively on the ground that they conflicted with the terms of the governor's instructions relating to appeals.[11] But the disallowance does not seem to have been reported to the province in due form and for half a century the judicial machinery continued to function according to these laws. Eventually a controversy broke out which went to the very bottom of the question of the assembly's right to establish courts. When the legislature passed the acts of 1699 and 1701 the settled area of the province was small and Portsmouth was chosen as the seat of all the courts. But with the expansion of the province to the west and north, complaints began to appear from the more remote parts that the holding of courts in Portsmouth only worked too great an inconvenience on the people. The inhabitants of the frontier towns demanded the division of the province into counties and the holding of sessions of the superior court in each county, in order that they might avoid the necessity of the long journey to Portsmouth whenever a suit arose. The assembly passed an act in 1730 which would have given partial relief to the more distant towns, but the privy council disallowed the measure as being against the royal interest.[12] The question came up again in 1755 in connection with an attempt on the part of Governor Benning

10 *Mass. Acts and Res.*, I, 367-372, 417-418.

11 The act of 1699 superseded an act of 1692. *N. H. Prov. Laws*, I, 541-544, 660-666, 702-705; Board of Trade report, July 19, 1706, *ibid.*, II, 862-863; *Acts, Privy Coun., Col.*, 1680-1720, p. 847.

12 *Acts, Privy Coun., Col.*, 1720-1745, § 328.

Wentworth to get adequate salaries for the judges. The assembly was willing to make such provision, but only if they might divide the province into counties with courts held in each. But the governor and councillors, nearly all of whom lived in or near Portsmouth, would not agree to such a measure, ostensibly on the ground that the lower house ought not to have a voice in the establishment of courts, but actually because their own interests would be adversely affected. The assembly naturally had no sympathy with such an attitude and refused to give way. The judges eventually declined to hold court unless they were paid. Faced with a crisis, the doughty governor rose to the occasion and paid the judges' salaries out of his own pocket, an action which won for him the thanks of the king.[13] Although the question of the judges' salaries was finally settled, nothing was done about the courts during the rest of the administration.

Meanwhile the continued expansion of the province added to the seriousness of the problem.[14] But the next governor, John Wentworth, displayed a more conciliatory spirit than his uncle had shown. In spite of the unwillingness of the councillors to yield to the demands of the frontier towns, he realized that a change was necessary. With the permission of the home authorities he used his

[13] An additional instruction was sent to Wentworth, Dec. 22, 1758, ordering the assembly to provide the judges with adequate salaries, and declaring that Wentworth's action was ''an instance of your zeal for our service and for the welfare of our said province [in which] we are graciously pleased to signify to you our royal approbation of your conduct.'' N. H. Prov. Laws, II, 654–655; III, 633–634.

[14] This controversy is fully discussed in Fry, New Hampshire as a Royal Province, pp. 456–465. See also, N. H. Prov. Paps., VI and VII, passim. The difficulties incident to the concentration of all judicial machinery in Portsmouth are illustrated by the experience of an inhabitant of Charlestown, the northernmost town of the province, who was ordered to take a prisoner to jail in Portsmouth during the spring of 1767. The round trip took nine days during the busiest part of the planting season. MS. Diary of Peter Labaree, May 5–13, 1767 (copy in possession of the author).

influence in 1769 to secure the passage of a bill dividing the province into counties and making the courts more accessible to the interior towns, with a clause suspending the operation of the measure until it should be confirmed in England. The privy council gave its approval in the following year and thus definitely conceded the position of the assembly that the representatives should have a voice in the establishment of county courts.[15]

The governors encountered much opposition from the assemblies in connection with the courts of special jurisdiction which they tried to establish without consulting the representatives. In particular, the people objected to the creation of chancery courts by prerogative action. By virtue of a clause in his commission giving him the custody of the provincial seal, each governor was *ex officio* chancellor of the province. Although the governors, especially in the West Indies, often associated the councillors or others with themselves in the exercise of chancery jurisdiction, opposition to such courts was widespread, either because they were constituted without the authority of the assembly, or because they heard cases without the assistance of a jury, or because they so often concerned themselves with the recovery of arrears of quit-rents. The rural population was particularly bitter on this last account. In New York especially, public sentiment was aroused against the chancery court and Governor Montgomerie stated with some truth that it had "occasioned more uneasiness to Mr. Hunter and Mr. Burnet [his last two predecessors] than all other parts of their administration."[16] Hunter erected a court of chancery whereupon the assembly resolved that such action without their con-

---

[15] *N. H. Prov. Laws*, III, 524–530; *Acts, Privy Coun., Col.*, 1766–1783, p. 580. See also L. S. Mayo, *John Wentworth*, pp. 35–37.

[16] Montgomerie to the Board of Trade, Feb. 14, 1729, *N. Y. Col. Docs.*, V, 874.

sent was "contrary to law, without precedent, and of dangerous consequence to the liberty and properties of the subjects."[17] The Board of Trade retorted sharply that this vote was "very presumptuous and a diminutions [sic] of her Majesty's royal prerogative, for that her Majesty has an undoubted right of appointing such and so many courts of judicature in the plantations as she shall think necessary for the distribution of justice."[18] The home authorities had no sympathy with the colonial opposition to these courts. Although they might tolerate the creation of certain courts by act of assembly, they would never consent to a denial of the royal prerogative in the erection of judicial machinery.

Here again the members of the assemblies and the royal officials came to take opposing views. The representatives felt that they had an intimate concern in the matter and that they ought to have a voice in deciding what courts were to be established and how they should function. The administration of justice was of vital importance to every colonist. However satisfactory from a British point of view a given type of court seemed to be, it might become the instrument of abuse and oppression unless its erection was legally authorized by the representatives of the people themselves. The establishment of courts "by royal grace and favor" alone was a menace to the liberties of the subject. Legislative action was a vital necessity. Such arguments explain the statement in the Declaration of Independence that "by refusing his assent to laws for establishing judiciary powers," George III had "obstructed the administration of justice."

Both English officials and colonial assemblymen agreed that the satisfactory administration of justice depended

[17] *Journal of the Votes and Proceedings of the General Assembly of the Colony of New-York*, I, 224. See also, *ibid.*, I, 150, 571.
[18] Board of Trade to Hunter, June 12, 1712, *N. Y. Col. Docs.*, V, 333.

largely on the type of men chosen to serve as judges and other officers of the courts. In general, responsibility for the selection of the right men rested primarily with the governors. The commissions for all the provinces except Massachusetts empowered the governors to appoint judges and other judicial officers on their sole authority.[19] From 1681 on, the instructions to the Jamaica governors somewhat vaguely implied that judicial commissions were to be granted only with the advice and consent of the council.[20] This apparent limitation upon the power conferred by the commission was extended to a few other provinces before 1700, and soon afterward was incorporated in the instructions to the remaining governors. At the time of the general revision of the instructions in 1752, the Board of Trade, realizing that some governors had not correctly understood the intent of the article, redrafted it so as definitely to prohibit a governor from making any judicial appointments without the approval of at least three members of his council.[21] As far as the commissions and instructions were concerned, all judicial officers of a prov-

[19] The province of Massachusetts Bay constitutes an exception to all the statements made in this paragraph. The charter of 1691 authorized the governor to appoint all judicial officers with the advice and consent of the council. Consequently the commissions and instructions for the province were entirely silent on the matter of judicial appointments.

[20] Article 27 of the instructions to Sir Thomas Lynch as governor of Jamaica in 1681 reads in part as follows: ". . . And to prevent arbitrary removals of judges and justices of the peace, you are not to express any limitation of time in the commissions, which you are to grant with the advice and consent of the council to fit persons for those employments. . . ." C.O. 138: 4, pp. 17–19. How far the words "with the advice and consent of the council" was a general restriction upon the free appointive power indicated in the commission, remained undetermined.

[21] Board of Trade representation on the instructions for Governor Thomas of the Leeward Islands, April 19, 1753, Acts, Privy Coun., Col., 1745–1766, p. 184. Thomas's instructions differed, however, from those sent soon after to the governors of other provinces in that he was required to get the consent of a majority, instead of three, of the councillors of the island concerned.

ince were apparently to be chosen by the governor and council from among the available men of the community.

Here was presented one of the greatest problems which the governors had to face. The choice of good judges was especially difficult in the early period when trained lawyers were scarce, and when even fair-minded men with any considerable degree of native ability were hard to find. The lack of good material to fill judicial offices was brought home to the Board of Trade again and again in the letters of the governors. The earl of Bellomont, writing from New York in 1698, drew a vivid picture of conditions in that province: "Colonel Smith, one of the council, is chief justice of the province, but is no sort of lawyer, having been bred a soldier. He is a man of sense and a more gentlemanlike man than any I have seen in this province, but that does not make him a lawyer. . . . As to the men that call themselves lawyers here and practice at the bar, they are almost all under such a scandalous character, that it would grieve a man to see our noble English laws so miserably mangled and profaned. 1 do not find that a man of 'em ever arrived at being an attorney in England. So far from being barristers, one of them was a dancing master; another a glover by trade; a third, which is Mr. Jamison, was condemned to be hanged in Scotland for burning the Bible and for blasphemy; a fourth, which is Mr. Nicolls, your lordships have had his character formerly from me; and there are two or three more as bad as the rest; besides their ignorance in the law, they are all, except one or two, violent enemies to the government, and they do a world of mischief in the country by infecting the people with ill principles toward the government."[22] Similar conditions prevailed in most of the provinces for many years.

[22] Bellomont to the Board of Trade, Dec. 15, 1698, *N. Y. Col. Docs.*, IV, 442.

An anonymous writer prepared a paper in 1700 describing the conditions of the courts in the colonies, with special reference to Barbados. The state of affairs was so bad, he declared, that even the English merchants were unwilling to venture much in colonial trade, for they "find more security and better and more speedy justice in the most distant provinces of the Ottoman dominions from their bashaws, than they do in some of the American colonies, though under the dominion of their own prince." As this writer felt, "the root and foundation of most grievances," in Barbados and the other colonies, was "that some persons fitly qualified" were not appointed to judicial office independently of the governor. He advocated the complete removal of the judiciary from the control of the governor.[23] During these years many other complaints were reaching England of the unsatisfactory administration of justice in the plantations. Numerous petitions to the king from aggrieved colonists and English merchants indicate that frequent adjournments, undue delays, ignorance and partiality on the part of the judges, and irregularities in procedure, were causing distress and injury to litigants in nearly all the colonies, but especially in Barbados.[24] Clearly something ought to be done to improve the colonial judiciary.

The Board of Trade set about the task of reform with

[23] "The Present State of Justice in the American Plantations and Particularly in the Island of Barbados, with Some Thoughts How the Same May (in a Great Measure) Be Amended for the Future," Sept. 4, 1700, C.O. 324: 7, pp. 311–331 (L.C.); *Cal. State Paps., Col.*, 1700, § 751. This paper was presented to the Board of Trade by one of its members, John Pollexfen, but its author is not indicated. In his preface to the next volume of the Calendar (*Cal. State Paps., Col.*, 1701, p. liii) Mr. Headlam suggests that this often-quoted paper was written by Thomas Hodges, a Barbados planter, and points out its practical identity with an anonymous pamphlet called *Plantation Justice*, printed at about the same time.

[24] *Cal. State Paps., Col.*, 1700, §§ 257, 975, 993, 1030; 1701, §§ 64, 300, 636, 1103.

energy and zeal. Under orders from the privy council they
wrote to the governors of all American colonies demanding the transmission of detailed accounts of all judicial
proceedings in their governments.[25] They wrote a special
letter to Governor Grey of Barbados ordering him to
send over copies of the minutes of the court of chancery
and the court of errors, lists of all cases depending and
of those concluded since his arrival in the island, and
exact reports as to how many days each court there had
sat during the same period.[26] They prepared the draft of
a royal letter to Grey, directing him to take care that justice be duly and speedily administered, and ordering him
to sit himself in the court of chancery and to exclude any
judge from sitting if he was likely to have a personal interest in the cases before the courts.[27] They prepared an
article to be inserted in the instructions to the next governor of Barbados, repeating and elaborating the provisions
of this letter, and later prepared another instruction to
the same effect for the governors of other provinces.[28] In
a new letter to all the royal governors they repeated their
former demand for reports of judicial proceedings and
added a paragraph recommending the establishment by
act of assembly of a court for the trial of small causes in

[25] Order in council, July 18, 1700, C.O. 324: 7, pp. 309–310 (L.C.); *Cal.
State Paps., Col.*, 1700, § 651; circular letter to the governors, Aug. 1, 1700,
C.O. 324: 7, p. 332; *Cal. State Paps., Col.*, 1700, § 679.

[26] Board of Trade to Governor Grey, Oct. 16, 1700, C.O. 29: 7, pp. 106–
110; *Cal. State Paps., Col.*, 1700, § 843.

[27] Board of Trade to the king, March 11, 1701, enclosing draft of royal
letter to Grey, C.O. 29: 7, pp. 299–303; *Cal. State Paps., Col.*, 1701, § 246;
Board of Trade to Grey enclosing above royal letter, March 25, 1701, C.O.
29: 7, pp. 303–304; *Cal. State Paps., Col.*, 1701, § 284.

[28] Instructions to Granville, Barbados, 1702, art. 31, C.O. 5: 188, no. 8
(L.C.). The more general instruction was first sent as the first paragraph of
a circular letter from the Board of Trade to the governors, April 20, 1703,
C.O. 324: 8, pp. 244–246 (L.C.); *Cal. State Paps., Col.*, 1702–1703, § 578.
See instructions to Handasyd, Jamaica, 1703, art. 41, C.O. 138: 11, pp. 195–
256.

each province.[29] Upon the disallowance of a habeas corpus
act of Barbados, they drafted a series of instructions
setting up rules by which some, though not all, of the
privileges of the English habeas corpus act were extended
to the inhabitants of the island.[30] By these and similar
methods the Board of Trade worked to improve the administration of justice and to convince the governors of
their personal responsibility in the matter.

As far as a board situated three thousand miles away
could accomplish anything by command or exhortation,
they were successful in their purpose. Complaints of obstruction in the courts decreased although they did not
entirely cease. But after all, the heart of the problem was
the choice of able and upright judges. However diligent
the governors might be in transmitting reports to England, or however often the courts might sit, the administration of justice could not be considered satisfactory
until the courts were presided over by able men, trained
in the law which they were expected to apply. And an adequate supply of such men was simply not to be had in the
colonies at the beginning of the eighteenth century. The
home authorities recognized this fact and already had
made some attempts to provide from England a more
efficient personnel for the provincial courts through the
appointment by the king of chief justices in a few prov-

[29] Board of Trade to the governors, April 20, 1703, C.O. 324: 8, pp. 244–
246 (L.C.); *Cal. State Paps., Col.*, 1702–1703, § 578. The reference to a
court of small causes was also introduced into later general instructions to
most governors.

[30] *Cal. State Paps., Col.*, 1700, §§ 960, 1005; 1702, §§ 737, 863; instruc-
tions to Granville, Barbados, 1702, arts. 32–41, C.O. 5: 188, no. 8 (L.C.).
These instructions were later sent to some of the governors of Virginia,
North Carolina, South Carolina, the Bahamas, and Nova Scotia. See A. H.
Carpenter, ''Habeas Corpus in the Colonies,'' *American Historical Review*,
VIII, 18–27, where is printed (pp. 24–25) a proclamation by Lieut. Gov.
Spotswood of Virginia setting forth in detail the provisions of these in-
structions.

inces. The complaints of Bellomont as to the dearth of
trained lawyers in New York, for example, led the Board
of Trade to recommend that two able lawyers be appointed as chief justice and attorney general respectively.[31] The suggestion was adopted, but unfortunately
the two men chosen, William Atwood and Sampson Shel-
ton Broughton, proved to be far from satisfactory, and
the province was clearly no better off than before. Nevertheless, from this time on the chief justices of many provinces and some attorneys general and clerical officers of
the courts were regularly appointed in England. The inferior judges, however, continued generally to be named
by the governors from among the available colonists. As
the eighteenth century advanced and the number of
trained lawyers in America greatly increased, the problem of selection became somewhat less difficult. But the
very improvement in legal education itself offered in some
cases a new obstacle, because, as Lieutenant Governor
Bull of South Carolina explained in 1770, trained lawyers
could get better pay as attorneys and counsellors than
they could as associate judges. To meet this difficulty Bull
expressed to the earl of Hillsborough his wish that "from
among the many gentlemen in London regularly bred to
the law, who are arrived at a time of life when the san-
guine hopes of rising to eminence or a comfortable share
of practice in the profession are extinguished by a very
moderate employment therein, some could be prevailed
upon to accept of such commission [that is, as associate
judges] in this province, where their advancing age would
be cherished by our mild climate, give dignity to their office, and authority to their decisions. Inland inhabitants of
England, I know, are terrified with ideas of Indians and
savage beasts behind every tree in our woods, but gentle-

[31] Board of Trade to the king, Dec. 14, 1699, *N. Y. Col. Docs.*, IV, 598–
599; order in council, Dec. 14, 1699, *Cal. State Paps., Col.*, 1699, § 1062.

men of a liberal education are superior to such vulgar
prejudices, and tho the circuits require riding 4 or 500
miles through woods, yet they are well inhabited, and there
are roads and accommodations for travellers, not to be expected equal to those in England, but the most comfortable
would always be given to the judges.''[32] This proposal,
illuminating as it may be as to current British views of
America, is hardly flattering to the character of the colonial judiciary at the very close of the period. The fact
that Bull, an American by birth, though educated abroad,
and himself a former assistant judge, seriously suggested
the recruiting of unsuccessful and broken-down English
lawyers for the colonial bench, shows that the problem of
an able judiciary had not been entirely solved even just
before the Revolution.

For the most part, the assemblies did not interfere directly with the activities of the governors and councils in
appointing judges. In some provinces, indeed, as in New
York, the representatives gained an indirect control over
the personnel of the courts through the practice of appropriating salaries by name.[33] But they never challenged
with permanent success the right of the king's agents to
name all judicial officers in the first instance. The royal
officials were quick to oppose any move which savored of
interference with this branch of the prerogative. They
even frowned upon suggestions that the governor received
his appointing power from an act of assembly rather than
from the king's commission. This attitude was illustrated
in connection with a South Carolina act of 1731, which
empowered and required the governor to appoint two or
more assistant judges for the court of common pleas at
Charleston, established by the act. Upon complaint of the

[32] William Bull, jr., to the earl of Hillsborough, March 7, 1770, C.O. 5:
379, pp. 222–223.

[33] See above, pp. 287, 308.

chief justice, the Board of Trade conducted a hearing and reported to the privy council committee "that the power of appointing judges being a right inherent in the crown, acts of assembly are therefore unnecessary for that purpose and may be considered as an encroachment upon his Majesty's prerogative." They recommended, therefore, that the act be disallowed and that an additional instruction be sent the governor directing him to appoint two assistant judges in each law court of the province with powers equivalent to those of the puisne judges in England.[34] The report was approved and the act was disallowed.[35] The prerogative basis of the appointing power was thus preserved.

But the question as to whether the king and his governor had a right to remove judges after they had once been appointed could not be settled quite so easily. A number of serious disputes arose over the tenure of judicial office. The commission was silent as to the governor's power to remove judicial officers within his province, although such authority was implied in the power to appoint, as the instructions clearly show. From about 1670 on, each governor was forbidden to displace any judge, justice, sheriff, or other officer without "good and sufficient" cause, which he was to explain to the authorities in England. This instruction, negatively worded though it is, indicates that the power of removal was understood.[36] The consent of the council, which was expected in the case of an appointment, was not required by the instructions in the case of

[34] Board of Trade to privy council committee, Aug. 12, 1735, C.O. 5: 401, pp. 150–154; additional instruction, submitted Aug. 12, 1735, *ibid.*, pp. 155–156.

[35] *Acts, Privy Coun., Col.*, 1720–1745, § 299.

[36] The rule was first given in this form in instructions to Lynch, Jamaica, 1670, art. 5: C.O. 1: 25, no. 107. It was included in the next instructions to governors of the other royal provinces, the Leeward Islands, Barbados, and Virginia.

a removal. But in 1674, the Council for Trade and Foreign Plantations, feeling that some further safeguard was necessary, proposed an additional instruction for Sir Jonathan Atkins of Barbados, by which, in order to "prevent arbitrary removals of judges and justices of the peace," he was forbidden "to express any limitations of time" in the judicial commissions which he might issue.[37] Just how such an omission could prevent an "arbitrary removal" when the power of the governor was otherwise unchecked, the council did not make clear. Nevertheless, the instruction was issued in the same vague terms and was soon included among the articles regularly given to each new royal governor. The futility of this rule was not pointed out until 1754, when in response to a request for comments on his instructions, Governor William Popple of Bermuda "humbly submitted" to the Board of Trade the question as to "how the not expressing any limitation of time in their [the judges'] commissions prevents their arbitrary removal."[38] Apparently the board had just been asking themselves the same question, for a few months before they had redrafted the article, omitting the vague phrases about "arbitrary removal" and "limitation of time." Instead they introduced a provision that the governors should appoint all judges and other officers "during pleasure only." In view of recent events in Jamaica, this new rule was much more to the point.[39]

During the seventeenth century and the first half of the eighteenth, the assemblies of the various provinces

[37] Council for Trade and Plantations to the king, April 13, 1674 (including draft of five additional instructions for Atkins), C.O. 29: 1, pp. 172–173.

[38] "Observations on the Instructions Given to His Majesty's Governor of Bermuda, etc.," by William Popple [no date, but indorsed "read Nov. 6, 1754"], C.O. 37: 18 (unpaged).

[39] Board of Trade representation on the instructions for Dobbs, North Carolina, June 17, 1754, Col. Recs. of No. Car., V, 1104; instructions to Dobbs, 1754, art. 62, ibid., pp. 1107–1144.

seem to have made no serious attempt to limit the right of the king or the governors to remove judges from office at will. Some appointments had been made "during good behavior," but as a general thing, a judge's commission read that he was to hold office "during our pleasure and his residence in our said province."[40] The British authorities learned with something of a shock, therefore, that the Jamaica assembly had passed an act in 1751, according to which all judges of the supreme court were to hold office during good behavior. The act allowed the governor to remove a judge on orders from the king, through the privy council, secretary of state, or Board of Trade, but he was not to do so on his own authority. If he wished to displace a judge of this court from his office, he must first get the consent of the council upon cause signified, then give twenty-one days' written notice to the misbehaving judge, and lastly conduct an open trial for the hearing of evidence on both sides. When this measure was referred to the attorney and solicitor general of Great Britain, they reported that it ought to be disallowed since it directly affected the prerogative "in a point of great moment," without indicating that the governors had abused their power in any way that made this limitation on their authority necessary. Such a change in the tenure of office, if brought about at all, ought to have been made by the king's own authority rather than by act of assembly. But the law officers denied that "it would be advisable, either for the interest of the plantations themselves, or of Great Britain, that the judges in the former should hold their places *quam diu se bene gesserint*."[41] The Board of Trade

[40] The most important case of a judicial commission granted during good behavior had been that given to Robert Hunter Morris as chief justice of New Jersey by his father, Governor Lewis Morris, in 1739 (*N. J. Arch.*, IX, 207–209), which had caused almost endless confusion.

[41] Attorney General Ryder and Solicitor General Murray to the Board of Trade, June 22, 1753, C.O. 137: 25 (unpaged).

and privy council agreed with this opinion and the act was
disallowed.[42] Thereafter the instructions directed the
royal governors to grant all commissions during pleasure
only.

Only a short time elapsed before several assemblies had
arrayed themselves in opposition to this instruction. The
scene of bitterest controversy was New York, where there
were several precedents for the granting of judicial commissions during good behavior. The assembly objected to
the instruction which required tenure during pleasure
only, on the ground that it violated precedent and tended
to increase the governor's authority over the judiciary.
Consequently, they tried in 1761 to pass a bill providing
that the judges of the supreme court should hold office
during good behavior. In spite of the instructions, the
lieutenant governor, Cadwallader Colden, was willing to
meet the assembly halfway. He told several of the members that he would consider the measure favorably if they
would add a clause permitting the governor to remove a
judge upon an address from the assembly, upon a signed
request from at least seven members of the council, or
upon a royal warrant under the signet and sign manual,
and if the assembly would make adequate provision for
permanent salaries for the judges. Such arrangements
would, he thought, sufficiently protect the prerogative and
at the same time would guard against arbitrary proceedings by the governor. The assembly was willing to allow
removals upon their own application or upon that of the
council, but would not recognize the validity of a royal
warrant for the same purpose. Neither would they agree
to provide salaries for more than a year at a time. Therefore, Colden refused to sign the bill.[43] The recent death of

[42] *Acts, Privy Coun., Col.*, 1745–1766, pp. 215–217.
[43] Colden to the Board of Trade, April 5, June 2, Aug. 12, Sept. 25, 1761,
N. Y. Col. Docs., VII, 462, 466–467, 467–468, 470.

George II, in whose name all commissions were issued, complicated the situation, for the judges, quite properly, asked for new commissions in order that they might legally continue to perform their duties. And they let Colden know that they would refuse reappointment unless they were to hold office during good behavior. The lieutenant governor feared that he might have to submit in order to prevent the entire stoppage of the judicial machinery.[44] The situation had indeed become serious.

In the meantime the Board of Trade had taken cognizance of the affair and soon presented a long representation to the crown on the subject of Colden's difficulties in New York. With regard to the tenure of judges, they cited the case of the Jamaica law and a similar experience with Pennsylvania as establishing precedents for future action by the king. The colonists compared their condition to the situation in England prior to the overthrow of James II, but the board believed the analogy was erroneous. "The change which the tenure of the judges' commissions underwent at the Revolution in this kingdom," they said, "was founded upon the most conclusive and repeated proofs of arbitrary and illegal interposition, under the influence of the crown, upon points of the greatest importance to the constitution and the liberty and rights of the subject; it was not, however, by the tenure of their commissions alone that they were rendered independent, but such salaries were settled upon them as not only rendered them less liable to be corrupted but was an encouragement for the ablest men to engage in that profession which qualified them for such high trusts."[45] Such conditions did not exist in the colonies, as the board pointed out.

---

[44] Colden to the Board of Trade, Oct. 6, 1761, *N. Y. Col. Docs.*, VII, 470–471.

[45] The rule that judges must hold office during good behavior subject to removal only upon a joint address of the two houses of parliament was not,

Salaries there were inadequate to attract able men and the
governors were frequently obliged to appoint such men
as offered themselves, "however unqualified to sustain
the character." Tenure during good behavior would prevent the governors from displacing these judges with
more capable men whenever the latter should be found.
All too often the governors had been forced to appoint
judges who had accepted office "with a view to make it
subservient to their own private interests, and who, added
to their ignorance of the law, have too frequently become
the partisans of a factious assembly upon whom they have
been dependent for their support, and who have withheld
or enlarged that support according as the conduct of the
judges was more or less favorable to their interests." The
board considered that it would be difficult to conceive a
state of government "more dangerous to the rights and
liberties of the subject" than one in which the judges were
made dependent solely upon "the factious will and caprice of an assembly." Such a proposition was "subversive of all true policy, destructive of the interests of your
Majesty's subjects, and tending to lessen that just dependence which the colonies ought to have upon the government of the mother country." The privy council agreed
heartily with these opinions and ordered a circular instruction sent to all royal governors, forbidding them to
pass any bills that dealt with judicial tenure and repeating
the former directions to grant all commissions during
pleasure only.[46] The British authorities left no room for

of course, made a part of statute law until the Act of Settlement in 1701
(12 and 13 Will. III, c. 2), although it had been suggested in 1689 in connection with the Bill of Rights.

[46] Board of Trade representation, Nov. 11, 1761, C.O. 324: 17, pp. 129–
148 (L.C.); *Col. Recs. of No. Car.*, VI, 582–586; order in council, Nov. 23,
1761, quoting the representation in full, *N. Y. Col. Docs.*, VII, 472–476;
Acts, Privy Coun., Col., 1745–1766, § 460; circular instructions to all royal
governors, Dec. 12, 1761, *N. J. Arch.*, IX, 322–323, 329–330.

doubt of their strong opposition to tenure during good behavior in the colonies.

The Board of Trade had much to justify its views on the matter. The assemblies were undoubtedly trying to make the judicial officers dependent upon themselves rather than upon the governors and the king, as they were attempting to do with every other branch of provincial government. "The factious will and caprice of an assembly" could certainly be as harmful to the true course of justice as what some Americans called "arbitrary and illegal interposition under the influence of the crown." And yet the Board of Trade ignored certain important considerations which influenced the colonial attitude. They failed to see that the analogy of the mother country herself involved more than a mere comparison of conditions which prevailed in England at the time of James II with those in the colonies. They could not understand the natural resentment of the assemblies at the exercise of a royal prerogative in America which had been forbidden in England itself, regardless of the differences in local conditions. Furthermore, the board paid no attention to the colonial belief that there was, after all, something in common between the state of affairs in England in the latter part of the seventeenth century and that in America in the eighteenth. Although the colonists could point to no cases, perhaps, in which the governors had influenced the judges quite so unduly as had James II, yet there were instances enough in which the control of the courts by the anti-popular party had resulted in serious injury to the rights of the subject. The mere appointment of a governor by the king was no guarantee that the governor would not become a strong partisan of one faction in the colony and be controlled in his own relations to the judiciary by personal motives. And lastly, the Board of Trade and other British officials utterly failed to comprehend the new conception of "government by the consent of the governed" which was coming more and more to influence the Americans in all their relations with the crown. The home authorities could not understand that a judiciary dependent upon a royally appointed governor for its tenure was repugnant to the very spirit of American political life. The Board of Trade's representation and the circular instruction which followed are illustrations of that failure to understand America which later lost the British half a continent.

When the circular instruction reached New York it did not find the judicial machinery of the province entirely stopped as Lieutenant Governor Colden had feared. Benjamin Prat, a prominent Boston lawyer, had recently arrived with a royal warrant directing Colden to appoint him chief justice during his Majesty's pleasure and Prat's residence in the province. Although the other judges refused to act without commissions during good behavior and the assembly refused to grant salaries on any other terms, Prat managed to keep the supreme court open intermittently.[47] But the assembly was affronted at the appointment as chief justice of a man from another province and determined to force the lieutenant governor to surrender. In the winter of 1762 they sent up a bill for the payment of all salaries for one year providing that the judges' salaries should be given to them only if their commissions ran during good behavior. Unless Colden signed this bill, all governmental business, civil and military as well as judicial, would come to a stop for lack of funds with which to pay the officers. If he did sign the bill, the assemblymen thought, their victory was won. But they reckoned without their host. The wily old lieutenant governor promptly approved the measure thus insuring the

[47] Colden to the Board of Trade, Jan. 11, 1762, *N. Y. Col. Docs.*, VII, 483–485; Prat to the Board of Trade, May 24, 1762, *ibid.*, VII, 500–502.

support of the civil government. But he still refused to issue judicial commissions during good behavior, so that that question was left exactly as it stood before. Yet Prat could not be expected to continue acting alone and without salary, as Colden pointed out to the Board of Trade after describing his skirmish with the assembly. An independent salary must be granted or the instruction withdrawn. And then he added this significant sentence: "I must with humble submission beg leave to observe that the putting the governor under restriction by instruction will certainly in many cases lay the governor under great difficulties but may have no effect on an assembly, and in such cases they tend to lessen the force of instructions in the minds of the people."[48]

This sentence points out the consequences of that rigidity which was a fundamental weakness of the system of "government by instruction" and which can be illustrated from the history of every royal province. The home officials insisted that the governor follow a predetermined course, expressed in the inflexible form of instructions. They refused to give their responsible agent in America that discretion and latitude of action which are as essential to success in political as in military operations. The Board of Trade, the secretary of state, and the privy council, did not, and probably could not, appreciate the actual conditions under which the governor labored. Certainly they could not anticipate the changes in the local situation which might have taken place before their long-deliberated orders should reach the colony. The governor was often placed in a dilemma: he must violate his instructions in order to accomplish some immediately necessary end, thereby incurring the displeasure of the home officials; or else he must blindly adhere to his orders in spite of

[48] Colden to the Board of Trade, Feb. 11, 1762, *N. Y. Col. Docs.*, VII, 489–490; *Col. Laws of N. Y.*, IV, 550–553.

changed conditions, submitting if necessary to defeat on some more vital issue when a little more freedom of action might possibly have enabled him to save the situation. In either case, the instructions would probably suffer a loss in prestige, the colonists would tend to grow more estranged from the home government, and the governor would have to endure severe criticism for his apparent failure to support the prerogative.

In response to Colden's letters the Board of Trade showed the attitude they characteristically took toward those who were trying to pull their chestnuts out of the provincial fires for them. While they agreed with the lieutenant governor's suggestion that the chief justice ought to have an independent salary and praised Colden's refusal to sign the tenure of office bill, they severely criticized him for approving the salary bill with its proviso regarding the judges' commissions. Utterly disregarding the fact that Colden had kept the government in operation without giving any commissions during good behavior— the real point at issue—the board chose to regard his very minor violation of the spirit of his instruction as due to selfish motives. They reported to the king that he appeared to them "to be blamable in having passed the act," and they informed the lieutenant governor that, although they were "sensible that great inconveniency must have followed from [vetoing the bill] to yourself and the rest of the officers, yet no conditions of that kind at least, ought to have induced you to acquiesce in such an unprecedented and unjust attack upon the authority of the crown."[49] Thus did they criticize a loyal official who had dared to use his discretion in carrying out his instructions.

But in the same month in which the Board of Trade was expressing its opinions in this way, the situation in New

[49] Board of Trade to the king, June 11, 1762, *N. Y. Col. Docs.*, VII, 505–506; Board of Trade to Colden, June 11, 1762, *ibid.*, VII, 503–504.

York was suddenly cleared up. Chief Justice Prat, whose health had been failing for some time, died, and one source of friction was thus removed. Governor Monckton, then on one of his occasional visits to the province, persuaded Daniel Horsmanden, the second judge and a bitter enemy of Colden, to accept the position of chief justice with tenure during the royal pleasure.[50] The triumph over Colden and his friends which this appointment signified was no doubt largely responsible for the willingness of Horsmanden and the other judges to give way on the question of their tenure. The issue was not raised again before the Revolution, but the bitterness which the controversy had caused while it lasted did much to make ineffectual Colden's later attempts to maintain the prerogative and the binding force of the instructions.

Similar contests over the tenure of judges took place in New Jersey and North Carolina at the same time as that in New York. Robert Hunter Morris, who had received from his father, Governor Lewis Morris, a commission as chief justice of New Jersey during good behavior, was still presiding over the supreme court when George II died. Governor Josiah Hardy proposed to give him a new commission during pleasure, as the instructions required, but Morris objected violently and the assembly threatened to grant no salary to the chief justice unless the commission was made to run during good behavior. In marked contrast to the attitude of Colden in New York, Hardy weakly gave way and, in spite of his instructions, granted Morris and his two associates the commissions which they demanded.[51] On hearing of this flagrant violation of the instructions by a newly appointed governor, the Board of Trade immediately requested his recall ''as a necessary

50 Colden to the Board of Trade, July 8, 1763, *N. Y. Col. Docs.*, VII, 528.
51 Hardy to the Board of Trade, Jan. 20, 1762, *N. J. Arch.*, IX, 345–347; Hardy to the earl of Egremont, Jan. 22, 1762, *ibid.*, pp. 347–349.

example to deter others in the same situation from like acts of disobedience to your Majesty's orders, and as a measure essentially necessary to support your Majesty's just rights and authority in the colonies, and to enable us to do our duty in the station your Majesty has been graciously pleased to place us in and effectually to execute the trust committed to us.''[52] Possibly Hardy got wind of this representation, for he immediately set about undoing the mischief he had wrought. He revoked commissions during good behavior granted by Governor Belcher that had expired with the death of the king, and by some means or other persuaded Morris and his associates to resign their new commissions and to accept others valid during pleasure only. Within four months after the Board of Trade had requested his recall, he was able to write that all commissions during good behavior were now at an end.[53] But this action was too late to save him. He received a curt note from the secretary of state announcing that, in consequence of the "strong representation" of the Board of Trade, he had been superseded by William Franklin.[54] Such vigorous disciplining of a royal governor was almost without precedent in the colonies. Whether entirely deserved or not, it served its purpose in New Jersey at least. There the question of judicial tenure was never again raised during colonial times.

North Carolina was the only one of these three provinces that apparently had no precedents in favor of judicial tenure during good behavior.[55] Yet it was the only one in which the crown failed to win at least a techni-

[52] Board of Trade to the king, March 27, 1762, *ibid.*, pp. 361–362.

[53] Hardy to John Pownall, June 22, 1762, *ibid.*, pp. 364–365; Hardy to the Board of Trade, July 16, 1762, *ibid.*, pp. 366–367.

[54] Egremont to Hardy, Sept. 11, 1762, *ibid.*, pp. 374–375.

[55] The commissions to the chief justices during the royal period regularly provided for tenure during pleasure. These commissions, or the royal warrants directing the governors to issue the commissions, are printed in *Col. Recs. of No. Car.*, III, 136, 490, 490–491, 492–493; V, 403, 962, 963–964.

cal victory before the Revolution. In 1760 the assembly passed an act relating to the courts, which, among other things, provided that the associate justices of the province should hold office during good behavior. This act was particularly obnoxious to the Board of Trade, not only because it directly violated the instructions, but because it placed the associate justices upon a more independent footing than the chief justice, who was appointed from England and who held office merely during pleasure. The act was consequently disallowed.[56] In the controversy that followed, the assembly showed no signs of giving way until 1768 when Governor Tryon secured an act providing the judges' salaries for five years and conceding for the time being the royal position as to tenure.[57] But after the expiration of this act the struggle was renewed, Governor Martin reporting that the assembly would grant no salaries to the judges unless the commissions were to run during good behavior.[58] The issue was still pending at the outbreak of the Revolution.

The widespread bitterness which the royal policy with regard to the tenure of judicial office aroused in America is indicated in the Declaration of Independence. Among the other evidences of a design on the part of the king to impose "an absolute tyranny" over America which that document contains is the statement that "he has made judges dependent on his will alone for the tenure of their offices and the amount of their salaries." That the Americans, with their well-developed repugnance to govern-

[56] *Acts, Privy Coun., Col.*, 1745–1766, pp. 504–505; *Col. Recs. of No. Car.*, VI, 587–591. Governor Dobbs had passed the act with reluctance and only after receiving written advice from the chief justice and attorney general of the province in favor of so doing. *Ibid.*, pp. 243–256.

[57] Tryon to Shelburne, March 7, 1768, *Col. Recs. of No. Car.*, VII, 693–694. In the meantime the commissions had run during pleasure. See Tryon's "View of the Province of North Carolina in the Year 1767," *ibid.*, p. 478.

[58] Martin to Dartmouth, May 5, 1774, *ibid.*, IX, 992.

ment "by royal grace and favor," would consider this policy as tyrannical, was only natural, especially in view of the fact that the judges of England herself had not been dependent on the royal pleasure for three quarters of a century. But tyranny was far from the thoughts of the British officials responsible for the adoption and enforcement of this policy. They saw in it only a device for keeping as high a standard among the colonial judges as possible and for supporting the royal prerogative by making the judicial officers independent of the political activities of the often unstable assemblies. The charge which should be made against the royal officials is not that they were tyrannical but that they failed to understand the attitude of the Americans and that they tried to maintain a system which was incompatible with the growing American ideals.

The lack of ability and legal knowledge which obtained among so many of the colonial judges, as well as the fact that their views were so often colored by local prejudices, made an adequate system of appeals seem a vital necessity to the responsible agents of the crown. The earliest provisions, however, for appeals in Virginia, the first royal province, took the form of an act of assembly and not of a royal order. One of a group of measures passed in 1623–1624 provided for the taking of appeals from the monthly courts of Charles City and Elizabeth City to the governor and council.[59] This very simple arrangement underwent several changes during the next four decades until, in 1662, a much more elaborate system was adopted providing that cases might be taken on appeal from the governor and council to the assembly as a court of last resort.[60] This

[59] Hening, *Statutes at Large*, I, 125.

[60] *Ibid.*, II, 65–66. An interesting feature of the act was the omission of any requirement of a minimum sum to be involved in an appeal "because there may be as great error in judgment or will in matters of small value as in the greatest." Cases from the Eastern Shore, however, did have to involve a specified amount until 1676, *ibid.*, pp. 362, 397.

law remained in force until 1679, when instructions were being prepared for Lord Culpeper as governor of Virginia. The Lords of Trade had recently become aware of the growing power of the colonial assemblies and had determined to check this development as far as possible. The exercise of judicial functions by the Virginia legislature as a court of highest appeals seemed to the Lords of Trade to be quite improper. Consequently they introduced an article into Culpeper's instructions authorizing appeals from the courts of the province to the governor and council "and to no other court or judicature whatsoever."[61] Three years later the act of 1662 was disallowed. In a new set of instructions prepared for Culpeper he was specifically forbidden to permit appeals from himself and the council to the assembly but was authorized instead to permit appeals to the privy council in England in cases involving more than £100.[62] These instructions naturally aroused much feeling in the province where the assembly had acted as a court of appeals for many years. Messages on the subject passed back and forth between the governor and the assembly and several petitions were sent to the king, but the English officials steadily refused to consider allowing appeals to the legislature.[63]

Beginning with the instructions prepared for the earl of Carlisle as governor of Jamaica in 1678, the Lords of Trade gave considerable attention to the system of appeals in the other royal provinces as well as in Virginia.[64]

[61] Instructions to Culpeper, Va., 1679, art. 60, C.O. 5: 1355, pp. 326–356 (L.C.).

[62] Cal. State Paps., Col., 1681–1685, § 371; instructions to Culpeper, Va., 1682, art. 64, Va. Mag., XXVIII, 41–52.

[63] Cal. State Paps., Col., 1681–1685, pp. 619, 620, §§ 1643, 1654, 1694, 1698; Journals of the House of Burgesses of Virginia, 1659/60–1693, pp. 196, 197, 202, 203, 204, 228–230, 243, 245, 370.

[64] Instructions to Carlisle, Jamaica, 1678, art. 41, C.O. 138: 3, pp. 216–241.

The English officials seem to have been groping their way along, somewhat uncertain as to the provisions that would best meet the varying conditions to be found in the different colonies. The instructions prepared by the Board of Trade in 1702 after the accession of Queen Anne were the first in which an approximately uniform and permanent system of appeals was provided for all the royal provinces. These instructions recognized the governor and council as the highest court with civil jurisdiction within the province. An appeal might be taken to this body if the appellant gave adequate security to pay the costs in case the decision of the lower court should be sustained. Any councillor who had sat upon the case as a judge in the court below was debarred from voting upon the appeal but he might be present at the hearing to give the reasons for the previous judgment. The minimum sum which a case had to involve before an appeal might be taken varied from £50 to £300 according to the wealth and economic standards of the province concerned.[65] If either party should not be satisfied with the decision of the governor and council, he might appeal to the king in council, provided that he entered his appeal within fourteen days after sentence and gave security for the prosecution of the case in Great Britain and for paying the costs in case the privy council should uphold the governor and council. Again the minimum for which such appeals might be taken varied from province to province, the figures ranging from £100 to £500.[66]

[65] In Virginia until 1727, in New Hampshire until 1728, and in Maryland during the royal period, the minimum was not fixed by the instructions but was left for the assembly to determine by law. In New Hampshire from 1728 on, in the Bahamas from 1729 on, and in Bermuda, the instructions set a minimum of £50. In New York, New Jersey, North Carolina, and South Carolina, the minimum was £100; and in Barbados, Jamaica, and the Leeward Islands, it was £300.

[66] The instructions fixed a minimum of £100 for New Hampshire until 1728, for Bermuda, and for the Bahamas; £200 for New Hampshire after 1728,

These provisions remained in force with only minor variations until 1753.[67] In that year the Board of Trade, reconstituted under Lord Halifax, asked the attorney and solicitor general of Great Britain to prepare new regulations, because they felt that the instructions had become obsolete and improper in some respects. The revised provisions were incorporated in the general instructions to Governor Thomas of the Leeward Islands, Osborn of New York, and Dobbs of North Carolina, and were sent as a circular instruction to the governors of all other provinces. In a few important particulars the regulations changed the system of appeals formerly in effect. In order to make more clear the fact that the appellate jurisdiction of the governor and council did not extend to criminal actions, the reference to appeals "in cases of error" was changed and the words "in all civil causes" were substituted. Upon application for such an appeal the governor was "to issue a writ in the manner which has usually been accustomed," returnable before himself and the council. In all provinces, regardless of their size

and for New Jersey; £300 for New York, Maryland, Virginia, North Carolina, and South Carolina; and £500 for Barbados, Jamaica, and the Leeward Islands, and for Nova Scotia after the establishment of normal civil government there.

[67] The most important change during this period had to do with the execution of sentence pending final appeal. Prior to 1718 the instructions directed the governors not to suspend execution because of an appeal to the privy council. From 1718 to 1727 the instructions forbade suspension in case the governor and council had confirmed the judgment of the lower court. But in 1727 the Board of Trade reported that many appellants, victorious in the privy council, were unable to get their property restored through the insolvency of the appellee or his withdrawal from the province. A circular instruction was therefore issued in 1727 and its provisions incorporated in later general instructions, authorizing the suspension of execution pending appeal to the privy council in all cases unless the appellee gave security for the restoration of the property if the privy council reversed the decision of the governor and council. *Acts, Privy Coun., Col.*, 1720–1745, § 100; *ibid., Unbound Papers*, § 350; circular instructions, March 23, 1727, *N. J. Arch.*, V, 157.

and wealth, the minimum sum for which appeals might be taken to the governor and council was now fixed at £300, and that for appeals to the privy council at £500. But in cases "where the matter in question relates to the taking or demanding any duty payable to us, or to any fee or office or annual rent or other such like matter or thing, where the rights in future may be bound," appeals might be taken to the privy council without regard to the sum involved.[68]

Only two slight changes were made in this instruction during the remainder of the period. The settlement of a boundary dispute between New Hampshire and Massachusetts resulted in a number of suits in the former province over titles to various parcels of land worth less than £500 separately but much more in the aggregate. The defendants asked for and secured an additional instruction to the governor of New Hampshire permitting appeals in these special cases.[69] But this provision was not incorporated in later general instructions. A more important exception was made in the case of Bermuda. By the earlier

[68] Circular instructions, Dec. 18, 1753, C.O. 324: 15, pp. 335–336, 341–347 (L.C.); *Acts, Privy Coun., Col.*, 1745–1766, p. 775; representation on instructions to Thomas, Leeward Islands, 1753, *ibid.*, p. 185; instructions to Thomas, 1753, art. 34, C.O. 5: 200, pp. 777–849 (L.C.); representation on instructions to Osborn, N. Y., July 5, 1753, *N. Y. Col. Docs.*, VI, 790; instructions to Osborn, 1753, art. 26, C.O. 5: 200, pp. 875–964 (L.C.); representation on instructions to Dobbs, No. Car., 1754, *Col. Recs. of No. Car.*, V, 1103–1106; instructions to Dobbs, 1754, art. 60, *ibid.*, pp. 1107–1144. A. M. Schlesinger (*Political Science Quarterly*, 1913, p. 284) and H. D. Hazeltine (*Amer. Hist. Assn. Report*, 1894, pp. 309–310) both state that these new provisions were first given in instructions dated Feb. 4, 1746. Their authority is W. Birge, *Commentaries on Colonial and Foreign Laws*, I, intro., xlvii, xlviii. But no instructions of this date have been found by the present writer and the new regulations have been first located in 1753. All the representations and other documents point to the fact that the change was made in 1753 and not seven years earlier.

[69] *Acts, Privy Coun., Col.*, 1745–1766, § 202; additional instructions to B. Wentworth, Aug. 6, 1755, *N. H. Prov. Laws*, III, 632.

instructions for this island appeals to the privy council had been permitted in cases involving as little as £100 and the figure thus established had been incorporated in a provincial act confirmed in 1708. Soon after the circular instruction of 1753 had been sent to all the provinces, including Bermuda, the Board of Trade realized that they had made a slip, since, as Governor William Popple later pointed out, the instruction conflicted with the law by authorizing appeals only in cases of £500 or more. Consequently, the Board omitted the new rules from the instructions given to Popple in 1755, but reinserted a former article which directed him to observe the provincial act in all matters relating to appeals.[70] Bermuda remained the only royal province from which appeals might regularly be taken to the privy council in civil cases involving less than £500.

In contrast to the instructions relating to appeals on civil actions, those dealing with criminal cases did not recognize an appellate jurisdiction in the governor and council. As far as these instructions were concerned, a convict was not entitled to appeal to the governor and council as was the loser in a civil case. The only local agency which could stay the hand of justice was the governor himself, who in his executive capacity had authority from his commission to remit all fines imposed in the provincial courts and to pardon all offenders except those convicted of treason or wilful murder. In such cases he might grant reprieves and refer the question of pardon to the king. But in spite of this broad power, the governor's discretion in the remission of fines was limited by his instructions which forbade him to absolve any one from the payment of a fine or forfeiture above the sum of

[70] William Popple to the Board of Trade, Dec. 16, 1755, C.O. 37: 18; Board of Trade to Popple, Feb. 4, 1756, C.O. 38: 9, pp. 147–148; instructions to Popple, Bermuda, 1755, art. 46, C.O. 38: 9, pp. 52–144.

£10, although here again he might suspend the execution of the sentence pending final decision in England. The instructions gave the right of appealing to the king to persons convicted of misdemeanors and fined fairly substantial amounts—£100 in a few provinces, £200 in most.[71] But in lesser cases of misdemeanor and in convictions for treason or murder the governor alone could decide whether to ask for the king's mercy or to order the sentence carried out at once.

The character and conduct of appeals from the colonies to the king have been so adequately treated by other writers that further comment here is unnecessary.[72] But the activities of the governor and council as a court of appeals for civil cases have not been so fully dealt with. In this capacity the council performed its third function as a part of the provincial government. Here it reached its position of greatest independence. As the upper house of the legislature it had a share in the passage of laws, but a share which the lower house was usually able to restrict in a very large degree; as an executive body advising the governor in the performance of his duties, the council was often under his influence and lost most of its individuality; but as a supreme court it could be bravely

[71] This instruction was first given to the earl of Inchiquin, governor of Jamaica, in 1689 (art. 54, C.O. 138: 6, pp. 247–271), but was not extended to the other provinces generally until 1702. In Nova Scotia, New Hampshire, North Carolina, South Carolina, Bermuda, and the Bahamas, and in Virginia after 1756, the sum of £100 was fixed; in all other cases, £200.

[72] The most complete treatment of this subject is by A. M. Schlesinger in "Colonial Appeals to the Privy Council," in *Political Science Quarterly*, XXVIII (1913), 279–297, 433–450. G. A. Washburne, *Imperial Control of the Administration of Justice in the Thirteen Colonies, 1684–1776* (Columbia Univ. Studies, CV, 2, 1923), also deals with the subject. Excellent accounts of appeals from corporate colonies are found in C. M. Andrews, "The Connecticut Intestacy Law," *Yale Review*, III, 261–294, and H. D. Hazeltine, "Appeals from Colonial Courts to the King in Council with Especial Reference to Rhode Island," in *Annual Report* of the American Historical Association, 1894, pp. 299–350.

independent. After the English government had stopped the carrying of appeals from the council to the assembly late in the reign of Charles II, the representative body had no effective way of controlling the judicial activities of the council. When sitting as a member of the highest court, each councillor attained a position of approximate equality with the governor himself, for in his judicial capacity the governor, as Sir Thomas Robinson of Barbados once remarked, was only "primus inter pares" in the council.[73] Although the governor presided in the judicial council, his authority there was no greater than his personality and the prestige of his office could win for him, and his position was not unlike that of the chief justice of the United States Supreme Court. Thus the councillors were less subject to domination by the assembly or by the governor when sitting in the court of appeals than they were when acting in either of their other capacities.

The judicial function of the council made necessary the taking of a special oath by its members, not required when performing their legislative or executive duties. The instructions made no mention of a judicial oath to be taken by the councillors until 1698 and apparently the English officials thought at first that an oath for the due execution of their places and trust would be sufficient to bind them in all their capacities.[74] But during the administration of Governor Andros in Virginia, complaints reached England that the councillors of that colony were acting in a

[73] Robinson to the Board of Trade, Dec. 3, 1743, C.O. 28: 26.

[74] The oath administered to all Jamaica councillors in 1698 read as follows: "You shall swear to be true and faithful unto his Excellency the captain general and governor in chief of this his Majesty's island and in everything to be of counsel with him, and to disclose none of his or his Majesty's secrets, and to declare, publish, and reveal whatsoever you shall find prejudicial to his said Excellency or leading or tending to the disturbance of this his Majesty's island or government. And in everything to perform your duty as a just and faithful councillor according to the best of your judgment, cunning, and discretion. So help you God." C.O. 137: 4, no. 95 i.

judicial capacity without being properly sworn. Andros denied that there was any impropriety in the situation, but the Board of Trade decided to allay any ill feelings by adding a clause in the instructions given to Governor Nicholson in 1698 requiring him to swear all councillors "to do impartial justice in the cases of all kinds whatsoever that may come before them as judges."[75] A few years later the board wrote to some of the other governors in the same terms, and after 1702 required a similar oath of the councillors in the instructions for all the provinces.[76] Thereafter the oaths taken by every councillor gave full recognition to his judicial responsibilities.

The earlier instructions specifically limited the council, when hearing appeals, to cases of error. But the substitution in 1753 of the words "in all civil causes" for the words "in cases of error," produced a bitter quarrel in New York, for, instead of clarifying the appellate jurisdiction of the council, as the Board of Trade intended, the change only served to confuse the matter. In 1764, before the reverberations of the quarrel over judicial tenure had wholly died away, a man named Thomas Forsey brought an action of trespass for assault, battery, and wounding against one Wadell Cunningham, and was awarded £1500 damages by a jury in the supreme court of the province. Cunningham considered the verdict excessive and moved for a new trial but the judges denied the

[75] Andros to the Board of Trade, July 1, 1697, C.O. 5: 1309, no. 23 (L.C.); *Cal. State Paps., Col.*, 1696–1697, § 1130; instructions to Nicholson, Va., 1698, art. 37, C.O. 5: 1359, pp. 266–303 (L.C.).

[76] Board of Trade to Governor Codrington, Leeward Is., May 23, 1701, *Cal. State Paps., Col.*, 1701, § 472; Board of Trade to Governor Beeston, Jamaica, May 23, 1701, C.O. 138: 10, p. 163; *Cal. State Paps., Col.*, 1701, § 473; Board of Trade to Lord Grey, Barbados, Aug. 20, 1701, C.O. 29: 7, pp. 379–380; *Cal. State Paps., Col.*, 1701, § 767. The instructions from 1702 on required the governor and councillors to take an oath for the "equal and impartial administration of justice in all causes" without specifying the exact phraseology to be used.

motion. The defendant's attorney then sought to appeal from the judgment and verdict to the governor and council, but in his petition to Cadwallader Colden, again acting governor, he alleged no error as the basis of the writ. As was customary in New York practice, the testimony of witnesses and the other evidence upon which the jury had based its verdict were not entered on the record of the trial court, so that the refusal of the judges to grant a new trial could not be deemed reversible error by the appellate court on the basis of the record alone. There was, in fact, no way in which the council could determine whether the jury had brought in a verdict in accordance with the weight of the evidence, short of an entire rehearing of the case on its merits. Colden, who knew more about medicine and botany than about law,[77] told the council that he thought Cunningham's appeal was warranted by the words of the instruction, which to his mind authorized an appeal to the council from the verdict in all civil causes without reference to any alleged error in law in the court below. He believed that justice demanded and the instruction permitted the council to sustain or reverse the verdict of the jury as well as the judgment of the court. In other words, the governor and council, when sitting as a court of appeals, might judge the facts as well as the law. He issued, therefore, two writs, one a writ of "inhibition," as he called it, directing the supreme court to stay all proceedings in the case there, and the other an unnamed instrument, apparently similar in purport to a writ of *certiorari,* ordering the chief justice to bring the proceedings before the council for a full hearing.

[77] Colden studied medicine in Scotland in his youth and practiced in Philadelphia for several years. He wrote several treatises on medical and other scientific subjects and corresponded with Linnaeus and other contemporary European botanists. See *Dictionary of National Biography* and Alice Keys, *Cadwallader Colden: A Representative Eighteenth Century Official.*

But Colden found little support for his views. To the chief justice and the other judges, the lawyers, and the people of the province generally, the lieutenant governor's interpretation of the instruction seemed to violate every principle and precedent of common-law procedure and to sweep away the very foundation of civil liberty—the jury system. In a long prepared statement Chief Justice Horsmanden refused to obey the second writ, informing the council that "the law warrants no such letters as those which the defendant sued out and delivered to me. We have taken the oath prescribed by the statute of the 18th of Ed. 3 and have sworn 'to deny no man common right by the king's letters, nor none other man's nor for none other cause,' but to proceed 'to execute the law notwithstanding the same letters.'"[78] After hearing the opinion of the other judges the councillors unanimously stated their belief that the instruction referred to writs of error only and they refused to take cognizance of the case, thereby overriding the action already taken by the lieutenant governor. Cunningham thereupon petitioned the privy council in England for an appeal from the verdict and judgment of the supreme court and from the subsequent determination of the provincial council. The privy council committee reported that appeals ought to come to Great Britain only through the regular channel provided by the instructions, and on their recommendation the privy council remanded the case to the governor and council with orders to admit Cunningham's appeal from the verdict and judgment of the supreme court and to hear the case as a court of appeals. Thereafter either party might bring a further appeal to the privy council.[79] In the

[78] Horsmanden's opinion, read in council Nov. 19, 1764, *The Colden Letter Books*, I, 407–415 (in *Collections* of the New-York Historical Society, 1876).

[79] Order in council, July 26, 1765, *Colden Letter Books*, II, 39–42 (in *Coll.*

light of later developments this order is surprising, since it seems to support the position taken by Colden, although neither the committee nor the privy council mentioned the central point of the controversy—the necessity of alleging error as the basis for an appeal. One can only believe that the privy council and its committee were more interested in the regularity of appeals from the colonies to England than in the procedure to be followed within the colony itself.

In the meantime the dispute continued to rage within the province. Colden was an old man of seventy-eight, embittered by a lifetime of political controversy, and he now assumed an attitude of suspicion and hostility toward those who refused to accept his arguments, charging one and all with conspiracy against him and against the interests of the king. He felt that in a province in which the lawyers dominated politics and actively allied themselves with the landed proprietors, no bar ought to be imposed to the fullest review of important cases, first by the governor and council in the province, and later by the privy council in Great Britain. He was convinced that where popular opposition to the prerogative was as strong as it was in New York, packed juries might jeopardize the rights of the king in cases where such rights were involved, unless the verdicts and the evidence upon which they were based could be fully reviewed by a higher authority than the trial judge. With such thoughts Colden filled his letters to the officials in Great Britain, while the judges, espousing the more popular side, delivered long harangues to approving audiences, and with the support of

of N. Y. Hist. Soc., 1877). The abstract of this order given in *Acts, Privy Coun., Col.*, 1745–1766, § 615, is quite misleading, since it indicates that the governor and council were to hear Cunningham's appeal "as a court of errors," which would imply denial to, rather than support of, Colden's contention.

the lawyers, disseminated their views even more widely
through the public press.[80]

There were two fundamental obstacles to the adoption
of Colden's views. In the first place, his system implied, if
not the complete abolition of the jury, at least the destruction of that body's importance as the sole judge of the
facts in every case of importance which might arise in a
court of common law. Most modern students of judicial
procedure would agree with the lieutenant governor that
a higher court ought to be able to consider the jury's
verdict, if only to the extent of determining whether it
was legally supported by the evidence. Few people will
assert that the trial judges ought to have the final right
to deny a new trial when sought on the ground of insufficient evidence or of an excessive verdict.[81] But the method
by which Colden proposed to reform the evils of the situation aroused intense antagonism because it violated the
principles of common law procedure. His interpretation
of the instruction seemed to imply that the governor and
council, and later the privy council, might set themselves
up as a sort of higher jury with power to bring in what
amounted to a fresh verdict, quite without regard to that
arrived at by the twelve "good men and true" in the trial
court. Whether the lieutenant governor really intended
to bring about this result is not entirely clear, but the
colonists certainly thought that such was his purpose.
Neither the people of the province nor the members of the

[80] For Colden's letters describing the dispute and elaborating on his views,
see *N. Y. Col. Docs.*, VII, 676, 679, 681, 695–702, 705, 706, 709, 768; *Colden
Letter Books*, I, 394, 421, 427, 446, 467, 469, 476; II, 49. See also extract of
council minutes, Nov. 19, 1764, *ibid.*, I, 415–416; petitions of R. R. Wadel,
Cunningham's attorney, Oct. 27 and 30, 1764, *ibid.*, pp. 416–419; Colden's
narrative, Dec. 13. 1764, *ibid.*, pp. 436–440; Colden to the council, Jan. 3,
1765, *ibid.*, pp. 441–442.

[81] In connection with this point, the reader will perhaps recall the criticism
directed against the rules of criminal procedure in Massachusetts at the
time of the Sacco-Vanzetti case.

legal profession would have permitted such a revolutionary change in the judicial machinery merely by a royal
instruction, without the bitterest kind of a fight. In the
second place, in spite of the support which Colden's position seems to have received from the privy council at the
time of Cunningham's appeal, his interpretation was directly contrary to the intention of the framers of the instruction in question. Neither the law officers of the crown
nor the Board of Trade had any idea that they were authorizing such a system of appeals as that which Colden
thought the instruction warranted. In the fall of 1765 the
Board of Trade submitted instructions for the new governor of New York, Sir Henry Moore. In the accompanying representation the board described the change which
they had made in the article on appeals in 1753 and explained that they had intended to do no more than prevent
the council from exercising appellate jurisdiction in criminal cases. They conceived that "the confining such appeals to cases of error only was upon the principles of
law a rule so absolute of itself and so well established by
the usage and constitution of this kingdom, that it was
thought unnecessary to point it out by express words in
the instructions." In order to prevent any further doubt,
the board now proposed that the instruction be rephrased
and the governor directed that "in all civil causes" he
should admit appeals to himself and the council "in cases
of error."[82] The attorney and solicitor general, to whom
this representation was referred, advised against making
any change in the wording of the instruction lest it prejudice the case of *Cunningham* v. *Forsey* which was still
depending, but they agreed that, in view of the practice
of the common-law courts of both England and New York
of omitting all evidence from the record, an appeal was

[82] Representation of the Board of Trade, Sept. 24, 1765, *N. Y. Col. Docs.*,
VII, 762–763; article 32 of draft instructions for Moore, *ibid.*, pp. 764–765.

inconceivable except in case of error in law upon the record of the judgment.[83] Because of this opinion, the Board of Trade's proposed change in the instruction was not adopted, although at the same time, Colden's well-meaning but revolutionary interpretation was repudiated.[84]

While the authorities in Great Britain were thus expressing themselves, the controversy in the province, which had largely died down during the summer of 1765, was revived by the arrival in October of the order in council authorizing Cunningham's appeal. When Colden read the order to the provincial council the members were convinced that his interpretation of the instruction had been sustained. On their advice he issued a new writ to the justices of the supreme court ordering them to send up their proceedings on the case on a date six weeks off.[85] But the triumph of the lieutenant governor was short-lived and he soon paid for his good intentions and his ignorance of legal principles. His unpopularity in the province, which had been pronounced for many years and had recently been intensified by the dispute over the tenure of judicial office, now reached a climax. His latest proposal for the review of the verdicts of juries by the council aroused the passions of his opponents as nothing before

[83] Attorney General Yorke and Solicitor General DeGrey to the privy council committee, Nov. 2, 1765, *ibid.*, pp. 815–816. The law officers added that in a court of equity, where the evidence was written, and the court judged of both fact and law, an appeal might lie for error in fact as well as in law.

[84] *Acts, Privy Coun., Col.*, 1745–1766, § 629; *ibid., Unbound Papers*, § 676; Board of Trade to Moore, Nov. 26, 1765, *Colden Papers*, VII, 95–96; instructions to Moore, 1765, art. 32, C.O. 5: 201, pp. 361–436 (L.C.).

[85] The principal source of information on the later proceedings in the case of *Cunningham* v. *Forsey* is the report of the grand committee of the assembly which investigated the matter, Dec. 14, 1765, *Journal of the Votes and Proceedings of the General Assembly of the Colony of New-York*, II, 803–806. See also *Calendar of Council Minutes, 1668–1783*, pp. 509, 510, 514, 515 (N. Y. State Library *Bulletin*, 58).

had done, and the colonists, especially the residents of
New York City, were ready to seize upon almost any excuse to demonstrate in no uncertain manner their hatred
of the old man. Thanks to Lord Grenville and the parliament that passed the Stamp Act, an occasion was almost
immediately offered. That unpopular measure went into
effect on November 1, only two weeks after Colden had
signed the writ for Cunningham's appeal. On that day a
mob collected and proceeded in disorderly fashion to the
fort where the lieutenant governor was living and where
the stamped paper was lodged, followed by a scaffold on
which were placed two images, "one representing their
old grey-haired governor, the other the devil, whispering
him in the ear." After a few verbal interchanges with the
garrison of the fort, the rioters burned the effigies together with several vehicles seized from Colden's coach-
house. No doubt this demonstration, so mortifying to the
lieutenant governor, was immediately due to the Stamp
Act, but unquestionably the main reason for the malice
of the populace and the personal indignities heaped upon
him was his attitude on the question of appeals.[86] Em-
boldened by this affair, Chief Justice Horsmanden defied
the council's order. He returned the writ with an endorse-
ment declaring that the judges "found it impossible (as
the law knew of no appeal from a verdict) to comply with
the command," although they were ready to send up the
record of the case as soon as they should receive a writ of
error.[87] A little later Governor Moore arrived, bringing
with him, presumably, information of the latest interpre-

[86] Colden to Secretary Conway, Nov. 5, 1765, Nov. 9, 1765, *N. Y. Col. Docs.*,
VII, 771–772, 773–774; Colden to the Board of Trade, Dec. 6, 1765, Jan. 13,
1766, *ibid.*, pp. 791–793, 803–804; Colden's "State of the Province of New
York," Dec. 6, 1765, *ibid.*, pp. 795–800, especially pp. 797–798; Sir William
Johnson to Colden, Jan. 9, 1766, *Colden Paps.*, VII, 101–103.

[87] Report of the grand committee of assembly, Dec. 14, 1765, *Journal of
Votes and Proceedings*, II, 805.

tation of the instruction by the British authorities.[88] The new governor and the council made. no effort to force the chief justice to obey Colden's writ and the case of *Cunningham* v. *Forsey* was allowed to drop.

But the assembly, inflamed against Colden, investigated the whole affair in grand committee and came to a series of resolutions. They declared that the recent attempt to introduce an appeal from the verdict of a jury was "illegal, an attack upon the right of the subject, and a most dangerous innovation, tending to encourage litigiousness and delay, promote perjury, prevent justice, subject the people to arbitrary power, and ruin the colony." The house believed that Colden had "to the utmost of his power endeavored to give success to that dangerous machination so naturally destructive to the security and peace of the subject." His conduct had "filled the minds of his Majesty's subjects in this colony with jealousies and distrust to the great prejudice of the public service and the repose of the inhabitants."[89] Discredited and insulted, Colden retired to his country home to brood over his wrongs, while the assembly turned to a consideration of that other "dangerous innovation," taxation with-

[88] We cannot be sure that Moore knew before he sailed exactly what interpretation was to be put upon the instruction. Being told not to wait for his instructions, he sailed about Sept. 5, 1765, and reached New York, Nov. 13, "after a long and dangerous passage of ten weeks." The Board of Trade representation on his instructions was dated Sept. 24 (about three weeks after Moore had sailed) and was read in the privy council Oct. 2. The instructions were finally signed Nov. 27, 1765. *N. Y. Col. Docs.*, VII, 762–763, 789, 794; *Acts, Privy Coun., Col.*, 1745–1766, p. 777; C.O. 5: 201, pp. 361–436 (L.C.). But the Board of Trade had known about the dispute in New York for a long time, and the probability is very great that they had talked the whole matter over with Moore before he sailed and that he knew their views even though they had not completed their representation on his instructions. Their letter to Moore of Nov. 26, 1765, formally notifying him of the final decision in England was not read to the New York council until March 22, 1766, *Colden Papers*, VII, 95–96.

[89] *Journal of Votes and Proceedings*, II, 786–794, *passim*, 803–806.

out representation.[90] But the incident as a whole shows more clearly than almost any other how the constant disputes over the royal system of government as laid down in the instructions prepared the way for, and later merged into, the colonial opposition to parliamentary authority. Had the royal administration and the crown officers both in Great Britain and in America been able to retain the confidence and full support of the colonists, the intervention of parliament in colonial affairs might have met with a more kindly reception.

The controversy also illustrates the lack of clarity which is so often noticeable in the instructions and which on several occasions led to other disputes only less dramatic in their final stages than the quarrel over appeals. There can be no doubt of the fact that both Colden and his opponents were sincere in their own interpretations of the instruction, although prejudice and personal enmity had their full share in bringing on the crisis. But in this case as in many others, the difficulty was aggravated by the absence of any machinery within the province for the effective and final interpretation of the instructions. Theoretically the governor to whom they were issued was expected to decide upon the meaning of his instructions for himself, perhaps after taking the advice of the council and the local attorney general, but he lacked power to enforce his views against organized opposition, and in cases such as this in New York, when the governor and council disagreed, the result was confusion worse confounded. Of course the final decision upon the meaning of an instruction was in the hands of the privy council in England, who could approve or disapprove the governor's action or issue a fresh instruction upon the subject. But this body was remote and invisible to the colonists, it was slow in

[90] For an account of the controversy that is highly sympathetic to Colden, see Alice Keys, *Cadwallader Colden*, pp. 300–328.

arriving at conclusions, and it failed to reflect the colonial point of view. It might even reverse itself within a short space of time, as it actually did on the question of appeals, thus adding to the difficulties of the provincial administration. If the instructions were to be an integral part of the constitution of a royal province, as all British authorities agreed they should be, some local agency was needed which could give to them an effective interpretation and to which both colonists and royal officials would listen with respect and obedience. Probably such an institution could never have been successfully established in the eighteenth century, but its very desirability lends emphasis to the weakness of "government by instruction."

On the whole, however, the instructions relating to the administration of justice aroused fewer controversies than did those dealing with almost any other part of the provincial system of government. Their chief purpose was to provide for a judicial system modeled on that of the mother country. With this object the colonists, who were mainly British in background and tradition, were largely in sympathy. The most important difficulties and problems in connection with these instructions arose from disagreement as to who should have the authority to establish the courts, upon what tenure the judges should hold office, and just how certain instructions ought to be interpreted. In all the disputes which grew out of these questions the colonists showed an increasing desire to regulate colonial affairs for themselves and to take from the British authorities control over provincial institutions. The unwillingness of the royal officials to grant such autonomy was not an evidence of tyrannical intent. It was rather a typical expression of conservatism and of man's common inability to admit the validity of a new and differing point of view.

CHAPTER X

GOVERNMENT BY INSTRUCTION

FOR all practical purposes the form of royal government which prevailed in some twenty-one British colonies at the time of the Declaration of Independence can be said to have been in existence for only a century before the American Revolution, although, strictly speaking, the system of direct royal control of colonial government had begun in 1624 upon the overthrow of the Virginia Company of London.[1] But the political machinery set up in Virginia and in the three island provinces which came under the direct authority of the crown at the Restoration —Jamaica, Barbados, and the Leeward Islands—underwent so many changes at first that no uniform and permanent system of government can be said to have existed

[1] The commissions and instructions to the governors of the following colonies and islands, which constituted the royal provinces at the time of the Declaration of Independence, have been made the basis for this study: the Bahamas, Barbados, Bermuda, Dominica, East Florida, Georgia, Grenada, Jamaica, the Leeward Islands, Massachusetts Bay, New Hampshire, New Jersey, New York, North Carolina, Nova Scotia, Quebec, St. John (Prince Edward Island), St. Vincent, South Carolina, Virginia, and West Florida. The governmental system of Massachusetts Bay differed from the normal prior to 1774, as did that of Quebec, especially after the same date. If the four subordinate governments of the Leeward Islands which had separate councils and assemblies—Antigua, Montserrat, Nevis, and St. Christopher— and the two similar governments under the chief executive of Grenada— Grenada itself and Tobago—be considered as separate colonies, the total number of royal provinces is increased to twenty-five. Maryland and Pennsylvania were also royal provinces at certain periods of their history but had been returned to their proprietors long before the Revolution. The inclusion of these two and of that short-lived experiment in colonial union, the Dominion of New England, would bring the number of royal provinces at one time or another to a possible total of twenty-eight.

before 1680. Of course, certain features of the final scheme
are apparent in the early commissions and instructions.
In all cases, royally appointed governors represented the
interests of the king; councillors assisted in the performance of executive, legislative, and judicial duties; and
elected representatives nearly always had a share in the
making of laws. But aside from these and a few other
points of similarity, the commissions and instructions
for different provinces, and even for the same province at
different times during these early years, varied widely in
detail. The first two governors of Barbados, Francis, Lord
Willoughby of Parham, and his brother, William, had, for
example, a certain proprietary interest in their domain
and were designated governors for specific terms of
years.[2] Generally, the councillors were named in either
the commission or the instructions to the governor, but
occasionally that official was left to choose all or part of
his associates himself.[3] Usually no time limit was imposed for the duration of provincial legislation; but the
laws passed by the early Jamaica assemblies were allowed
to remain in force for only two years unless confirmed by
the king—which they never were.[4] In matters of less importance the commissions and instructions show even

[2] The appointment of Francis, Lord Willoughby, in 1663, for seven years
was to cover the unexpired portion of his twenty-one-year lease of the Caribbee
Islands from the former proprietor, Lord Carlisle. His brother, William,
Lord Willoughby, was appointed in 1667 for the three years that still remained after his death. Commission to Francis, Lord Willoughby, 1663, C.O.
1: 17, no. 41; commission to William, Lord Willoughby, 1667, C.O. 29: 1,
pp. 51–64. See V. T. Harlow, *A History of Barbados, 1625–1685*, chap. IV.

[3] *E.g.*, commission to Francis, Lord Willoughby, Barbados, 1663, C.O.
1: 17, no. 41; commission to Modyford, Jamaica, 1664, C.O. 1: 18, no. 20.

[4] Instructions to Windsor, Jamaica, 1662, art. 20, C.O. 324: 1, pp. 37–56.
This provision was continued in the instructions until 1674 when it was
transferred to the commission to Vaughan, C.O. 138: 3, pp. 1–11. The whole
legislative system of Jamaica was changed in 1678. For an account of the
early system see Agnes M. Whitson, *The Constitutional Development of
Jamaica, 1660–1729*, chaps. II and III.

more clearly that the governmental system was in a state of flux during these early years.

But a marked change took place during the decade from 1670 to 1680, and especially during the last five years when the Lords of Trade were in charge of colonial affairs. What might be called the period of haphazard experimentation in colonial government began to draw to a close, although one of the greatest experiments of all— the attempt to apply the Irish system of legislation in Jamaica and Virginia—occurred during this decade.[5] Many changes were made in the commissions and instructions. Some of these changes involved only phraseology, but in the great majority of cases the old articles were discarded and entirely new paragraphs were written. Furthermore, many clauses containing entirely new matter were added, reflecting the experience of the previous years. The changes and additions were so extensive that the general instructions prepared for Sir Richard Dutton as governor of Barbados in 1680 contain half again as many words as do those given to William, Lord Willoughby of Parham in 1667. Not a single sentence from the earlier instructions is repeated in those of the later date.[6] But the commissions and instructions issued during the years from 1670 to 1680 have a strong similarity to each other and to those which came later. They mark the end of the old experimental days and the beginning of a new, permanent, and generally uniform system.

During the next hundred years the commissions and instructions to the governors underwent no fundamental change. In so far as these documents created constitutions for the royal provinces, the commissions and instructions

---

[5] See above, pp. 219–222.

[6] Instructions to William, Lord Willoughby, Barbados, 1667, C.O. 29: 1, pp. 65–73; instructions to Sir Richard Dutton, Barbados, 1680, C.O. 29: 3, pp. 37–53.

issued during the American Revolution, except in the cases of Quebec and West Florida, do not differ vitally from those given to the governors of Virginia, Jamaica, Barbados, and the Leeward Islands during the last years of the reign of Charles II. Some important, though temporary, changes appear during the century, such as the special legislative arrangements tried out in Jamaica and Virginia, already referred to, and the omission of provisions for elective assemblies in the Dominion of New England and in New York during the reign of James II, and in a few other provinces during the first years of royal control. The commissions and instructions for Massachusetts, also, differ from the normal because the charter of 1691 allowed that province to have an elective council and to keep some other features of the earlier form of government there. But even these variations tend to disappear. By 1775 the special privileges of Massachusetts had been wiped out and normal legislative bodies had been provided for all other provinces except Quebec and West Florida. The most striking characteristic of the royal provinces in the eighteenth century is the general uniformity of their governmental systems.

This uniformity is illustrated in the commissions to the governors, which contained the essentials of the provincial constitution as planned by the English officials. Thus the commission given to Sir Richard Dutton of Barbados in 1680 is surprisingly like that given to James Cunninghame as governor of the same island in 1780. If allowance is made for the fact that Dutton was expected to set up governments in the lesser Windward Islands subordinate to Barbados while Cunninghame's authority was limited to Barbados alone, and for the further fact that the oaths required of all officials were often changed during the century by act of parliament, the differences between the two commissions, except in matters of unimportant phraseology, are few and far between. Four clauses in Dutton's commission are not included in Cunninghame's, because by 1780 the matters with which they deal were generally taken up only in the instructions. Dutton was authorized to dissolve assemblies only, while Cunninghame was permitted to adjourn or prorogue them as well. Dutton was given slightly more specific powers in connection with trade and commerce than was Cunninghame, but had no definite authority, as had the latter, to take custody of lunatics and idiots. The clauses in the two commissions relating to military and naval authority, to the issuing of money, and to the devolution of government upon the death or absence of the governor also differ in varying degrees. Otherwise the two documents are identical.[7] Equally striking is the similarity that exists in the commissions for different provinces. For example, the commissions to Dunmore of Virginia in 1770, Tryon of New York in 1771, and Hay of Barbados in 1772 differ from each other in only four out of thirty-two paragraphs, and in these four only slightly, although Tryon's commission has an extra paragraph authorizing him to command the Connecticut militia.[8] The differences which one might expect to find in the constitutions of such widely separated provinces, after generations of growth and development, are not indicated in the commissions. As far as the home authorities could control the situation, the fundamental structure of government was the same in all royal provinces throughout the eighteenth century.

Even in the instructions, which deal with the details of administration, the uniformity is impressive. Naturally,

[7] Commission to Dutton, Barbados, 1680, C.O. 29: 3, pp. 25–37; commission to Cunninghame, Barbados, 1780, C.O. 29: 19, pp. 169–187.

[8] Commission to Dunmore, Virginia, 1770, C.O. 5: 1369, pp. 61–89 (L.C.); commission to Tryon, New York, 1771, C. Z. Lincoln, *Constitutional History of New York*, III, 696–710; commission to Hay, Barbados, 1772, C.O. 29: 18, pp. 415–452.

these instruments could not be expected to remain as fixed and uniform as the commissions. Variations from governor to governor of the same colony and from province to province at the same time were inevitable. But the articles prepared for one governor were based upon those given to his predecessor and the Board of Trade and privy council made only such changes as they thought absolutely necessary. When an alteration was needed, the Board of Trade seems to have striven intentionally to keep as much of the former phraseology as possible. In contrast with the complete dissimilarity between Dutton's instructions in 1680 and Willoughby's of thirteen years before, the wording of over half the articles given to Dutton is repeated in whole or in part in the instructions to Cunninghame a century later.[9] In the same way, the instructions given to the governors of different provinces tend toward uniformity. Articles dealing with such peculiarly local problems as the distribution of land naturally show marked differences from province to province, but similar variations do not so commonly appear in the instructions which relate to political, commercial, military, and religious affairs. Most of the instructions given to any one governor are identical with those given to his contemporaries in other provinces. Changes and additions were not always made at the same time in the form of circular instructions to the various governors, but the Board of Trade usually put into each set of general instructions all new or revised articles which they had recently prepared for other governors and which they thought were at all pertinent. The decisions of the home authorities on questions arising in any one province were usually reflected before long in the instructions drawn up for the guidance of royal governors elsewhere. Each set of instructions is much like every other set of the

9 Instructions to Dutton, Barbados, 1680, C.O. 29: 3, pp. 37–53; instructions to Cunninghame, Barbados, 1780, C.O. 5: 207, no. 5 (L.C.).

same period, for all were based upon the same foundations.

The fact that instructions were so often sent to other governors than those for whom they were originally prepared gives to the West Indies an especially prominent place in the history of colonial administration. At least two thirds of the more important changes and additions in the instructions, the origins of which can be traced to a single province, were first drawn up with either Jamaica, Barbados, or the Leeward Islands in mind. Outstanding examples of such instructions are the articles changing the succession in administration from the council as a whole to the senior councillor alone, prescribing the form for appropriating money and the rules for enacting laws, requiring all judges to hold office during pleasure only, prohibiting duties on the importation of slaves, and restricting legislation "of unusual and extraordinary nature and importance" prejudicial to the royal prerogative or the property of subjects. Any one who fails to include the West Indies in a study of the political growth of the colonies cannot fully explain the development of British governmental policies toward the continental colonies and of the resulting colonial unrest. As the instructions to the governors show, a large proportion of the restrictive measures which the continental leaders found most oppressive had their origins in the islands which are still parts of the British Empire.

The inhabitants of the royal provinces lived under a system of "government by instruction," which underwent no fundamental change during the century before the American Revolution. Details of the system were modified from time to time and from place to place. But these changes lay on the surface. At bottom the system was fixed, static, and unchanging, an expression of what the Board of Trade loved to call "the true principles of a provincial constitution." In keeping with these principles, the British officials provided that the governor should exercise in the province all those broad powers which various officials exercised in England in the name of the king; that the governor should be assisted in his duties by a group of councillors chosen for their loyalty, ability, and standing in the community; that the assembly, even though modelled on the House of Commons, should be sharply limited in its powers; that a "balance" should always be kept between the executive and the legislature, whereby the improper aspirations of the assembly might be checked at all times; that the judiciary should be efficient but subject to the control of the crown rather than of the popular assembly; and that the interests of the province should be subordinated to the interests of the mother country whenever the two came into conflict. Drafted with these ends in view and issued in the spirit of government "by royal grace and favor," the commissions and instructions for all the royal provinces maintained their uniformity throughout the century.

But however uniform the commissions and instructions were and however proper in British eyes were the principles upon which they were drawn up, the actual constitution of the royal provinces underwent great changes in this century. Members of the old Lords of Trade set up under Charles II would have approved all the articles of a set of instructions signed by George III, could those men have been brought back to life in 1775. But they would not at first have understood why some of the more restrictive clauses were necessary. Upon further investigation of conditions in America they would have been aghast at the number of instructions that the assemblies were coolly ignoring. These English Rip Van Winkles would have felt—and rightly—that the system of government which they had so carefully worked out for the four little royal provinces of their time, though spread to many other colonies, had lost most of its vitality and force through the rise of an institution which they themselves had feared and fought—the provincial assembly. And indeed, could they have but realized it, their own defeat in 1680 at the hands of the Jamaica assembly on the issue of the initiative in legislation marked the beginning of a movement which, within a hundred years, had substituted government "by the consent of the governed" for government "by royal grace and favor" as the controlling principle in the actual working of the provincial constitution. The prohibitions which were added in the later instructions bear witness to the fact that a new spirit was abroad in the land, a spirit which changed the balance of power in the colonial government from the prerogative to the assembly thereby greatly modifying the actual constitution of the royal provinces.

Undoubtedly the assembly leaders were largely responsible for their own success in the contest with the prerogative. At the start the assemblymen were mere novices at the parliamentary game, holding good cards, if they only knew it, but inexpert at their play. However, they proved quick to learn. Practice and experience soon developed masters among them who showed themselves able and willing to outmaneuver their opponents in ways made famous by the House of Commons. Delays, evasions, claims of privilege, short-term revenue acts, detailed and specific appropriations, "riders" attached to money bills—these were among the trumps which the provincial leaders learned to play so skilfully that the champions of the king were forced to the defensive in the hope of staving off complete defeat.

The assemblymen had certain advantages on their side which helped them greatly in their efforts to take from the governors the direction of provincial affairs. For one thing, they had the undisputed right, after 1680, to initiate all laws. The right to determine what bills should be brought forward for passage, what undertakings should be financially supported, and what governmental policies should be sanctioned by legislation was an essential part of the authority of the lower house and gave to the leaders of that body a positive voice in all important decisions. An able and popular governor might, and sometimes did, have a good deal to do with the shaping of legislation, but in the last analysis the chief executive's authority was limited to the approval or rejection of such bills as were laid before him. As compared with the governor's negative voice in lawmaking, the assemblymen's right of initiative gave them an advantage of great strategic importance.[10]

A second advantage to the assemblymen grew out of the fact that the assembly was modeled on the House of Commons. Because the assembly was similar in structure to the lower house at Westminster, its leaders naturally claimed for it a position in local affairs similar to that which the elective branch of parliament occupied in England. Whenever a controversy arose over privilege or procedure, the assemblymen were able to cite English precedents which put the governor at once upon the defensive. Instead of attacking his opponents for their ''unwarranted'' innovations, he had to take the less convincing position of declaring that English precedents did not

[10] Professor Notestein's words on the importance of the shift in leadership of the House of Commons from the privy councillors to the ''Country Party'' early in the seventeenth century might well be applied to the colonial assemblies: ''So long as the Commons was a ratifying body, with the right of occasional refusal, their interference with government would be at best slight. Once they were in charge of initiation, formulation, and passage of laws, once they had caught the reins of policy and begun to drive, there was no saying where they might draw up.'' Wallace Notestein, ''The Winning of the Initiative by the House of Commons,'' in *Proceedings* of the British Academy, 1924–1925, p. 175.

apply to the case in hand. Even more important in the minds of the colonial leaders than the practices of the House of Commons in such matters of detail as freedom from arrest and the approval of the speaker was the fact that parliament had, through a period of many years, gradually but effectively taken from the king the personal exercise in England of most of his prerogatives. The royal officials, on the other hand, were trying to keep the prerogative unimpaired in the colonies. As Governor Colden of New York once said, they believed that "the prerogative cannot be limited in these new countries by usage and custom."[11] The instructions to the governors were drafted in accordance with this principle and the whole system of royal government gave to the crown a much more important place in the provincial constitution than it occupied in the British constitution in the eighteenth century. In combating this situation the assemblymen felt themselves supported by common sense. They took the position that "the king can do nothing in the colonies which he cannot in England."[12] They used English precedents as weapons not only in defending themselves against the demands of the governors but in launching their own attacks against the authority of the prerogative. England's own history was thus one of the most effective aids to the assemblymen in their opposition to the system of royal government.

A third advantage on the side of the assembly was its control of provincial finance. Except in a few cases, the English officials conceded the principle that the colonies could be properly taxed only by parliament or by their local assemblies. The home authorities did not set up a comprehensive program of parliamentary taxation while the provincial system was still developing. They allowed

[11] Colden to the earl of Halifax, Dec. 13, 1764, *N. Y. Col. Docs.*, VII, 683.
[12] *Ibid.*

the assemblies to raise their own revenues until the colonies had fully established the principle of self-taxation. By failing to use the taxing power of parliament during most of the colonial period, the ministers left in the hands of the assemblymen a powerful instrument which was destined to do great injury to the prerogative and at the same time to increase enormously the assemblymen's sense of their own importance. Instead of trying to get parliament to impose the necessary taxes, the royal officials adopted the policy of the local permanent revenue; that is, they urged the passage by the assemblies of perpetual laws for raising enough revenue to take care of the ordinary needs of local government. This policy proved entirely mistaken. Only a few of the provinces ever passed such laws, and in those that did, the taxes levied soon proved inadequate to support the governments. Sooner or later the assemblies of all the provinces were called upon to grant sums for ordinary as well as for extraordinary services. The financial supremacy of the assembly was thus established throughout the British colonial world. The harmful effects of this situation were of course apparent to the royal authorities, but they did not fall back upon the other alternative, that of taxation by parliament, until nearly the end of the period. By then the time for such action had long since passed. The assemblies had grown too strong to submit tamely to parliamentary interference with their fiscal affairs. The measures commonly associated with the names of Grenville and Townshend proved to be dismal blunders. The century-old policy with regard to colonial taxation could not be even partially reversed without calling forth a serious protest.

In the meantime the assemblymen had learned how to use their control of finance to reduce the influence of the prerogative to a minimum. By passing revenue laws for short periods only, by making detailed and specific appropriations, by refusing to accept amendments from the council, by controlling the appointment of the treasurer, and by arranging as far as possible that money should be paid on their authority rather than on that of the governor and council, the members of the lower house of every royal province placed themselves in a position from which they could dominate the administration and safely defy the orders of the home government. They became especially adept at picking the right moments for their maneuvers, as Governor Benning Wentworth of New Hampshire explained: ''The prerogative of the crown, his Majesty's instructions, and the passing of laws inconsistent therewith are matters that the assemblies are exceedingly averse to submit to, and therefore upon every occasion when the necessity of the government calls for an immediate supply of the treasury, they never fail of invading the one or the other, and the greater the necessity or emergency is, the greater they esteem their advantage.'"[13] This control of finance, whereby the assemblymen gain their ends, was not limited to one or two issues or details of local administration. Every field of governmental activity, civil, military, or judicial, which needed financial support, was fertile ground for controversy, and sooner or later, in one province or another, yielded its crop of discord. In many provinces the British authorities were measurably successful in placing the governor's salary out of the assembly's reach, but even where the lower house kept control, the salary issue was only one of many paths to legislative supremacy. The ultimate effect of the assembly's financial power was well summed up by Governor Knowles of Jamaica in 1752:

Your Lordships is sensible of the difficulties most of the governors of this island have labored under to execute his Majesty's

[13] Benning Wentworth to the Board of Trade, Oct. 23, 1754, C.O. 5: 926, fo. 222.

instructions, by the balance of power being constantly in the House of Representatives (an error, I am inclined to believe, in its first concoction).

One who is thought to have understood the nature of government as well as any who ever wrote on that subject [James Harrington], says "That national or independent empire is to be executed by them who have the proper balance of dominion in the nation; wherefore provincial or dependent empire is not to be exercised by them who have the balance of dominion in the province, because that would bring the government from provincial and dependent to national and independent." Now as the assembly of this island have long (though contrary to his Majesty's instructions) assumed to themselves the sole power of raising and appropriating money exclusive of the council (for they will not so much as receive or admit of a literal amendment from them in any money bill) they are indeed the government.[14]

[14] Knowles to the Board of Trade, Nov. 18, 1752, C.O. 137: 25 (unpaged). The quotation is from James Harrington's *The Commonwealth of Oceana* (1656), p. 8. By stopping where he did, Knowles failed to do justice to Harrington's political insight. The context explains the passage which may be roughly paraphrased as follows: "Political power in an independent government is exercised by those who possess the property (primarily the land) of the territory: by the king in an absolute monarchy, by the nobility in an aristocracy or 'mixed monarchy,' or by the people in a commonwealth. But political power in a provincial government ought not to be controlled by those who possess the wealth there, because the government would thereby be changed from provincial and dependent to national and independent." Knowles's thought, therefore, was that the Jamaica assembly, representing the property owners of the province, had acquired the "balance of dominion," that is, political supremacy, through control of the purse, and had thereby made the island in effect "national and independent." Had Knowles pursued Harrington's analysis a little further, he would have found a prophecy of just such a development. Harrington explains (p. 9) that the basis of provincial government is "the overbalance of a native territory to a foreign," that is, that the province is controlled by the home country: because of the latter's superiority in government, as in the case of Rome; because of its greater military power, as in the case of the Mamelukes in Egypt; because of its superior situation, as in the case of Denmark's power in the Sound: or because of the colony's immaturity, as in the case of the Indies. As to the colonies in the Indies, "they are yet babes that cannot live

Certainly the assembly's "sole power of raising and appropriating money" was second to nothing in importance as a means of making that body actually "the government" of the royal province.

The three great advantages that the assembly enjoyed in its contest with the prerogative—the initiative in legislation, the historical example of parliament, and the control of finance—were not the only causes of the final outcome. In addition, there were certain features of the system of "government by instruction" itself which weakened the authority of the governors and contributed to the decline of the prerogative.

Uncertainty as to how much discretion the governor might use in interpreting and enforcing his instructions was one factor tending toward the decay of the royal authority. The opinion has been held by some historians that the Board of Trade and the privy council considered the instructions as merely formal guides which the governors were not expected to obey too literally. Nothing could be farther from the truth. Again and again a provincial act was disallowed, not because it was a bad law in itself, but because it failed to comply with some detail of the instructions. Again and again the board wrote to one governor or another expressing in the strongest possible terms their disapproval of his failure to obey orders. They felt so keenly on this subject that they sent a circular letter to all the governors in 1752 in which they pointed out that "the experience of late years furnishes

without sucking the breasts of their mother cities, but such as I mistake if, when they come of age, they do not wean themselves; which causeth me to wonder at princes that delight to be exhausted in that way." A century after Harrington wrote, the English colonies in America were very obviously coming of age, and were busily engaged in weaning themselves from dependence upon England, a fact which neither Knowles nor the other British officials were able to understand.

too frequent instances in which many of those instructions have been dispensed with and neglected upon slight and unwarrantable pretenses." They urged the governors to "have a proper regard to the regulations contained in your instructions" especially in the passing of laws.[15] In self-protection the Board of Trade told the privy council in 1767 that they did not believe the neglect of the governors to protect British interests in colonial legislation was "owing to the want of frequent admonitions from this board to the said governors, who have been from time to time called upon by our predecessors in office to a more regular observance of their instructions relative to the passing and assenting to laws."[16] There can be little doubt but that the home authorities intended the instructions to be literally obeyed.

Of course, there were times when the interests of the crown and of the colony would have been ill served by too strict an application of one or another of the formally worded instructions. Even the Board of Trade admitted this fact in their circular letter of 1752, when they cautioned the governors "strictly to adhere to your instructions and not to deviate from them in any point but upon evident necessity justified by the particular circumstances of the case." At such times the governors were to explain their reasons at once, and, if time allowed, to ask for directions from England before taking action. But who was to decide when a deviation from the instructions was immediately necessary? It was well enough for the duke of Portland to say that he believed he ought not to disobey his instructions "but on such emergencies as, when told, carry their reasons along with them, so that my behavior may be justified and my honor and integrity not

---

[15] Circular letter from the Board of Trade to the governors, June 3, 1752, C.O. 324: 15, pp. 318–323 (L.C.); N. Y. Col. Docs., VI, 760–761.

[16] Acts, Privy Coun., Col., 1766–1783, pp. 43–44.

called in question.'"[17] But several governors found to their sorrow that emergencies which seemed very real and pressing to them in the colonies often appeared quite the reverse to the officials in England, and that their letters explaining their violations of instructions proved much less convincing to the readers in England than the writers had hoped. The slowness of ocean transportation in those days prevented easy consultation between the king's officers in England and America. Governors had a hard time getting the home authorities to understand the true state of affairs in the colonies and persuading them to excuse the occasional violation of an instruction. The colonial executives seldom knew just how far they dared go in disregarding their orders without being brought sharply to book. An easy-going governor was likely to have his acts publicly repudiated in Great Britain and even to find himself ignominiously recalled if he interpreted his instructions too liberally. On the other hand, a conscientious governor was likely to hesitate so long before disregarding an instruction that the assembly would look upon any indulgence that he finally showed them as a forced surrender rather than a voluntary act of generosity. His concession, therefore, would weaken rather than strengthen his position in the province. The uncertainty of the governor's discretionary power made difficult the game of give and take, which every successful politician must play, and seriously handicapped the royal governor in his contests with the assembly.

An even more important reason for the decline of the system of government by instruction was the fact that the governor had the sole responsibility for the enforcement of the instructions. They were directed to him alone and related almost exclusively to the manner in which

---

[17] Portland to the Jamaica council, enclosed in his letter to the Board of Trade, Dec. [18?], 1725, C.O. 137: 16, fo. 158.

he was to exercise the authority given to him by his commission. The Board of Trade made this fact clear in a letter to Governor Knowles, written in 1754 during the dispute over the use of the suspending clause in certain types of legislation. The board declared that the instruction in question was "not directory to the assembly as to the manner of framing their bills, . . . but to you only, as to the manner in which you are to apply your assent or negative to the bills which they have so framed."[18] On the other hand, the home authorities repeatedly insisted that the instructions were to be accepted as an essential part of the constitutional system of the province. If the instructions were to receive the attention and respect which they deserved as a constitutional document of the highest importance, they should have been issued, as was the commission, in the form of a public document. They should have been openly read at the governor's installation and recorded in the office of the provincial secretary. They should have contained, as the commission did, a clause calling upon all officers, ministers, and other inhabitants to assist the governor in the execution of their provisions. They should have been "directory to the assembly as to the manner of framing their bills," and not simply to the governor as to his use of the veto. Instead the instructions were issued as a private paper for the eyes of the governor alone. Although he was told to show some of the articles to the council and was allowed to lay extracts before the assembly when occasion required, everyone was made to feel that the governor alone was responsible for their enforcement. In this sense, then, the instructions were a very narrow type of constitutional document.

If any moral or legal obligation rested upon any officers of the province to assist the governor in executing the in-

---

[18] Board of Trade to Knowles, Oct. 15, 1754, C.O. 138: 20, pp. 89–91. See above, p. 259.

structions, it surely rested most of all upon the royally appointed councillors. Sometimes, especially when their own interests coincided with those of the crown, the members of the council took an active part in supporting the governor and in resisting the encroachments of the assembly. But even they often stepped aside when a crisis occurred and left the governor to uphold the prerogative alone. The councillors repeatedly showed their willingness to evade responsibility, especially on the frequent occasions when, in their legislative capacity, they passed a bill because it was desired in the province and then, in their executive capacity, solemnly advised the governor to veto the measure because it was contrary to his instructions. One Jamaica councillor frankly wrote a member of the Board of Trade that when certain very improper bills came up during a period of distress in the island, he and his colleagues ''chose to give way to the necessity of the times and leave the supporting the king's instructions to the king's ministers, who had the framing of them, and who have sufficient power to do it, had they the leisure for such remote considerations; and the visible want of that encourages these men in their insolence.''[19] When councillors were so indifferent, assemblymen could hardly be expected to show greater loyalty.

Actually, the representatives paid no more attention to the instructions than they absolutely had to. Probably all the royal governors, in the West Indies as well as on the continent, would have agreed with Benning Wentworth of New Hampshire when he wrote: ''In this government, and I believe in some other of the northern colonies, for want of a more perfect understanding of the intention and use of the king's instructions and the royal prerogative, they are esteemed by the assemblies as burdensome and useless and therefore they take every advantage to

[19] Thomas Bernard to John Chetwynd, Feb. 20, 1720, C.O. 137: 13, no. 41.

force acts contrary to both as opportunity offers; from which behavior it appears to me that nothing less than an act of parliament will be binding on the assemblies to pay a due obedience to his Majesty's instructions. I have laid before the present assembly, which I deem as well disposed as any I have had, a paragraph in your Lordships' letter wherein I am commanded to adhere to my instructions and not to deviate from them on any occasions. It had no effect upon them. They say among themselves that the instructions are binding on the governor but not on them.''[20]

Ten years before this letter was written, the Board of Trade had tried to get parliament to pass a bill which, among other things, would have required all governors, lieutenant governors, councils, and assemblies ''to pay strict obedience to such orders and instructions as shall from time to time be transmitted to them or any of them by his Majesty or his successors or by any under his or their authority.'' The bill would have automatically made invalid all ''acts, orders, votes, or resolutions'' contrary to the instructions.[21] The opposition of the colonial agents and the jealousy in the Commons of the prerogative prevented any such sweeping measure from being enacted by parliament.[22] But even if such a bill had become law in 1744 it would have come too late to accomplish its purpose. The members of the Board of Trade must have been optimistic, indeed, if they thought the assemblies would accept with docility as late in their development as this, any constitutional change so revolutionary as the proposal

---

[20] Wentworth to the Board of Trade, Oct. 23, 1754, C.O. 5: 926, fos. 222–223.

[21] *A Bill to Prevent the Issuing of Paper Bills of Credit in the British Colonies and Plantations in America to be Legal Tenders in Payments for Money*, § 12 (1744), bound in *Parliamentary Papers Printed by Order of the House of Commons, From the Year 1731 to 1800*, I, no. 19 (British Museum).

[22] See above, pp. 33–35.

to give the instructions the binding force of law. The assemblies had already taken the position that the instructions related to the governor alone and that under the constitution the legislatures could not be bound by royal orders. When news of the bill of 1744 reached New York, a committee of the assembly reported that the measure would, if enacted, "establish such an absolute power of the crown in all the British plantations as would be inconsistent with the liberties and privileges inherent in an Englishman whilst he is in a British dominion."[23] By this time two full generations of colonists had grown up with the belief that the governor alone was responsible for carrying out the instructions. The proposed act of parliament would hardly have changed this belief, and although it might have increased the apparent power of the crown in the colonies, it would hardly have led the assemblies to give the governors more sympathetic support.

As matters stood, the royal governor to whom the instructions were addressed could count on very little certain support from any quarter in carrying out his orders. A few administrative officials whose appointment and removal he controlled, here and there an officer directly appointed from England, some members of the council nearly always, and others less frequently, and such friends as he might have made among the assemblymen, could be relied upon to give him a helping hand. But none of them had the same sense of responsibility that the governor had. No wonder that he found the task of enforcing the instructions so difficult; no wonder that his powers proved so often quite unequal to that task.

A third feature of the instructions which made them hard to enforce was their evident partiality. In drafting

[23] *Journal of the Votes and Proceedings of the General Assembly of the Colony of New-York* (March 15, 1645), II, 49.

instructions on controversial points, the Board of Trade nearly always favored British rather than colonial interests. Emphasis has been placed in earlier chapters on the influence of the merchants in preparing orders for the royal governors.[24] The assemblymen could not fail to understand this influence. They realized that whenever a law was passed in a province designed to protect local interests against those of the British merchants, the latter could nearly always get the law disallowed and could often persuade the Board of Trade and privy council to send an instruction to the governor forbidding him to approve any similar bills in the future. Such realization hardly increased the assemblymen's respect for the instructions or their willingness to obey such prohibitions as seemed to be harmful to the colonists as a whole. The representatives of Jamaica, for example, knew that the article restricting the duties on slaves was continued for seventeen years at the instigation of the British traders, in spite of the protests of every royal governor and their assertions that the slave trade as carried on was bad for the island. Such knowledge was not likely to make the Jamaica assemblymen respect the instructions in general; rather would it suggest to them the necessity of evasion at every possible point. The colonists knew that their local interests were not the foremost consideration of the British officials who prepared the instructions. Had it been otherwise, they might have felt differently about the whole system of government by instruction. But the number of cases in which the representatives of the prerogative completely disregarded the colonial point of view was so great as not only to increase the difficulty of enforcing the instructions, but, in the end, to lower the influence of the crown in controlling the affairs of the royal provinces.

The last and undoubtedly the most important feature of

24 See above, pp. 60–63, 229–247.

the instructions that contributed to the decline of the
royal authority in America, was their inflexibility. In
theory the commission and instructions were easily ad-
justable tools with which to build the constitutional system of the provinces. A new commission and set of general instructions were prepared for every province on an
average of once in every five and a half years,[25] and
changes in detail were made during the intervals by the
very simple method of issuing additional instructions.
Even a radical alteration in the draft of a commission or
instruction from the form previously in force needed only
the recommendation of the Board of Trade and the approval of the privy council on the advice of its committee,
and the privy council could dispense with the recommendation of the Board of Trade if it so wished. Few
constitutional documents in all of history have offered
such frequent opportunities for, or such easy means of,
amendment. With the two hundred and more commissions
and sets of general instructions which were issued during
the century before the American Revolution, the British
authorities had a magnificent opportunity to experiment
in colonial government. They could modify the constitutional system almost at will; introduce new principles
whenever such seemed desirable; try out some new feature in a single province and later apply it to the others
if it proved successful. In short, they could do anything
to keep the colonial constitution up to date so long as they
did not violate the acknowledged liberties of the colonists.
The colonial world was a splendid laboratory for the contemporary student of political science, and the commis-

[25] The statement has been made (p. 126 above) that the average length
of a governor's administration was almost exactly five years. The apparent
discrepancy between the two statements is explained by the fact that lieutenant governors or presidents of the councils often administered the government between the death or departure of one governor and the arrival of
his successor.

sions and instructions were almost perfect instruments for the experimenter.

But in Great Britain the eighteenth century was not an age of conscious experimentation in constitutional government, as the seventeenth century had been or as the nineteenth and twentieth centuries were destined to be. Between the collapse of the Dominion of New England and the passage of the Stamp Act the British officials showed no inclination to change the constitutional system of a single royal province, except in the case of Massachusetts whose special privileges they would have gladly destroyed. Their only contributions to the theory of colonial government during this time are to be found in their partly successful efforts to royalize the proprietary and corporate colonies, in the half-hearted and abortive attempts to bring the various colonies into closer union for defense, and in their ill-timed suggestion that parliament give the royal instructions the force of law in all the colonies. As far as the internal affairs of the royal provinces themselves were concerned, the Board of Trade and privy council made no fresh experiments after the late seventeenth century when the principle was established that each province was to have a local assembly endowed with the right to initiate legislation. Even in setting up the vice-admiralty courts in the continental colonies after the passage of the act of 1696, the home authorities merely extended and enlarged the powers of an institution which had existed in the West Indies for a generation. The parliamentary measures which the Board of Trade advocated, such as the Hat Act, the Molasses Act, and the Paper Currency Act, all dealt primarily with trade and commerce. None of them was passed for purposes of constitutional revision. Parliament passed no laws directly relating to colonial government before 1763, and even the measures enacted after that date were signs that the royal officials had failed to maintain their long-established system rather than proof of any particular effort to improve the system of colonial government. In their attitude toward royal government in America the Board of Trade and privy council showed an almost fanatical reverence for the *status quo*.

In letter and in spirit the commissions and instructions reflect this fundamental conservatism. The similarity of these documents from province to province and from governor to governor shows the lack of originality in the minds of their authors. Only two noteworthy changes in the organization of the provincial governments were made during the period before the Stamp Act. These two were the removal of the governor's right to give orders to officers commanding vessels of the royal navy in provincial waters and the substitution of the senior councillor for the whole council as the successor in administration to the governor and lieutenant governor. These were minor matters after all. Although the assemblies were growing in maturity and in ability to handle their own affairs, the Board of Trade modified the governors' instructions in favor of the assemblies only three times—once when they permitted the Jamaica assembly to lay a "reasonable duty" on slaves purchased in the island,[26] again when they let Governor Belcher of Massachusetts accept an annual salary,[27] and lastly when they allowed Governor Hardy of New York to approve temporary appropriation acts because of the impending war with France.[28] Not one of these reversals of policy was made willingly; each was wrung from the board only after the most convincing evidence had been given that the concession was absolutely necessary. In a few other cases the board gave way when they found that acts had previously been passed and inadvertently approved by the king which made illegal the

[26] See above, pp. 243-244.   [27] See above, pp. 365-366.
[28] See above, pp. 293-294.

instructions the board had issued. With such exceptions as these, the changes in the instructions were all made with the intent of tightening the royal grip upon the colonies rather than of loosening it, and of counteracting the growing power of the assemblies rather than of conforming to it. The British authorities had no intention of experimenting with colonial government or of changing the commissions and instructions in the direction of greater liberality and freedom.

One incident deserves to be mentioned, however, because it stands so completely apart from the normal attitude of the English authorities toward the situation in the colonies. When the Quebec Act was passed in 1774, a new commission and new instructions were necessary for the governor of the province, Guy Carleton. This act was in considerable measure the work of Carleton himself, and, as he was in England while the new instructions were being prepared, the Board of Trade naturally called upon him for assistance. Carleton was a man of common sense and vision. The results of his activity are striking. He was unquestionably responsible for the omission of many of the usual paragraphs of the instructions and the inclusion of many new ones based on the recent act of parliament. Thanks to him the new orders were phrased in fresh and unhackneyed language. The meaningless formulae of the past century were discarded. Provincial problems were presented in a simple and informal manner. Throughout the document there flow a current of liberalism and a spirit of adventure. Confronted with a vast domain and an alien population, the British officials at last seemed bent on a great experiment. The instructions show the desire of these officials to give the governor the soundest advice possible and yet to allow the utmost freedom and discretion possible that he might bring order out of what must have seemed like chaos. Whatever may or may not have been the merits of the governmental plan laid down, whatever the success or failure of the administration in Quebec, the freshness and vigor of Carleton's instructions are a welcome contrast to the staleness and ineptitude of the orders given to the governors of the other provinces.[29]

The inflexibility and uniformity of the instructions contributed directly to the failure of the royal system of government in America. No constitutional system can long survive the conditions which called it into being, unless the necessary steps are taken to adapt the system to changes in the community. In the case of the British colonies the constitutional system as embodied in the commissions and instructions was established in the seventeenth century when most of the provinces concerned were small and undeveloped. Even in those communities, such as the West Indies, which were foremost in wealth and population, the inhabitants had very limited political experience and the assemblies had not yet had time to establish strong traditions of self-government. The commissions and instructions then issued were based upon principles of government by royal grace and favor which, although distasteful to some individuals, were not entirely out of keeping with the immaturity of the colonies. A hundred years later conditions were wholly changed. In the continental colonies, population had increased enormously, territorial expansion had been continuous, and wealth had accumulated. Both in the West Indies and on the continent, the assemblies had created precedents, had established fixed rules of procedure, and had won recognition of their parliamentary privileges in fact if not in theory; they had gained control of finance and by these

[29] Instructions to Carleton, Quebec, 1775, *Report Concerning Canadian Archives for the Year 1904*, pp. 229–247; A. Shortt and A. G. Doughty, *Documents Relating to the Constitutional History of Canada*, I, 419–433.

means they had come to dominate provincial affairs. The propertied classes, to whom the franchise was extended, had gained not only familiarity with political methods, but the habit of self-government. But during these hundred years the instructions had undergone no fundamental change; they still rested on the principle of government by royal grace and favor; they continued to give the governor, as the representative of the prerogative, the same large powers that he had received when the assembly was first created. The officials in Whitehall who drafted these documents were as unmoved by the changes in America as they would have been if those changes had taken place on another planet. Inevitably, therefore, the system of government by instruction proved more and more unworkable the longer it was in force.

The British authorities remained blind to the causes which underlay the decline of royal authority. They never offered a workable solution for the problem before them. They were suspicious and critical whenever a governor exercised any real discretion in applying his instructions. They made only futile and half-hearted attempts to help him share responsibility for observing the instructions with the council and assembly. They never receded from the position that the colonies existed primarily for the benefit of Great Britain and that the instructions ought to protect British rather than colonial interests when these came into conflict. And the royal officials never saw any need for liberalizing or modernizing the instructions, which they repeated from governor to governor with monotonous regularity. Instead of modifying the system from time to time so as to preserve the influence of the crown and insure the cooperation of the assemblies, they rejected all proposals of this sort as contrary to "the true principles of a provincial constitution." For the new wine of colonial conditions and ideals they offered only the old wineskins of an ancient and inflexible system. Responsibility for the catastrophe that followed must rest primarily upon the shoulders of those who prepared the commissions and instructions and who failed to see that the system of "government by instruction" was no longer suitable as the foundation of the colonial constitution. For they thought only in terms of the past and of government "by royal grace and favor," ignoring the new principle of government "by the consent of the governed," which not only was soon to become the corner stone of a republic in America, but was in time to have an important place in the reconstruction of the British Empire itself.

BIBLIOGRAPHICAL NOTE

LISTS, GUIDES, AND BIBLIOGRAPHIES

THE works of Hubert Hall, entitled *Studies in English Official Historical Documents* (Cambridge, 1908); *A Formula Book of English Official Historical Documents*, Part I, *Diplomatic Documents* (Cambridge, 1908), Part II, *Ministerial and Judicial Records* (Cambridge, 1909), have been of assistance in studying the diplomatic character of the instruments of royal authority in the colonies, although the volumes relate almost entirely to an earlier period of English history. By far the most important work designed to assist the student of English colonial history has been done by Professor Charles M. Andrews. His *Guide to the Materials for American History, to 1783, in the Public Record Office of Great Britain*, vol. I, *The State Papers* (Washington, 1912), vol. II, *Departmental and Miscellaneous Papers* (Washington, 1914), and the *Guide to the Manuscript Materials for the History of the United States to 1783, in the British Museum, in Minor London Archives, and in the Libraries of Oxford and Cambridge* (Washington, 1908) by Professor Andrews and Miss Frances G. Davenport, are invaluable to the worker in these collections or in transcripts therefrom. Fuller in detail, though more restricted in scope, is the *Guide to British West Indian Archive Materials, in London and in the Islands, for the History of the United States* by Herbert C. Bell, David W. Parker, and others (Washington, 1926). Professor Andrews has published also a number of special lists. These are "Lists of the Journals and Acts of the Councils and Assemblies of the Thirteen Original Colonies, and the Floridas, in America, Preserved in the Public Record Office, London," in the *Annual Report* of the American Historical Association for 1908, I, 399–509 (Washington, 1909); "List of the Commissions and Instructions Issued to the Governors and Lieutenant Governors of the American and West Indian Colonies from 1609 to

1784," in the *Annual Report* of the American Historical Association for 1911, I, 393–528 (Washington, 1913); and "List of Reports and Representations of the Plantation Councils, 1660–1674, the Lords of Trade, 1675–1696, and the Board of Trade, 1696–1782, in the Public Record Office," in the *Annual Report* of the American Historical Association for 1913, I, 319–406 (Washington, 1915). The "List of Commissions and Instructions," though needing some revision, has been most useful in gathering material for the present study. Without it, the labor involved would have been immeasurably increased. The reader in search of a more extensive bibliography on the subject of the British colonies than is contained in the following pages is referred to the very elaborate and satisfactory bibliography in *The Cambridge History of the British Empire,* edited by J. Holland Rose, A. P. Newton, and E. A. Benians, vol. I, *The Old Empire from the Beginnings to 1783* (Cambridge, 1929).

MANUSCRIPTS

BY far the great majority of manuscripts used have come originally from the Colonial Office Papers in the Public Record Office, London. For the purposes of this investigation they may be described in three parts. One part consists of transcripts from the original papers in the Division of Manuscripts of the Library of Congress at Washington, indicated in the footnotes by the symbol "(L.C.)." The most important set of documents used there is the collection known as Public Record Office, Colonial Office, series 5, vols. 188–208 (designated as C.O. 5:188–208) containing a large percentage of the commissions and instructions issued between 1702 and 1783. Another group of transcripts of great value is C.O. 324:3–19, 21, 48–58, 60, consisting of entry books, royal warrants, licenses, lists, and other material under the classification of "Plantations General." Almost equally useful to the present study is C.O. 5:1–10, 65–76, containing various papers, letters, reports, petitions, etc., which also deal with the colonies at large. Wide use was also made of the material transcribed from C.O. 5:1305–1375, which contains almost all the commissions, instructions, correspondence, and other similar documents relating to Virginia. Less useful were the transcripts from C.O. 5: 540–569, relating to East Florida. Other documents, too miscellaneous in character to describe fully, were also used.

The second part of the manuscripts consulted is a series of transcripts made for the Colonial Society of Massachusetts under the supervision of Mr. Albert Matthews and now deposited in the custody of the Massachusetts Historical Society. It comprises a selection of material chiefly from C.O. 5: 764–923, and includes all the Massachusetts instructions and other communications from British officials to the governors of this province. The letters from the governors in America to the officials in England are not included. These transcripts were made available for investigation through the courtesy of Mr. Matthews, who sent them to New Haven at his own expense. They are designated in the footnotes by the symbol "(Mass.)."

The third part of the Public Record Office manuscripts consulted is composed of originals in London, which I have examined at the Record Office itself or which I have had transcribed for my personal use. References to such documents in the footnotes have no special symbol. A large part of these papers are the instructions to governors not found either in print or in the transcripts at Washington or Boston. They include instructions to the governors of North Carolina, New Jersey, and New York (in scattered volumes of C.O. 5); the Bahamas (in C.O. 24); Barbados (in C.O. 29); Bermuda (in C.O. 38); Jamaica (in C.O. 138); the Leeward Islands (in C.O. 153); and Nova Scotia (in C.O. 218). I have also made a careful examination of many Barbados papers (C.O. 28: 4–33; C.O. 29: 7–18) and Jamaica papers (C.O. 137: 1–26; C.O. 138: 1–18) and a less complete study of various volumes and bundles among the Bermuda papers (C.O. 37 and C.O. 38), the Leeward Islands papers (C.O. 152 and C.O. 153), and the papers relating to New Hampshire, Massachusetts, and South Carolina (gathered in C.O. 5). Some other documents in the Public Record Office not among the Colonial Office Papers have also proved useful, as indicated in the footnotes.

I have also examined numbers of volumes and individual documents among the Newcastle Papers in the British Museum (general classification, Additional Manuscripts 32,686–33,057) either in the originals or in transcripts at Washington. While making no pretense of an exhaustive search in this rich collection of historical material, I have found the volumes consulted useful primarily for the light they shed on the patronage system and the many applications to Newcastle for appointment to colonial governorships. To the manuscript material from the Public Record Office and the British Museum here listed should be added passing mention of the use of an occasional document from the Massachusetts Archives and from the collections of the Huntington Library, the latter kindly copied for me by Professor Andrews.

PRINTED DOCUMENTS: GENERAL

INDISPENSABLE to any study in colonial history is the *Calendar of State Papers, Colonial Series, America and the West Indies* (London, 1860–1926) which has now reached a total of 22 volumes, covering the period from 1574 to 1714. Volumes I–IV were edited by W. Noël Sainsbury, volume V by W. Noël Sainsbury and J. W. Fortescue, volumes VI–XI by J. W. Fortescue, and volumes XII–XXI by Cecil Headlam. They constitute by far the most important collection of documents for the period that they cover, but should, when possible, be supplemented by examination of the full documents which are calendared. This the present writer has been able to do in many cases. Of almost equal importance to the student of British control of the colonies are the volumes entitled *Acts of the Privy Council of England, Colonial Series,* 6 vols. (London, 1908–1912), edited by W. L. Grant and James Munro under the general supervision of Sir Almeric W. Fitzroy. Covering as they do the entire period from 1613 to 1783, they shed much light on events to which the *Calendar of State Papers, Colonial,* has not yet been extended. They present, often with much detail, the determinations of the privy council and its committee on matters relating to the colonies. *The Journal of the Commissioners for Trade and Plantations* (commonly known as the Board of Trade) which has been separately printed in full for the years 1704–1734 in six volumes (London, 1920–1928) instead of in abstract as a part of the *Calendar of State Papers, Colonial,* as formerly, has proven a mine of information on the activities of the Board of Trade and on colonial administration generally.

Three sets of calendars of Treasury documents are of great value for a study of the financial relations of the mother country and her overseas possessions. These series are: *Calendar of Treasury Books*, 1660–1689, 8 vols., in 15 parts, prepared by William A. Shaw (London, 1904–1923); *Calendar of Treasury Papers*, 1557–1728, 6 vols., prepared by Joseph Redington (London, 1868–1889); and *Calendar of Treasury Books and Papers*, 1729–1745, 6 vols., prepared by William A. Shaw (London, 1897–1903). Because of the developments in provincial finance, these volumes are more useful in connection with the West Indies than in connection with the continental colonies. A most promising beginning has been made toward a compilation of parliamentary material relating to the colonies by Leo Francis Stock in his *Proceedings and Debates of the British Parliaments respecting North America*, of which only two volumes have as yet been issued covering the years 1542–1702 (Washington, 1924, 1927). When this work is finished the student of colonial history will no longer have to plow his laborious way through the pages of the *Journals of the House of Lords*, the *Journals of the House of Commons*, and the *Parliamentary Histories*, which are enumerated in detail in the preface to the first volume of Mr. Stock's work. But the *Statutes of the Realm* to 1713, 12 vols. (London, 1810–1828), and *Statutes at Large*, 109 vols. edited by Danby Pickering (London, 1762–1866), are still indispensable.

George Chalmers, *Opinions of Eminent Lawyers, on Various Points of English Jurisprudence, Chiefly Concerning the Colonies, Fisheries, and Commerce, of Great Britain*, 2 vols. (London, 1814), is perhaps the most useful non-official collection for the constitutional history of the colonies. To it should be added a work of a different sort, *British Royal Proclamations Relating to America, 1603–1763*, edited by Clarence S. Brigham, in the *Transactions and Collections* of the American Antiquarian Society, vol. XII (Worcester, 1911), which, though not complete, contains many important proclamations. The United States government has published *The Federal and State Constitutions, Colonial Charters and Other Organic Laws of the States, Territories and Colonies Now or Heretofore Forming the United States of America*, 7 vols., edited by Francis Newton Thorpe (Washington,

1909). These volumes, however, are quite useless for the constitutional history of the royal provinces since they omit the only organic documents of these colonies, the commissions and instructions to the governors. Of occasional value are the *Reports* of the [Royal] Historical Manuscripts Commission. In particular, the report on the Marquess Townshend Manuscripts (vol. XI, appendix 4, London, 1887) contains a calendar (pp. 254–328) entitled "Papers Relating to the American Plantations," which consists chiefly of letters to Lord Wilmington, president of the council.

PRINTED DOCUMENTS: INDIVIDUAL PROVINCES

FOR Quebec, the northernmost royal province of our period, *The Report Concerning Canadian Archives for the Year 1904* (Ottawa, 1905) is useful, since it contains all the general instructions and many of the additional instructions issued to the governors of Quebec between 1763 and 1786. Many of these documents are also printed in Adam Shortt and Arthur G. Doughty, *Documents Relating to the Constitutional History of Canada*, vol. I, 1759–1791 (Ottawa, 1907), which also includes many letters and other papers, helpfully annotated. The published documentary material relating to the constitutional history of Nova Scotia is comparatively scant. The only collection of value is found in part V of *Selections from the Public Documents of the Province of Nova Scotia* (cover title: *Nova Scotia Archives*) edited by Thomas B. Akins (Halifax, 1869), containing most of the correspondence and other documents relating to the establishment of an assembly in that province.

The journals of the lower house of New Hampshire and the legislative and executive journals of its council are printed in *Documents and Records Relating to the Province of New Hampshire* (cover title: *Provincial Papers*), 7 vols., compiled by Nathaniel Bouton (Concord, 1867–1873). This series also contains a few letters and some of the commissions and instructions to the governors. In the last respect, however, it is completely superseded by the *Laws of New Hampshire*, vols. I–III, *The Province Period*, edited by Albert Stillman Batchellor (Manchester, N. H., 1904–1915), which includes not only a well-annotated collection of the laws but an almost entirely complete set of the commissions and instructions to the governors. No other state has so adequately published its royal commissions and instructions. The correspondence of the New Hampshire governors, however, is unfortunately not in print.

The published material for Massachusetts is abundant but at the same time exasperatingly deficient in some important particulars. The inaccessibility of the legislative journals, long felt by historians, is now being remedied by the publication by the Massachusetts Historical Society of the *Journals of the House of Representatives of Massachusetts*, with introductions by Worthington Chauncey Ford and Gardner Weld Allen. The work has now extended to ten volumes covering the period 1715–1732. Some compensation for the disappearance of the earlier journals is afforded by the existence of a little pamphlet entitled *A Collection of the Proceedings of the Great and General Court or Assembly of His Majesty's Province of the Massachusetts Bay, in New England, Containing Several Instructions from the Crown to the Council and Assembly of that Province, for Fixing a Salary on the Governor and Their Determination Thereupon. As Also the Methods Taken by the Court for Supporting the Several Governors Since the Arrival of the Present Charter*, printed by order of the House of Representatives (Boston, T. Fleet, 1729). The chief value of this rare pamphlet, of which I have used the Library of Congress copy, is in connection with the salary disputes, as its title suggests. For the closing years of the colonial period a useful compilation is that by Alden Bradford, entitled *Speeches of the Governors of Massachusetts, from 1765 to 1775; and the Answers of the House of Representatives to the Same; with their Resolutions and Addresses . . . and Other Public Papers, Relating to the Dispute between this Country and Great Britain* (Boston, 1818). To this may be added the appendices in Thomas Hutchinson's *History of Massachusetts Bay*, vol. III (London, 1828), which contain many of the messages and addresses for the same period. The council journals of Massachusetts have not been published, but in *The Acts and Resolves, Public and Private, of the Province of the Massachusetts Bay*, 20 vols. (Boston, 1869–1918), edited by Albert Cheney Goodell, A. S. Wheeler, and W. C. Williamson, is to be found not only the finest edition of provincial laws which has yet been published but an abundance of editorial material, including many documents of great importance. Few of the Massachusetts instructions have been printed, but Albert Matthews has edited *Massachusetts Royal Commissions, 1681–1774*, in the *Publications* of the Colonial Society of Massachusetts, II, *Collections* (Boston, 1913). Nearly all the commissions are there, and most of the omissions are supplied in vol. XVII of the *Publications* of the same Society, *Transactions, 1913–1914* (pp. 150–155), which also contains (pp. 2–111) the very valuable "Notes on the Massachusetts Royal Commissions" by Mr. Matthews. The correspondence of the governors of the province has never been printed in its entirety.

Of the printed collections relating to individual provinces, one of the most exhaustive and satisfactory is that entitled *Documents Relative to the Colonial History of the State of New York* (commonly known as *New York Colonial Documents*), 15 vols., procured by John Romeyn Brodhead and edited by E. B. O'Callaghan (Albany, 1853–1887). It contains a very nearly complete collection of the letters between the governors and the home authorities as well as a considerable number of commissions, instructions, orders in council, representations, and other documents emanating from British sources. It omits, however, the important enclosures in the letters from the governors, which are now being copied for the Library of Congress. Of some supplemental value is *The Documentary History of the State of New York*, 4 vols., arranged under the direction of the Hon. Christopher Morgan, secretary of state (Albany, 1849–1851), which contains material on a number of special topics. The *Journal of the Votes and Proceedings of the General Assembly of the Colony of New-York*, 1691–1765, 2 vols. (New York, 1764, 1765), and a third volume for the years 1766–1776 (Albany, 1820), together with the *Journal of the Legislative Council of the Colony of New York*, 2 vols. (Albany, 1861), give information on the activities of the legislature. *The Calendar of Council Minutes, 1668–1783*, in New York State Library *Bulletin* 58, History 6 (Albany, 1902), is disappointingly condensed. On the other hand, *The Colonial Laws of New York from the Year 1664 to the Revolution*, 5 vols. (Albany, 1894), is conveniently edited.

The first ten volumes of the *New Jersey Archives,* First Series, designated as *Documents Relating to the Colonial History of the State,* edited by Frederick W. Record and William Nelson (Newark, 1880–1886), contain the correspondence of the governors and similar matter generally as that in the *New York Colonial Documents.* Vols. XIII–XVIII of the same series contain the *Journals of the Governor and Council,* by the same editors (Newark, 1890–1893). Neither the legislative journals nor the provincial laws of New Jersey have been satisfactorily compiled. *The Acts of the General Assembly of the Province of New-Jersey,* 1702–1761, 2 vols. (I, no place, 1752; II, Woodbridge, N. J., 1761), compiled by Samuel Nevill; and *Acts of the General Assembly of the Province of New-Jersey from . . . 1702, to . . . 1776* (Burlington, 1776), compiled by Samuel Allinson, are both very inadequate.

More complete are the journals of the governmental bodies of Maryland in the *Maryland Archives,* 46 vols. (Baltimore, 1883–1929). The first thirty-two volumes were edited by William Hand Browne, the next three by Clayton Colman Hall, the next ten by Bernard Christian Steiner, and the last by J. Hall Pleasants. Assembly proceedings and acts passed during the royal period are in vols. XIII, XIX, XXII, XXVII, XXIX, XXX, and XXXVIII. The proceedings of the council for the same period are in vols. VII, XX, XXIII, and XXV.

The most elaborately issued among legislative and executive journals are those of Virginia, published by the State Library and edited by H. R. McIlwaine. These are: *Legislative Journals of the Council of Colonial Virginia,* 3 vols. (Richmond, 1918–1919); *Journals of the House of Burgesses of Virginia,* 13 vols. (Richmond, 1905–1915), which contain many short gaps; *Minutes of the Council and General Court of Colonial Virginia, 1622–1632, 1670–1676* (Richmond, 1924); and, most recently, *Executive Journals of the Council of Colonial Virginia,* now in three volumes covering the period 1680–1721 (Richmond, 1925–1928). Many of the papers and minutes of the executive council are also printed in various numbers of the *Virginia Magazine of History and Biography.* In this quarterly journal, which first appeared in 1894, many early commissions and instructions and other useful documents have also been printed. The laws of the province are collected in William Waller Hening, *The Statutes at Large, Being a Collection of All Laws of Virginia, from the First Session of the Legislature, in the Year 1619*, 13 vols. (Richmond, Philadelphia, New York, 1809–1823). Appended to several volumes of this series are various historical documents, particularly some relating to the seventeenth century. A very inadequate and disappointing collection of documents is given in *Calendar of Virginia State Papers and Other Manuscripts*, 1652–1781, arranged and edited by William P. Palmer (Richmond, 1875), but the complete correspondence of the governors of this important colony still awaits publication.

North Carolina has followed the commendable example of New York and New Jersey in bringing together in one series the letters to and from the governors, many of the commissions and instructions, and much other British material relating to the province. The first ten volumes of the collection entitled *The Colonial Records of North Carolina*, edited by William L. Saunders (Raleigh, 1886–1890), cover the period from 1662 to 1776, supplemented by some additional documents in vol. XI (Winston, 1895). Volume XXIII contains the provincial laws (Goldsboro, 1904). The legislative and executive journals are interspersed through the first ten volumes, so that this one series provides most of the materials for the constitutional history of the province.

South Carolina has lagged behind its northern neighbor in the publication of its documentary history. Only *The Statutes at Large of South Carolina*, edited by Thomas Cooper and David J. McCord (Columbia, 1836–1841), vols. II–IV, 1682–1786, deal with the royal period, although much other material has been transcribed for the Historical Commission of the State. *The Statutes at Large* suffer from a desire on the part of the editors to conserve space, with the result that many laws are printed by title only.

The Colonial Records of the State of Georgia, 26 vols., edited by Allen D. Candler (Atlanta, 1904–1906), contain the journals of the council and Commons House of Assembly. Vols. VII–XII include minutes of the governor and council; vols. XIII–XV, the journals of the Commons House; vols. XVI–XVII, those of the upper house; and vols. XVIII–XIX, the statutes, all of these during the royal period only. The correspondence of the governors has not been adequately published.

For the Floridas no collections of published documents comparable to those described above exist. The printed documents for the British provinces in the West Indies, for Bermuda, and for the Bahamas are scanty and often very rare. None of those listed below have been used in the present work. Of collected laws the most important are: *Acts Passed in the Island of Barbados, 1643–1762* . . . edited by Richard Hall and Richard Hall, jr. (London, 1764); *Acts of Assembly Passed in the Island of Jamaica from 1681 to 1737 Inclusive* (London, 1738); *Laws of Jamaica,* 5 vols. (St. Jago de la Vega, 1792); *Acts of Assembly Made and Enacted in the Bermuda or Summer Islands, 1690–1713* (London, 1719) and continued to 1736 (London, 1737). These collections do not generally include disallowed or obsolete laws, unless by title only. Legislative journals in print include: *Votes of the Honorable House of Assembly of the Bahama Islands,* vols. I–IV (Nassau, 1910–1911); *Ancient Journals of the House of Assembly of Bermuda,* from 1691 to 1785, 3 vols. (Bermuda, 1890); and *Journals of the House of Assembly of Jamaica, 1663–1826,* 14 vols. (Jamaica, 1811–1829). For more complete lists see the bibliography in *The Cambridge History of the British Empire,* I, 830–831 (mentioned above) and Frank Cundall, *Bibliographia Jamaicensis* (Kingston, 1902) and *Bibliography of the West Indies, Exclusive of Jamaica* (Kingston, 1909).

PRINTED DOCUMENTS: CORRESPONDENCE OF INDIVIDUAL GOVERNORS

As indicated above, the correspondence of the governors of only a few provinces, New York, New Jersey, and North Carolina, has been published with any degree of completeness. However, there are some printed collections of the letters of individual governors, although no one series is entirely complete. The following have proved most useful in the present work: *The Belcher Papers,* in *Collections* of the Massachusetts Historical Society, sixth series, vols. VI and VII, with prefaces by Charles C. Smith (Boston, 1893–1894), which contains much of Jonathan Belcher's correspondence while governor of Massachusetts and New Hampshire; *Correspondence of William Shirley, Governor of Massachusetts and Military Commander in America, 1731–1760,* 2 vols., edited under the auspices of the National Society of the Colonial Dames of America by Charles Henry Lincoln (New York, 1912), which also contains the commission and general instructions to Shirley; *The Colden Letter Books,* 2 vols., in *Collections* of the New-York Historical Society for 1876 and 1877 (New York, 1877, 1878); and *The Letters and Papers of Cadwallader Colden,* 7 vols., in the *Collections* of the same society for 1917–1923 (New York, 1918–1923), which together contain a mass of material; *The Papers of Lewis Morris, Governor of the Province of New Jersey, from 1738 to 1746,* in the *Collections* of the New Jersey Historical Society, vol. IV (Newark, New York, 1852), which lacks adequate references in the supplemental notes; *The Official Letters of Alexander Spotswood,* 2 vols., with introduction and notes by R. A. Brock, in the *Collections* of the Virginia Historical Society, new series, vols. I and II (Richmond, 1882, 1885); and *The Official Records of Robert Dinwiddie,* 2 vols., in the *Collections* of the same society, new series, vols. III and IV (Richmond, 1883–1884), which contains only the letters written by Dinwiddie himself and not those which he received.

PRINTED WORKS: MISCELLANEOUS CONTEMPORARY

IN addition to the various classes of documents above described, there are several treatises or histories written by contemporaries, which must be considered as source material within certain natural limits. The most important of these which deals with general subjects is *The Administration of the Colonies,* by Thomas Pownall. The second edition (London, 1765) has been used. Pownall had an excellent opportunity to observe the British system of administration, both as the governor of Massachusetts and as the brother of the secretary of the Board of Trade. His dispassionate treatment of his subject and his keen insight into the heart of the colonial problem make his treatise one of the utmost value to the student of colonial history. Far less penetrating are the works of another former royal official in America, George Chalmers: *Political Annals of the Present United Colonies from Their Settle-*

ment to the Peace of 1763 (London, 1780); *Continuation of Political Annals,* in *Collections* of the New-York Historical Society for 1868 (New York, 1868); and *An Introduction to the History of the Revolt of the American Colonies* (London, vol. I, 1782; Boston, 2 vols., 1845). Of little value as narratives, these volumes are important as illustrations of the current though mistaken British view that the colonists were striving for many years to achieve total independence rather than that freedom for self-government under the British flag which was their actual goal until after hostilities had begun. A small volume by the former royal chief justice of Georgia, Anthony Stokes, *A View of the Constitution of the British Colonies in North-America and the West Indies* (London, 1783), is useful chiefly as a source of information on various governmental precedents and customs and on the formulae and uses of several types of documents relating to provincial government.

A number of histories of individual provinces were written in the eighteenth century by men familiar with the more recent events with which they dealt. Of these the best known, as well as the most impartial, is Thomas Hutchinson's *History of Massachusetts Bay,* 3 vols., of which the last two volumes deal with the period of royal government (London, 1768, 1828). Hutchinson's account of the years which coincided with his own administration (1760, 1769–1774) is particularly valuable. His opposition to the assembly is unmistakable, but he is always careful to present his antagonists' arguments. Almost as well known, but by no means as impartial, is William Smith's *The History of the Late Province of New-York, from its Discovery, to the Appointment of Governor Colden, in 1762,* 2 vols., in *Collections* of the New-York Historical Society for 1829 and 1830 (New York, 1829). The work is accurate and informative, although not always fair to those with whom Smith or his father disagreed. Two histories of West Indian provinces must also be mentioned. Bryan Edwards, *History Civil and Commercial of the British Colonies in the West Indies,* 4 vols. (London, 1793; second edition, 3 vols., London, 1794–1801, used here), deals with all the British possessions in the Caribbean and may be considered as almost a contemporary account. Edward Long, *The History of Jamaica,* 3 vols. (London, 1774), was written by a judge of the vice-admiralty court in the island and contains much reliable information.

SECONDARY AUTHORITIES

IN the sections which follow no attempt is made to give an exhaustive list of books dealing with the constitutional and political development of the colonies. What is offered is a selection of such as are most valuable for the purpose of supplementing or amplifying the present study.

GENERAL

IN a class by itself, as containing the only comprehensive study that has been made of the colonies which participated in the American Revolution is the work of the late Herbert Levi Osgood: *The American Colonies in the Seventeenth Century*, 3 vols. (New York, 1904, 1907), and *The American Colonies in the Eighteenth Century*, 4 vols. (New York, 1924–1925). Discussing with minute detail, as these volumes do, the settlement, administrative development, and political and religious characteristics of these thirteen colonies, they stand in the front rank of scholarship within their field. The author's point of view is that of the colonies themselves, hence their internal development is fully treated, while British administration receives only secondary consideration, in spite of the inclusion of a few chapters of great value. Also occupying a place of prominence in the field of colonial history are the works of George Louis Beer: *The Origins of the British Colonial System*, 1578–1660 (New York, 1908); *The Old Colonial System, 1660–1754*, Part I, *The Establishment of the System, 1660–1688*, 2 vols. (New York, 1912); and *British Colonial Policy, 1754–1765* (New York, 1907). In contrast to Osgood, Beer lays emphasis not on the American side of the story, but upon the origins and growth of British policy. Unfortunately, the author did not live to treat of the period from 1688 to 1754, but for the years with which these volumes deal they present a very informative and thoughtful discussion of the workings of the British system. An important cooperative work has recently begun to appear under the title of *The Cambridge History of the British Empire*, J. Holland Rose, A. P. Newton, and E. A. Benians, general editors, of which the first volume, *The Old Empire from the Beginnings to 1783* (Cambridge, 1929), deals with our period. The most useful chapter for the present study is No. xiv, "The Government of the Empire," by Charles M. Andrews.

Within the compass of a single volume of four essays, *The Colonial Background of the American Revolution* (New Haven, 1924), Charles M. Andrews gives a satisfactory discussion of the significance of colonial development and of the place which the events of the seventeenth and eighteenth centuries had in the eventual break between the colonies and the mother country. Briefer still, but no less satisfactory in its conclusions, is Professor Andrews's presidential address before the American Historical Association in December, 1925, "The American Revolution: an Interpretation," printed in the *American Historical Review* for January, 1926 (vol. XXXI, no. 2, pp. 219–232).

One other work must be mentioned here to which the writer owes much. That is *The Provincial Governor in the English Colonies in North America*, by Evarts Boutell Greene in the Harvard Historical Studies, VII (New York, 1898). Though seriously handicapped by the scantiness of his material, Professor Greene wrote a pioneering work of real significance. Its chief structural defect lies in its confinement to an analytical investigation of the mechanism of provincial government, without a full discussion of the underlying policies and problems. In spite of its defects, the volume has been most helpful to the present writer.

SPECIAL SUBJECTS

A NUMBER of excellent monographs have appeared within the last twenty years dealing with special phases of the subject of colonial administration and government. Three works deal with the important Board of Trade: Oliver Morton Dickerson, *American Colonial Administration, 1696–1765* (Cleveland, 1912); Arthur Herbert Basye, *The Lords Commissioners of Trade and Plantations, Commonly Known as the Board of Trade, 1748–1782*, Yale Historical Publications, Miscellany, XIV (New Haven, 1925); and Mary Patterson Clarke, "The Board of Trade at Work" in the *American Historical Review*, for October, 1911,

XVII, 17–43. A definitive history of the board throughout its existence has yet to be written. A monograph by Elmer Beecher Russel, entitled *The Review of American Colonial Legislation by the King in Council,* Columbia University Studies in History, Economics, and Public Law, vol. LXIV, no. 2 (New York, 1915), deals, on the whole, quite adequately with this subject. It needs to be supplemented, however, by Charles M. Andrews, "The Royal Disallowance of Colonial Laws" in the American Antiquarian Society *Proceedings,* new series, vol. XXIV, 342–362, and by a more specialized discussion of the same subject by Arthur Garratt Dorland, *The Royal Disallowance in Massachusetts,* in the *Bulletin* of the Departments of History and Political and Economic Science in Queen's University, no. 22.

Aspects of the judicial system are treated by Arthur Meier Schlesinger in "Colonial Appeals to the Privy Council" in the *Political Science Quarterly,* 1913, XXXVIII, 279–297, 433–450; and by George Adrian Washburne in *Imperial Control of the Administration of Justice in the Thirteen American Colonies, 1684–1776,* Columbia University Studies in History, Economics, and Public Law, vol. CV, no. 2 (New York, 1923). The system of appeals is further illustrated, though from corporate colonies, in "Appeals from Colonial Courts to the King in Council, with Special Reference to Rhode Island," by Harold D. Hazeltine, in the *Annual Report* of the American Historical Association for 1894, pp. 299–350; and "The Connecticut Intestacy Law," by Charles M. Andrews in the *Yale Review,* III, 261–294. Although an old book, Richard S. Field's *The Provincial Courts of New Jersey, with Sketches of the Bench and Bar,* in *Collections* of the New Jersey Historical Society, III (New York, 1849), is useful because it prints the ordinances for the establishment of courts within the province. Few similar documents have been published elsewhere.

Reference should also be given to Arthur L. Cross, *The Anglican Episcopate and the American Colonies* in the Harvard Historical Studies, IX (New York, 1902), which, because of its excellent treatment of the problems arising from the ecclesiastical jurisdiction of the Bishop of London, has made unnecessary here more than a brief mention of the instructions on this subject.

INDIVIDUAL PROVINCES

THE monographs and other works dealing with individual provinces vary greatly in quality. Because of its more general nature, mention should first be made of *Controversies Between Royal Governors and Their Assemblies in the Northern American Colonies*, by John F. Burns (Villanova, Pa., 1923), which deals with the four provinces of Massachusetts, New Hampshire, New York, and New Jersey. Father Burns has made a careful use of his materials and has arrived at sound conclusions but he has made the volume difficult to handle by his sectional and chronological treatment. Nevertheless, it remains a convenient source of information on the subjects within its scope and a useful contribution to the general topic. Frank Wesley Pitman deals with a different geographic area in *The Development of the British West Indies, 1700–1763*, in the Yale Historical Publications, Studies, IV (New Haven, 1917). As an economic study this volume is of great importance, though its usefulness for the constitutional history of the West Indies is more limited.

In *The Dominion of New England: A Study in British Colonial Policy*, Yale Historical Publications, Miscellany, XI (New Haven, 1923), Viola Florence Barnes has performed a real service to colonial history by demonstrating that the Dominion of New England was not an instance of "Stuart Tyranny" but the "most complete expression of British Colonial policy in the seventeenth century." James Truslow Adams in his *Revolutionary New England* (Boston, 1923) deals with the subsequent history of this region, particularly with that of Massachusetts. Although an excellent corrective to the undue reverence long shown the Puritans, the book is inadequate in its explanation of the revolutionary movement.

An important group of institutional studies was prepared at Columbia under the direction of the late Professor Osgood, each analyzing the institutions of a particular province. Those relating to the royal provinces are: W. Roy Smith, *South Carolina as a Royal Province, 1719–1776* (New York, 1903); Charles Lee Raper, *North Carolina, A Study in English Colonial Government* (New York, 1904); William Henry Fry, *New Hampshire as a*

Royal Province, in the Columbia University Studies in History, Economics, and Public Law, vol. XXIX, no. 2 (New York, 1908) ; Edwin P. Tanner, *The Province of New Jersey, 1664–1738,* in the same series, vol. XXX (New York, 1908) ; and Edgar Jacob Fisher, *New Jersey as a Royal Province,* in the same series, vol. XLI (New York, 1911). The present writer has found the volumes by Drs. Smith and Fry the most useful. But all of these works suffer from being too closely bound up with the details of the system as it existed in the province in question to enable the authors to appreciate the background of British policy or the similarity of conditions throughout the colonial world as a whole. Much less open to criticism on this score are the somewhat similar studies of Percy Scott Flippin: *The Royal Government of Virginia, 1624–1775,* in the Columbia University Studies in History, Economics, and Public Law, vol. LXXXIV, no. 1 (New York, 1919) ; and "The Royal Government of Georgia, 1752–1776," in the *Georgia Historical Quarterly,* vol. VIII, nos. 1, 2, 4; vol. IX, no. 3; vol. X, nos. 1, 4; vol. XII, no. 4; vol. XIII, no. 2 (1921–1929).

Alexander P. Bruce has written an *Institutional History of Virginia in the Seventeenth Century,* 2 vols. (New York, 1910), one of a series of studies of this colony by the same author. The work is admirably done and is filled with information.

Considerable progress has been made in recent years in the study of the West Indian provinces. C. S. S. Higham has written two useful studies of the Leeward Islands: *The Development of the Leeward Islands under the Restoration, 1660–1688; A Study of the Foundations of the Old Colonial System* (Cambridge, 1921) and "The General Assembly of the Leeward Islands" in *The English Historical Review,* April and July, 1926, XLI, 190–209, 366–388. Vincent T. Harlow, *A History of Barbados, 1625–1685* (Oxford, 1926), is largely political in character but highly informative. In *The Constitutional Development of Jamaica— 1660 to 1729* (Manchester, 1929), Agnes M. Whitson has dealt very adequately with the growth of the legislature of that island and with the struggle over the perpetual revenue. Other topics are intentionally omitted from her study. If one may judge solely by the abstract printed in the *Bulletin* of the Institute of Historical Research, June, 1928, VI, no. 16, pp. 36–39, J. W. Herbert has arrived at worth-while and sound conclusions in his unpublished thesis "Constitutional Struggles in Jamaica, 1748–1776."

BIOGRAPHIES OF GOVERNORS

IN spite of what has been accomplished and what is now in progress, many opportunities remain for needed biographies of colonial governors. The most readable account of any royal governor is by Estelle Frances Ward, *Christopher Monck, Duke of Albemarle* (London, 1915), which is devoted to the life of this Restoration favorite and governor of Jamaica. The book deals only briefly with the period of Albemarle's actual administration of the province, but it conveys a fine flavor of court life in England at the time and shows clearly the influences involved in colonial appointments. *The Public Life of Joseph Dudley*, Harvard Historical Studies, XV, by Everett Kimball (New York, 1911), successfully analyzes the character of this Massachusetts governor. In two short articles, Viola Florence Barnes has made a careful study of the character and career of one of Dudley's predecessors, Sir William Phips: "The Rise of William Phips," *New England Quarterly*, I, 271–294; and "Phippius Maximus," *ibid.*, pp. 532–553. Other biographies of Massachusetts governors are: *William Shirley, Governor of Massachusetts, 1741–1756, A History*, vol. I, Columbia University Studies in History, Economics, and Public Law, XCII (New York, 1920), by George A. Wood, which carries the account only to 1749, since the projected second volume has never appeared; *Thomas Pownall, M.P., F.R.S., Governor of Massachusetts Bay, Author of the Letters of Junius* (London, 1908), by Charles A. W. Pownall, which, as the title shows, makes some rather extravagant claims for a man who, even without them, has an assured place in history; and *The Life of Thomas Hutchinson, Royal Governor of the Province of Massachusetts Bay* (Boston and New York, 1896), by James K. Hosmer, which is detailed and impartial but narrative and uncritical. Lawrence Shaw Mayo has written a life of *John Wentworth, Governor of New Hampshire, 1767–1775,* which adequately explains the popularity of this last royal governor of the province, but belittles the successful administration of his uncle and predecessor, Benning Wentworth. The only biography of a New York governor which has yet appeared is *Cadwallader Colden: A Representative Eighteenth Century Official* (New York, 1906) by Alice Keys, a sympathetic and defensive treatment of this stormy petrel of New York politics, but a not entirely adequate account of the problems of his times. A somewhat disappointing sketch of one New Jersey governor appears under the inaccurate title of "Lewis Morris, First Colonial Governor of New Jersey" by Charles W. Parker, in the *Proceedings* of the New Jersey Historical Society, July, 1928, new series, XIII, 273–282. Morris deserves a careful full-length biography. Percy Scott Flippin's "William Gooch: Successful Royal Governor of Virginia," in the *William and Mary College Quarterly Historical Magazine*, V, 225–258; VI, 1–38 (1925–1926), is as much concerned with conditions in Virginia during Gooch's administration (1727–1749) as with the personality and work of the man himself. But Dr. Flippin has given a satisfactory account of this truly successful administration. Two North Carolina governors are treated by Marshall Delancey Heywood in *Governor George Burrington, with an Account of His Official Administration in the Colony of North Carolina, 1724–1725, 1731–1734* (Raleigh, 1896), and *Governor William Tryon and His Administration in the Province of North Carolina, 1765–1771* (Raleigh, 1903). The only West Indian governor of the period besides the duke of Albemarle to receive adequate biographical study is the younger Christopher Codrington. Vincent T. Harlow's *Christopher Codrington, 1668–1710* (Oxford, 1928), is an entertaining and sound study of that versatile personality.

Articles of varying worth on many of the more prominent governors appear in the *Dictionary of National Biography*, 63 vols. (London, 1885–1901), edited by Leslie Stephen and Sidney Lee, and the lives of about fifty of the royal governors of continental colonies will eventually be included in the *Dictionary of American Biography* edited by Allen Johnson, now in progress (vols. I and II, New York, 1928, 1929).

INDEX

Absenteeism, of patent officers, 103; of councillors, 148.

Accounts, transmitted to England, 273.

Acts, parliamentary, effect of, on trade instructions, 70; number of, relating to colonial trade, 121; act to punish governors, 123; Townshend Acts, 159, 340; Boston Port Act, 197; Massachusetts Government Act, 197; Triennial Act, 211; Septennial Act, 211; Act of Settlement, 392 n.; Stamp Act, 416; Hat Act, 443; Molasses Act, 443.

Acts, provincial, see Legislation and names of individual provinces.

Adams, Samuel, 370; on non-binding character of instructions, 196–197.

Admiralty, instruments from, classified, 7; seal of, 72 n.

Admiralty, commissioners of, letters from, classified, 28; consulted in preparing instructions, 56; share of, in preparing vice-admiralty commission, 71; provide frigate for governor, 83; on relations of governor and navy officers, 111.

Admiralty, High Court of, 25; share of, in preparing vice-admiralty commission, 71.

Admiralty, receiver general of rights and perquisites of, advises on instructions, 60.

Admiralty, solicitor of, prepares vice-admiralty commission, 71.

Admiralty, vice-, governor's commission of, described, 25–27, 109; preparation of, 71; courts of, see Courts and Vice-admiralty.

Agents, provincial, fail to get orders in council, 225.

Albany, Congress at, 293; county of, divided, 187.

Albemarle, duke of, governor of Jamaica, accommodations required by, 83; hoists admiral's flag, 84 n.; gets perpetual revenue act, 276.

Albemarle, earl of, governor general of Virginia, death of, 48; son of, suggested to succeed, 49 n.

Alexander, James, supports Van Dam against Cosby, 161.

Allen, Samuel, governor of New Hampshire, gets no salary, 346.

Amendment of laws, difficult under instructions, 251.

Amherst, Sir Jeffrey, commander in chief in America and governor of Virginia, 38; instructed on supplies for navy, 57.

Andros, Sir Edmund, governor of Dominion of New England, Virginia, Maryland, career of, 41 n.; power of, to pass laws with council, 175; salary of, 337 n.; on judicial oath of councillors, 409.

Antigua, disputes over issuing money in, 302.

Appeals, to governor and council, 99, 402; to privy council, 5, 99, 402; Massachusetts act respecting, 376; importance of system of, 401; in criminal cases, 406.

Appointments, method of making, 102.

Apportionment, only occasionally prescribed in instructions, 179.

156; early ordinance power in, 175; choice of speaker in, 201 ff.; duration of assemblies in, 212; legal tender act in, 230; instruction on duration of acts modified in, 249 n.; 4½ percent duty granted in, 271; council's amendment of money bills in, 299; naming of treasurer in, 301; governor's salary in, 313, 316, 318, 323, 326, 327; gifts to governors in, 318; prices in, 321 n.; maladministration of justice in, 383; habeas corpus in, 385.

Barbados Gazette, rejection of speaker discussed in, 202–203.

Beeston, Sir William, governor of Jamaica, salary of, 320.

Belcher, Jonathan, governor of Massachusetts, New Hampshire, and New Jersey, applies for South Carolina governorship, 47; inauguration of, 87; complains of injustice done him, 98; objects to appointment of naval officer, 105; opposes instructions against repealing laws, 254; salary of, 344, 348, 444; appointment of, 363; instructions to, on salary, 364; contest over salary of, 365 ff.

Belhaven, Lord, governor of Barbados, asks for change in salary, 325; death of, 81 n., 82, 130, 326.

Bellomont, earl of, governor of New York, Massachusetts, and New Hampshire, salary of, 337 n.; grants to, 346, 353; on dearth of good lawyers in New York, 382.

Berkeley, Sir William, governor of Virginia, 9 n.; length of administration of, 126 n.; power of, to erect courts, 373 n.; salary of, 313, 315 n.

Bermuda, title of governor of, 19 n.; secrecy of instructions in, 97;

suffrage in, 188; election of speaker in, 200; duration of assemblies in, 212; unnotified of disallowed acts, 225; reenactment of disallowed law in, 253; disputes over issuing money in, 303; governor's salary in, 319, 323, 326, 328; governors' oppressive acts in, 321; appeals from, to privy council, 406.

Bernard, Francis, governor of New Jersey and Massachusetts, instructions to, 68 n.; council meets without, 159; on power to act without council, 170; removes assembly to Cambridge, 194; salary of, 344 n.; dispute over salary of, during absence, 368.

Betts, Thomas, recommended for Jamaica council, 137 n.

Bill, parliamentary, against paper currency (1744), 33, 439; (1749), 34.

Bill of Rights, 193.

Bill of Rights Society, South Carolina assembly makes gift to, 306.

Bills of credit, instructions limiting acts for, 68 n., 227 n.

Bishop of London, suggests instructions, 55; licenses ministers and schoolmasters, 68 n.; ecclesiastical jurisdiction of, 115 ff.

Bladen, Martin, recommends governor for Bahamas, 45.

Board of Trade, see Trade, Board of.

Bolton, duke of, recommends councillor, 137 n.

Boone, Thomas, governor of New Jersey and South Carolina, salary of, 331, 344 n.

Boston, Mass., as meeting place of assembly, 193 ff.

Boston Massacre, 194.

Boston Port Act, 197.

Botetourt, Baron de, governor of